Collisions

T0282817

Collisions

*The Origins of the War in Ukraine
and the New Global Instability*

MICHAEL KIMMAGE

OXFORD
UNIVERSITY PRESS

OXFORD
UNIVERSITY PRESS

Oxford University Press is a department of the University of Oxford. It furthers
the University's objective of excellence in research, scholarship, and education
by publishing worldwide. Oxford is a registered trade mark of Oxford University
Press in the UK and certain other countries.

Published in the United States of America by Oxford University Press
198 Madison Avenue, New York, NY 10016, United States of America.

© Michael Kimmage 2024

All rights reserved. No part of this publication may be reproduced, stored in
a retrieval system, or transmitted, in any form or by any means, without the
prior permission in writing of Oxford University Press, or as expressly permitted
by law, by license, or under terms agreed with the appropriate reproduction
rights organization. Inquiries concerning reproduction outside the scope of the
above should be sent to the Rights Department, Oxford University Press, at the
address above.

You must not circulate this work in any other form
and you must impose this same condition on any acquirer.

CIP data is on file at the Library of Congress

ISBN 978–0–19–775179–4

DOI: 10.1093/oso/9780197751794.001.0001

Printed by Sheridan Books, Inc., United States of America

Dedicated to my daughters, Ema and Maya,
and to the conviction that we can learn from history

Contents

It may be that the lack of a romantic element in my history will make it less of a pleasure to the ear; but I shall be content if it is judged useful by those who will want to have a clear understanding of what happened—and, such is the human condition, will happen again at some time in the same or a similar pattern.

Thucydides, *The Peloponnesian War*, Book 1:22

Preface

On a Kyiv side street stands the residence of the US ambassador, an elegant yellow neoclassical building. Located in the fashionable Podil neighborhood, this small villa is close to the river that divides the city. A hilly park runs from near the residence up toward Saint Michael's Golden Domed Monastery, which had been torn down between 1935 and 1936, when Kyiv was in the Soviet Union and when Joseph Stalin was in power. After Ukraine broke away from the Soviet Union in 1991, the monastery was rebuilt. Up the hill one walks from Podil to the monastery, past the statue of Bogdan Chmelnitsky, a symbol of Ukrainian nationhood and of independence from the Polish-Lithuanian Commonwealth. Down the hill one walks in another direction into the Maidan Square, the place where European history changed course in November 2013. It is a wide square or set of squares, too big to be medieval or early modern, a little bit like a calm Times Square, and ideally suited to public assembly. In November 2013, a protest movement took shape on the Maidan. An institution founded in the eleventh century, Saint Michael's Monastery harbored protestors escaping a fierce government crackdown on the Maidan. In that November and in the December that followed, discontent built up until it issued in revolution. In the early months of 2014, this revolution issued in war.

In January 2016, I attended a dinner with several State Department colleagues at the Kyiv residence of the US ambassador. An academic, I had joined the State Department's Office of Policy Planning very late in 2014, months after the annexation of Crimea and amid heavy fighting in Ukraine's east. The situation was superficially calmer in 2016, resembling neither war nor peace. Ukraine had settled into a period of stability after its revolution, drawing closer to Europe than it had been in 2013, though still far from membership in the NATO alliance or in the European Union. The United States, ten months before the election of Donald Trump, was the country edging closer to revolution—unbeknownst to our State Department delegation in Kyiv that January, when Trump was not yet the Republican nominee. Taking a seat at the ambassador's candlelit table were representatives of Ukrainian civil society; they were think tankers, activists, and academics. Among them was Mustafa Nayyem, a well-spoken advocate for Ukraine's European path and for good reason a famous man. It was his Facebook posting that had brought a handful of people to the Maidan back in November 2013. In the beginning was his injunction not to accept the status quo, and his wish had been granted. The status quo—in Ukraine, in Russia, in Europe—did not survive the winter of 2013–14.

In the course of our official visit, we met with many prominent Ukrainians. We spoke to the prime minister, Arseniy Yatsenyuk, who looked young and was effortlessly voluble (in English). We had a meeting with the major of Kyiv, Vitaly Klitschko. Gracious and irreverent, he was a former boxing champion who towered over his staff and over us. We sat down as well with Leonid Kuchma, Ukraine's president from 1994 to 2005, one of the country's founding fathers, a cagey intelligent man whose manner and appearance were vaguely Soviet.[1] He was a reminder—in 2016—that independent Ukraine stood atop layers of complicated history. Kuchma's father had been wounded in World War II. Born in 1938, Kuchma himself had joined the Communist Party, rising up the Soviet ranks until he drifted away from the communist project in the 1980s. Kuchma's presidency was a period in which Ukraine was basically democratic but hardly free from government abuse of power, including at the hands of Kuchma and his associates. During his time as president, much of the country's post-Soviet promise had been squandered, having been sold to the highest bidder. Yet in 2016 Kuchma had the virtue of being an ex-president. His successors had been elected, not installed, and power had been transferred to other leaders. The open question in 2016 was whether the work-in-progress Ukraine of Yatsenyuk and Klitschko would be different from the struggling Ukraine of Kuchma, whether the past was prologue or whether it was truly past.

The most memorable of our many meetings in Kyiv was not with the political eminences of 2016 and of yesteryear. It was with a group of students from Taras Shevchenko National University and from the National University of Kyiv-Mohyla Academy, two of Ukraine's elite universities. The students were eager to speak with us, to get the word from the State Department, and to give us their impressions of Ukraine after the Maidan. We discussed governance good and bad, and for quite a while we discussed Alexis de Tocqueville. Tocqueville was a European who, in dissecting American democracy, had emphasized the importance of "voluntary associations." It was the stuff of seminars and almost a caricature of American diplomacy, with its transatlantic enthusiasm and its unquenchable fondness for democracy. Yet it was also—in a way it might not have been back in Washington, DC—the stuff of real life. It was to an imagined voluntary association that Mustafa Nayyem had appealed in his Facebook posting. Voluntary associations had driven the Maidan Revolution and proliferated in 2015, and they still mattered in 2016. Voluntary associations seemed to hold more appeal for these students than the government jobs that surely awaited them. Six years later, I am haunted by these brilliant young Ukrainians, by the curiosity, decency, and idealism they projected. In February 2022, all of them in their mid-twenties by then, they must have found themselves on the front lines of an unexpected and terrible war. Not surprisingly, a distinguishing feature of this war has been the voluntary associations spurring the Ukrainian war effort.[2]

* * *

Collisions is anything but a memoir or an eyewitness account. For two years, I was a mid-level functionary at the State Department, a "senior official" at best, but in reality, not much more than an observer of great events—during the initial phase of Russia's war against Ukraine. Instead of journalism or autobiographical writing, *Collisions* is an early draft of the history that will one day be written about the 2022 war, which began in 2014, if not earlier. It is a narrative of the events that have culminated in a major European war and an inquiry into the causes behind these events. With this book, I have aspired to the objectivity of a scholar and to the conscious avoidance of advocacy: it is neither a justification of US policy nor a *mea culpa*. At the same time, while striving to provide an even-handed account of the war, I have tried to imbue *Collisions* with the immediacy of my government experience, focusing on the choices leaders and governments have made, on mistakes of judgment and of prediction, on triumphs of judgment and prediction, on the play of personality that is so determinative for diplomacy, on the economic and political constraints under which governments operate, and on the clash of ideas between Russia and the United States, going back not just to the 1990s but to the Cold War. Washington and Moscow fiercely disagree about politics and about Europe, and they have disagreed on these points for time immemorial, which is an invitation to historical reflection. Without this disagreement in the background, there might well have been a war but there would have been no global collision over Ukraine in 2022.

In the writing of this book, I have had an illustrious model in mind. In the first sentence of *The Peloponnesian War*, its author describes himself as "Thucydides of Athens [who] wrote this history of the war fought against each other by the Peloponnesians and the Athenians." Then he continues, as if writing about someone else: "He began his work right at the outbreak, reckoning that this would be a major war and more momentous than any previous conflict." Thucydides had been a general in the war and was a witness to a few of the events he mulled over as a historian. With some transposition, his famous explanation of the Peloponnesian War eerily anticipates Russia's 2022 war against Ukraine: "In my view the real reason, true but unacknowledged, which forced the war was the growth of Athenian power and Spartan fear of it." Both the deep underlying causes and the "openly proclaimed grievances," the acknowledged disputes that led directly to the war, fascinated Thucydides, but most important were the underlying causes.[3] Enamored of its openly proclaimed grievances, Russia did not precisely fear the growth of Ukrainian power in 2022. Putin feared the alignment of Ukraine with Western power. It would be as valid to say that he resented this alignment, that he perceived it as a personal affront. This fear and this resentment forced the war. In the fifth century BCE, Thucydides of Athens did not write to validate Athenian power (or Spartan fear). He wrote in order to understand such power and such fear, to understand this double helix of force and emotion, which is the prime mover of international relations. More than two millennia after it was written, *The Peloponnesian War* is not just a good book. It is still a relevant book.

Two caveats about *Collisions* are worth noting at the outset. It is not a history of Ukraine. I do not have the linguistic or academic background to write the history of Ukraine as such. My training is as a historian of the Cold War with three points of emphasis: the history of Russia and the Soviet Union, the history of Europe, and the history of the United States. I have done what I can to link the history of Ukraine, which lies at the heart of the 2014 and 2022 wars, with the European, Soviet, Russian, and US material that is more familiar to me. This helps with the global frame that the 2022 war requires. It is, however, a necessarily partial interpretation of the war. Another caveat is that as time passes, historians will gain access to more and better information about the war, bringing greater empirical heft and more grounded insight to the question of why it broke out. Eventually, historians will know how the war ends, which will help them to assess the changes wrought by the war. I envy these historians, but I also see the value in picking up the historian's pen "right at the outbreak" of a war—rather than waiting for a finality that will be a long time coming. In their radicalism and in their horror, wars threaten to erase history, to rush past history or to render it invisible, to substitute ephemeral news cycles and jittery rumors for historical context and analysis, especially when the outcome of a war is not yet in sight. To prevent such erasure and to move toward a reasoned understanding, wars must be approached as events in history before all the archives can be assembled, all the monuments erected, and all the museums built, and even before the guns have fallen silent.

Acknowledgments

Written in haste, this book was nevertheless years in the making. Its origins lie in the two years I spent at the State Department Office of Policy Planning. There, from 2014 to 2016, I was fortunate to have as colleagues Lauren Baer, Max Bergmann, Charles Edel, Eddie Fishman, Ziad Haider, Andrew Imbrie, Arslan Malik, Drew McCracken, Amanda Monsour, Jonathan Stromseth, Bart Szewczyk, Jonathan Temin, Ian Klaus, and my brother, Daniel Kimmage. I was equally fortunate to have as bosses David McKean, and Jon Finer. The collective standard of excellence at Policy Planning gave me an invaluable education in policy formation, which is a primary theme of this book.

Since 2014, I have had the good fortune to work on issues related to Russia, Ukraine, and Europe at the Wilson Center's Kennan Institute, the German Marshall Fund, and at the Center for Strategic and International Studies. Colleagues at these and at other think tanks have added immeasurably to my understanding of international relations and of US–-Russian relations. They include David Cadier, Sam Charap, Derek Chollet, Heather Conley, Karen Donfried, Joe Dresen, Matt Duss, Jeff Edmonds, Nick Fenton, Jeff Gedmin, Jim Goldgeier, Fiona Hill, Jonathan Katz, Andrea Kendall-Taylor, Margarete Klein, Hans Kundnani, Miriam Lanskoy, Robert Legvold, Eric Lohr, Jeff Mankoff, Jade McGlynn, Julie Newton, Olga Oliker, Victoria Pardini, Will Pomeranz, Matt Rojansky, Eugene Rumer, Kori Schake, Jeremy Shapiro, Maria Snegovaya, Mary Sarotte, Constanze Stelzenmueller, Angela Stent, Izabella Tabarovsky, Jan Techau, Andrew Weiss, and Stephen Wertheim.

The editors at *Foreign Affairs*—Daniel Kurz-Phelan, Justin Vogt, Hugh Eakin, Kate Brannen, Kanishk Tharoor, Stuart Reid, Elise Burr, and many others—have done so much to help me to formulate my own thinking about the war and about international affairs. It has been a joy to work with them. The same is true for my cherished co-authors in the pages of *Foreign Affairs*: Michael Kofman, Maria Lipman, Hanna Notte, and Liana Fix, all of whom are also friends. Conversations with Josh Yaffa, Valerie Hopkins, Linda Kinstler, Anton Troianovsky, and Keith Gessen are always illuminating; so too is reading their writing.

As was the case (by now) with three of my previous books, conceptualizing *Collisions* was jumpstarted by time spent at the Center for Advanced Studies at the Ludwig Maximilian University of Munich, where Annette Meyer and her colleagues provided their signature intellectual hospitality and day-to-day sociability. Their doing so in the summer of 2021, during a pandemic not always conducive to reading and writing and thinking, holds special importance for me. It was a rare gift.

Great thanks to Professors Michael A. Reynolds and Jennifer Wistrand for invitations to discuss this book at Princeton University and at the Miami University of Ohio, respectively. Thanks as well to Luiza Bialasiewicz and George Blaustein for instruction on European affairs and to Stephen Kotkin for his mentorship. Anna Vassilieva is a dear friend and colleague in the academic domain: she made it possible for me to start writing this book beneath the blue California sky. Conversations with Jeremi and Zachary Suri did much to shape this book. I am grateful to the many non-expert audiences I have had the opportunity to address while writing *Collisions*. Peter Schmidt in particular does wonders bringing serious talk to the general public. Questions from this public are the point of departure for *Collisions*.

Catholic University, especially Dean Thomas Smith and Associate Dean Caroline Sherman, has tendered much support for this book, some of it material and some in the form of non-material encouragement.

It was a pleasure to work with my agent, Don Fehr, on the idea behind this book and on its journey into print. David McBride has been a wonderful editor, and he belongs to an expert crew at Oxford University Press.

My parents, Ann and Dennis Kimmage, have a hand in this book. They may not agree with all of its arguments, but they provided the foundation for it to be written, which is their capacious interest on all of the regions and themes covered in *Collisions*. Avid students of twentieth-century history, they are always finding ways to relate it to twenty-first-century developments, making them my best teachers.

Collisions is dedicated to my daughters, Ema and Maya, who in countless ways have made it worth writing and brought happiness to the writer. When they are adults, they will be able to regard the collisions of 2022 and 2023, which we all lived through in real time, as history, and they can learn from them as history. My wife, Alma, may not fully accept (or fully forgive) the title of this book, but she brought her wit, her wisdom, and her kindness to the task of getting it across the finish line.

Introduction

> The Anglo-American relies upon personal interest to accomplish his ends, and gives free scope to the ingrained strength and commonsense of the people; the Russian centers all authority of society in a single arm. The principal instrument of the former is freedom; of the latter, servitude. Their starting point is different, and the causes are not the same; yet each of them seems marked by the will of heaven to sway the destinies of half the globe.
>
> Alexis de Tocqueville, *Democracy in America* [1833][1]

"Beware the Ides of March," a soothsayer remarks in Shakespeare's *Julius Caesar*, warning of that moment in March when everything would go wrong. Julius Caesar, who should have paid heed, carries on to the Senate and is assassinated. A twenty-first-century soothsayer might have focused on February rather than March. Back in the twentieth century, February was an ill-omened month for Europe. According to the Russian empire's Julian calendar, Czar Nicholas II found himself impossibly embattled in February, the Russian army disintegrating all around him, the social order turning in upon itself. On February 23, 1917, Nicholas II ended the Romanov dynasty, launching the "February Revolution" and a long time of troubles for Russia—with enormous repercussions for a Europe itself awash in revolution. A provisional government would be overthrown by the Bolsheviks in the more famous October Revolution of 1917, giving birth to the Soviet Union after several years of civil war. On February 24, 2022, Russia launched a massive invasion of Ukraine, shattering normal life across this country, dragging Europe back to the misery of full-scale war and plunging US-Russian relations into permanent crisis. The February 2022 invasion was a wrinkle in political time, a caesura, a rupture, and the termination of the thirty-year period that began with the Soviet Union's collapse in 1991, three of the most peaceful, most promising, most prosperous decades in European history. Caution was warranted in the tense months of diplomatic back and forth that preceded war in 2022.

Caution was warranted in January 2014 as well. Eastern Europe was not an obvious crisis zone at that time, and nobody had expected Viktor Yanukovych, the unimpressive president of Ukraine, to flee the country. In Ukraine and throughout Eastern Europe, he was a familiar type. Yanukovych had grown up in eastern Ukraine, a young man in trouble with the law. He adopted some of his political style from the local mafias—those that had proliferated after the fall of the Soviet Union—and as his career went forward, he made little effort to shed his past. Ukraine's president since 2010, Yanukovych understood the politics of personal gain and the art of quid pro quo. When in the mood, he advocated a European path for Ukraine. He was also comfortable with a Ukrainian tilt toward Russia, for which there was some foundation in a country historically intertwined with Russia, and this made him an attractive partner for Russia's president, Vladimir Putin. Yanukovych did not have Putin's hunger for glory or Putin's consuming grievances. Yanukovych was not obsessed with his historical legacy or even with high politics as such. No Julius Caesar, he was out to muddle through and to squeeze what he could from Ukraine, and with his self-serving, provincial, and essentially criminal mindset, Yanukovych purchased Putin's benign neglect. Putin let Ukraine be, while Yanukovych lined his pockets. More than political allies, they were partners versed in self-dealing and survival.

Yanukovych's relationship with Putin explained a curious about-face Yanukovych made in November 2013. For months, Yanukovych had been on the verge of signing an Association Agreement (AA) with the European Union. The agreement did not entail membership in the EU, which was at best a distant prospect for Ukraine in 2013. The AA was more prosaic than that. It concerned the EU as a system for managing and regulating trade. The AA would open European markets to Ukraine by aligning Ukraine's rules and regulations with those that were set in Brussels: its culmination was to be a DCFTA or Deep and Comprehensive Free Trade Agreement. The AA and the DCFTA would give substance to the image of a European Ukraine. To the east, Ukraine bordered Russia; to the north, Belarus; and to the west it bordered multiple EU member states—Poland, Slovakia, Hungary, Bulgaria, Romania. It made perfect economic sense to draw closer to them. It was a step toward European markets or toward a vision of Europe, which, once finalized, could lead to further steps in the same direction—Europe the summit of normalcy, modernity, and prosperity. By 2013, Ukraine had long ago left the Soviet Union, and in 2013 Ukraine was in its twenty-second year of sovereignty and statehood. Why not affirm Ukraine's place in Europe, long a geographic and historical fact, whatever the word "Europe" had meant over the ages and whatever it might mean in the fall of 2013?

Well before the Ides of February, in late November 2013, Yanukovych had traveled to Vilnius for an EU meeting. Prior to arriving in Lithuania's capital city, he had admitted he would *not* sign the AA, but some uncertainty about his decision lingered on; he was still scheduled to show up in Vilnius. Putin had been pressuring Yanukovych not to sign. Quite possibly private threats had been voiced. Putin openly offered some $15 billion to Yanukovych if he could save

Ukraine from sliding into Europe, an incentive to sweeten Moscow's strong-arm diplomacy. In the fall of 2013, the world was not waiting to see what would happen in Vilnius. Ukraine was not then center stage, and the fate of Europe did not hinge on the question of whether Ukrainian fisheries were to be regulated according to EU or non-EU standards. The EU itself could seem a layering of bureaucracy on bureaucracy, rule on rule, agreement on agreement, something slow, stodgy, boring. Pro-European in his own eyes and very much aware that many in Ukraine looked admiringly toward the EU, Yanukovych wavered. He would have preferred not to choose between Russia and Europe, keeping his options open, but the time for choosing had finally come. At the moment of truth, he went with Moscow. It was the more intuitive choice for Yanukovych, the more familiar choice, and it was the more immediately lucrative choice.

Back in Ukraine, the protests started small. They were not just about the EU Association Agreement. They were also about its symbolic meanings and about the poignantly un-bureaucratic questions embedded within the symbolism. Where did Ukraine's future lie? What would Ukraine be inside of Europe? What would Ukraine be outside of Europe? And who were Ukrainians? Yanukovych had many abuses of power on his conscience and even more on his record. His past misdeeds mattered when he found himself the focal point of an unpopular decision—especially with younger Ukrainians, whose aspirations to join Europe (and not just to finalize an Association Agreement with the EU) mingled with anger at Yanukovych's abuses of power and at his coziness with Putin, who was after all a foreign leader. The protests grew and grew. Unable any longer to sign the AA, having delayed his decision until he could delay no longer, Yanukovych was flummoxed by the protests. From the beginning, he employed violence, further stimulating the appetite to protest. In January and February of 2014, his orders to shoot protestors backfired. He was an inept dictator, and the protests not only continued but expanded until in only a few months, he had lost his grip on power. On February 21, 2014, the president of Ukraine abandoned his gaudy home outside of Kyiv and left in hiding for eastern Ukraine, then for the Crimean peninsula, then for Russia, running unsurprisingly into Putin's arms. Even his escape from Ukraine was a zigzag.

Over time, the low comedy of Yanukovych's escape came to resemble the curious drama of Archduke Ferdinand's assassination in June 1914. A seemingly random occurrence on Europe's periphery, an accident that somehow precipitated a major European war, had taken place exactly a hundred years earlier in Sarajevo. It all unfolded faster in the twentieth century than it did in the twenty-first. By August 1914, the world was at war, whereas Europe's first major twenty-first-century war was eight years in the making. What could be ignored by some in 2014—and what was ignored by many—could not be ignored by anyone in 2022, when Russia lunged at Kyiv, sending tank and infantry sorties into Ukraine's north, east, and south, accompanied by missile strikes and aerial bombardment. Ukraine is Europe's second biggest country after Russia (if Russia counts as Europe). Ukraine is roughly the size of Texas or of France, its population around 40 million people. In February 2022, the Kremlin dreamed of conquering half the country. It had assured itself that Ukraine's government was the artificial construct of the United States and of a handful of Ukrainian nationalists. Perhaps Ukraine was a house of cards like the Western-backed Afghan government that had so unceremoniously collapsed in August 2021, when the Taliban appeared on the outskirts of Kabul and Afghanistan's US-backed president slipped into exile. Putin intended to rewrite the rules of international politics, making it a game played by great powers, and to reinscribe the rules of Russian history on the territory of Ukraine, making it once again a part of a Russian empire. Long suppressed countries like Russia could finally exert themselves and call the shots in their neighborhoods, while a decadent, exhausted United States and its anemic European allies walked the gangplank of decline.

Putin made many miscalculations in February 2022, underestimating Ukraine and overestimating his own military. He did get one thing right. His war would be the start of a new era, newly dangerous and newly bloody. It would substitute a Russian-initiated phase of instability for the languorous Pax Americana that had come to Europe in the 1990s. In his own eyes, Putin's invasion would be a February Revolution guided by a Russian leader's foresight and agency rather than by the defeat and the abdication of power that had broken Russia in February 1917.

* * *

No war begins at an opportune moment. World War I arose from a Europe mostly at peace with itself and very much enjoying the pleasures of globalization, which had bankrolled the Belle Époque, a turn-of-the-century European renaissance. World War II took Poland, France, and Britain largely by surprise. Without knowing it, Europe's great powers had not kept pace with the German war machine. It was the luck of the Allies that the British could evacuate their soldiers at Dunkirk; that the Soviet Union did not fall in 1941, when Hitler invaded; and that the United States got pulled into the war, when Japan attacked Pearl Harbor. In 1947, the Cold War was wanted by nobody—not by Moscow, not by Washington, not by Europe. It proceeded from years of limitless destruction, the European continent in ruins, millions of refugees wandering from place to place, the Soviet Union barely recovered from its wartime losses in the mid-1940s, and the United States preoccupied with labor unrest and with its default instinct *not* to go out in search of monsters to destroy.[2] Europe's major modern wars have all been inopportune since they have rippled directly and indirectly outward, drawing in millions of non-Europeans. Europe's wars have been more than inopportune for the countries engulfed in them, for the populations suffering invasion from without, for the countries unprepared militarily and for the countries unprepared psychologically, as France was unprepared in the summer of 1940 and as the United States was unprepared in the winter of 1942.

February 2022 was another such inopportune moment for war. Ukraine had been subjected to the evils of war since 2014, to Russia's prior annexation of Crimea and invasion of eastern Ukraine, a few of the many consequences of Yanukovych's February flight from office. For eight years, Ukraine had been forced to live with the uncertainties and the anxieties of an unended war. Back in 2014, Ukraine had been among Europe's poorest countries, rural Ukraine in particular. Not authoritarian, its political system was still post-Soviet, thin on rule of law and burdened by a kleptocratic ruling class. Its political imperfections notwithstanding, Ukraine was making its way after 2014 as it had been since 1991; it was moving ahead. It was building bridges to international markets and to European institutions, making technological advances. It was culturally and politically vibrant, with a will to move beyond its twentieth-century past and to piece together a better future. The last thing Ukraine needed in 2022 was a brutal war—and a brutal war administered by an adversary with nuclear weapons, with Europe's biggest conventional military, and with a leader, Vladimir Putin, who did not believe in the existence of a Ukrainian state or in the integrity of a Ukrainian culture. Though they quickly adjusted, Ukraine's leadership and population were not psychologically prepared for the war Russia unleashed in 2022.

Ukraine's president in February 2022 was Volodymyr Zelensky, a man not previously steeped in war. Ukraine's first post-Soviet leader, he was no former *apparatchik* or KGB officer, and he was no oligarch. The Ronald Reagan or the Arnold Schwarzenegger of Ukraine, Zelensky had come to prominence as an entertainer.[3] He was a performer and producer, and in a textbook case of life imitating art he had made and starred in a television show, *Servant of the People*, which ran from 2015 to 2018. It featured Vasyl Holoborodko, a history teacher whose rant about corruption goes viral when a student films it and puts it on social media. This newfound celebrity results in his becoming—against all odds—the president of Ukraine. Zelensky followed in the footsteps of his good-hearted fictional alter ego, winning a well-administered election on April 21, 2019. Representing a new departure and himself a young man, Zelensky had a great deal to overcome in 2019, and three years later he was in a tough political spot. This too had been anticipated in *Servant of the People*: it is not easy for an honest man to serve the people. As president, Zelensky was smaller than Ukraine's oligarchic political system, more dominated by it than he was able to dominate the system, and in 2022 he was no closer to bringing Ukraine into NATO or the EU than his presidential predecessors had been. Zelensky's approval ratings were middling in January 2022. Right until the war began, he was insisting that there would not be a war.

Ukraine's European neighbors were no better prepared. Europe had witnessed many wars since 1945: civil wars; separatist movements; invasions (Hungary in 1956, Czechoslovakia in 1968); the bitter conflicts in former Yugoslavia in the 1990s; expeditionary wars in Mali, Iraq, Libya, Afghanistan; and of course, the shooting war in Ukraine that had run from February 2014 to February 2015 without ever getting adequately resolved. War shadows the history of Europe, a never-ending succession of violent contestations, but by 2022, many Europeans had convinced themselves that the future of Europe was a future of perpetual peace.[4] Dropping their swords for plowshares, France and Germany had set aside their centuries-old differences. So had Germany and Britain. So had Germany and Poland, and on and on it went, the shocking story of a Europe that had finally understood the hazards of war and the harmonies of peace. A Germany hostile to war was one pillar of the new Europe, and an EU hospitable to integration was another—the same integrationist EU Viktor Yanukovych had tip-toed up to in 2013 before he took Vladimir Putin's advice and turned down the Association Agreement. Europe was unprepared for war in 2022 in large part because it did not believe a major war in Europe was possible. Europe was unprepared—psychologically, intellectually, militarily—for the terrifying revelations of February 2022.

Europe faced a challenge other than war in 2022. It was in between cycles of political leadership. In 1989, a remarkable group had coalesced in Europe: Helmut Kohl in Germany, Francois Mitterrand in France, Margaret Thatcher in the United Kingdom, Lech Walesa in Poland, and Václav Havel in Czechoslovakia.[5] Together they fashioned a post-communist Europe, a Europe of independent nation-state democracies, a civilized Europe that had evaded the demons of petty nationalism and world war. In 2022, no such cadre of leaders existed. In Germany, Angela Merkel had just retired after sixteen years at the center of European politics, a canny German leader more than she was a great European leader. Italy was governed by a technocrat, by a man without a movement or a party behind him. Having departed from the European Union, the United Kingdom was governed by a man mired in a scandal no less urgent for its absurdity: Boris Johnson's hypocritical flouting of pandemic lockdown rules. France had Europe's most visionary leader in Emmanuel Macron, but one who did not always have the mandate (outside of France and not always inside of France) to act on his expansive ideas. Poland and Hungary were European outliers. Skeptical of the "European project," they could be dismissive of the EU as too accepting of immigrants and not accepting enough of Christianity. They were less dismissive of the EU's financial support for Poland and Hungary. Hungary's Viktor Orban and Poland's Andrzey Duda enjoyed inveighing against Brussels and Berlin. Where was the European center in 2022? Not quite in

Brussels, not quite in Berlin, not quite in Paris, and definitely not in London. Europe was missing a center.

Across the Atlantic, the United States was a mystery to itself and to others in 2022. On the surface, the United States was what it had almost always been. It was globally engaged and invested in order and stability. The Biden administration was speaking self-confidently in the name of democracy. It was an excellent partner to Europe, a supporter of the NATO alliance and a firm believer—unlike such European countries as Poland and Hungary—in the European project. The more integration the better. Harry Truman and Dwight Eisenhower would have easily recognized this United States. Beneath the surface, the United States was in the grips of a difficult-to-define malady. Its political culture had splintered into pieces. The man who had lost the 2020 presidential election could not admit his loss, while many of his supporters could not admit that he was lying about his loss. A few of these supporters had stormed the US Capitol on January 6, 2021, almost disrupting the transfer of power from Donald Trump to Joe Biden, a near-death experience for the American Republic. Biden, who rejected everything about Trump and promised greater foreign-policy competence, bungled the US departure from Afghanistan in August 2021. A month later, he managed to alienate France after a stretch of secret diplomacy related to Australia and nuclear submarines. An abiding mystery was all that had changed in Washington since the 1990s, when the world had only one superpower, a democracy intent on exporting democracy.

In the enigmatic United States, the 2020 election had not been haunted by war in Europe. Mercifully, it was not an election about Russia, which had acquired a sinister hold on the American political sub-conscious in 2016: the never-ending accusations that Trump was a Russian asset; the weird connections between Russia and Trump's campaign and personal entourage; the nervous awareness that Russia had meddled in the 2016 American election and was poised to do so again in 2020. Perhaps it was the COVID pandemic of 2020 that broke the Russia fever. If so, the beneficiary was Joe Biden, whose appeal was his familiarity and his normalcy. He was not abnormally linked to Russia, not abnormally enraged by Russia, not abnormally *interested* in Russia. When he entered the White House in January 2021, Biden did not prioritize Russia; nor was he expected to by his party or electorate. His foreign-policy agenda was to manage the global repercussions of the pandemic and to orient the US government and American society toward containing climate change, an agenda as much domestic as diplomatic. Most important, perhaps, Biden wanted to succeed in the worldwide competition with China, whether that meant building alliances in Asia or considering industrial policy at home or exploring the subtleties of deterring China from invading Taiwan. In January 2021, a war with Russia was closer to science fiction than it was to policy planning in Washington. The war for which the United States was conspicuously starting to prepare in 2021 was a war in Asia.

Though a war of choice for the Kremlin, Putin's invasion came at an inopportune moment for Russia too. The country had vast internal problems. It was rigidly unequal, much of its wealth concentrated in the country's two major cities, Moscow and Saint Petersburg, while the rest of Russia lagged behind.[6] Russians often did well outside of Russia, but Russia was not itself a center of great business or technological innovation. Its government had the tell-tale hallmarks of oil wealth—the underinvestment in human capital and the co-existence of wealth with stagnation. War would help with none of the country's structural challenges. Nor had Russians been whipped into a frenzy before the February 2022 war. Putin had built his regime on apathy, on a lightly coerced and wan patriotism, on a population unaccustomed to ideological or to wartime mobilization. Before the war, Putin spoke of ruthless NATO expansion and of a Ukrainian "genocide" directed against ethnic Russians in Ukraine, but NATO posed no direct threat to Russia and there was no genocide taking place in Ukraine. It was not just an untrue narrative. It was not an especially persuasive narrative. Once the war began, Putin would find himself in a bind. The Russia that had not been attacked and that had not been mobilized for war in February 2022 was also the Russia that failed to deliver a knock-out blow to Kyiv. Yet the scale of Russia's Blitzkrieg drove the West to support Ukraine with money and with sophisticated weaponry, compounding the strategic blunder of Putin's decision to invade. Russia was acutely unprepared for the war it found itself having to fight by the summer of 2022, which was a long, bruising war of attrition.

* * *

The February 2022 war was not one collision. It was several wars simultaneously, each with different points of origin, with different levels of conflict and with different degrees of danger. Front and center was a war between two states, Russia and Ukraine, a war tied up in centuries of convoluted history. The war's second collision was between Russia and Europe, a collision likewise steeped in history, in the many wars France, Britain, Poland, Sweden, Germany, and Russia had fought with one another since the seventeenth century. If the 2022 war has a clear origin, it is in February 2014, in Yanukovych's flight, which was itself caused by a regional tug-of-war over Ukraine, in which Europe was at every point involved. Europe wanted Ukraine as one more independent democracy in Eastern Europe, standing on its side of the political ledger, not necessarily against Russia but unimpeded by Russia, whereas Russia wanted to control Ukraine's destiny; Putin could only accept an independent Ukraine that was deferential to Moscow. The third collision was between Russia and the United States, two countries that had the potential to be allies, as the United States and imperial Russia were in World

War I and the United States and the Soviet Union were in World War II. Yet Moscow and Washington were most recognizable to each other as adversaries. Reared in the tradition of being adversaries, they made the most sense to one another as adversaries.[7] The Cold War had ended in 1991, a mere thirty-one years before some version of it returned in 2022, or perhaps it had never ended.[8] US-Russian tension over Ukraine shifted Russia's war from a European conflict in 2022 to a global conflict and, because of the stakes, to a conflict with the potential to turn nuclear. One war: three collisions.

Russia's imperial purview had for centuries been fixed on Ukraine. From this point of view, the eastern territories of Ukraine had been incorporated into the Russian empire in 1654. The Habsburg empire had incorporated the western territories, and until the eighteenth century, Crimea had belonged to the Ottoman Empire. When World War I was going well for Russia, in 1915 and early 1916, the conquest of all of Ukraine was conceivable for Czar Nicholas II. By 1917, this dream had dissolved into defeat and revolution. At first, the Soviet Union controlled only eastern Ukraine, turning it into the Ukrainian Soviet Socialist Republic, a state within the Soviet Union. (After a brief period of independence, western Ukraine found itself divided among Poland, Czechoslovakia, and Romania after World War I.) World War II changed the equation once again. Not only did Moscow possess all of Ukraine by 1945; the Soviet imperium extended to Czechoslovakia and East Germany, stranding Ukraine deep within the Soviet fold. An unusual stasis settled on the region from 1945 to 1989, the stasis of imperial dominion, after which the borders were once again in flux. The 1950s, 1960s, and 1970s were marked by the Soviet Union's control of Eastern Europe and by its policies of Russification, which never eliminated the hunger for nation states liberated from Moscow's rule.[9] Though Ukraine won its independence in 1991, Russia's political leadership did not cease seeing Ukraine through an imperial lens. It was the only lens through which Putin ever saw Ukraine.

The Russian imperial purview merged military, historical, and civilizational concerns. Ukraine was mountainous only in its southwest. With Belarus to the north, Ukraine was the military highway to Russia for Napoleon and Hitler. Ukraine was highly vulnerable to invasion, rendering Russia vulnerable to invasion from the west. For many of the makers of Russian foreign policy, a key instrument of outside attack was the turning of Ukrainians—its nationalists in Russian parlance—into an eternal fifth column (for Russia). Poland had used Ukrainians as a cudgel against the Russian Empire. Hitler had exploited Ukrainian nationalism during World War II, granting occupied Ukraine its own SS Division. The Kremlin could also define Ukraine as Russia proper, as an extension of itself: centuries of imperial Russian history in Ukraine plus the blood shed by Russians to defend Ukraine's land and cities during the Great Patriotic War were proof positive that Ukraine and Russia were one. Crimea could be at the center of this narrative. Imperial Russia had fought a war against Britain, France, and Turkey in the 1850s, the Crimean War, and the Soviet Union expelled Nazi Germany from Crimea and from western Ukraine, a hinge connecting Russia and Ukraine within this line of historical thinking. Ukraine might be deemed culturally Russian as well. Orthodox Christianity was a bond. The millions of Russian speakers in Ukraine could be another perceived bond. The claim that modern Russia was a child of medieval Ukraine, of Kievan Rus', a state that existed from the ninth to the thirteenth centuries, was a further bond. Ukrainian-born writers like Mikhail Bulgakov and Nikolai Gogol, both of them giants of Russian literature, could be yet another bond, as were such Soviet leaders as Nikita Khrushchev, Leonid Brezhnev, and Mikhail Gorbachev, all of whom had family or biographical ties to Ukraine.[10] By no means did the Soviet period erase the Russian imperial purview.

As the career of Viktor Yanukovych attests, post-Soviet Ukraine did have its philo-Russian elements. In addition to the Russian speakers, many Ukrainians were bi-lingual or they went back and forth between Russian and Ukrainian. Some in Crimea, in eastern Ukraine, and in southern Ukraine may have thought of themselves as Russians and wished for close cooperation with Russia; a few may have wished for the formal incorporation of Ukrainian territories into Russia. In Russia as well as Ukraine, millions upon millions of families had Russian *and* Ukrainian heritage, a complicating factor for those committed to a homogeneous Russia or a homogeneous Ukraine. Ukraine had its regional distinctions in politics and cultural affinity, which dictated a more benign view of Russia in some corners and a less benign view in others. But there was no doubt that the Ukraine born in 1991 was the nation state Ukrainians wanted to have and to preserve, and that it was a nation state separate from Russia. *Ukraine Is Not Russia* was the no-nonsense title for the memoirs of Leonid Kuchma. He was Ukraine's president from 1994 to 2005 and a man who was by no means anti-Russian.[11] Those Ukrainians who came of age before 1991 knew a Soviet system designed to transcend national belonging and in the case of Ukraine to repress national belonging. Those Ukrainians who came of age after 1991 knew only their own country. Whether they spoke Ukrainian or Russian, whether or not they had relatives in Russia, whether they worshipped in the Ukrainian Orthodox Church (Moscow Patriarchate) or at some other church or religious institution, their reference points were Ukrainian: the political capital in Kyiv, the Ukrainian sports teams, the Ukrainian currency and economy, the Ukrainian flag. For them, Ukraine was not an aspiration. It was not a question mark or a historical conundrum. It was a fact of life, and it was theirs.

In hitting up against the fact of Ukrainian nationhood, the Russian imperial purview ran into two other inconvenient facts. One was the stubborn Ukrainian longing to join the West or to join "Europe," what Yanukovych had tried and failed to finesse in 2013. This could be an economic-political venture or it could be a civilizational orientation—Europe as a well-regulated market and desirable neighbor or Europe as a bastion of Western civilization, an alternative to Russia's Asiatic civilization or to Russia's lack of civilization, as some Ukrainians might put it. (For others, the connecting link between Russia and Ukraine could be a shared "Eastern" Slavic civilization, a link connected to the claim that Russia, Ukraine, and Belarus were naturally affiliated.) The Russian imperial tendency was also in friction with Ukrainian ethno-nationalism, a diffuse movement going back to the late nineteenth century and popular in the far-flung Ukrainian diaspora. The ethno-nationalist impulse, which was most widespread in western Ukraine, in those areas that had once been under Austro-Hungarian and Polish control, posited Ukraine as necessarily apart from Russia, distinct in language and ethnicity, and as long-standing victim of Russian or Soviet imperialism. Ethno-nationalist constituencies sometimes designated Ukraine as indigenously Western and Russia as indigenously Eastern, much as Poland or Hungary could at times define themselves against a Muslim other. Quite often, the Russian imperial purview and ethno-nationalism in Ukraine were symbiotic, somewhat like the British imperial purview of the 1760s and 1770s and the evolution of a distinctly American national identity in these decades.[12]

The war of February 2022 demonstrated the irreconcilable differences that had arisen between Russia and Ukraine, many of them after 2014. Putin would accept only a sovereign Ukraine that paid homage to Russia, that limited its ties to Europe and to the West, and that acknowledged explicitly or tacitly Ukraine's place within a Russian sphere of influence. These were the Kremlin's conditions for peace and for non-interference in Ukrainian affairs, and with Putin they were not up for debate. With the insight of a tragic hero, Viktor Yanukovych understood Russia's unbending terms. He knew they were harsh, and he knew that they were less and less grounded in Ukrainian society and politics. Ukraine certainly considered itself a nation. It felt more and more the attractions of Europe and the EU, though since 1991 Kyiv had had to balance an ethno-nationalist element with the Russophone or non-nationalist constituencies that persisted throughout Ukraine. Starting in 2014, with Yanukovych gone and with war in the air, Ukraine was moving rapidly away from Russia. It expanded its ties with the West and did what it could to escape from a Russian sphere of influence. This choice was not without costs, but these costs did not sway most Ukrainians from the basic decision made between November 2013 and February 2014. This was that Ukraine was better off turning West than turning East.

A Russian collision with Europe was not less historically fraught than the Russia-Ukraine collision. Imperial and Soviet Russia twice achieved a lasting peace with Europe, at both times when Russia was militarily ascendant. After the Napoleonic wars—the War of 1812 for Russia—a victorious Russia had joined the Concert of Europe and was with Britain, Prussia, and the Habsburg empire a conservative guarantor of European order and stability. Intermarried with royal families across Europe, the Romanov dynasty was a lynchpin of European peace until 1914. That year brought seemingly endless strife to Europe, wars hot and cold, until in 1975 the Soviet Union (at the peak of its power) completed negotiations with Western European nations and with the United States in Helsinki, Finland—the Helsinki Final Act, as it came to be known. Better remembered in the West for its endorsement of human rights and boost to the Eastern European dissident movements of the 1980s, the Helsinki Final Act also secured Europe's borders. Since 1945, these borders had been perilously open to readjustment, threatening war. On a landmass all too welcoming to imperialism and to conquest, Cold War Europe's most continuous flashpoint had been West Berlin, which the Soviet Union would have loved to have readjusted into East Germany, although it never did. The Helsinki Final Act gave Europe forty years of relative peace, no small achievement for the diplomats who negotiated it, until Russia annexed Crimea in 2014, consigning the Final Act to history. The right question is not why the Helsinki Final Act failed in 2014. By the standards of European history, the right question is why the deal survived for as long as it did.[13]

Even when a negotiated peace predominated, Russia tended to combine offensive and defensive strategies toward Europe. The defensive strategies have revolved around buffer zones in Belarus and Ukraine. Situated between Poland and the Baltic Republics on one side and Russia on the other, Belarus was once a part of the Soviet Union and before that of the Russian empire (and before that of the Polish-Lithuanian Commonwealth). Control of Ukrainian territory erects a buffer zone for Russia south of Belarus through to the Black Sea. In the name of self-defense, Russia has often gone on offense in Europe. Russia annexed parts of Poland together with Latvia, Estonia, and Lithuania in the late eighteenth century. The Soviet Union invaded Poland in 1920, an invasion Poland successfully repelled. Via the Molotov-Ribbentrop Pact of 1939, the Soviet Union colluded with Nazi Germany to carve up Poland and to take control of the Baltic Republics, a tenuous buffer zone against Hitler. The Soviet Union invaded Finland in 1940. The Soviet Union's conquest of half of Europe (by 1945) was offense as defense and defense as offense: the acquisition of new buffer zones in Central Europe had been enabled by Hitler's invasion of the Soviet Union. Russian soldiers, already stationed in post-Soviet Moldova in 1991, never left; Russia invaded Georgia in 2008, biting off two pieces of Georgian territory; it waged war against Ukraine in 2014 and 2015. Unprovoked, Russia invaded Ukraine again in February 2022. One could go back into early modern and medieval history to find other examples of Russia's many collisions with Europe, of invasions from one direction and then from another and then from another.

In 2022, Putin had to know that invading Ukraine would provoke Europe's wrath. It would be a rerun of 2014, he may have hoped, when Europe rallied on behalf of Ukraine and the EU imposed sanctions on Russia but when Europe steered fully clear of war. Before the 2022 war, Putin lamented Europe's hold on Ukraine, invoking the defense of an embattled Russia by emphasizing Ukraine's possible entry into the NATO alliance, his motivating nightmare scenario. Russia's misfortune, he complained, was Western encirclement. He had been boxed into a corner. Factually speaking, Ukraine's military relationship with the West had been advancing since 2014. It would progress further with the election of Joe Biden in 2020, Biden a stalwart transatlanticist and seasoned friend of Ukraine. But Putin's narrative was in many ways misleading, and it was intended to mislead. Putin's invasion of Ukraine reflected his low opinion of Europe, his contempt even. He looked down on Europe—in the form of the EU and of its myriad nation states—as a rhetorical superpower. Europe acted as if it could, simply by speaking up, ensure that Ukraine had the right to choose its trading partners, its political system, its alliances. Unbelievably, after centuries of imperialism and of imposing its terms on others, Europe acted as if all countries had full autonomy and independence by virtue of being "sovereign" countries. Yet the EU commanded no army. If France and Britain had real armies, unlike militarily bashful Germany, they would never use them in Ukraine, Putin must have surmised, whatever they said about Ukrainian liberty and Russian aggression. A tempting gap may have existed between Europe's perception of its power and its actual power, in Putin's eyes. On the eve of war, he may well have seen a Potemkin village in Europe's military setup, a vacuum waiting to be filled. To Russians Putin spoke only of defending Russia. In Europe, though, he was going on the offensive in 2022.

* * *

Europe's twenty-first-century collision with Russia was more reactive than Russia's collision with Europe. Among the thorniest questions in European politics and in modern European history is where the border with Russia should be. (Russia has the same problem with Europe.) Where does Europe end? Where does Russia begin? Napoleon had set out to forge a European Russia by conquering it, by ridding Russia of czarist autocracy, and by fashioning a Russia that was a vehicle and not an opponent of the European Enlightenment. Napoleon's invasion ended with Russian soldiers in Paris. After Napoleon, Europe resolved its Russia problem via the Concert of Europe. For this resolution, Poles, Lithuanians, Latvians, Estonians, and many other peoples paid the price of subordination to Saint Peterburg. World War I destabilized the dividing lines between Russia and Europe, borders moving monthly with the war. The end result was a Soviet Union vastly smaller than the Russian Empire had been in 1914. In the 1920s and 1930s, freshly minted nation states of Eastern Europe arrived at an unsteady equilibrium, interrupted by Nazi-Soviet collaboration in 1939 and then by Operation Barbarossa in 1941. Hitler's effort to transform the Soviet Union into German-controlled *Lebensraum* was Napoleon's fantasy without the Enlightenment behind it. In 1945, Churchill and Truman resented Stalin for leaving the Red Army in Eastern Europe, knowing this was the beginning of a vast Soviet empire at Europe's core, but they accepted this regrettable state of affairs. Militarily, they could not do otherwise, and so things stood for a long time. Some forty-five years after the end of World War II, the Soviet Union withdrew from Europe. Then, it vanished from the international stage altogether. When a diminished Russia emerged from the wreckage of the Soviet Union, its emergence did not settle the question of Europe and Russia. It brought this question back to life.

With the question of Russia and Europe in play again after 1991, so too was the question of war in play. It took a Europe based on the elimination of war some time to realize and to accept the dangerous relationship between an unfinished Russia and an unfinished Europe. The Kremlin was not just dissenting from the status quo in February 2022, not just criticizing the EU for having gotten too close to Ukraine, or objecting to NATO expansion in speeches and at diplomatic gatherings. Russia was bent on transforming the European status quo through war. It was, as Putin openly said, at war with "the collective West." Were Russia to realize its plans in Ukraine, this war would not be over; it might just be starting. The war might spread outside of Ukraine by accident, as World War I had come to Europe by accident; intentional or unintentional run-ins and cyberattacks could occur at any time. Even if the war did not spread, Russia was going to use all the means at its disposal to destabilize the EU and NATO: disinformation, espionage, active measures, the withholding of gas and oil, nuclear brinksmanship. Fully aware of where they stood with Russia after February 2022, European countries poured money and military assistance into Ukraine not just for Ukraine's sake but also out of self-defense, though assessments of self-defense varied from country to country. They levied sanctions on Russia as they never had before. Grudgingly in some cases, avidly in others, European countries accepted that their national security was in peril and that a state of semi-war had broken out between Europe (broadly construed) and Vladimir Putin's Russia. Even Germany underwent a change of heart due to the war, one that Poland, France, Britain, and the United States greeted with gratitude.[14]

* * *

The third layer of the collision confirmed in February 2022 was between Russia and the United States. It passed through stages on both sides. In the active memory of both countries, as the tension mounted, was the Cold War, which had begun to the west of Ukraine—in the vicinity of Germany. The Cold War had begun in Europe, though, and it was in Europe that the Cold War had ended, when the Berlin Wall came tumbling down. Moscow and Washington were accustomed to colliding in Europe. Woodrow Wilson and Vladimir Lenin had competed for Europe, one to democratize it and the other to make it communist, setting a precedent. After 1991, after four decades of Cold War, Russia and the United States never really found a way to cooperate on Europe. They succeeded only at avoiding overt disaster when times were bad. When times were good, they kept their distance capably, perhaps by not listening too closely to what the other was saying. Accustomed to ideological competition, in some respects excited by ideological competition, the United States and Russia were accustomed to militarized competition on a global scale. The United States returned to Cold War form when it framed the 2022 Russian invasion as an assault on democracy and as the epitome of authoritarian cruelty. In 2022, Russia returned to Cold War form by reaching out to the non-Western world and by blaming the war on the West's neo-colonial arrogance. Russia found sympathy in China, the same Communist China that had allied with the Soviet Union for some of the Cold War; in India, which had been non-aligned, though often philo-Soviet in the Cold War; in Africa, in the Middle East, and in Latin America, where the Soviet Union had been an active and at times an accepted or invited presence during the Cold War.[15]

The United States loomed large for Putin. At issue was its irritating strength and beguiling weakness. US strength lay in the combination of its military power and its powers of attraction. Since 2014 the various governments of Ukraine had *wanted* to ally with the United States: it was the United States keeping Kyiv at arm's length on entering NATO or on finalizing a treaty alliance. In Europe, the United States was everywhere, the hyperactive guarantor of regional security. It was hemming Russia in, and it would not close NATO's door for Ukraine out of deference to Russian sensitivities. It would not close the door on the Balkans or the south Caucasus. But the power of the United States, ubiquitous as it was, might be hollow. How else could victory have eluded the United States in Iraq? How else could the United States have lost a war in Afghanistan? How else could the United States claim red lines in Syria that were not actually red and not actually lines? How else could the United States stand by and watch as Russia walked into Syria in 2015 and seeded the American political landscape with fear and loathing in 2016? And why was the United States such a mess at home? Even the Americans themselves were asking this question incessantly, and never with as much sincerity or severity as after the attempted putsch of January 6, 2021. For Putin, American strength *and* American weakness were very likely provocative. The weaknesses modified the strengths, and for Putin the weaknesses could ideally be exploited to neutralize the strengths.

In 2022, Putin waged war in Ukraine in part to push the US perimeter of influence farther west. This could be achieved by dividing Ukraine in two, which was Putin's initial war aim. If the government in Kyiv fell, that would demonstrate the emptiness of US support. It would be Afghanistan in Europe. Perhaps European countries would then start to regard the United States as a distant, self-absorbed, and inept ally, a superpower in word but not in deed. That may have been the grandest of Putin's ambitions when he opted for war. The less specific aim was to foster chaos through war: not only to gain control over Ukraine, Putin's first-order intention, but to add to the balance sheet of dilemmas and crises that the faltering hegemon and its effete European sidekicks would have to face. That China was on Russia's side—though it was not a co-combatant in Ukraine—may have encouraged Putin in his assessment of the war's global stakes. When selecting February 2022 as the moment to strike, he had to have doubted US leadership. Since 2014, the United States had never been able to clarify its position on Ukraine, treating Ukraine as a quasi-ally and as a neutral state at the same time, and since September 11 and the ensuing global war on terror, the United States had been stumbling from one foreign-policy fiasco to another; or so it could seem to an unsympathetic observer. Watch and wait five years and Ukraine would be in Washington's pocket, Putin may have felt. Watch and wait five years and Washington might, as it had after the Vietnam War, find its global footing again, pitching forward with all its wealth and its technology and its self-confidence about how American the international order was supposed to be. Better not to watch and wait.

By no means did the United States want war with Russia in 2022, in 2014, or earlier. If Russia had faded away as a partner in 2011 and 2012, coming into focus as a semi-adversary, the United States still counted on Russia not to be a serious obstacle in 2022. When Moscow challenged Washington, Washington tended to pull back and to keep lines of communication open. In 2008, Russia invaded Georgia, and that did not upend the US-Russian relationship. In 2014, Russia annexed Crimea and invaded eastern Ukraine, and the United States was outraged but unable to reverse the annexation of Crimea or to expel Russian soldiers from the Donbas. Washington tolerated Russia's incursion into Syria in 2015. The US response to Russia's election interference in 2016 was muted. President Obama did not want to skew the 2016 election. Trump appreciated the interference while campaigning and wanted it to be forgotten (or misunderstood) once he won the election. Washington was always saying goodbye to "business as usual" with Russia until these goodbyes became an aspect of "business as usual" in a dysfunctional but somehow unchanging diplomatic relationship. When Joe Biden and Vladimir Putin met in the summer of 2021 in Geneva, both of them had the same message. They could do business with one another. For the United States, it was, as Samuel Johnson said of second marriages, the triumph of hope over experience. For Russia, the Geneva summit was likely stage-managed diplomacy meant to distract from a war that nobody was predicting in the summer of 2021.

Russia's invasion in February 2022 changed everything. Week by week, month by month, the United States rushed past inhibitions that had been established in the Cold War and taken for granted after the Cold War. US sanctioning of Russia reached record levels. US soft power was marshaled to stigmatize and shame Russia. A global coalition was formed—with Washington at its center—to counter Russia in Ukraine and to counter Russia per se. Most consequentially, the United States forged a military partnership with Ukraine that was not camouflaged, as such partnerships had tended to be during the Cold War, and that included intelligence sharing, targeting, and the provision of high-powered weaponry. The military partnership between the United States and Ukraine predated the war. Washington had sought this partnership not to embolden Ukraine but to deter Russia from further invading Ukraine. Once Russia began its massive war, the US military was already on the battlefield, although without uniformed soldiers on the ground and with care taken to distinguish between Ukraine's defense and attacks on Russian territory.[16] As was Europe, the United States was in a state of semi-war with Russia by February 2022, a war less circumscribed than the Cold War had ever been in Europe. The spheres of influence imposed on Europe after 1945, the rampant worries about escalation, the iron curtain and the diplomatic back and forth that typified the Cold War were all relics of the past by February 2022. On all sides, there was very little about the war in Ukraine that was cold.

* * *

Collisions is the story of this war. Or more precisely it is the story of the war's origins. Of Caesar's murder in *Julius Caesar*, Cassius, Brutus's accomplice, asks a prescient question—"how many ages hence/Shall this our lofty scene be acted over/In states unborn and accents unknown?" Ages hence will know how the war in Ukraine ends, and that knowledge will affect the question of its origins. Whether speaking in known or unknown accents or in states long standing or unborn (in the early twenty-first century), historians from ages hence will have another advantage. They will have government documents from the decision-makers; they will have access to archives; they will conduct interviews and make their way through memoirs, altering the debate over the war's origins. Putin's mind and motivations are a black box as far as empirical evidence goes. His thinking can be inferred from his speeches and from his actions: it can be the object of educated guess work, a very imprecise science. The Russian archives may never open, and members of Putin's inner circle may never speak. If they do, they may not have definitive or trustworthy answers to the question that overshadows this book. Why on February 24, 2022, did Putin invade Ukraine in the manner that he did? Whatever transpired in the Kremlin on the eve of the invasion was a scene more sordid than lofty. (Shakespeare's Cassius was himself romanticizing a brutal assassination as "our lofty scene.") Like Caesar's murder and like the murder of Archduke Ferdinand in 1914, Putin's decision will reverberate throughout the history of the twenty-first century. It may be acted over at some point. It will certainly be mulled over and argued over.

Collisions aligns the origins of the war in Ukraine with four intersecting causes. The first is Russia's will to control Ukraine, to hold the keys to its foreign policy, and to do so though persuasion or through manipulation or, if necessary, through force. The means have varied over the years in line with Ukrainian politics and Russian capabilities. The ends have stayed the same. The second cause is the precarious situation of Ukraine, a country with many friends and neighbors but without allies, a strategically vital country, a large country not easy to defend, and in 2022 a country that had already been invaded by Russia. Russia had been a military presence inside of Ukraine in the 1990s, not to mention in the Soviet or imperial Russian past. Putin's contempt for Ukraine spurred him to overestimate Ukraine's precarity: Ukraine would show Putin that it was less vulnerable than he thought it was. The third cause concerns Europe and the United States—the West—which were lazy about Ukraine after 2014 or perhaps since 1991, when Ukraine gained its independence. The West overpromised and underdelivered, compounding the practical difficulties of defending Ukraine from Russian invasion. Western policy did not crystallize around achievable aims. It was simultaneously too much (publicly promising Ukraine NATO membership); too little (refusing to arm Ukraine comprehensively after it was invaded in 2014); too optimistic (assuming this part of Europe would take care of itself); and too pessimistic (assuming that Ukraine could not defend itself). And fourth: Putin would not have invaded had he considered the United States capable of defeating Russia's ambitions in Ukraine. Putin's war was, among other things, a high-stakes bet against the United States or a bet on American decline. Any one of these causes might not have been enough to spark a war. It was the *confluence* of these four causes that made for the shattering collisions of February 2022.

Though *Collisions* often dips back into the twentieth century and before, it begins in 2008. This was the year a financial crisis broke out, a young man took the reins in the Kremlin, and another young man prepared to take the reins in the United States. Even with chaos bearing down on the global economy, it was a time of possibility in Washington and in Moscow. Russia was set to continue modernizing, gathering foreign styles and ideas into the Russian fold, tying Russia's economy to the outside world, refurbishing its two most splendid cities, and rejoicing at the growth of a Russian middle class. The United States was in the throes of democratic renewal, changing gears politically, moving grudgingly beyond the racial exclusions so common to American history, and eliminating excesses (it was hoped) from the global war on terror. To begin in 2008, with Dmitry Medvedev in the Kremlin and Barack Obama readying himself for the White House, neither of whom had any desire for war with Ukraine or for a serious US-Russia confrontation, is to begin outside the realm of inevitability. It is to begin in the realm of contingency, when no soothsayers' warnings were audible, when the horizon was neither cloudless nor cloudy but still open, when the script was not yet written. The story of *Collisions* begins at this indeterminate point and progresses, event by event, personality by personality, decision by decision, year by year to the anguish of a sprawling war. The Russia-Ukraine, Russia-Europe, Russia-United States collisions that were *not* predestined to occur when Barack Obama was first elected became the collisions that nevertheless did occur fourteen years later. This is the story of the winding road from an imperfect and in some ways star-crossed peace, complacently held yet beginning to fray in 2008, to the catastrophe set in motion in February 2022.

PART I
OPEN QUESTIONS, 2008–2013

1

Yes We Can

Bliss was it in that dawn to be alive,
But to be young was very heaven!

William Wordsworth, *The Prelude*

For seven years, the United States had lived in the shadow of the fallen towers, the damaged Pentagon, and the crashed airplane in rural Pennsylvania. September 11, 2001, had been the day on which—allegedly—everything changed. The fear and the insecurity were tenacious. Airports and government buildings started to resemble fortresses. Suspicion about the outside world, suspicion of foreign lands, and suspicion of the foreigner within were mounting. The cascading fear inundated American foreign policy. Fear underwrote two major overseas wars, enhancing the federal government and justifying the torture of terrorists or of people said to be terrorists (without too much legal handwringing over the difference). Elected in 2000, George W. Bush pushed vigorously for these changes. He fought a war in Afghanistan that would probably have been launched by any American president, and he decided for a war in Iraq that was his alone. Only in his second term did support for the Iraq War start to melt away. Only slowly did the fear started to dissipate. To a great degree, trust in the government diminished, an unintended consequence of September 11. As had happened so many times before in American history, domestic political concerns chipped away at the primacy of foreign affairs, reasserting themselves in a financial crisis that percolated in 2007 and boiled over in September 2008. Moral and strategic overreach was the unavoidable story of Bush's second term, dooming the candidacy of John McCain in 2008, although the global war on terror had been underwritten not just by the Republican Party. Most Democrats had gone along willingly, even enthusiastically, for the ride.

Had it not been for September 11, Barack Obama might not have become president. In the dynasty-driven era of the Bushes and the Clintons, of politics as a family business, Obama was a self-made man. He was from Hawaii, far from Washington, DC. In 2008, Obama was the owner of a superb but limited resume—the Illinois State Senate, three years in the US Senate, and before that his tenure as a law professor and community organizer. Obama was also Black. Until the moment he was elected, this could seem an insurmountable hurdle for

American voters, or so it was commonly argued before the election. Obama's policy ideas were in tune with those of the Democratic Party mainstream. They were fairly conventional. What got him noticed—in addition to his eloquence, his youth, and his skin color—was his position on the Iraq War. He had been critical of the war when most Democrats had been rallying around the flag and smoothing the Bush administration's path. Obama was the candidate of the hour in 2008, not least because he promised to save the United States from itself—and especially from what it had become after September 11. He spoke modestly of nation building at home, which could be interpreted as an anti-war message. He spoke warmly of international cooperation. He spoke pointedly about an end to the United States dividing the world into friends and foes. Throughout his campaign, Obama spoke implicitly about an end to the fear that for so long had inundated American politics. "Hope" was the fearless mantra of his presidential bid.

A careful reader of the American political tradition, Obama extracted an affirmative storyline from it. He interpreted Thomas Jefferson's obsession with rights—best articulated in the Declaration of Independence—as a precursor to the modern age of human rights. He read Abraham Lincoln's speeches on self-government as a fleshing out of the US Constitution and the Declaration of Independence: the labor of self-government, the value of deliberation, the appeal of mixed government, and the majesty of the law.[1] Two philosopher kings from the hinterlands, two lawyers-turned-politicians from Illinois, neither of them to the manor born, Lincoln and Obama had somehow made it to the White House. Obama had a quote from Martin Luther King Jr. stitched into the Oval Office carpet: the arc of the moral universe is long but it bends toward justice. For Obama, Martin Luther King Jr. fused two story lines: the civil-rights revolution fought for by Black Americans, their appeal to be treated as citizens of the United States; and the post-colonial struggles of the 1950s and 1960s, those that had minimized European empires in Asia, the Middle East, and Africa, unsettling the racial hierarchies fostered by centuries of colonial rule. Obama was no less invested in gay rights or women's rights than in the rights of ethnic and racial minorities. He placed these movements in the same continuum from Seneca Falls, New York, birthplace of the movement for women's rights in 1848, to Selma, Alabama, where in 1965 Black Americans had survived violence and abuse for the sake of affirming their constitutional rights. His election in 2008 was the latest data point in this continuum.

From Seneca Falls to Selma, as Obama was fond of saying. This progressive continuum did a great deal to inform Obama's view of international affairs. Much like his predecessor George W. Bush and his successor Donald Trump, Obama did not arrive at the White House with a deep diplomatic or international-affairs background. (The last president who had had this kind of background was

George H. W. Bush.) Obama's father was from Kenya and his mother was an anthropologist fascinated by the world outside the United States. Cosmopolitan and curious, Barack Obama had lived in Indonesia as a child and was widely traveled as an adult. He was an avid reader of books from different cultural and intellectual points of origin. He promised to lead the United States away from a unilateral war on terrorism and to scale back American militarism. He deplored the tendency of George W. Bush to dictate terms, especially to US allies, and he deplored Bush's simplistic binaries: with us or against us, new Europe versus old Europe. Obama cherished an interconnected or globalized world, and as president he sought to make the international scene more cooperative and more humane, more amenable to human rights, and in a subtle sense more American, which is to say more deliberative and more democratic. Merge the philosophical idealism of a Thomas Jefferson, the more tortured idealism of an Abraham Lincoln, the hortatory idealism of a Martin Luther King Jr., and you get the audacity of hope as Barack Obama articulated it in 2008, and as he would continue to articulate it as president.[2]

The Obama administration had a term for its foreign-policy vision—the liberal international order. Not the stuff of campaign rallies, the liberal international order was a guiding light to those who knew and believed in it. It was superior to the chest-thumping "free world" and to the ad hoc coalitions of the panicked war on terror. The liberal international order was less chauvinistic and less encumbered by culture, history, and civilization than *the West*, which for decades had been the organizing principle of American foreign policy. The liberal international order fit the dimensions of a globalized world, extending in all directions. The idea was born in 1945, if not in the eighteenth-century Enlightenment, and it was born in the devastation of the Second World War. Far-sighted policymakers saw that integration was crucial and could be achieved through laws and institutions, through commerce and trade, through the exchange of ideas and the free movement of people.[3] The United Nations embodied the spirit of the liberal international order. So too in its initial phases did the NATO alliance insofar as it performed one of its core functions, which was keeping the peace in Western Europe. The European Union (EU) was the liberal international order in microcosm. Eager to correct the excesses of counterterrorism, Obama thought the United States could revive the liberal international order in 2008 and universalize it through persuasion as well as through the appeal of the project itself. Obama disliked Bush's reliance on military power. More than that, he considered it old-fashioned, more nineteenth than twenty-first century, despite the association of war with September 11 and of September 11 with the most contemporary of foreign-policy challenges.[4]

Obama's advantage was the boldness of his vision. Were it to succeed, he would be a president in the grand manner of Woodrow Wilson, Harry Truman, or George H.W. Bush. These statesmen had enacted versions of the liberal international order in Europe and elsewhere: Wilson the visionary advocate of international cooperation and of a democratic Europe; Truman the progenitor of NATO and of peace in Western Europe; and Bush the president who witnessed Soviet influence evaporate from Eastern Europe, opening the East to democratic vistas that would have delighted Woodrow Wilson and Harry Truman alike.[5] In Obama's first term, he made great strides—in Europe, in Russia, in Africa, and in the Middle East. Obama's disadvantage was no less the boldness of his vision. The idealism and universality behind it hid some of the dangers that were coalescing in his first term: a stubborn streak of sectarian and authoritarian politics in the Middle East, and a China that had its own notions of international order, none of them liberal. China would use Obama's liberal international order as a station on the highway to Chinese progress in Chinese terms, but the coming collision—nowhere in sight in 2008—would not be with China or with authoritarianism in the Middle East. It would not be with the stateless terrorists who had provoked a vast war against them in 2001. The coming collision would be with Russia, and in the eight years of his presidency Obama's most formidable enemy turned out to be President Vladimir Putin, who clashed with the American president not just over international order in the abstract and not just over whose vision was nobler, wiser, and shrewder, but over a particular country, and one that was very far from the headlines in 2008. They would clash in 2014 over Ukraine.

* * *

On entering office, Obama's easiest foreign-policy job was to repair relations with Europe. They had been torn asunder by the Iraq War. Not all of Europe dissented from the hard-edged policies of George W. Bush. He had the support of the United Kingdom, the support of Spain, and the support of new Europe in Secretary of Defense Donald Rumsfeld's memorable phrase. New Europe was Eastern Europe, where Bush's "Freedom Agenda," his crusade against tyranny and authoritarianism, had a positive resonance; it resonated with memories of the 1989 revolutions. In Eastern Europe, many states had a fear of Russia, a reverence for the NATO alliance, and a close attachment to the United States, which they regarded as Europe's indispensable military power—not Britain, not France, not Germany, and not the European Union. In old Europe, the United States cut a different figure. As it had with the Vietnam War, this America could go off the rails. It could err on the side of aggression, and it could be culturally suspect, a consumerist behemoth overly enthusiastic about guns, religion, and laissez-faire capitalism. Western Europeans might enjoy stereotyping the United States. They were habitually drawn to caricatures of American politics, and then along came George W. Bush, who gave them the picture-perfect caricature of the American cowboy, reckless, trigger-happy, and ignorant. Perhaps Bush's war in Iraq was nothing more than the misadventure of a foolish president. Though old and new Europe may still have existed in 2008, five years into the Iraq War, the argument over the war had mostly been settled. Old Europe had been right. The Iraq War was an ongoing disaster, and saying so had helped to get Barack Obama elected in 2008.

The most remarkable defection from George W. Bush's war had been Germany. (Had France eagerly joined in an American war, that would have been no less remarkable.) On September 11, 2001, Gerhard Schroeder was Germany's chancellor, a social democrat from a working-class background whose party, the SPD, had pioneered *Ostpolitik*, a phase of outreach to the communist East, in the 1960s and 1970s.[6] Schroeder was not by nature the most pro-American of German chancellors, and neither was his foreign minister, Joschka Fischer, a member of the Green Party, who in the 1960s had been a prominent anti-war activist—anti–Vietnam War, that is. In 2001, Germany was not structured to oppose the United States. To the contrary, it was a close ally and member of NATO that had been occupied by the United States after World War II. Germany was a key staging ground for US military activities in Europe and the Middle East; US bases in Germany would end up being pivotal to the Iraq War. Twenty-first-century Germany was sovereign but not completely sovereign. It had no nuclear weapons and a small army, meaning that Germany was still dependent on the United States. This was why Joschka Fischer's remarks at the 2003 Munich Security Conference were so startling. "I am not convinced," he said in English to Donald Rumsfeld, who was in Munich to elicit support for the war.[7]

Schroeder stepped down from the German chancellorship in 2005. His political career over, he would enact his own version of *Ostpolitik* by becoming a handsomely paid lobbyist for the Russian government. He was replaced by someone very different from himself. Angela Merkel had grown up in East Germany, the daughter of a pastor. A physicist by training, she was living and working in Berlin when the wall came down in November 1989. The upheaval of this moment cast her not into the ardor of political activism but into the discipline of party politics. She joined the rival party to the SPD, the Christian Democrats (the CDU). Due to her own political gifts and to a corruption scandal that knocked a generation of CDU bigwigs off course, she enjoyed a spectacular journey from East German obscurity to the inner sanctums of power in a unified Germany. Merkel was many things. She was measured, cerebral, patient, taciturn, risk-averse (most of the time), and hard to read. She would be Germany's chancellor for sixteen years and the continent's most important political personality and decision-maker, bestriding Europe like a thoughtful colossus. The years between 2005 and 2021 were the age of Merkel in Europe, and a perplexing age it was, culminating by 2021 in a Europe that had survived fiscal and migration crises *and* a Europe that was descending once again into war.

Unlike Schroeder, Merkel was definitely an Atlanticist, and more than a conservative, she was a centrist. She was also unapologetically pro-American. Germany should stay close to the United States, she believed, and Merkel had almost ended her political career by supporting Bush's war in Iraq. She had served as minister for the environment, and like many Germans Merkel wanted to see swift progress on climate change. Not a free-market enthusiast on par with Ronald Reagan or Margaret Thatcher, Merkel had no desire to dismantle the German welfare state, but she favored markets and especially those markets that received German exports. After all, Germany had profited tremendously from the fall of communism in the Soviet Union and from the rise of capitalism in China. Merkel was not as sentimental a Europeanist as her political mentor, Helmut Kohl, the hero of German reunification, had been, though she was certainly a believer in the EU.[8] Never a dissident in East Germany, Merkel had hated its police state, and as chancellor she took what opportunities she could to champion democracy and human rights, while defining German relations with Russia (and with China) according to Germany's economic interests and not to any controversial human-rights agenda. Internationally, her beau ideal resembled a global *Rechtsstaat*, a panoply of states imbued with the rule of law. This was the liberal international order that Barack Obama had upheld while campaigning in 2008. For Obama and Merkel alike, it was a decent alternative to George W. Bush's penchant for division and for war.

Even though Obama and Merkel were an excellent match, not everything went smoothly between them. Obama had to manage Merkel's anger when she learned (in October 2013) that US intelligence had been tapping her cell phone, not just an annoyance to Merkel but a reminder to the German public of all that had gone haywire in the United States after September 11. The shadowy legality of the global war on terror elevated the concern that Germany was a *Rechtsstaat* and the United States was not. When Edward Snowden left government service, publicizing the scope of US surveillance programs, many Germans sided with Snowden and not with the Obama White House. The Afghanistan and Iraq wars continued with Obama, who expanded the parameters of drone warfare in places where the United States was not formally at war. Despite Obama's campaign-trail vows to close it, the detention center in Guantanamo Bay Cuba stayed open.[9] But the larger, more important story was of Obama's popularity in Germany and throughout Europe, of his infectious idealism, his way with words and his ability to demonstrate that in 2008 the United States had turned a corner. Perhaps "new Europe" missed the forthright toughness of a George W. Bush. Many Eastern European states had joined NATO while Bush was president. "Old Europe" audibly breathed a sigh of relief in 2008. The Texas cowboy was gone. A more European American partner was in evidence, and there was much to be done.

Germany was at the heart of Europe, and Europe was at the heart of Obama's international order. Having pioneered the worst forms of tyranny and authoritarianism in the 1920s and 1930s, Germany had turned itself into a European and a global role model. Hitler had pulled Europe and the world into war, committing unfathomable crimes, chief among them the Holocaust. It was world disorder at its lowest ebb. Then, advocates of the liberal international order believed, the US and Allied occupation had wrought a miracle after 1945, constructing (and reconstructing) the *Rechtsstaat* of which Angela Merkel was so proud. West Germany's restoration paid countless dividends inside and outside of Germany, manufacturing international order. (Japan did the same in Asia.) Having learned the art of deliberation in West Germany, Germans impressed this art on Western Europe. Franco-German cooperation on coal and steel was the germ of a new Europe—not in Donald Rumsfeld's sense but in the sense that Europe would rely on law and integration rather than on war and nationalism to move ahead. That this was a winning proposition became clear in the 1980s, when an integrated, democratic, and prosperous Western Europe outshone the economies and polities of Eastern Europe—West Germany over East Germany, West Berlin over East Berlin. Germany had been Europe's bellwether from start to finish. A country unified along West German lines after 1989, Germany had grown into a superpower of cooperation and integration. So too had the European Union in which Germany was enveloped. As Obama wrote in his memoirs, EU members had given up "some elements of their sovereignty." In exchange, they "had enjoyed a measure of peace and widespread prosperity perhaps unmatched by any collection of people in human history."[10]

For Merkel, this Obamian view of postwar Europe made intuitive sense. It was one of the reasons she was pro-American. In East Germany, she had been told to be skeptical of the United States, the plutocratic hegemon. Never blindly admiring of American politics, Merkel associated the United States with a nexus of virtues. It was the country that led the NATO alliance, subduing militarism in Western Europe by bringing Western Europe countries into the alliance; the country that had sustained a non-authoritarian political system, a democracy, from the 1770s into the twenty-first century, illustrating to outsiders, like the West Germans of the 1940s, that democracies could be stable and sustainable; and the country that embedded international affairs in institutions, practices, and procedures that were democratic in spirit. In the 1940s, the United States had strongly promoted Western European integration. Europeans later established the EU as a deliberative confederation similar to the League of Nations, which Woodrow Wilson had unsuccessfully promoted after World War I and which Congress had not allowed the United States to join. Wilson's contributions to integration were the best of the American bequest to Europe. Merkel had been chancellor for three years of George W. Bush's presidency, and she had never given up on *this* United States. With Bush, she deftly balanced her Atlanticism with the mainstream German disapproval of Bush's war-like foreign policy. With Obama as president, an internationalist and an institutionalist like Merkel herself, she had someone with whom she could accomplish great things.[11]

The Europe of 2008 was mostly at peace. The Balkan wars of the 1990s were over. The EU and NATO had dramatically expanded after 1991, very much with the approval of Barack Obama's Democratic predecessor, Bill Clinton, and with the hearty approval of George W. Bush, whose troubles with Europe were particular to the Iraq War and to his own political and diplomatic style. For the many countries that joined the EU and NATO, border disputes and military conflict, the cause of countless European wars, had been retired. To those who remembered the Cold War that had sputtered out between 1989 and 1991, Europe was a magical place in 2008. Travel had been freed from the iron curtain, and crossing national borders was easy. Many EU member states adopted the Euro between 1999 and 2002, a common currency that brought its own conveniences and its own unifying momentum.[12] In 2004, the American sociologist Jeremy Rifkin published a book titled *The European Dream: How Europe's Vision of the Future Is Quietly Eclipsing the American Dream.*[13] A bit breathlessly, Rifkin made good on its title, outlining Europe's dream of integration and cooperation, its generous social safety net and its plausible claim on the brightest of futures. Established in 1987 and named after an itinerant humanist intellectual, the EU's Erasmus Program sent students to universities across Europe, another version of the European dream, in which students, having received a broadly European education, would be spiritually European, and they could be Europeans in their political and professional lives as well. Numbering in the tens of millions by 2008, "Erasmus students" were the beneficiaries of Europe's peace dividend after a twentieth century of extreme nationalism and unfathomable bloodshed.

Merkel's and Obama's shared problem when Obama was inaugurated in 2009 was a financial crisis. American banks had been reckless. They had gamed the US housing market on the assumption that prices would always go up, that the US government would stand behind mortgages, and that there was no practical distinction between high-risk and low-risk housing loans. The high-risk loans had permeated the financial system. By exposing themselves to speculation in the US housing market, European banks had been reckless too. The financial crisis, which exploded in September 2008, was a classic case of the United States sneezing and of Europe catching a cold, though it took a while for the aftershocks to be felt in Europe. This crisis revealed an acute policy difference between Merkel and Obama. Obama propped up the banks, and he flooded the US economy with cash, for which the US government assumed considerable debt. Obama looked to Merkel to do the same in Europe and thus to minimize US exposure to knock-on maladies coming *from* Europe—to Europe sneezing and the United States catching a cold. He pushed Merkel so hard on the issue at the 2011 G-20 summit in Cannes that she burst into tears.[14] She did not change her mind, however, arguing that excessive debt would overburden Germany's aging population. She referenced the connection between debt and inflation that many Germans associated with the collapse of the Weimar Republic in 1933. Though Merkel preferred "German" austerity to "American" spending, Merkel's and Obama's relationship survived such disagreements. It was a policy disagreement among friends.[15]

Pressing as Europe's financial woes were after 2008 and pressing as these woes were in the United States, Merkel and Obama did not confine their gaze to the transatlantic West. Both had their sights set on China, the market-driven engine of the twenty-first century economy and confusingly a country still in the grip of the Communist Party. Neither Merkel nor Obama admired China's human-rights record, its one-party political system, its denial of political rights to all Chinese, and its furious denial of human rights to various minority populations—the Falun Gong, Buddhists in Tibet, Muslims in Xinjiang. Merkel looked past this record to the enormous Chinese market. Much more than the United States, Germany excelled at industrial output and manufacturing. It produced goods—like cars—that the Chinese were eager to buy. Meanwhile, Obama's "pivot to Asia," announced in the fall of 2011, was not a shift away from Europe to Asia but a basketball metaphor of the kind that was second nature to the sports-loving Obama. He sought a foreign policy that would enable the United States to pivot between Europe and Asia.[16] A son of Hawaii who had spent years of his childhood in Indonesia, Obama could not forget that the United States was a Pacific—and therefore an Asian—power in a way that no twenty-first-century European country was. Obama wanted his pivot to Asia to improve US alliances and working relationships in the Indo-Pacific, from Australia to Japan to India. The Quad, a security dialogue among Japan, India, Australia, and the United States, predated the Obama presidency; it had come into existence in 2007. Obama valued the Quad as an American gateway to Asia and not just as a discussion forum. He emphasized Asia's booming economies and populations, its dynamism, and its status as the driving force of global economic growth. The pivot to Asia was, in his view, a means of paying attention to this important and mostly beneficial trend.

President Obama's dedication to the liberal international order could give a positive spin to the Chinese future. The Chinese Communist Party might have evolved into a vehicle of Chinese nationalism, hostile to a Taiwan outside of China and keen at times to flex its economic and military muscle. China might not endorse the liberal international order. Its government was designed to suppress democracy, and China was hardly appreciative of American power and leadership,

but a twofold process would iron out the wrinkles over time. The Chinese government would see the value of international institutions, and by doing so it would
bend toward the cooperation that was the lifeblood of these institutions. In 2005,
Robert Zoellick had coined the phrase "responsible stakeholder" for China, more
aspirational than descriptive but on target for US policy: stakeholder first, responsible by and by.[17] In a separate groove, Chinese society would gravitate toward
greater democracy. Though the Tiananmen Square student uprising had been put
down in May 1989, the residual hunger for democracy was still there in Hong
Kong and in mainland China. A new post-communist generation was waiting to
be born. In 1989, the Soviet Union and Communist China had had to contend
with the magnetism of liberal societies. The Soviet Union could not withstand the
pressure. Given its staggering rates of economic growth, China could now compete with the United States and even outcompete it at times, but the arc of the political universe was long, and it bent toward democracy.

In the Middle East, the liberal international order was distant in 2008. George
W. Bush had tried to emancipate the Middle East by the sword. He had broken
from decades of cautious precedent by declaring that authoritarianism itself was
the problem in the Middle East, the lack of political freedom a root cause of terrorism and by extension of the September 11 attacks. (Before September 11, the
United States had partnered extensively with authoritarian states in the Middle
East, and many of these partnerships continued after September 11.) From
the end of the Cold War, Bush had learned a resounding lesson: that Ronald
Reagan had won it. Reagan's recipe was to confront and democratize. He had
confronted Soviet leaders in the 1980s, saying out loud that the Soviet Union
was an evil empire and enjoining "Mr. Gorbachev" to tear down the Berlin Wall.
Europe's democratization was the result. Bush's wars in Afghanistan and Iraq
were meant to alter the political destiny of Central Asia and the Middle East.
Afghanistan and Iraq would be exemplary states. Their path to democracy would
show that Afghans and Iraqis were democrats at heart, as was the entire human
race. Flourishing democracies in Afghanistan and Iraq would bring elections,
women's rights, and the best of American modernity not just to these two countries but to the world at large. In his second inaugural address, George W. Bush
spoke of a world freed from tyranny. His extravagant program for human emancipation flickered out not long after that speech in January 2005.[18] Both Merkel
and Obama saw a wealth of cautionary examples in Bush's attempted remaking
of the Middle East. Democratization could not be a military venture, and perhaps it was not as universal as Bush had made it out to be. Bringing the Middle
East into the liberal international order would have to be a long-term political
venture.

On June 4, 2009, President Obama traveled not to Bagdad but to Cairo to
sketch his dream for a better Middle East. There in one of the most discussed

speeches of his presidency, his "Cairo speech," he bid farewell to the stridency of George W. Bush. Obama acknowledged the West's imperial history in the Middle East, something that many in the Middle East associated with the unended Iraq War. Co-hosted by Cairo University and Al-Azhar University, the Cairo speech was a gesture of respect. The United States was not locked in a clash of civilizations with Muslims. It was instead a multi-cultural society in which Islam had a recognized home. Obama the American president had a modulated message in Cairo. He was there to espouse American values and through them the multiple paths to the promised land of rights and liberties, technological innovation and economic growth, international deliberation and cooperation. He was not in the Middle East to impose American values on anyone. His vision was of "democracy, human rights and women's rights, religious tolerance and the need for a true and lasting peace between a secure Israel and an autonomous Palestinian state," as he described the speech's themes in his memoirs.[19] The more countries, regions, and civilizations that adopted this vision, the stronger the liberal international order would become. Coercion was illiberal, whereas a liberal order had to be willingly joined. Were it to be only transatlantic, were it to belong only to the West, the liberal international order would fall short of the cosmopolitanism for which Obama wished to speak as an American president. It would also bypass the rapidly integrating communities and the connective promise of the twenty-first century.

About a year and half after Obama gave the Cairo speech, the Middle East cracked open. One country after another experienced the crumbling of the *ancien régime*, starting in Tunisia, where a spontaneous act of protest toppled an authoritarian government and pointed the way to politics in another mode: not the heavy, militaristic strong-man states of the past but an innovative merger of youth, civic activism, and democracy. It was the season of the Arab Spring, and its pace and scale were breathtaking. An indispensable medium of the new politics was the internet, as it had been in Barack Obama's 2008 campaign and as had been anticipated in the popular thesis (during the first decade of the twenty-first century) that the internet democratized by its very nature.[20] Making full use of social media, young people could challenge the state's powers of oppression, as they did on Cairo's Tahrir Square, granting themselves the freedom of assembly. Obama's dilemma was the international appeal and progressive spirit of the protest movements in North Africa and the Middle East. They had erupted from the degradations of authoritarian rule, and as revolutions they were intentionally turning the status quo upside down. Yet much of this status quo was underwritten by the United States either because of US economic interests (oil), because of US commitments to Israeli security, or because the regional balance of power was thought to depend on aid to authoritarian leaders like Egypt's Hosni Mubarak.[21] Obama, who vacillated but could not simply stay silent and back Mubarak, felt personally and politically obliged to encourage the Arab Spring. He openly called for Mubarak to step down, which Mubarak did on February 11, 2011.[22]

In the sunshine of the Arab Spring, Libya devolved into a conundrum for the liberal international order. US actions in Libya would be augmented by a corollary of this order, the right to protect, to use military force for humanitarian purposes, associated with Obama's advisor Samantha Power, "one of my closest friends in the White House," as he described her in his memoirs. Her 2005 book, *A Problem from Hell*, a study of genocide across time and place, had been a tour de force, and Obama had read it carefully: it was "one of the reasons I'd brought her to the White House."[23] Samantha Power had come of age politically with the Balkan wars of the 1990s. Twentieth-century history had taught her, an activist by nature, the lesson that only state power can curb genocidal intent. World War II was the paradigmatic, if imperfect example: the Holocaust had not gone further because Nazi Germany was defeated on the battlefield. NATO's corralling of Serbia in the late 1990s also proved that American power might impose itself between tyranny and genocide. When Libyan forces threatened to commit atrocities in February 2011, Obama himself wavered. He was not going to start an Iraq War of his own, though Power and others in his administration convinced him to go to the United Nations and to go to NATO. In this way, the United States would honor the responsibility to protect and fulfill the non-pacifist imperatives of the liberal international order. By October 2011, Muamar Gaddafi the tyrant had fallen. He was attacked and killed on the street, but US intervention in Libya, limited to the application of air power, had become a case study of the liberal international order devouring itself. Having chosen not to send in ground troops, Obama did not have any more of a political plan for Libya than George Bush had had for Iraq. Libya descended into a disarray that was neither liberal nor orderly. Obama would later call his use of force in Libya the greatest mistake of his presidency. Surely, the souring of the Arab Spring in Libya and elsewhere was one of the greatest disappointments of his presidency.[24]

Obama's stewardship of the liberal international order bore fruit in Africa, where he had better prospects for building on George W. Bush's record than he did in the Middle East. Bush had strengthened African countries' capacity to fight communicable diseases, the collective problem-solving at the core of the liberal international order. To Bush's impressive legacy Obama added a new intensity of outreach.[25] During his often emotional visits to the continent, Obama did not treat Africa as an afterthought—as so many American presidents had done previously. Obama could believably promise to avoid the drawbacks of the Cold War approach to Africa: the shameful partnership with South Africa under apartheid; the reputation of the United States for racism in its foreign policy, for not treating African countries as the agents of their own destiny, for taking up the mantle of European imperialism and for deep-seated racism at home; and the Cold War dirty dealing in many parts of Africa. (The Soviet Union and post-Soviet Russia had large networks of support in sub-Saharan Africa, not least because of the many Africans who studied in Russia or earlier in the Soviet Union and not least because of a common desire in Africa for alternatives to the United States.) A less ennobling continuity between Bush and Obama surfaced in the global war on terror in Africa and elsewhere. Though he began no new wars, Obama was not less globally active than Bush. This included quite a bit of low-grade and undeclared war in places where the threat of terrorism was perceived.

As in Africa, the liberal international order framed President Obama's approach to Latin America. There the signature issue became the US opening to Cuba, the *bête noire* of US foreign policy since its turn to communism in the 1950s. The site of the 1961 Bay of Pigs invasion, an American debacle, Cuban history harbored many instances of US meddling. Cuba was also the home of Fidel Castro, for many in the United States, and for many Cubans who had emigrated to the United States, a hated symbol of the anti-American revolutionary. With September 11 and the Cold War in mind, Obama had speculated about a less confrontational, less us-them attitude in his Cairo speech. The winner of a transformative election, Obama reached for a transformative foreign policy, the motors of which would be respect and dialogue. Through negotiations carried out by Obama's close advisor, Ben Rhodes, the Obama administration mended a broken Cold War relationship that made no sense to the president. What was the point of an ideological antipathy toward Cuba when so much more could be achieved through interaction and through Cuba's integration into the economic and social structures of the Western hemisphere? Obama's outstretched hand to Cuba—together with his opening gambits in Asia, the Middle East, and Africa—was a bet on the next generation in Cuba and in the United States, on their collective tolerance and creativity, on their desire not to repeat the mistakes of the past, whether these mistakes emerged from colonialism, from inequality, from the excesses of the Cold War, from ingrained prejudice, or from the fearsome anxieties unleashed by terrorist attacks.

* * *

Russia and Ukraine each had assigned spots in the liberal international order, and Washington could regard both with modest optimism in 2009. So could leaders in Europe, who since 1991 had witnessed so many advances toward peace, prosperity, growth, and integration. The problem concerning Ukraine and Russia was not the ill intentions of Europe and the United States. Europe and the United States thought they had the best of intentions, and in many respects they did. The problem in transatlantic capitals was all that the liberal international order hid from view. It obscured the fact that some choices are zero-sum, such as (eventually) the choice Ukraine would have to make between Russia and Europe.[26] It obscured the true contours of Europe after the Cold War: a success story to be sure but with acute instability under the surface. Europe was flexible and brittle at the same time. It was brittle because of its flexibility: some of Europe was in the EU; some was not. Some of Europe was in NATO; some was not. Yet the doors to NATO and to the EU were perpetually open, meaning in theory that Europe was without end. Obama and Merkel did not overlook any easy solution to the problem of Europe's flexibility and brittleness; there was no easy solution. In Eastern Europe, though, the intrinsic optimism of the liberal international order, the premise that it was a conflict-ending mechanism per se, running on some invisible engine of global cooperation, was an intellectual burden. It encouraged the untroubled sense that everything would work out well, oddly enough in a part of Europe where nothing had ever worked out peacefully—not for long. As it had been throughout the twentieth century, Eastern Europe (taken as a whole and not just as the Eastern Europe within the EU and NATO) would be inhospitable soil for the liberal international order in the twenty-first century.

The Eastern Europe Obama inherited in 2009 deserves some historical context, starting in Ukraine. The story of independent Ukraine is a story of European ambiguities. Some of this ambiguity originated in Ukraine, which did not cast its lot fully with Europe after 1991. The EU and NATO were not necessarily its terms of reference in the 1990s, when the EU and NATO were only beginning to expand eastward and were still far from Ukraine. For Ukraine, economic and other ties to the former Soviet Union and to post-Soviet Russia were profound. Transportation systems and pipelines, folkways and habit linked political economy in post-Soviet Russia and in post-Soviet Ukraine. There was no categorical or simple way of orienting Ukraine away from Moscow and toward Brussels, and in the 1990s Kyiv oscillated between presidents who leaned toward Russia and those who leaned toward the West. Leonid Kravchuk, a former communist and the first president of independent Ukraine, looked West to the extent that he could. Leonid Kuchma, who succeeded him, looked not only to Russia but he looked East as much as he looked West. Viktor Yushchenko, who came to power in 2004, irritated Russia, while in the West he was appreciated as a reformer. Viktor Yanukovych, Russia's preferred candidate in 2004, was democratically elected in 2010. Prior to 2014, Western leaders did not make it a priority to achieve Ukraine's "Euro-Atlantic integration," a phrase they would use for Ukraine after the Maidan Revolution of 2014. Nor was it a Western priority to bring Ukraine into NATO and the EU. Even if it had been a priority, Western countries would have run up against friction within Ukraine, where NATO and the EU had defenders and detractors. That was the internal ambiguity.[27]

The external ambiguities mattered too, and they go back at least to the end of World War II. European integration and NATO both got their start in the 1940s and 1950s, though the European Union came about later. European integration and NATO were designed for the delimited geography of Western Europe and for a Europe that was rigidly divided into East and West. The iron curtain was an immutable fact of European life until 1989. This tragic dividing line lent coherence to the EU and NATO as they were originally conceived. The EU could pursue integration within a circumscribed set of countries at peace with each other, while a NATO condemned to sitting still was a defensive military alliance. It had everything it needed to defend Western Europe against the Soviet Union. So superlative was NATO that it could deter the Soviet Union from attacking in the first place, which it expertly did. For the duration of the Cold War, pan-European institutions developed quickly and profoundly but within a territory bounded by the Atlantic Ocean to the west, by the Mediterranean Sea to the south, and by the iron curtain to the east. NATO had an open-door policy from the beginning: any country could apply to join, and by the 1950s NATO stretched from Turkey to Iceland and from Portugal to the United States. It was enormous, but like "institutional Europe" it existed within Europe's Cold War confines. When the Berlin Wall came down in 1989, Europe was all of a sudden wide open.[28] NATO and European institutions such as the European Union, established in 1993, no longer faced any natural barriers to expansion.

When the Soviet Union disappeared, NATO enlargement was not the immediate rallying cry in Washington, Berlin, Paris, or London. Enlargement came in the 1990s because of Eastern European countries that very much wanted to join NATO and because Washington preferred a unified to a piecemeal approach to Eastern Europe. Washington's twinned worries were that countries in a non-aligned Eastern Europe or a non-NATO Eastern Europe might seek nuclear weapons; and that an Eastern Europe without the incentive to join Western institutions like NATO and the EU might falter politically. Its democracies, novel inventions in a region historically prone to autocratic governance, might backslide. A new system for Europe that was not NATO redux could be devised on paper, encompassing East and West. Yet it was the EU and NATO that were there on the ground in Europe; they were both real and familiar. It was far simpler to have them be the vehicles of the new system and to have both the EU and NATO grow to meet the needs of a Europe without an iron curtain than it was to invent new institutions. NATO membership delighted Warsaw and Prague, whose leaders, Lech Walesa and Václav Havel, respectively, were esteemed and eloquent advocates for NATO enlargement.[29] Figures of moral authority, they were hard to turn down. A bigger NATO would be fine for Eastern Europe, according to a gathering consensus on European security. It would be fine for Western Europe, which would be the controlling element in the EU. It would be fine for Washington, which would be the controlling element in NATO. NATO and EU expansion enhanced peace, democracy, and Western leadership in Europe. It was win-win.[30]

It was not win-win for everyone in Eastern Europe. The drawback of taking a decades-old institution like NATO and grafting it onto new territories was that it functioned less well in Eastern Europe, where the geography and the history differed from Western Europe's. Western Europe had established nation states, going back to its early modern history: France, Britain, Switzerland, Spain, the Netherlands, and the nineteenth-century newcomers, Germany and Italy. Western Europe's nation states, which emerged from and overlapped with the many empires of early modern Europe, had ancient histories of enmity and two world wars to their credit. One could say, though, that the entire problem of Western European security had been soluble in the late 1940s, and because it was soluble it had been solved. By contrast, Eastern Europe was territorially amorphous: the Balkans in the south, including Turkey perhaps; the Central European states of Poland, Hungary, Czechoslovakia (later the Czech Republic and Slovakia) in the west; the Baltic States in the north. That was one half of Eastern Europe. The other half was Belarus, Ukraine, and Moldova. It might also be the south Caucasus: Georgia, Armenia, and Azerbaijan. Down to 1991, most of the countries of this "other Europe" had been shackled to the history of empire. The preeminent Eastern European empire was of course Russia, an Eastern European empire since the seventeenth century, and many of its structures and purposes had been incorporated into the Soviet Union. At various times, the Polish-Lithuanian Commonwealth, Sweden, Austro-Hungary, Prussia, the German *Kaiserreich*, and the Ottoman Empire had crisscrossed Eastern Europe as well, a patchwork quilt of competing (and at times complementary) empires. It was not as if this history fell by the wayside or became irrelevant simply because the Soviet Union committed suicide in 1991 and because its self-erasure allowed NATO and the EU to advance.[31]

By expanding eastward, NATO made itself a central actor in the geopolitical story of Eastern Europe, possibly the central actor because of its immense military resources. NATO enlargement proceeded on the unwise premise that NATO expansion was itself resolving the problem of Eastern European security. In truth, by expanding, NATO was absorbing the age-old problem of Eastern European security in the 1990s and thereafter. It was embarking on a project far more demanding and dangerous than what NATO had set out to do in 1949, when it was created. What made NATO's ambitions in Eastern Europe bewildering as well as dangerous was that NATO comfortably accepted some Eastern European countries, while uncomfortably failing to accept all Eastern European countries into the alliance. Turkey had been a member since 1952. The Baltic Republics were waved in in 2004, following the path of the pioneering Central European nations. A few Balkan nations got in, and a few did not. Russia did not get in. Nor did Ukraine or Belarus, Georgia, Armenia, or Azerbaijan. Why Estonia and not Belarus? Why Latvia and not Ukraine? Why Croatia and not Serbia? There were ample logistical, historical, and cultural answers to these questions, but there were few good strategic answers to them. NATO was unifying Europe by dividing it, and dividing it by uniting it. There was no Eastern European empire able to dissuade NATO from expanding in the 1990s, no Ottoman Empire, no Austro-Hungarian empire, no Prussia, no *Kaiserreich*, no Nazi Germany, no Russian empire, no Soviet Union. They had all died their ignominious deaths, leaving the illusion of an open, uncontested playing field in one of history's least open and least uncontested playing fields.

Ukraine was among Europe's non-NATO "in between" states in the 1990s, and with Ukraine, the United States was accustomed to going slow. In July 1991, shortly before the Ukrainian Soviet Socialist Republic voted to leave the Soviet Union, George H. W. Bush had given his "chicken Kyiv" speech. So called by the *New York Times* columnist, William Safire, a wordsmith and a wit, the "chicken Kyiv" speech was Bush's attempt to muffle Ukrainian zeal for independence. Do not rock the boat, he recommended, cautioning in particular against nationalism. The Ukrainian Soviet Socialist Republic had a sizable nuclear arsenal, and the United States had a long history of arms-control negotiations and agreements with Moscow. These were some of the most meaningful achievements of Cold War diplomacy, achievements that did not cease to matter after the Cold War. Throughout the 1990s, the will to keep the Soviet nuclear arsenal under Moscow's control and not to have it dispersed among post-Soviet nation states or sold off to unscrupulous independent actors guided US and European expectations for Ukraine. Ukraine's *not* being a nuclear power would be its contribution to international order. NATO accession was remote for Kyiv, an abstraction, and so it was for Washington as well. Diplomacy, which thrives on specific objectives, fell into place for the West around two goals—the existence of Ukraine as a sovereign European state, a fait accompli by 1991, which Russia's president Boris Yeltsin respected, and the existence of Ukraine as a non-nuclear state, which would be a fait accompli by the mid-1990s.

Ukraine signed the Trilateral Statement in January 1994, consenting to deliver its nuclear weapons to Russia. (Already in 1992, Ukraine had signed the Lisbon Protocol, establishing its status as a non-nuclear state.) It was a concession, though Ukraine would have had to invest and recalibrate dramatically if it were to become a functioning nuclear power; the last of its nuclear weapons was given up in 1996. In return, Ukraine got the Budapest Memorandum. Signed in December 1994 by the United States, Russia, and Ukraine, the Budapest Memorandum guaranteed Ukraine's territorial sovereignty. A memorandum is a diplomatic uncertainty, a publicly signed document but also not a treaty: it is closest perhaps to a pledge, resting on the sincerity of those making the pledge.[32] The other development of 1994 was Ukraine's joining the Partnership for Peace, a collaboration with NATO and an attempt to adapt Eastern Europe to NATO and NATO to Eastern Europe. Russia too was invited to join, and Boris Yeltsin applauded the Partnership for Peace, not because he accepted NATO or liked its expansion but because he wanted some Russian say in things or at least the appearance of a Russian say in things. These three developments—the Trilateral Statement, the Budapest Memorandum, and Ukraine's and Russia's entry into the Partnership for Peace—gave the impression that the region had positive momentum. The nuclear weapons had been handled. Ukraine had a security guarantee of sorts with the Budapest Memorandum. Russia was cooperating with NATO. A better, more peaceful Europe was everywhere on the horizon, in the East and in the West.[33]

The fourteen years between 1994 and 2008 were years of Western inattention to Ukraine. Although the EU was expanding in Central Europe and the Baltics, the path to EU membership had (by 2008) long ago stalled for Turkey, which had been more interested in applying for EU membership than Brussels was in accepting its application: Turkey had been officially recognized as a candidate for EU membership in 1999. Geography distanced Ukraine from Brussels. A post-Soviet state stymied on rule of law and weighed down by an all too post-Soviet economy, Ukraine did not endear itself to an EU that had already moved precipitously eastward. Ukraine could seem another Turkey with an awkwardly big population. Either Ukraine was not as self-evidently European as the Baltic Republics managed to appear or it was more resolutely Eastern European.[34] No less post-Soviet than Ukraine, though each had been an independent country in the interwar years, which was not the case with Ukraine, the Baltic Republics had walked into the European club. Together with Belarus, Ukraine could seem an extension of Russia to Europeans unfamiliar with the region. Moreover, for many Europeans, the surprise of the 1990s and of the new millennium was not that too few countries were entering into Europe. It was that so many countries, erstwhile colonies of Moscow orphaned behind the iron curtain, were suddenly full-fledged members of the European family.

Center stage during the Cold War's final chapters, Eastern Europe fell in stature after the Cold War. In Washington, the foreign-policy revolution between 1994 and 2008 was less NATO expansion, which was merely the growth of a venerable institution, than the global war on terror. President from 1992 to 2000 and a child of the Cold War, Bill Clinton had lavished attention on Europe and Russia. From the Cold War, he had learned the destructive potential of war: he had protested the Vietnam War as a student, something that got rehashed in the 1992 campaign.[35] As president, Clinton did everything he could to preserve the gains of 1989, to solidify the norms of peace in Europe, and to initiate a decent working relationship with Russia. Another child of the Cold War, for whom Reagan's full-throated defense of freedom was far more pertinent than the Vietnam War, George W. Bush coasted for the first few months of his presidency.

When tragedy struck on September 11, the consuming mission of his presidency was thrust upon him. Not since the Second World War had the United States reoriented its foreign policy and military posture so comprehensively: a new cabinet-level department, the Department of Homeland Security; multiple overseas wars; a rapid expansion of the intelligence community; and the combined diplomatic-military-intelligence community dedication to "counterterrorism," with the lion's share of resources and attention going to September 11–related concerns. Apart from its local counterterrorism challenges, Europe fell into the background after 2001. The Middle East and Central Asia—plus parts of Asia and Africa—were the geographic locus of American foreign policy. Ukraine fell off the map, and Russia was at best an afterthought.[36]

George W. Bush's views on Ukraine followed from his Reagan-esque convictions about freedom. The claim that freedom would drain the swamps of despair in the Middle East, thus eliminating terrorism, applied to countries untouched by the global war on terror. Freedom might mean democracy, or it might mean a country's freedom to choose its international course. Bush regarded Georgia and Ukraine in the light of such freedom: they were both democracies, and both countries were endowed with a God-given right to determine their alliances. Facing a formidable neighbor in Russia, they were out there in the geopolitical ether. Their leadership looked with interest to the Article 5 security guarantee that comes with NATO membership. NATO's Article 5 was no memorandum. It was a definite commitment, and it was backed up by the world's sole superpower. In April 2008, Bush came to the NATO summit in Bucharest eager to hand a Membership Action Plan (MAP) to Ukraine and to Georgia, opening their paths to accession.[37] Both countries were interested in applying, and NATO's proverbial door had never not been open. Yet at Bucharest Bush got blocked by France and Germany, leading to a peculiar Euro-American compromise. No MAP would be forthcoming, but a statement was released affirming that one day Georgia and Ukraine *would* be NATO members.[38] The sloppiness of the decision-making and the incoherence of the agreed-upon compromise are hard to imagine without the global war on terror in the background, without the energy expended (by the United States) on issues other than NATO expansion, without the prevailing sense that Europe had figured itself out after 1991, that broadly speaking NATO was the solution to Europe's security problems regardless of when NATO would usher in Ukraine and Georgia. After all, the world's worst real-time challenges and crises were elsewhere, and for many decades NATO's track record in Europe had been flawless.[39]

From the ashes of the Bucharest summit and its insincere promise to Georgia and Ukraine arose a new EU project. It was not just for Georgia and Ukraine. It was for six of the "in between" states: Belarus, Ukraine, Moldova, Georgia, Armenia, and Azerbaijan, all former Soviet Republics. The non-aligned status of Ukraine,

Moldova, Georgia, and Azerbaijan was indication of a job unfinished; Armenia and Belarus had military partnerships with Russia. The EU was not ready to admit any of these six countries, and NATO had just withheld a MAP from two of them. What Europe's leaders refused to say openly was that these six countries were *not* slated for NATO or EU membership, but they could instead be given a partnership with the EU. It would be win-win. The EU would escape the travails of actual membership for these countries, each burdened by corruption and democratic deficits, and these countries would in turn come closer to the EU; the prospect of future membership would always be there. Devised by Carl Bildt, a Swedish diplomat, and Radek Sikorsky, a Polish diplomat, the Eastern Partnership Program (EaP) was launched in 2009. Its aim was "to create the necessary conditions for political association and further integration between the European Union and its Eastern partners."[40] The partners would have to adopt the *acquis communitaires*, the rules and regulations that would facilitate trade and exchange, to take advantage of the EaP. As they did, the EU would become more and more of a partner. An economic and legal logic predominated, but, in the program's own parlance, the partnership between the EU and these six countries was to be more than an agreement about rules. It was to be a "political association."

The liberal international order was on the move. The EaP embodied the German notion of transformation through commerce, since commerce created dependencies as well as human contact, decreasing the likelihood of war.[41] The *acquis communitaires* were a web of legal arrangements, the stuff of a transnational *Rechtsstaat*, and for Merkel and Obama alike the EaP was attractively institutional. It echoed Obama's faith in young people, in the next generation, which, whether in Georgia or Ukraine, would surely prefer contact with the EU to isolation. A new generation of leaders would prefer peace and freedom of movement to the imperialist depredations of the Eastern European past. It would be genuinely win-win on one condition. For the liberal international order to lift up the EaP, the country to Ukraine's east and to Georgia's north would have to accept or at least not oppose the program. The entire arrangement—the haphazard enlargement of NATO and the compromise offer of Eastern partnership rather than EU and NATO membership—rested on a compliant Russia. All the headwinds would be right if Russia were to be tied up with its own affairs or, better yet, if Russia could be yet another pillar in an integrating European home. Russia had as much to gain from a quiet and prosperous Europe as the United States, did it not? The EaP might have begun with Russia's neighbors; it might have been invented to save these neighbors from unwanted Russian influence. Yet the EaP might culminate in an acceptance of the *acquis communitaires* by the ultimate Eastern partner, which is to say by Russia itself. Not part of the original plan, this was not unthinkable in 2009.

* * *

Back in the 1990s, the Clinton administration had labeled Yeltsin a demo-crat not least because Yeltsin labeled himself a democrat. Yeltsin had invited American economic advisors to join in on the creation of a market economy in Russia. This they enthusiastically did, jolting the protean Russia of the 1990s with "shock therapy." While the Russian economy was being therapeutically shocked into life, Yeltsin removed many of the police-state attributes that had marked the Soviet Union. The boy from Hope, Arkansas, Clinton had excel-lent rapport with Yeltsin, who had come of age in the Urals, in the Russian provinces. They were Bill and Boris, and together they addressed nuclear non-proliferation in the former Soviet Union. Boris did not block Bill's effort to expand NATO, not that he had a good way of doing so, and his non-resistance helped Bill to get money into Boris's hands. Tension did arise between Yeltsin, the valiant Russian democrat, and Russian democracy, never more notice-ably than during the 1996 presidential election in Russia, which Yeltsin contemplated canceling and which he struggled to win. From Washington, Clinton did what he could to promote Yeltsin, as did Germany's chancellor, Helmut Kohl, who during the campaign declared Yeltsin "the best president for Russia."[42] Clinton feared Russia's regression back to communism a mere five years after the Soviet Union's collapse. He also feared Russia's descent into manic nationalism, something that might throw Europe off kilter by disrupting Russia's relations with its neighbors, none of which were yet in NATO by 1996. Washington left no doubt about the candidate it preferred, politely delaying the visible work of NATO enlargement until after the election. To Clinton's great relief, Yeltsin came out ahead.

US-Russian relations deteriorated over time. Yeltsin the democrat deviated from democratic practice in late 1999.[43] His health was bad, and he was visibly tired. When stepping down from Russia's presidency, he would apologize to Russians for not having done more to improve their lot. Yeltsin wanted a young, effective leader to succeed him and to protect his family from the retribution of political opponents. Not quite trusting the Russian electorate, Yeltsin installed his prime minister, Vladimir Putin, as acting president on New Year's Eve 1999. When Putin stood for election in the spring of 2000, he had the incalculable ad-vantage of already being president. Yeltsin was the king maker, and Clinton did not much like the king he made. Presidents Putin and Clinton met only once, the whole light-hearted drama (or farce) of the "Bill and Boris show" having come to an end. Putin coldly received Clinton at the Kremlin. Clinton later conveyed his unease about Putin to his successor, George W. Bush. As with Clinton, Bush's re-lations with his Russian counterpart would worsen over time, but they began on a high note, and Bush conveniently isolated two from the many available Putins, recognizing a modernizing pragmatist and a pious Christian in the Russian leader. He got a glimpse into Putin's soul during their 2001 meeting in Slovenia.[44]

This was a projection of modern America, as Bush envisioned or idealized it, onto Putin's Russia. For an American president who loved to speak about his own religiosity, Putin was seemingly a kindred spirit, whose willingness to help came in handy after September 11, when he was the first foreign leader to call Bush. Putin presented Russia to Bush as a country that could subdue Islamist extremism and terrorism of all kinds, doing so as the partner and the equal of the United States. Bush must have liked what he heard from Putin.[45]

Within the global war on terror, Russia waxed and waned as a US partner. Russia offered its assistance in Central Asia, doing what would have been impossible during the Cold War, when the United States and Soviet Union clashed in Afghanistan. Given how far Central Asia was from the United States, Russia's help with basing rights in Uzbekistan and Kyrgyzstan simplified the US war effort in Afghanistan. US and Russian interests could overlap in the global war on terror. The United States wanted to curtail Islamist extremism everywhere. Russia, with its large and historic Muslim community, its struggles against Chechen separatism, its proximity to the Middle East and to Central Asia, wanted to prevent Islamist extremism from becoming a regional threat or a threat within Russia itself. Putin initially saw September 11 as a chance to let go of the Cold War rivalry. Meanwhile, Bush was busily applying broad moral categories to his foreign policy, not just to the Middle East but globally. He invoked an axis of evil, vaguely reminiscent of World War II and comprising Iraq, Iran, and North Korea. Russia did not symbolize goodness in Washington, and it was not exactly on the side of the United States in Bush's terminology of being "with us" or "against us." But it was not against, and in the immediate aftermath of September 11, Russia and the United States were as close and as cooperative as they had ever been.

With the Iraq War of 2003, Russia drew away from the United States and the United States from Russia. Putin tried to talk Bush out of the Iraq War. Russia had an old relationship with Saddam Hussein, one that went back to Soviet times and one that Putin wished to preserve. Bush's antipathy to authoritarianism must also have struck Putin either as unintentional nonsense or as deliberate folly. Putin had correctly assessed some of the war's negative consequences. The war would not democratize Iraq and stabilize the Middle East. It would destabilize Iraq and destabilize the Middle East—to the detriment of the United States and Russia. Not only did the Iraq War, a showcase for American power, end the illusion of US-Russian parity. The war devalued the UN Security Council, one of the few objective indices of Russian superpower status and a check in theory and at times in practice on American hegemony. The Iraq War was truly a problem for the Kremlin—beyond the problems it caused in Iraq and beyond the economic ties it destroyed for Russia. Putin was not being capricious in opposing it.[46]

In 2008, Russia and the United States did not experience a spectacular breakup. For the Bush administration, Russia did not greatly matter. It was not a foe, and its economy was diminutive compared to China's. Russia did not stand for anything big in international affairs—not democracy, not communism, not good. It did not even have the distinction of being an evil empire. On the assumption of Russia's relative non-importance, it made more sense to encourage freedom in Georgia and Ukraine. The Czech Republic, Hungary, and Poland had joined NATO in 1999, and in the "big bang" of 2004 the three Baltic Republics as well as Bulgaria, Romania, Slovakia, and Slovenia came through the door. For the Bush White House, every Eastern European country had the freedom to join NATO, and joining NATO would make them more free.[47] As late as June 16, 2007, though, Bush hosted Putin at his family's compound in Kennebunkport, Maine. A year later, Putin's successor, Dmitry Medvedev, responded to Bush's Freedom Agenda and to developments on the ground in Georgia by going to war there. It was the eleventh hour of the Bush presidency—three months before the presidential election and one month before the financial crisis that would overtake the headlines in September 2008. Despite Bush's best efforts, Georgia was not in NATO; it was not a treaty ally of the United States. The war itself was relatively quick, and Russian forces refrained from attacking Tbilisi, the capital city. For these reasons, the United States stayed on the sidelines: Bush was not going to send in the Marines. Russia had long presided over a "frozen conflict" in Moldova, leaving Russian soldiers parked on Moldovan territory throughout the 1990s and thereafter. Over time, the frozen conflict in Moldova became a forgotten conflict. Another "frozen conflict" followed the war in Georgia.[48] The Russian soldiers stayed in the north, while Moscow occasionally retouched the borders of territory it neither annexed nor let back into a sovereign Georgia. This was not the Russia Bush had hoped for. Yet in the eight tumultuous years of his tumultuous Russia's infringement on the territorial integrity of Georgia and Moldova was a sideshow.

* * *

The Georgia War did not dispel Washington's hopes for Russia. Badly as things had gone between Bush and Putin, annoyed as Putin had grown with Bush and Bush with Putin, Bush was about to step down in 2008. In a satisfying symmetry, Putin was finishing out his constitutionally mandated term as well. Vladimir Putin exited the office of the president and Dmitry Medvedev entered (in May 2008). George W. Bush exited the White House and Barack Obama entered. Between 2000 and 2008, Putin had characterized himself as a modernizer, and in these years Russia had indeed modernized. Medvedev was more emphatic: a first-class modernizer he would be.[49] It clicked for Obama, who in no sense approved of Putin's war in Georgia or of Putin's disregard for democracy but who tied the downturn in US-Russian relations in part to the "go it alone" ethos of the Bush team. During the campaign, Obama said he would talk to Iran. As president,

Obama did talk to Iran and to Cuba. Of course, Obama would talk to Russia, which was not Iran or North Korea or Saddam Hussein's Iraq. The Obama "reset" with Russia was a computing metaphor: reload, reboot, reset, the terminology of modernization.[50] Not everything was mired in the past; not everything had to be. If George W. Bush admired Reagan for being courageous enough to win the Cold War, Obama admired Reagan for being forward-looking enough to end the Cold War. Let not war burden the US-Russian relationship—not the Cold War, not the Iraq War, not the global war on terror, not the Russian war in Georgia. Let the relationship crystallize around economic growth, technological innovation, and peace. This had to be what the common folk of Russia and the United States expected of their leaders.

The reset could be sweeping, and it could be practical. Because the war in Afghanistan was very much ongoing, the United States needed transportation routes into the country, which Russia could help provide. Hardly a relic of the Cold War, arms control had to be maintained, and both countries could save money through successful arms-control agreements. Russia was an increasingly important part of the global economy, a major producer of gas and oil and a market for Western goods and services, a Eurasian hub. Keeping US-Russian relations steady, not letting them get out of hand, was a gift to the crisis-ridden global economy in 2009, and it was imperative that Russia not interfere with US allies in Europe, the beating heart of the liberal international order. Russian-occupied territory in Georgia and Moldova was an ugly fact, though a fact that was more outlier perhaps than precedent. For the White House, the reset was, finally, a step toward Russia's intended democratization. It would bring more of America to Russia—the American way of doing business, the American way of engaging the public sphere, the American way of enlisting youth and technology in social change. By preventing Russia from closing itself off—with the occasional nudge from Washington, if need be—the reset would elevate the democratic spirit in Russian life. It would consolidate the rocky political pluralism of the 1990s, the economic expansion between 2000 and 2008, and the basic global tendency toward democracy since the 1970s. When Russia would finally consolidate its democracy, it was not only the Russian citizens who would reap the rewards. It was the United States too that would gain. A Russian democracy, once secured, would equal permanent peace in Europe and permanent peace between the world's two major nuclear powers. Win-win-win.

The US-Russian reset had its tragi-comic debut in March 2009. In Geneva, Secretary of State Hillary Clinton presented Foreign Minister Sergey Lavrov of Russia with a button on which a non-English word was imprinted. It was supposed to be the word for "reset" in Russian, *perezagruzka*, but somehow the wrong word got put onto the button—*peregruzka*, meaning "overload." A veteran of Russian diplomacy even in 2009, Lavrov was a man with a mordant sense of humor. He took the button and laughed. While promising to put the button on his desk, he could not resist pointing out the spelling mistake.[51] Captured on video, the personal interaction of Secretary Clinton and Foreign Minister Lavrov betrayed charm and awkwardness, a reset baptized in laughter and error. Reset or overload? It was the right question. A *peregruzka* had seemed likely if Putin had been in the Kremlin: a collision of interests and worldviews of which the 2008 war in Georgia was emblematic. Yet a *perezagruzka* had its seductions in March 2009, especially if Medvedev would have the fortitude to open Russia more and more to democratic practice, if he would open Russia more and more to the outside world and to the United States. Much depended on Russia itself, that creation of Boris Yeltsin's and Vladimir Putin's in the eighteen years since the Soviet Union's collapse. Would it blossom into a mature democracy, untying geopolitical knots in Europe, the Middle East, and Asia? Or would it travel down some other path? The riddle wrapped in a mystery inside an enigma, in Winston Churchill's oft-quoted characterization of Russia, was back—not that it had ever gone away. However unresolved, this legendary enigma did not preoccupy the White House after the "yes we can" optimism of Obama's presidential campaign. An overloaded Cold War past need not stand in the way of an expertly designed reset. In a Russia more modern than ancient, a reset was bound to gain traction. It was bound to gain traction in the Russia of Dmitry Medvedev.

2

The Allure of a Modern Russia

> Russia is part of European culture. I cannot imagine my country
> in isolation from Europe and from the so-called, as we often say,
> civilized world. So I find it difficult to imagine NATO as an enemy.
> It seems to me that . . . even posing the question this way can be
> damaging.
>
> Vladimir Putin in an interview with David Frost, March 5, 2000[1]

The Soviet Union had once been modernity par excellence. Having traveled there
in the 1920s, the American journalist Lincoln Steffens declared that he had seen
the future "and it works."[2] The Soviet Union was the first country to base its political and social life on the philosophy of Karl Marx, the first country where communist theory had been turned to praxis. The Soviet Union was in every respect
the product of revolution. In the name of progress, the Bolsheviks eliminated the
Russian aristocracy, executed Czar Nicholas II and his family, and hobbled the
Russian Orthodox Church. They believed in the new man, the new woman, the
new family. Waves of avant-garde art swept through the Soviet Union in the early
1920s, after which Joseph Stalin, who took charge in the late 1920s, built the first
communist superpower, a country so modern that it eviscerated the Nazi leviathan, took control of half of Eastern Europe, and sat at the table with Britain and
the United States, dividing up the world.[3] Soviet modernity had immense global
appeal after World War II. By the late 1940s, China was imitating it. So too would
North Korea, Vietnam, Cuba, Cambodia, Angola, Mozambique, and a host of
other countries enamored of the Soviet model in the second half of the twentieth
century. The Cold War was a forty-year competition over which was the more
modern country, the Soviet Union or the United States. The winner of the competition was not a foregone conclusion. In the 1970s, many in the Soviet Union
and many in the United States thought that the Soviet Union might claim the
laurel wreaths of modernity. The Vietnam War could seem a turning point that
confirmed both American decline and Soviet ascendance.

By the 1970s, modernity appeared to be shunning the Soviet Union. The
Soviet war in Afghanistan, begun in 1979, was an unintelligent and costly war.
The Soviet economy delivered certain goods in high volume, but it was ever
less vibrant, ever less agile. Leonid Brezhnev became a leader synonymous with

doing nothing, and after his death in 1982 a film of crisis settled on the selection of the Soviet leaders. One after another of the Union's elderly leaders was dying in office. From the Brezhnevite stasis emerged a general secretary who was a forward-looking reformer. A man from a simple background in southern Russia, Mikhail Gorbachev had climbed to the heights of Soviet politics, and he loved the heritage of Soviet modernity. Gorbachev truly believed in the Soviet Union and believed he could bring it forward. His touchstone was communism itself, the doctrinal theories of Marx and Lenin. The least bloodthirsty leader the Soviet Union ever had, Gorbachev did not adequately appreciate the role that coercion played in uniting the many peoples and nations of the Soviet Union, a giant multi-ethnic, multi-confessional empire. He would learn quickly the shortcomings of his reforms, which could not bridge the distance between the Soviet Union and a viable economic system. Pushed from power in the fall of 1991, Gorbachev was forced to watch as the Soviet flag was taken down from the Kremlin on Christmas Eve 1991. To forestall its steady unraveling, the Soviet Union had abolished itself.

The trauma of post-Soviet Russia was its objective backwardness. Its birth was the death of a revolutionary empire, and in the 1990s Moscow's sway over Eastern Europe declined to almost nothing. Each of the other fourteen countries that arose from the carcass of the Soviet Union, several of them with histories of liberation from imperial Russia, could characterize its creation as independence gained. Only Russia seriously contemplated this transition as paradise lost. Post-Soviet Russia wrestled with its political vacancies. The Soviet Union had been familiar in its institutions and rituals, its party congresses, its newspapers, its slogans, its nightly news. Post-Soviet Russia had to invent itself from scratch. Nor could it invent itself in opposition to Russia as many other post-Soviet countries did, having undergone revolutions of national independence in 1991. Post-Soviet Russia had to invent itself as a Russia that was no longer Soviet, whatever that meant in light of Soviet and pre-revolutionary Russian history, and as a Russia pledged to democracy. Russia's most immediate trauma was economic, a bruising loss of security, a disruption felt in the life of every family and every individual. The irony was bleak and unforgiving. Soviet citizens had become impatient with Soviet rule in part because of its relative consumer poverty. They got what they were asking for, an end to communist rule, and the result was a rapid drop in the standard of living.[4] "Everything they told us about communism was a lie," ran a 1990s-era joke about the Bolsheviks, whereas "everything they told us about capitalism was true."

For Russia in the 1990s, backwardness meant catching up with the West. The Soviet Union or Soviet Russia had lost the Cold War by being increasingly unable to wage it, irrefutable proof that Soviet communism had lost the race. Had the Soviet Union been able to generate greater wealth, had it been able to keep pace with the computer age, the Soviet Union might have stayed in the Cold War. It might have held its own in the Cold War. Instead, the Soviet Union's failure to change, despite its official commitment to revolution, had amounted to an inability to be modern. After 1991, the West was transparently modern because it had won the Cold War, having lived to bury the Soviet Union. It recovered from the setbacks of the 1970s—the energy crisis, the Vietnam War—and from the doldrums of Watergate and its accompanying malaise. It got a wealth bump in the 1980s. It raced ahead with computing technology, giving it manifold economic and military advantages. While conventional great powers rose and fell, the West, its decline so often predicted, rose and rose. Such were the common perceptions of the 1990s. For post-Soviet Russia, these clichés drove home a simple lesson: to become modern, Russia had to become more like the West. Fast-food restaurants cropped up in Moscow. So did billboards and advertising. Democracy was the word of the hour, and everything in Russia came on the market, the very market that was supposed to have been redirected into a planned utopia in 1917. Most poignant was the Soviet memorabilia that was sold to Western tourists, the fur hats with the red stars on them and bric-a-brac with Soviet military insignia, the unloved detritus of a fallen empire.[5]

Despite its alleged backwardness, Russia after 1991 was following the allure of modernity. This was not an illusion. The allure was real enough, and the country was Europeanizing more than it was Americanizing, its society unconstrained. Russia was joining the outside world, improvising a political order that was not unfree. If its economy bestowed benefits haphazardly, it did bestow benefits. The image of a modern Russia was integral to US foreign policy after 1991, almost its emotional center. It oriented the US approach to Russia, since a market-oriented, prospering Russia was necessary for Europe to work as it was supposed to work and for the liberal international order to work as it was supposed to work. At some point, because Russia was becoming modern, it would grow itself into a proper democracy. Where America was, Russia would follow. The EU and NATO expanded eastward on the basis of an overall optimism about relations with Russia, which in Washington was an optimism about a viable modern Russia. Because the allure of a modern Russia was real, the United States and Europe could be justified in thinking that their conflicts with Russia, which were frequent, were destined to be temporary. Many thought this even after the annexation of Crimea and invasion of eastern Ukraine in 2014. Wishful thinking can be irresistible, as can expectations of a better future. So can the perceived superiority of one's own political model be irresistible, especially when legitimate evidence supports these frames of reference. For far too long, the allure of a modern Russia made it hard to notice the dilemma of a modern Russia, of a Russia that was a modern adversary, drawing life from technology and from global markets, without turning its back on the world, a modern and therefore a formidable adversary. This is the realization that came to the West, if it truly did, only in February 2022.

* * *

Vladimir Putin became Russia's appointed president at the apex of American excitement about globalization. The September 11 attacks had not yet happened, and the supercharged globalization that preceded them had coincided with the fall of the Soviet Union. Just as excessive state control had destroyed the Soviet Union, the cohesion and power of countries like the United States (many concluded) had to be a function of open markets. Open markets required free trade among national markets, and free trade required open markets, a moratorium on Berlin Walls and iron curtains. During the Cold War, the iron curtain had been more than a metaphor: the restrictions on travel imposed by the iron curtain were severe. It was an ordeal to go from East Berlin to West Berlin, from Bratislava to Vienna (some fifty miles away), from Leningrad to Helsinki (some 250 miles away). The lifting of the iron curtain engendered an astonishing liberty of movement and much excited speculation about a new age of integration and progress.[6] Globalization was the movement not just of goods but of people and ideas across national borders. A third aspect of globalization, hard to discern in the America-saturated 1990s, was the rise of China, booming because of its access to non-Chinese markets and to investment from outside of China. The density of economic wealth and power enjoyed by Western Europe, the United States, and Japan after 1945 was shifting farther eastward—not so much to struggling Russia in the 1990s but in a way that placed post-Soviet Russia between two powerhouses of innovation and wealth, the established economies of the West and the flourishing economies of Asia.

No doubt Boris Yeltsin, Russia's leader since 1991, had personal reasons for promoting Putin. Yeltsin must have sought the loyalty he would get from Putin, but the Yeltsin who chastised himself for not doing enough to modernize Russia also promoted Putin to continue his own unfinished work. Born in Leningrad in 1952, Putin was not of the Soviet elite and not of the intelligentsia; his was a typical Soviet family. Having spent some time on the city streets, learning their lingo as a youth, Putin took up judo and benefited from its emphasis on self-discipline. Step by step, he advanced toward his dream of government service. He was the Soviet equivalent of a self-made man, less rags to riches than rags to the KGB. Emotionally attached to the Soviet Union, the young Putin also admired the KGB's code of conduct, *its* emphasis on self-discipline, and the chances it presented for travel and social advancement. Putin's KGB posting in East Germany gave him an affection for his host country and for its culture. In Soviet Russia (as in many other countries), Germany carried the connotation of being orderly, advanced, and modern. What Putin endured in his tenure in

Dresden was the erosion of the old Soviet order and the momentous grassroots revolutions of 1989, which he watched with consternation. When he telephoned headquarters in Moscow, amid unrest in East Germany, he got the message that Moscow is silent. It is one of the archetypal Putin anecdotes, the supposed key to his political psyche. Once the KGB disappeared in name, together with the Soviet Union—Moscow's silence having been fatal—Putin had to begin anew.

Putin distinguished himself in the 1990s, having returned to his hometown of Saint Petersburg, formerly known as Leningrad. These were the extraordinary chapters in Putin's biography, shrouded in later embellishments and stylized narratives. When Putin went to work for the mayor's office in Saint Petersburg, it was not as a starry-eyed democrat, desperate to rid Russia of its Soviet past and to have it adapt to Western ways. Neither was he surreptitiously trying to resurrect communism or to erect a reactionary dictatorship in Russia. His political fortunes were tied to Anatoly Sobchak, a self-declared liberal who had been one of Putin's law professors in 1970s Leningrad. (Dmitry Medvedev was another of Sobchak's law students.)[7] Putin's instinct for the intersection of money and power drew him to politics, and in post-Soviet Saint Petersburg he handled the business contracts through which the intersection of money and power came to life. He had organizational talent and was not overtly corrupt. Yet he was not squeamish about the corruption that coursed through Saint Petersburg in those violent, hard-pressed years. His work ethic was notable enough for him to be called to Moscow, where he vaulted into the upper echelons of political power: a Hollywood tale of pluck and transformation. Putin was appointed head of the FSB (Federal Security Service, in English), the successor to the KGB. The KGB had proven to be a valuable alumni network in post-Soviet Russia, as it was in many post-Soviet countries. Enterprising figures in the KGB had amassed hard-currency reserves and business assets before the fall of the Soviet Union, which they translated into status and political clout in post-Soviet Russia.[8]

Yeltsin made Putin's career by bringing him to Moscow, by placing him at the head of the FSB (the internal-security successor to the KGB) and then by making him prime minister. What Putin was *not* may have impressed Yeltsin. Putin was not old, and Yeltsin had lived through the jokes and the mockery that attended Leonid Brezhnev's later years: Brezhnev the cognate for stagnation and the bumbling, inarticulate Soviet leader who had died in office. Yeltsin had witnessed the deaths of one aged general secretary after another in the early 1980s. Burdened by health problems, Yeltsin was not a young man himself in 1999, whereas Putin was forty-eight years old in 2000. Putin was not obviously ideological, and that suited a society with the ideological hangover Russia had in the 1990s. Yeltsin had bested Gorbachev in the late 1980s in part because he had been less ideological, less of a communist than Gorbachev, or not a communist at all, and Yeltsin did not govern Russia as an ideologue. In the 1990s, Russia was a potpourri of ideologies: still Soviet, yet capable of being zealously capitalist; still westernizing in aspiration, yet capable of being zealously nationalist. Perhaps Yeltsin felt that Russia needed a leader who could manage Russia's many and contradictory ideological leanings without adhering too rigidly to any one of them. Putin was also discreet and dedicated to his work. He was not a drinker like Yeltsin, who, by the 1990s, was trailed by a long list of embarrassing anecdotes: the time his plane landed in Ireland and he was unable to walk out of it; the time he picked up a baton and started conducting a band in Germany; the time he wandered around the nighttime streets of Washington, DC, in his underwear, trying, as was later explained, to get hold of a pizza. These (often embellished) anecdotes were damaging to Russia's international reputation. By comparison, Vladimir Putin could come across as a staid technocrat and as such, a steadying influence.

Putin could deliver what Yeltsin was seeking. The nine years between 1991 and 2000 had been among the most complex in Russian history. Depending on the observer, they could be remembered as a moment of anarchic freedom, of pure becoming, or they could be remembered as the time when the floor dropped out and everyone was suspended mid-air.[9] Personal and political freedom were at hand as never before in Russian history, yet one person's intoxicating freedom might well be another's abyss. Not up for debate was the scale of the transitions. They were enormous, and all the transitions, good and bad, were given a harder edge by a financial crash in 1998, when many Russians lost their personal savings, lost their jobs, or saw their pensions dwindle in value. More so than the supposedly classless Soviet Union, post-Soviet Russia was money driven, and throughout the 1990s money was asserting itself more than the Russian state was asserting itself. The market was supposed to be Russia's salvation, its path out from the communist dead end—in a society that had once had an extensive social safety net and that had exchanged this safety net for the mercies of the market. In 1998, money and markets showed how cruel they could be, turning planning for the future on its head. Yeltsin felt personally responsible for Russians' loss of confidence in the late 1990s and for the common intuition by the decade's end that the country was going off course.

Putin's appeal was the promise of stability—not too much stasis, not too much reform, and no hint of revolution. This too would be a part of the Putin mythology, disseminated in later cycles of government propaganda, not entirely fiction and not entirely fact. The 1990s were without form, after which there was order in the world: and that order was Vladimir Putin. What is not after-the-fact mythology was the merger of stability and globalization that Putin pursued in 2000. By stability Putin meant predictability, something that had been in short supply ever since the Soviet Union's sudden implosion. Yeltsin's Russia may have been exciting, and it may have been free, but nobody could say that it was predictable. Here Putin could draw on his personality, which was more measured than Yeltsin's. He could draw on his KGB past, as if to say that he had been a highly trained professional in the Soviet Union and would be highly trained professional president of Russia. He could draw as well on his law degree, most likely a plagiarized PhD dissertation, but in Putin's manicured biography a sign—in addition to his being a Germanophile—that he stood for law and order, order and law. Putin implied that with him there would be a system. That was what the Soviet Union had had, the mighty Soviet Union, the conqueror of worlds, and that was often what was missed in Yeltsin's Russia, which had placed such heavy responsibilities on the individual. If Russia were to compete on the bewildering playing field of globalization, the field on which the Americans and the Western Europeans had such an unfairly long head start, it would have to have a system. As so often in its history, Russia was reconstituting itself with reference to the West. Yeltsin had given Putin this task, which he himself had been given by the collapse of the Soviet Union.

The formula for Putin's system was stability within globalization. In 2000, there was not much of an alternative for Russia. To swear off globalization, as the Soviet Union had mostly done, was to condemn Russia to poverty, which would make people restless and leave post-Soviet Russia a stunted great power. Putin's version of globalization, lightly Soviet in some respects, was not necessarily to let the market have its way. That Yeltsin had tried to the dismay of many Russians, leaving Yeltsin horrified by the results of shock therapy. Putin's version of globalization did not empower the market at the expense of the Russian state: it empowered the Russian state through the productive energies of the market. That was very far from the Washington consensus of the 1990s, the "neoliberal" practices often said to be preconditions for globalization, which idealized the self-limiting, streamlined state, a networked and highly international economic environment and everywhere the unbridled market.[10] Putin's thinking harmonized better with the Chinese version of capitalism—capitalism with a statist face. In the early 2000s, the Chinese model had a prestige outside of Europe and the United States that the Soviet Union had enjoyed in the 1950s and 1960s: China showed how a non-Western and formerly anti-capitalist country could keep pace with and maybe overtake the West. Putin the modernizer wanted the Russian economy to be rule-bound in the sense that he wanted it to be orderly, stable, and constant. It was the law of rules, rules that people could know and abide by (and bend), much more than it was the rule of law, for which there was little precedent in Russia, going back to medieval and to czarist times.[11] Such stability would stimulate wealth in Russia, Putin understood, and attract investment from abroad, benefiting the Kremlin. No less important, over time it would enable Russia's military modernization.[12]

Putin's quest for stability within globalization mirrored the particularities of Russian politics circa 2000. A near universal trait of post-Soviet countries, from

Latvia to Georgia, was the proliferation of oligarchs. Oligarchs had access to capital, to inside information, to government contracts, to assets and resources inherited from Soviet times or gathered quickly in the post-Soviet free-for-all. Rarely did these oligarchs confine themselves to amassing fame and fortune. They dabbled in politics or they plunged into politics because political power and wealth walk hand in hand and because the acquisition and preservation of wealth in these post-Soviet countries depended on the goodwill of political elites. Media—especially television—attracted the post-Soviet oligarchs, who could use media access to shape the political scene. Putin had the chance to study oligarchs' behavior from the mayor's office in Saint Petersburg, where he could scrutinize the transformation of oligarchs into political forces in their own right, a country's unelected governors.[13] As president in 2000, Putin set about corralling Russia's many oligarchs, demonstrating to them that they were not the country's unelected governors and that they could not meaningfully challenge the state. The state would challenge them first, something that had populist appeal. Putin intimidated, imprisoned, and forced into exile those oligarchs who considered themselves above the state or outside the state. Putin, who never fetishized the free market, fetishized the centralizing authorities of the Russian state. In the language of Russian politics, he was a *gosudarstvennik*, a statist.[14]

Globalization's appeal to a modern Russia was certainly financial. A stable Russia within a globalized world could be counted on to sell its reserves of gas and oil, and in a globalized world the demand for gas and oil was constantly increasing. Even before the Russian Revolution, Russia had been an oil-producing country. The Soviet Union found its way back to this status in the 1970s, gaining a lot from oil revenue. The drop in global oil prices was one of Gorbachev's many headaches in the late 1980s and a cause of the Soviet Union's general discontent. Once the Soviet Union was gone, the construction of pipelines to Europe, the large-scale export of gas and oil, was not initiated by Putin; it had been a key feature of Yeltsin's Russia.[15] It was Putin, though, who reaped the rewards. As if by pipeline, money flowed into Russia between 2000 and 2008, yielding the "new Russian" of the era, the clownish nouveau riche with disposable income and no taste, and yielding a Moscow inundated in conspicuous consumption.[16] The money enriched the Russian state through the siphoning off of private-sector profits or through state-owned enterprises in the energy business or in other businesses. The private sector did not mean in Russia what it meant the West. It was never genuinely private. Yet the money trickled down and generated a Russian middle class, whose standard of living was better than in Soviet times and better than it was in the 1990s. For the first time since 1917, Russia had and was happy to have a consumer culture, creating new forms of unevenly distributed abundance. Without globalization, Russia might have gotten eternally stuck in "the 1990s" or in the post-Soviet blues that many associated with the 1990s.

Without stability, the dividends of globalization might have eluded Russia. They would certainly have eluded the Russian state.

* * *

The articulation of a Russian foreign policy after 1991, more Putin's job than Yeltsin's, was long a work in progress. Though Yeltsin had started out as a local politician, he had no shortage of ideas about foreign policy. Capable and energetic, he came to Moscow from Sverdlovsk (now Yekaterinburg), where he had risen up in the construction industry. He was less of a cosmopolitan than Gorbachev and less of an internationalist, but he threw himself into the creation of post-Soviet Russia and into guiding its career on the international stage. However energetic, Yeltsin grappled with two near insurmountable constraints while he was president. Russian was in dire financial straits. The money available for investment and state revenue was inadequate, and to keep things going Yeltsin had to come to Washington or to Western financial institutions hat in hand, asking for money; this made it next to impossible for Yeltsin to assert himself against the West. Yeltsin's other foreign-policy challenge was military. Post-Soviet Russia was still a nuclear power. It had a vote on the UN Security Council, but its conventional military was not what the Soviet Union's had been. The Russian military's technological deficiencies, which had their source in Soviet isolation and sluggishness, were wide ranging, as were its problems of morale. In this sense, Yeltsin's two foreign-policy difficulties intersected. The cash-strapped Russian state needed income to function, and it needed wealth to modernize the Russian military. Nuclear weapons are a foreign-policy tool of last resort, useful for intimidation but not for much else. Only with an effective conventional military could Russia have the day-to-day leverage sought by powers great and small.[17]

All of Yeltsin's difficulties confronted Putin in 2000, when the Russian economy still showed the wounds of the 1998 financial crisis and Russia's military was not in any sense on par with the US military. That had been Yeltsin's lot, and it defined President Putin's first forays into foreign policy. Another continuity between Yeltsin and Putin was the belief that Russia deserved to be respected as a great power. When they looked back at Gorbachev, Yeltsin and Putin were aware how unpopular Gorbachev's foreign policy was in post-Soviet Russia. Behind Gorbachev's folly they could see his charity, his desire to do Europeans a favor, which in the end had been Russia's charity. Yet the United States was convinced it had won the Cold War. *Germany Unified and Europe Transformed: A Study in Statecraft* was the 1995 book that two NSC staffers, Philip Zelikow and Condoleezza Rice, wrote about the end of the Cold War, placing the United States in the starring role.[18] (In 2001, George W. Bush appointed Condoleezza Rice as his national security advisor and in 2005 as his secretary of state.) Perhaps

Helmut Kohl imagined that he had unified Germany and transformed Europe. Perhaps Margaret Thatcher imagined that it had been her doing. Looked at from Moscow, this was interpreting history backward. The peaceful resolution to the Cold War and Europe's miraculous transformation had proceeded from a *Soviet* choice, not a European or an American choice. It was the Soviet Union that voluntarily withdrew its troops, not because it had lost a war but because it was giving Europeans their freedom. The Soviet Union stood by as East Germany, Poland, Czechoslovakia, and Hungary went their separate ways, peacefully departing from the Soviet imperium. (A botched crack-down in Lithuania, in January 1991, got swept under the carpet in this narrative, as did the paralysis of foreign-policy decision-making under Gorbachev, paralysis that could be dressed up as charity.) A post-Soviet Europe had been the Soviet Union's final gift to Europe. When had an empire ever treated its subjects so graciously?

What Yeltsin and Putin wanted in return for Gorbachev's prior charity was a relationship of equals among Europe, the United States, and Russia. This Russian aspiration might or might not be interpreted as a Russian sphere of influence in Eastern Europe. It was open-ended when Putin became president. Asked in 2000 by the British journalist David Frost about Russia joining NATO, Putin responded positively, and this was *after* many of the major decisions had been made about enlarging NATO. The Kremlin's later claims about its point-blank opposition to NATO expansion distort the historical record. Neither Yeltsin nor Putin liked NATO expansion. That was self-evident, but in no way was the die cast in 2000. In 2003, the State Department Office of Policy Planning generated a memo on the possibility of including Russia in NATO.[19] The fact that this was the path not taken does not mean that it was never a path—with all that being a path implies. NATO expansion was partially a hedge against a revanchist Russia: that was a motivation in Eastern Europe for widening the NATO alliance. In the United States and Western Europe, NATO expansion could also be a wager on future partnership with Russia. Russia signed onto the Partnership for Peace with NATO in 1997, when Moscow knew full well that NATO was growing and would continue to grow. Putting the question of NATO aside, Russia had after 1991 the most quiescent Europe it had ever dealt with. Napoleon and Hitler were Europeans from the distant past. Europe had no intention and no capacity to invade Russia, and it may have been this suite of encouraging circumstances that Putin had in mind when he speculated about Russia joining NATO. No threat, no problem, no big deal.

Developing cooperation between Putin and George W. Bush had rested on Bush's sense of Putin as a proto-democrat, an illusion that died gradually in Bush's second term. It had rested as well on Putin's sense that the United States would work with Russia on an equal footing, an illusion that died suddenly with the Iraq War. Yet Bush's and Putin's partnership had a firm basis. It advanced Putin's project of stability within globalization. The United States was the world's preeminent economic and military power. It had done a lot to jump-start globalization, to which it was much more symbolically tied in 2000 than China. The United States was not to be escaped or ignored. Decent relations with the United States would bolster stability within Russia, and they were of a piece with the needs of a globalized Russia, needs that included access to technology, investment, and markets. In a world dominated by terror and by counterterrorism, there was considerable room for US-Russian collaboration. Russia had home-grown and regional problems related to terrorism—in the north and south Caucasus and in Central Asia. Trying to overlook the American rhetoric of democracy promotion and the United States' unilateral withdrawal from the Anti-Ballistic Missile Treaty (ABM) in June 2002, Moscow could highlight the realpolitik that fueled the global war on terror. Putin valorized his own toughness and his own skill at realpolitik: unlike so many Europeans he did not mind getting his hands dirty. He visited George W. Bush's ranch in Crawford, Texas, in November 2001 to demonstrate that they could fight terrorism together, two leaders who were both Texan at heart. It was a fine opportunity for Putin to elevate Russia not against but alongside the United States.

After the 2003 invasion of Iraq, Putin would have more than cosmetic disagreements with Bush. When Russia invaded Georgia in August 2008, Bush had more than cosmetic disagreements with the Kremlin. Even these more than cosmetic disagreements, though, were never absolute. Much as Putin regretted the war in Iraq, much as it pained him to see George W. Bush ignore his advice about the unwisdom of invading, Putin did not use his regional influence to block US military activity in Central Asia, which helped the United States fight its war in Afghanistan. He did not contest the United States in Afghanistan, which is considerably closer to Russia than it is to the United States. Much as Bush was shocked and disgusted by Russia's invasion of Georgia, he did not consider kicking Russia out of the G8, which Russia had joined (when it was still the G7) in 1998, or directly opposing Russia in Georgia, which in 2008 was a partner of the United States, an exemplar of Bush's Freedom Agenda.[20] A modern Russia entirely aligned against the United States might not have been viable in 2003 or 2008, and an international order in which Russia was treated only as a pariah may not have been viable for the United States in 2008. Washington was committed to countering terrorism globally, the agenda that set the tone for all other agendas, and to ensuring peace in Europe, to which Russia was integral; some overlapping interests remained. Russia had not ceased to be a nuclear power, and the United States had not ceased being the economic and military trendsetter. If Russia was too big to ignore, it was too small in its aggregate power to fear.

The Russian constitution granted the president only two terms, and in the spring of 2008 Putin's two terms were up. How could Putin proclaim that he was the leader of a modern Russia and not abide by the Russian constitution?

* * *

With Dmitry Medvedev, the allure of a modern Russia had its heyday. He did not cultivate the overtones of menace that emanated from Putin's KGB past, from Putin's now-and-then guise as a Leningrad tough guy, and from the blunt irritation that often crept into Putin's official speeches, especially those on foreign policy. By contrast, Medvedev cultivated the style of a modern manager. He was, in Barack Obama's description, "young, trim, and clothed in hip, European-tailored suits."[21] He smiled more than Putin did. A bit boyish in demeanor, he did not seem to take himself very seriously. As Putin did, Medvedev had a fitness routine: neither would betray the poor style sense and bad physique of the typical Soviet-era leader. Medvedev acknowledged that modern political leadership had to be media savvy; it had to blend a personal story with image making, not so bland as to be un-interesting and not so severe as to appear un-democratic. Like Putin but more so, Medvedev was a kind of everyman, and what helped him to be average was his truly impeccable mediocrity. He was not exceptionally handsome, he was not exceptionally smart, he was not exceptionally charismatic; in fact, he was not charismatic at all. Putin had consciously surrounded himself with mediocrities in 2000, many of them friends from the past, and Medvedev was one of them. The mediocre Medvedev was a Russian leader with a light touch. His aim was to bring Russia forward, to perpetuate patterns of modernization begun by Yeltsin and Putin, and to do so gently. Medvedev gave off no authoritarian vibes.

In July 2009, Medvedev hosted Barack and Michelle Obama in his Moscow dacha. Barack Obama would describe this evening in his memoirs. "Our conversation barely touched on politics," he recalled. "[Dmitry] Medvedev was fascinated by the internet and quizzed me about Silicon Valley, expressing his desire to boost Russia's tech sector. He took a keen interest in my workout routine, describing how he swam for thirty minutes each day. We shared stories about our experiences teaching law, and he confessed his affection for hard rock bands like Deep Purple." The ease of communication between these two presidents is striking. No less interesting is the personal affinity Obama felt for Medvedev—and assumed that Medvedev felt for him: "Medvedev and I had more than a few things in common. Both of us had studied and taught law, gone on to marry and start families a few years later, dabbled in politics, and been helped along by older, cagier politicians."[22] In these recollections, Obama gave no indication of essential differences between Russia and the United States, no essential difference in national interest, no essential difference in history, no essential difference in attitude toward international affairs. If the political systems in Russia and the United States could produce two such similar leaders, they must have had more than a few things in common.

Medvedev had the obsession with Silicon Valley typical of the early 2000s. This oasis of California entrepreneurship was the ultimate signifier of modernity. It was not the government-directed research center of Cold War vintage—Los Alamos in the United States and its many secret counterparts in the Soviet Union—though Palo Alto's ascent into the business stratosphere had countless ties to government and to military funding. Silicon Valley encapsulated the free market at work. Linked more to the university than to the state, it was the knowledge economy at work, and Silicon Valley conveyed a message about lifestyle. It was insouciant, casual, and ruled by the young. It was intrinsically democratic. Through its genius for innovation, Silicon Valley contributed to research and development in the US military. It was lionized by Washington—whether Bill Clinton, George W. Bush, or Barack Obama was in the White House—as an iteration of American power and economic power, the same power that in the 1980s had buried the Soviet Union in backwardness. Silicon Valley was no less the high church of consumerism. Steve Jobs, the brilliant protagonist of its self-told story, was no military man and he was no bureaucrat. He was an iconoclastic pioneer and a counter-culture entrepreneur, whose most developed talent was for marketing. Silicon Valley invented the demand for products more imaginatively than it invented the products themselves. The wealth it generated for the United States, whether used for consumption or for military spending, whether for guns or for butter, was stupefying. In 2008, it could seem the very elixir of geopolitical success.

Medvedev's fascination with Silicon Valley gave him the nickname of Iphonechik in Russia, little IPhone. This derisive nickname could never have been applied to Putin, who was short but not little and not to be confused with a cell phone. At the same time, Medvedev represented far-reaching transitions that had been occurring in Russia since 1991, abruptly and disruptively in the 1990s, and more fluidly after that. The IPhone may have been the era's paradigmatic consumer good. Personalized, it enabled the quick assimilation and spread of information. For much of its history, the Soviet Union had concentrated on heavy industry, on getting people standardized cars, apartments, washing machines, and refrigerators. Its primary task was the transformation of peasants into factory workers and village dwellers into city dwellers. Efforts at creating a mass society defined Soviet life. By contrast, the IPhone was unique, and as Steve Jobs intuited, the IPhone was a magnifier of individualism. Though mass-produced, it inverted standardization, making the IPhone and the personal computer the least Soviet products imaginable. (In 1984, Steve Jobs commissioned an ad for Apple computers based on George Orwell's anti-communist masterpiece, *1984*: the point of this peculiar ad was the threat personal computers posed to Soviet totalitarianism, a way of equating accessible technology with emancipation.) In post-Soviet Russia, the IPhone was an import, and with Coca-Cola and Levi Jeans, it had the prestige of being a foreign product. Iphonechik was the kind of leader who borrowed willingly from abroad, doing so at a time when many Russians were likewise borrowing styles, dress, business methods, and cuisine from abroad. Medvedev registered in Russian politics as a westernizer.[23]

In June 2010, Iphonechik made the pilgrimage to Silicon Valley. There he met Steve Jobs in person and sent his first Tweet, while the co-founders of Twitter, Biz Stone and Evan Williams, looked on appreciatively.[24] Medvedev may have been trying to hoodwink Barack Obama by journeying to Palo Alto; he may have been faking his admiration for American-style innovation. Most likely he had simpler motivations—the importation of Silicon Valley's magic into Russia. If so, Obama had an alter ego in Dmitry Medvedev: each could see himself in the other; each was riding the wave of the future; each was trying to break down his country's resistance to change (in his own eyes); each was convinced that places like Silicon Valley were the secret to economic growth; each believed that economic growth was an organizing principle of domestic politics and indirectly of a nation's international clout. Obama's reset with Russia had started inauspiciously with the button Secretary of State Clinton handed to Foreign Minister Lavrov, hinting at the overload to come. Yet the reset took flight with Medvedev. The progression from Putin to Medvedev was a helpful step, and Medvedev's stated aspirations for Russia made sense to Obama. Having sent them in, Medvedev did not withdraw Russian soldiers from Georgia, but he invaded no other country in the four years he was Russia's president. He treaded lightly on the fraught terrain of Russian history, eschewing confrontation and helping the Obama administration to disassociate Russia from its invasion of Georgia, its wars in Chechnya, and its occupation of Transnistria. Medvedev's political style stimulated the hope that Russia could exist in concert with the liberal international order.

On June 24, 2010, Obama and Medvedev ducked out of the White House for hamburgers. The photos and videos of them eating at Ray's Hellburger in Arlington, Virginia, are not less evocative than the photos (snapped on July 24, 1959) of Nixon and Khrushchev arguing over domestic appliances in a mock American kitchen or the many photos of Reagan and Gorbachev tailored as statesmen and basking in the personal warmth between them. In the photos taken at Ray's Hellburger, Obama and Medvedev sit at a table crowded with condiment bottles. Their jackets are off and their sleeves are rolled up. Medvedev has a plastic Coca-Cola bottle in front of him. Behind them are the visuals of an American diner—with the incongruous detail of a *Cabinet of Dr. Caligari* poster on the wall behind them, a horror movie from Weimar Germany, giving off just a touch of visual overload. The two men are at ease. There is no pretense or formality, despite their not meeting on neutral ground. It is hard, though not impossible, to envision Barack Obama with his sleeves rolled up in a simple Russian restaurant in Moscow, joining Medevev for a plate of *pelmeni*. Their ease in Arlington, Virginia, came from the shared American terms, from Medvedev's familiarity with hamburgers (and with Coca-Cola), and from Obama's comfort hosting Medvedev in such a stereotypically American setting. It was almost as if in Arlington, Virginia, Medvedev were a smaller version of Obama.[25]

Obama's and Medvedev's big-ticket achievement was arms control. When they signed the New Start treaty, they knew that arms control was the classic Cold War meeting point between Moscow and Washington. It was important for what it was, and it was important for what it accentuated, which was the undercurrent of negotiation and expertise in the US-Russian relationship. Arms control signaled an escape from the arms race and a willingness to reduce risk through compromise. It upheld an image of the world's two major nuclear powers as the responsible stewards of the nuclear age, role models to the many countries that had or were seeking to acquire nuclear weapons. Successful arms control negotiations suggested that nuclear weapons might not be tools of coercion or devastation. They could validate the power to control technology's destructive potential, almost as if nuclear weapons were non-violent in nature, guaranteeing peace rather than war. US-Russian arms control could have a ripple effect on international politics, fostering a stability that for different reasons mattered to both Obama and Medvedev—the liberal international order in microcosm for Obama and a token of Russia's great-power status for Medvedev. Reassuring as all of this was, arms control could seem an old-fashioned diplomatic pursuit in 2010, a throwback to the Cold War, almost an anachronism. Arms control was something that twentieth-century statesmen worried about. It did not have the futuristic elan of Silicon Valley.[26]

Silicon Valley helped burnish Medvedev's vision for Russia. He decreed the construction of a Russian Silicon Valley called Skolkovo, which was to be constructed outside of Moscow. Russian excellence in mathematics, engineering, and computer science was world renowned. In general, Russian achievement in science extended back to imperial Russia and was one of the signature attributes of the Soviet Union, most memorably for Americans when the Soviet Union launched the Sputnik satellite in 1957, displaying research and development capacities in the Soviet Union that the United States did not have. With seed money from the government, Skolkovo could do what Silicon Valley did: it could gather youth, reward creativity with money and status, and capture for Russia the benefits that Silicon Valley had amassed for American society and for American foreign policy. Skolkovo was the height of American-style modernity assimilated and translated into Russian terms. Peter the Great had gone to Holland as a young man, working in shipbuilding to learn Dutch production methods. To entrench such methods at home, he severed Russia from its pre-modern, pre-Western self. Vladimir Lenin had pored over the theories of Karl Marx, which contained the secrets of modernity in his view. Stalin had summoned American engineers to the Soviet Union to align the Bolshevik Revolution with the Industrial Revolution. Then, in 2010, Dmitry Medvedev went to California and returned to Russia inspired. Skolkovo would be the tip of Russia's modernizing iceberg.[27]

In the end, Skolkovo would never rival Silicon Valley. It would never really emulate it, but what did get impressively modernized between 2008 and 2012, when Medvedev stepped down as president, was the city of Moscow. The city had grown shabby in the 1980s, in the dying days of the Soviet Union, long after the delirious architectural redesigns of the 1930s and after the construction of socialist suburbia in the 1950s and 1960s. In the 1990s, Moscow was once again in flux and very much at the center of the Russian story. It was the epicenter of Western luxury and of the harsh post-Soviet inequalities, of the crime and poverty that the Soviet Union had kept hidden and of the "new Russian" hedonism that repurposed the city: the sushi bars, the high-end car dealerships and boutiques, and the uninhibited night clubs that were reality and cliché for Moscow in the 1990s. What arose in the first decade of the twenty-first century was Moscow the European capital and Moscow the Russian capital, the sophisticated city, the city of the small detail, the renovated historic building or the corner café or the hipster bar. Moscow was not Russia, just as New York was not America or Berlin was not Germany. All three cities circa 2010—Moscow, New York and Berlin—were starting to have more in common with each other than with the countries in which they happened to be located. Driven forward by Sergey Sobyanin, who became Moscow's mayor in 2010, twenty-first-century Moscow was an urban playground like New York and Berlin, and like these two cities it was an extraordinary cultural center.[28] It was also a hub of globalization, a magnet for capital, for the exchange of ideas, and for the ceaseless movement of people to the city from Russia's provinces and from all over the world. Who needed Skolkovo when Moscow was on its own volition carrying Russia emphatically into the modern world?

Medvedev was not a Moscow intellectual, and despite his suits he was not exactly a Moscow hipster. Rather than encouraging a vibrant political culture in Russia, he chose not to oppose a vibrant political culture. He did not care about intellectuals. He let them be, and he was not by nature dismissive of political pluralism or democracy. Russia had elections—parliamentary elections in 2011—and it had (weak) political parties. In many ways, this was the veneer of democracy more than democracy itself, but what was not veneer was Russia's everyday political culture, its civil society, in the years between 2008 and 2012.

Moscow and other Russian cities were a varied landscape of media outlets, think tanks, NGOs, and artistic creativity (in film, in literature and in academic scholarship) that could pose probing questions about Russian history and politics, coming up with answers to these questions that adhered to no party line. In the two decades after the collapse of the Soviet Union, Russian universities had pulled up from the financial disarray of the 1990s and were places of research, debate, and learning. They were also bridges to the world outside Russia and bridges for non-Russian students to encounter Russia, many of them from Europe and the United States. This free-form internationalism had another home online, merging, for those who had the interest and the foreign-language skills to explore the internet, inquiry within Russia with everything that was happening elsewhere in the world. The Soviet Union had never been entirely closed off. It had its own rich sub-cultures, its own internationalism, its own autonomous intellectual life and its under-the-radar civil society. Yet the intellectual and media restrictions that had hampered Soviet life were long forgotten by 2008. So too was the Soviet Union's relative isolation. The allure of a modern Russia was this very openness, all the more precious (unlike Skolkovo) for not having been mapped out in the offices and meeting rooms of the Kremlin.

* * *

In January 2011, President Medvedev went for the second time to Davos, Switzerland. As Russia's prime minister, he had made his debut on the international stage in 2007 at Davos. The World Economic Forum held there occurred at the summit of globalization, a festival of wealth and internationalism and purported problem solving in which the powers of governments blended together with the powers of business. Political scientist Samuel Huntington had fun mocking "Davos man," the soulless avatar of globalization, who did know that there was such a thing as civilization. Even more obtusely, Davos man had forgotten that civilizations clash, Huntington would argue in his 1996 blockbuster, *The Clash of Civilizations*.[29] Prone to a certain homogeneity, as Huntington astutely noticed, Davos attracted the somewhat insecure and the status-conscious, which is to say that it attracted politicians like Medvedev, whose political legitimacy after 2008 had been less electoral than situational. In the end, it was not much more than Putin's permission to serve as president. The World Economic Forum could enhance Medvedev's international image. It could give him its blessing as one of the world's leaders, and in Davos, Medvedev could conduct some business of his own. He had been working with Obama to get Russia into the World Trade Organization, a prestige affiliation that demanded regulatory reform in Russia and would in turn give Russia greater access to global markets. Founded in 1971, the World Economic Forum in Davos would earlier have been anathema to any Soviet leader, capitalism at its most despicable. For personal and political reasons, Davos was a natural place for Medvedev to visit in his third year as Russia's president.[30]

At Davos, journalists asked Medvedev about the Arab Spring, which was incipient in January 2011. The United States was still feeling its way toward a position. The world was watching the Middle East, and Medvedev did not shy away from questions at Davos. "When governments fail to keep up with social change and fail to meet people's hopes," he told them, "disorganization and chaos ensue, sadly. This is a problem of governments themselves and the responsibility they bear."[31] A month later, in Moscow, Vice President Biden quoted Medvedev on the merits of democracy and on the responsibility governments had to keep up with social change. (Medvedev's anodyne phrases about North Africa and the Middle East might, depending on context, be daring statements about the democratic responsibilities of the Russian government.) At Davos, what was startling was that Medvedev's words were *not* startling. They did not cause a scandal or leave Medvedev's audience shocked at the audacity of the Russian president. Three years into Medvedev's tenure—and whatever the actual state of democracy back in Russia—he could credibly appear in international and internationalist venues like Davos, placing himself on the side of hope and change, his political vocabulary conspicuously Obama-like. (Hope and change had of course been the guiding lights of Obama's 2008 presidential campaign.) To many if not to all observers, Russia had modernized and globalized itself enough for Medvedev's words not to come off as hypocrisy or salesmanship. By every indication, Medvedev was not consciously dissembling when he spoke positively about the Arab Spring.

On May 18, 2011, Medvedev affirmed at a press conference (held at Skolkovo) that Ukraine had a right to pursue European integration.[32] This was long after the major rounds of NATO enlargement and two years after the EU had devised its Eastern Partnership Program for Ukraine. When governments fail to keep up with social change, chaos can ensue. (At this same press conference, Medvedev also warned about missile deployments in Eastern and Central Europe.) In 2011, Medvedev was not quite running for president. He was the president. It was unknown to him (perhaps) and certainly to the Russian public whether he would stay on as president for another six years. In 2008, the Russian constitution had been amended since Putin stepped down to allow for six-year presidential terms. What the actual arrangement was between Putin and Medvedev no one may ever know. Medvedev could sound like he wanted to remain in office, and his case for remaining was the leitmotif of his entire presidency: it was Russia's modernization. As Medvedev put it at a rally with Putin, in September 2011, his holy grail was the creation of "a modern political system" for Russia.[33] By making himself the man of the future he was pegging Putin as the man of the past, the older of the two men and the one who was much more tied by affinity to the Soviet Union.

Medvedev's relative youth notwithstanding, he had too little personality to pass *himself* off as an example of modern Russia's allure. Instead, he could campaign on Russia's arrival as a modern country. To the extent that he was running in 2011, Medvedev was running on his record of modernization.

Medvedev's foreign policy was a notable aspect of his modernizing record. Putin had gone back and forth with George W. Bush. Medvedev had hit it off with Obama. Medvedev's pitch was a Russia at ease with the world—not with the whole world, as Georgia and Moldova would have reminded him. Obama was by no means anti-Russian, and NATO expansion was effectively over in Eastern Europe, despite the mixed messages from the 2008 NATO summit in Bucharest. It took little geopolitical insight to say that the United States and Europe held many of the keys to Russian prosperity in 2008, as they still did in 2012. The absence of antagonism, in this line of argument, was the presence of a Russian advantage. And what would have been the reason for antagonism? Where did Russian and Western interests implacably clash in these years? Obama had conceded some of the "Russian" arguments about the Iraq War. He thought ill of it, and Obama wanted a more inter-connected, more globalized world, one based on cooperation, mobility, and economic growth. Russia could fit well within this vision; it could prosper within it. In the 1990s, Russia had been poorly connected and far from globalized. By 2011, Russia was impressively connected, globalizing, and frequently cooperating with its neighbors in Central Asia and with Ukraine. As a result, Medvedev could say, Russia was thriving in 2011. If Obama was right about the best path for Russia, then arms-control agreements, trade agreements, and presidential summits with the United States were not just episodic goods and not just a matter of diplomatic routine. They were in Russia's overall strategic interest. Had televised presidential debates been held in Russia in 2011, prior to the 2012 election, Medvedev could have spelled all of this out. Chances are, his message would have met with the approval of many Russians.

The Arab Spring turned out to be a test case for Medvedev's foreign policy. He had spoken his lofty words about social change in January 2011. Tunisia and Egypt were then renegotiating their social contracts: epochal shifts were on the horizon. In March, spring came to Libya. The Arab Spring was a referendum on dictatorship, as Medvedev had noted at Davos, putting himself forward as the representative of a Russian democracy, as if Russia had gone through these same motions in 1991, when it terminated decades of Soviet dictatorship. Those protesting Arab dictatorships hated dictatorship as such, and they felt held back—the Arab Spring being a movement of the young—by aging dictators sitting atop aging regimes. As in Europe in 1989, the proof of success in the Arab Spring was a dictator's fall from grace, precisely the destiny Libya's Muammar Gaddafi was desperate to avoid. He was one of the world's most flamboyant dictators with a dictator's typical mannerisms and hang-ups. Facing a national protest movement amid many regional protest movements, he did not concede to the protesters, and he did not flee the country. He went into battle. The country fragmented rapidly, while Gaddafi marshaled his military power to quell the protests and to regain control. Unlike Egypt's Hosni Mubarak, another target of Arab Spring protests, Libya's Gaddafi had been anathema to the West well before 2011. Though he had modulated after the Iraq War, agreeing to give up his nuclear weapons program, Gaddafi was regarded in Washington as a dictator who traded in terrorism. Most notably, he was held responsible for the downing of Pan Am Flight 103 in 1988.

In Libya, the West was quick to consider military force. When Vice President Biden was in Moscow in March 2011, citing President Medvedev's words about the merits of democracy, he was also pushing Medvedev to go along with the West on Libya. Biden was not asking Russia to commit its military forces to Libya. He had in mind a crucial source of geopolitical power for post-Soviet Russia—its vote on the UN Security Council. Medvedev did not reject Obama's position on Libya. Were Gaddafi left to his own devices, a bloodbath might follow: better order imposed from without than chaos welling up from within. Foreign-policy decisions can also be made for the sake of instilling goodwill, since agreement builds political capital. A Medvedev who was with the program—who was with the Obama administration—might be more powerful than a Medvedev who was not. The built-up good will could later be cashed in on issues more vitally significant to Russia than the fate of Muammar Gaddafi. Though Medvedev was not going to go out of his way to depose Gaddafi, he found it reasonable to accede to the White House's request and to abstain at the UN Security Council. He gave Russia's blessing to a military operation designed to protect the imperiled people of Libya. The operation in Libya lasted for eight months, and it was anything but Yugoslavia redux. Russia and the West were no longer parsing events by some matrix of mutual antagonism.[34] By accepting a NATO operation outside of NATO territory, Russia was launching a new era in international affairs.

Medvedev's own Foreign Ministry was angry about the president's decision. Gaddafi was not beloved in Moscow, but Russia did have assets and interests in Libya, as it did throughout North Africa and the Middle East (and as it had had in Saddam Hussein's Iraq). The Soviet Union had been a player in the Middle East and North Africa, its allegiances shifting over time, and before that, imperial Russia had understood itself as a major power in the Middle East. In addition to ceding regional influence by abstaining, Medvedev—in the eyes of his Russian critics—was giving up on energy projects in Libya, rail projects, and other deals that might have been possible with Gaddafi. In Libya, Medvedev was also agreeing to a changed orientation for the NATO alliance. NATO's charter had designated NATO a *defensive* military alliance, one that its members joined for the sake of protecting one another. A Cold War construct, NATO's raison d'etre was deterrence. Yet the September 11 attacks had brought NATO to Afghanistan, far afield from Europe, and Medvedev's critics regarded NATO's leading member, the United States, as being everywhere all at once, replacing deterrence with expeditionary ventures, while mixing up its soft and hard power in the American manner. It was blindness or madness not to see the implications of this arrangement for Russia. At will, NATO might choose to operate far outside its own borders or on the borders with Russia it had in Poland, Latvia, Estonia, and Lithuania. NATO might wage war without being attacked, without being at the risk of attack, as was the case with Libya in 2011. Gaddafi threatened no NATO member state, meaning that by unleashing NATO in Libya, the West was giving itself global carte blanche, including the option of stirring up trouble when it wished and then inserting itself militarily to eliminate the trouble. What the West did was the West's unseemly business. The last thing Russia should do, Medvedev's critics felt, was to give NATO its blessing.

NATO's course of action in Libya emboldened Medvedev's critics. The mandate for NATO's mission had been vague. After the UN vote, Medvedev was expecting a limited operation. Instead, the operation was fairly ambitious, though without an obvious strategic goal: the West was not fighting terrorism in Libya or pursuing economic interests. At stake was the "responsibility to protect" championed by President Obama's advisor, Samantha Power. In Russia, this could give the impression that Medvedev had been played, that he had been tricked by the West's humanitarian rhetoric, that he had been nice, and that he had been taken advantage of. Putin did not help matters by criticizing the UN resolution as "defective and flawed. It allows them to do what they like, to undertake any manner of actions against a sovereign state. It reminds me of a medieval crusade."[35] In two ways did Russia look weak by abstaining. It had not been listened to—it was the one listening to the West—and within Libya it had lost its network of relationships. Lose-lose. Then, in October 2011, Qaddafi was murdered on the street. (Putin is said to have watched the video of this assassination repeatedly.)[36] Thus could it be argued, in the long shadow of the Iraq and Afghanistan wars, that the United States and its NATO accomplices were still committed to regime change. The West had endless military ambition, and it had endless political ambition, with not much demarcation between the two ambitions. Neither China nor Russia could curtail these ambitions. Medvedev's critics could argue that the West was remaking the world in its own image, as it had been doing for centuries. A less West-centric narrative of the Arab Spring—by the fall of 2011—was that it was destabilizing the Middle East, not democratizing it. This too could reflect poorly on Medvedev's comments at Davos. Channeling President Obama, he had contended that chaos and disorganization come about when governments oppose social change. Might it be that chaos and disorganization come about when social change unseats governments?

In his return as Russia's president, Vladimir Putin would lament Medvedev's weakness on Libya. The West was eating Medvedev alive. If true, Putin was coming back unwillingly in 2011: he was being pulled from the semi-retirement of the prime minister's office. Most likely, Putin had planned to all along to come back, and Medvedev's yielding to US pressure was an easy justification for doing so.[37] Even that, though, is telling about the public Putin was addressing or at least about Putin's notion of this public, which he pegged as eager for greater assertiveness. Medvedev's 2011 abstention at the United Nations was the high point of his relationship with the United States, with NATO, with the West. The allure of a modern Russia still went both ways in 2011. It had appeal in Russia and in the West. Following the West's lead, Medvedev was concluding post-Soviet Russia's attempts to modernize itself along Western lines. As it had been since its inception, Medvedev's Skolkova was a place and a metaphor, a Russian Silicon Valley and a metaphor for progress or, depending on one's point of view, a metaphor for self-abasement and the excessive deference to foreignness. Medvedev himself would drift toward a vulgar, almost vaudevillian Russian nationalism later in his career. Or his vulgar nationalism, having been suppressed for years, would voiced in the dictatorship he had wittingly or unwittingly helped to build. Between 2008 and 2012 Medvedev could claim to be traveling away from Russia's authoritarian past. For a few years, it was not unreasonable to think that a modern Russia had incentives to live in peace with its neighbors, that Ukraine was Ukraine in Moscow as well as Kyiv, that Ukraine was not Russia and that a Ukraine in Europe was a more than tolerable proposition. More than tolerable for the Kremlin, a Ukraine in Europe, Medvedev suggested when addressing the topic, was uncontroversial. It made sense for Ukraine and for Russia.

* * *

The allure of a modern Russia had its coda in 2018, six years after Medvedev slid into relative obscurity and four years after Russia's annexation of Crimea and invasion of eastern Ukraine. In 2018, Russia hosted its own festival of globalization, which had been years in the making. The World Cup was held in Russia, and it came off beautifully. Ukraine and Poland had co-hosted the Euro Cup in 2012, a smaller tournament than the World Cup but no less a moment of international bonhomie than the World Cup. Several of the sites associated with the Euro Cup—the Donetsk airport most poignantly—were destroyed in the 2014 war, a commentary on what Europe was in 2014 or what it was becoming. Nevertheless, in 2018 Europe and the world flowed into Russia without war or destruction in mind. The games took their course, the common line of much journalism and social-media commentary being that Russians were friendly and indeed overjoyed to have so many international guests in their country. Moscow and Saint Petersburg could proudly show themselves off. The transportation system held its own. For most of the soccer fans, Russia did not have the aura of a police state. It did not seem to be drowning in nationalism or uninterested in technology or keen to shut itself off from Europe (or anywhere else). To the contrary, as a ritual of globalization the 2018 World Cup in Russia was no different from a World Cup in Brazil, Japan, or Germany. Russia *had* rescued itself from the 1990s doldrums, from an unforgiving poverty and isolation, traversing station after station on the highway of its post-Soviet modernization. The success of the 2018 World Cup was Medvedev's handiwork, not just Putin's.[38]

Yet already by 2012, well before the seamless World Cup, the Medvedev interlude was the road not taken, and it all vanished very quickly. Medvedev had been a ceremonial president responsible for non-ceremonial decisions. While he was prime minster, Putin could play it both ways: he could condescend to Dmitry Medvedev the political non-entity, or he could oppose himself to President Medvedev the leader taking Russia in the wrong direction. Medvedev's Russia also vanished for reasons other than Medvedev's fecklessness. No country is modern in only one way: countries contain within themselves competing modernities, competing variants of their future selves. Lurking behind Medvedev's air-brushed modernity and his democracy-promoting statements at Davos was a separate Russian modernity, one that drew on globalization for sustenance more than for guidance. Vladimir Putin had built up the military to compete with the United States, pursuing modernization for the sake of a Russia that stood among the global powers. His was a modern Russia outside the liberal international order and quite often a Russia enraged by the international order for which Washington presumed to speak. Rather than a democracy, it was a unified state subservient to the will of a single man. Having grown tired of a Russia fashioned in the image of the West, Putin was driving in 2012 for a modern Russia that could chart its own course, not so much a new departure as the confirmation of a position with deep historical roots in Russia. Though impossible to prove, it is possible that Russians preferred Putin's to Medvedev's modernizing path. Where a unified state subservient to the will of a single man had little appeal was in Europe and the United States. In the West, Putin's formal return to power in 2012 was almost immediately a dilemma.

3

The Dilemma of a Modern Russia

... the tragedy of the collapse of our state. ... It was precisely those people [the Bolsheviks] in October 1917 who laid a time bomb under this edifice, the edifice of a unitary state, which was called Russia. They divided our homeland into separate territories, which previously did not even appear on the map of the globe.

Vladimir Putin in a February 1992 television interview[1]

The Munich Security Conference takes place every February in the Bayerische Hof, a luxury hotel in the center of Munich. The conference was founded in 1963 to showcase Germany as a site of diplomatic connection, a meeting place for Europe and the world. Held in Bavaria, the US zone of occupation after World War II, the Munich Security Conference has always had a transatlantic tenor. Its themes, panels, and speakers often laud the close bonds between Europe and the United States and the salience of democracy to international affairs. Munich, the *Hauptstadt der Bewegung*, the place of origin for the Nazi movement of the 1920s, had been destroyed in the war. The rebuilt city, thriving and democratic, could be said to embody the promise of the liberal international order. Much like the UN General Assembly held in New York City every September, the Munich Security Conference is as much a ritual as it is a meeting of the minds. As a ritual, the conference helps politicians to recycle talking points, to articulate the conventional wisdom, and to enjoy being photographed in Munich without having to say anything particularly vivid or memorable. Diplomacy can be the art of not saying much in public, and the Munich Security Conference mostly takes the temperature of international politics, though this temperature can seem strangely monochrome and unchanging over time. More precisely, the conference tends to take the temperature of the transatlantic status quo.

In 2007, Vladimir Putin came to the Munich Security Conference in a foul mood. His speech was a conscious assault on US foreign policy, his critique a medley of arguments. The United States had too much power, and American power insulated Washington from hearing and seeing the world around it. Putin accused the United States of being a selfish superpower, one that made its own plans, served its own interests, listened to no one—and arrogantly claimed to be the steward of an international order based on deliberation. Putin decried the hubris of the United States. His other argument was about Washington's reck-lessness, its provocation of instability in the name of stability. As corroborating evidence Putin had the wars in Iraq and Afghanistan and a metastasizing global war on terror. By making this speech in Europe rather than in Russia, Putin was playing on the discontents many Europeans harbored about the war in Iraq. He was echoing Joschka Fischer, the German foreign minister who four years earlier had confronted the United States at the Bayerische Hof, questioning the merits of invading Iraq. By making this speech at a media-saturated conference, Putin was also pitching his criticisms to international audiences uneasy with the global war on terror, which the United States had been conducting for the past six years. Putin voiced his ideas not as an Atlanticist but as someone who nevertheless belonged to the European club. He was conveying his indignation, and for those who agreed with him he was conveying his righteous indignation. As few diplo-matic speeches do, this one made a mark.[2]

Putin's sine qua non for Russian foreign policy was the autonomy of Russia, not the defeat of the United States. In 2007, much was not yet broken in the US-Russian relationship. There were extensive diplomatic and economic ties. There was arms control, and there was the logistical cooperation in Central Asia. At the Munich Security Conference, Putin was hardly predicting war with the West. Despite Putin's loathing of NATO enlargement, Putin did not suggest that Russia was directly threatened by the United States—apart from the instability inching toward Russia from the Middle East—even if the specter of regime change and color revolutions informed Putin's speech. Putin knew that George W. Bush had spent most of his time since September 11 worrying about countries other than Russia. In Munich, Putin was complaining about the United States as an ob-stacle to the autonomy of many international actors, including Russia and also countries like Germany and France. At this stage and in this venue, Putin was upholding the desirability of a less US-centric world in 2007. He had brought Russia far enough along, he must have felt, to acknowledge a confrontation that had become unavoidable. Though a modern Russia might be many things, it would not be subservient, Putin was saying, and in particular it would not be subservient to the United States. Russia needed to be modern, it needed a modern economy and a modern military, in order *not* to be subservient to the United States. With their dislike of war and their iron-clad security guarantees from Washington, Europeans might let the United States take the lead, but in this, Russians were not Europeans (in Putin's terminology). Russia's history and geography demanded that Russians travel their own path, and on this path the United States had gotten in the way.

As a politician, Medvedev had operated on the easygoing surface of things. Developing below this benign surface until 2012, when it became more visible, was Putin's Russia, which was less conciliatory and less easygoing. Medvedev was much more a part of Putin's Russia than he let on when he interacted with Western leaders like Barack Obama. When he was not Iphonechik or playing Iphonechik, Medvedev was the understated ambassador of another Russia, of which Putin had been the architect. A KGB officer, Putin began his professional life as a servant of the Soviet state: a formative experience for him was of course the dissolution of this state. As Putin climbed the political ladder in the 1990s, his goal (beyond personal ambition) was the restoration of the Russian state, merging Soviet and pre-revolutionary Russian traditions of statehood. As he took the helm in 2000, modernization meant order within Russia to him, a calm population, secure borders, an expanding economy, power projection abroad (as opposed to power projection into Russia by other countries), and a state in which Russian citizens could believe. Joining Europe or having a Russia that resembled Europe or the United States was a peripheral concern and possibly an undesirable one. Wealth played a role in Putin's restoration of the Russian state. It was the glue but not the essence of the (Putinist) state and of a modern, autonomous Russia. Essential were the institutions of the state, first and foremost the security services, to which Putin was so intimately tied. Likewise, the military could be a source of pride—after the humiliations of the 1990s—and a tool of Russian influence in the world. Hardly a Jeffersonian, Putin might call his state consolidation "democracy," by which he would have meant a patriotic and self-sufficient Russia that expressed (in his terms) the will of the Russian people. Popular will, as he construed it, was the source of his power, and by ruling Russia he could empower the popular will. Elections and political parties had nothing to do with this notion of democracy.

Between 2008 and 2013, the United States and Russia sailed past one another, a slow process muddied by mutual incomprehension. Putin's characterization of American foreign policy at the Munich Security Conference was distorted and crude. It was a reduction of American foreign policy to Putin's interpretation of the Iraq War. The United States had extended many a helping hand to Russia after 1991, and there were countless issues on which Russia could profit from cooperating with the United States in 2007—in the spirit of the liberal international order. Put differently, Russia benefited from Europe's tranquility in the 1990s and 2000s, and security-wise, this tranquility was underwritten by the United States. The liberal international order's rules opened Europe's markets to Russian gas and oil, while the contracts signed by Russian businesses in a tranquil Europe brought immense riches to Russia. Putin was exaggerating America's flaws in Munich. His envy and resentment of the United States colored his vision. The speech's subliminal message was the pitch of Putin's intensifying anger and the doors he had decided to close. As such, it was a real turning point. Meanwhile, the United States was placing Russia into narratives of its own invention: Medvedev's fervent embrace of democracy; Russia as another piece in the mosaic of uplifting globalization; the drift of young people toward the internet, toward the wider world, and therefore toward civil society; Russia as some congenial, peace-loving, pro-American democracy of the future. These romantic images enticed American policymakers, but they were idealizations of the Medvedev era. Attuned to the issue of corruption in Russia, Washington imperfectly grasped the political system that had arisen in Russia under Boris Yeltsin and in Vladimir Putin's first two presidential terms. Far too beholden to the allure of a modern Russia, far too certain that modernization and Americanization were identical, Washington was exceedingly slow in recognizing the dilemma of a modern Russia. This dilemma, which was as much military as political in nature, would come to dominate Obama's second term. The antipathy to the United States that Putin articulated at the Munich Security Conference did not recede when Obama was sworn in as president in January 2009.

* * *

The spectacle of executive power and the figure of the leader connected post-Soviet Russia back to the Soviet Union. So much else had been discontinuous since 1991. The ethno-nationalist balance of the Soviet Union, established through coercion and compromise in the 1920s and 1930s, were completely upended by the Soviet Union's collapse: one country became fifteen independent nation states, each of them the product of the Soviet Union's decades-long schemes for mixing ethnic populations.[3] The popular thesis that the Soviet Union had lost faith in itself, that it had gotten its head turned by the West in the 1980s, and that communism had dissipated into a defunct ideology—all of this was not untrue, but it was only partially true. The Soviet Union melted down while some (primarily those in the Russian enclaves of the Soviet Union) retained their faith in the Soviet past and in elements of the Soviet system, especially where this faith dovetailed with the memory of World War II or where it was associated with economic security. The bewilderment of 1991 stayed with post-Soviet Russia. Not all Russians wanted to leave behind their Soviet baggage. Not all Russians wanted to separate their Soviet patrimony from the birth of a new nation, which was real enough in Russia in 1991 and thereafter. What softened the bewilderment was the continuity between Boris Yeltsin, formerly a Soviet politician, and Boris Yeltsin, the president of the Russian Federation. The same man who bested Mikhail Gorbachev in 1991, on the premise that the Soviet Union was a dead end, took charge after 1991. Yeltsin, the son of the Soviet Union, and Yeltsin, the Russian president, tied together two historical eras.

Yeltsin was not insincere in his hopes for a Russian democracy. A tactical democrat, he was hardly an authoritarian by nature, but all politicians seek to enhance their power, and Yeltsin had many pressing reasons to amass greater executive power. Political instability was his constant concern, coming from machinations within the Russian government or from the rough and tumble of Russian politics and civil society in the 1990s.[4] President Yeltsin could not have forgotten the August 1991 coup staged by communist hard-liners to depose Mikhail Gorbachev, and amid the post-Soviet jockeying, Yeltsin could never be certain of his own hold on power. On October 4, 1993, he had Russian troops shell the Russian parliament to stave off his impeachment. This attack on the legislative branch of government was a display of raw executive force. Checks and balances there were in the Russian constitution, and checks and balances are the way of democracy, but checks and balances and constitutional restraint were anything but settled norms in Russia in 1993. Czar Nicholas II had toyed with the prospect of a constitutional monarchy between 1905 and 1917, without putting an enduring constitutionalism into practice; the Bolsheviks made sure the Constitutional Assembly scheduled for 1918 never took place; and Soviet politicians proudly quoted from a constitution that had little bearing on Soviet political practice. After his run-in with the parliament, Yeltsin reworked the Russian constitution in such a way as to grant himself more executive authority. However justifiable his reasons, however real his personal decency, he was setting a precedent, and in Yeltsin's second term (from 1996 to 2000), the reformers and the westernizing democrats who had populated his first term were fading into the background. In 1998, Yeltsin made Yevgeny Primakov prime minister. Sometimes referred to as Russia's Henry Kissinger, Primakov had a background in academia and in intelligence work, and as prime minister, Primakov often hired people from the intelligence services. Primakov pushed for more state action in economic affairs and for a less soft-spoken Russian foreign policy, which is to say a foreign policy less accepting of Western decisions, Western rules, and Western ideals.[5]

Yeltsin's most consequential decision as Russia's president was to promote Vladimir Putin. A non-descript bureaucrat until he reached the presidency, Putin's rise to power sent several strong signals.[6] One was Yeltsin's ignoring the standard democratic procedure of having a political party select its leader and then put that leader up for a vote.[7] Russians could vote for or against Putin in the spring of 2000, and Putin was elected in March and sworn in in May of that year. By March 2000, he had already been given the double advantages of Yeltsin's imprimatur and of a few months in office as Russia's acting president. Succession had been plotted in the Kremlin. Another signal was sent by Putin's resume. Putin had never won an election before 2000. He was anything but a retail politician, unlike Yeltsin who had served as the first secretary of the Sverdlovsk Oblast' Party Committee, a big job, before going to Moscow. Putin arrived in the halls of power from within the halls of power. His KGB career was not accidental to his ascent: it was necessary, and before Putin became prime minister in 1999 Yeltsin had put Putin in charge of the FSB, the institution that had taken up where the KGB had left off, when the KGB went the way of the Soviet Union.[8] Putin's national-security credentials were on display in August 1999, when military tensions in Chechnya flared once again, and when a mysterious spate of apartment bombings occurred in Moscow and elsewhere.[9] However close to power and money he had come in the 1990s, Putin was not an oligarch. Nor was he a product of the Russian intelligentsia, someone who might have been philosophically opposed to the Soviet system in the 1980s and emotionally invested in building up an alternative to it (Western or otherwise). Despite his legal education, Putin was not a lawyer. When Yeltsin anointed him as Russia's next leader in 1999, Putin was a bit of a populist and a discreet administrator of state power, nothing more and nothing less. Choosing Putin in the way Yeltsin did was inconsistent with Yeltsin's democratic ideals. It was not inconsistent with Yeltsin's personalized manner of governing post-Soviet Russia.

Strange as Putin's Russia might look by comparison with the West, it could look normal by comparison with China. With variations from country to country, the West placed a premium on political pluralism and civic engagement in politics. These were virtues in and of themselves and they were, in the Western reading of history and geopolitics, what made countries and alliances stable and powerful. Political pluralism and civic engagement create legitimacy for states and for governments. Legitimacy helps with continuity, while vigorous debates about politics, fueled by media freedom, weed out corruption and expose the mistakes and pathologies endemic to political life. China's twentieth-century path foregrounded state power rather than political pluralism. After putting down the Tiananmen uprising in May 1989, Beijing had smothered civic engagement in state control. Legitimacy and continuity came through history, through Chinese civilization, through nationhood, through the Communist Party, and through the state. This state-driven approach to politics was not at all incompatible with capitalism or globalization, with an enriching outreach to the world's many markets. Circa 2000, China's rate of economic growth was much greater than the West's. Having evolved into a genuine superpower, China set about redressing a century of humiliation: European and Japanese colonialism and always the relative poverty compared to Japan and the West. Communism and nationalism were not necessarily antipodes in China as they sometimes had been in the Soviet Union, which had been both a Russian and an irrepressibly multicultural state. China's combination of one-party rule (the communist bequest) with national self-advancement (the post-colonial bequest) held many lessons for Putin, the freshly minted president of Russia in 2000.

Whatever Putin's sources of political inspiration, he improvised his way to a political order in Russia more structured than it had been in the 1990s. It had three components. First was further investment in the security services, Russia's most significant network of government institutions, combining police, intelligence, and military.[10] This was the world that Putin knew from the inside. It served the complimentary functions of keeping the peace inside Russia and of projecting Russian power abroad. The Soviet Union had not been loved for its communist accomplishments as much as it had been feared for its Red Army, and with that fear in mind it had acted on its interests. The second component of the Putinist structure was the pursuit of wealth within globalization, which would transform Russia between 2000 and 2008: the welcoming in of foreign capital, the requisite openness to the outside world (requisite for doing business), and the deal-making brokered by the Russian state. These deals enabled the sale of weapons, gas, oil, grain, and other commodities, which, together with the building of nuclear power plants, were Russia's key exports. More of a novelty than the other two structural features was the elaboration of a governing ideology, a political style, a language of politics, and a set of government-authorized assumptions about Russia and the world. Putin gathered the mass media into the state, starting with television. Through these media, a national idea (one part glorious Russian nation, one part glorious Russian state) was propagated, though much more loosely than in Soviet times. Then the communist idea had been imposed. Adherence to the national idea was not required in Putin's Russia, but woe to the journalist or civic activist or aspiring politician who too noticeably questioned this ideology and the power it was meant to underpin.[11]

In 2008, Medvedev had fit awkwardly into this structure. He had experimented with another structure or with a reconfiguring of the three-part Putinist structure. Given more time, he might have experimented more freely; but there was the unavoidable limitation of his own political mediocrity, not to mention the prowess of the security services surrounding him. There was the limitation of his coming to power in the same way Putin had come to power—through behind-the-scenes arrangements—and there was Putin himself, the puppeteer biding his time. Between 2008 and 2012, Putin was cloaked in the sheep's clothing of the prime minister's office, where the clothing (and the wolf beneath) were more apparent to some than to others. Medvedev might stand in Davos and empathize with the protestors decrying authoritarian rule in North Africa and the Middle East. Medvedev might bask in the applause of appreciative Western audiences, while back in Moscow the political structure Putin had nailed together after 2000 was unaffected. Russia's police, intelligence, and military services were continuing to gain in resources and prestige after 2008. The state's growth from globalization—via state-owned enterprises and the state's parasitic dominance of the economy—was proceeding apace. Under Yeltsin, the intellectual and ideological landscape had diversified profoundly in an era of laissez-faire—and not only in the economic domain. Yet the Russian state never handed over its tools of propaganda and ideological manipulation entirely to the free market or to civil society or to the public sphere: in 1996, Yeltsin had quite conspicuously used state power to get himself reelected. Putin acquired all of these tools in 2000, and Medvedev may have used them less than Putin did before 2008; and he may have liked them less. The crucial point, though, is that the toolbox was still there in 2012. It was still available when Putin gave up on pretending *not* to be president. Putin's military-minded modernization did not contradict Medvedev's superficial westernization of Russia. Without difficulty, Putin could bend the Medvedev interlude to his will.

* * *

On foreign policy, Putin and Yeltsin had more in common than either of these two post-Soviet leaders had in common with Mikhail Gorbachev. In the turbulent years before the Soviet Union fell, Gorbachev had speculated earnestly about a common European home from Lisbon to Vladivostok. Some of his concessions to the West were imposed upon him by circumstance and in particular by the Soviet Union's economic deterioration. Some of his concessions Gorbachev made for the sake of a new Europe. Gorbachev believed that by making concessions he could achieve a kind of moral parity with the West. The Soviet Union would freely abandon its domination of Eastern Europe, and another Europe would come into being, which Gorbachev envisioned as a shared arena of international governance—partially dictated by Europe, partially dictated by the United States, and partially dictated by the Soviet Union.[12] Interested bystanders in the Soviet Union's end phase, Yeltsin and Putin considered Gorbachev hopelessly naïve. Perhaps a bit of Gorbachev's idealism had rubbed off on Yeltsin, but not that much, and by the late 1990s Yeltsin was seriously frustrated with life after communism and with the United States. The Bill and Boris show of the 1990s admits two conflicting interpretations. It was the high point of the US-Russian relationship, the best this relationship had ever been, and it was a worrisome sign of things to come, especially if Russia were to have more power at its disposal. The United States pursued one vision of Europe, while Yeltsin's Russia, which never managed to lay out a coherent vision for Europe, had fault to find with the US vision and with the emphasis Washington put on the NATO alliance. Yeltsin had the greatest fault to find in those areas that directly concerned Russia, in the Balkans and in Eastern Europe.

Yeltsin anticipated Putin in his frustration with the United States and in the proper role Yeltsin ascribed to Russia in Europe. Apart from personality, a cardinal difference between Yeltsin and Putin was the diminutive military power available to Yeltsin and the palpable threat of political upheaval in the 1990s. Yeltsin's conciliatory position vis-à-vis the West reflected Moscow's reduced hard power as much as it did the personal rapport between Yeltsin and Clinton or the European future Yeltsin believed Russia should have. The United States regarded NATO's open-door policy as irreversible. It had been policy since NATO was founded in 1949, and to suggest that one country could veto the foreign policy of another (by forbidding it to join NATO) was to revert to nineteenth-century imperialism, to the time when Europe carved up the world through spheres of influence. Yeltsin disagreed with the open-door policy. For him, NATO could advance only by impeding Russian influence in Eastern Europe. It was an institution in which Russia had no direct decision-making authority, an institution led by the United States and an institution that was far more dynamic after the Cold War than it had been during the Cold War. In some places, NATO was expanding institutionally. In some places, NATO was simply broadening its scope—in countries that had once been under Soviet dominion and in countries (Poland and the Baltics) that many in Russia considered innately anti-Russian. For Yeltsin, NATO expansion was a foreign-policy problem, and it was a domestic political problem. By making Russia look passive and weak, it made him look passive and weak.[13]

Yeltsin's foreign policy was not all negative, and it was not all just a reaction to the United States. Yeltsin dreamed of a Russian version of the European Union. The Soviet Union had of course been a union, a confederation in name and sometimes in practice as well. The Soviet Union had excelled at uniformity across its many time zones and many ethnic populations; this uniformity contributed to the efficacy of its economy (such as it was). Hoping for a viable Commonwealth of Independent States, Yeltsin's early efforts at post-Soviet partnership concentrated on Central Asia, Belarus, and Ukraine.[14] The Commonwealth of Independent States was an umbrella institution created in December 1991, and it linked many post-Soviet states after 1991, from Central Asia to the south Caucasus to Belarus, though it did not include Ukraine. Were Russia able to construct an integrated zone running to its east, south, and west, it would be bolstering both its commercial opportunities and its security, just as the United States had done with its many overlapping commercial and military partnerships. Why not learn from what the institution-building United States had accomplished after 1945? Russia did not shy away from coercive arrangements. Moldova, a state between Ukraine and Romania, was tied to Moscow by the stationing of Russian soldiers who, working in tandem with pro-Russian separatists in Transnistria, dug themselves in in the early 1990s.[15] On a small scale, the situation in Transnistria proved that Russia could ride roughshod over another state's sovereignty when it chose to or that the sovereignty of post-Soviet states could be what Russia said it was. Andrey Kozyrev, Russia's pro-Western foreign minister under Yeltsin, wrote in *Foreign Affairs* in 1994 that "Russian foreign policy inevitably has to be of an independent and assertive nature."[16] The greater Russia's integration with its neighbors, brought about by persuasion or by force, the greater the potential for Russia to realize its independent and assertive nature.

The first US-Russian collision after the Cold War came in the Balkans. Unlike the northeast of Europe, where the push for joining NATO and the European

Union was strong and fear of Russia was widespread, the southeast of Europe was less uni-directionally European in the 1990s, and its place on the map of international politics was more unsettled. The languages were mostly, though not exclusively, in the south Slavic family. Parts of the Balkans were Catholic, parts were Muslim, and parts were Orthodox Christian, a circumstance that in the nineteenth century had drawn czarist Russia into the Balkans, the protector of fellow Slavs and fellow Christians trapped in the Ottoman Empire. (The Crimean War of the 1850s had as one of its origins a Russian commitment to Christians in the Holy Land, which led to conflict with the Ottoman Empire as well as with Britain and France.) A bond formed between Russia and Bulgaria in the late nineteenth century. The bond between imperial Russia and Serbia had been a catalyst for the First World War, which began (as a world war) with the collision between the Russian and the Austro-Hungarian empires. Yeltsin was not trying to relive czarist glory days in the 1990s or to start a world war, but he did feel invested in the Balkans. When the religious and ethnic tensions boiled over after 1991, in the one part of Europe that did not navigate a bloodless escape from the Cold War, Russia took Serbia's side. A revanchist Serbia shelled Sarajevo in February 1994, leading to a crisis that was temporarily resolved, and mostly because the United States, led by the hard-driving diplomat Richard Holbrook, devoted itself to resolving it. As a keeper of the peace in southeastern Europe, the United States played a bigger role than either Russia or Western Europe was able to do.[17]

The more intense US-Russian collision over the Balkans came later. In 1996, Yeltsin replaced Foreign Minister Kozyrev with Yevgeny Primakov—the Primakov who would be named Russia's prime minister in 1998. Even more than Kozyrev, Primakov argued for an independent and assertive foreign policy; he was highly critical of Kozyrev's acceptance of NATO expansion.[18] He rejected the idea of American primacy and assessed the world of the 1990s to be multi-polar. One pole was the United States, another was Europe, another was China, and another was Russia, and there were other poles as well. Coined in 2001, the BRICS designation—uniting Brazil, Russia, India, China, and South Africa—came from the business world.[19] It would popularize the basic thrust of Primakov's multi-polarity thesis. A turning point came in 1999, the year in which NATO welcomed three new members—to the displeasure of Yeltsin and Primakov alike. Operating outside of NATO territory in March 1999, NATO used its air power to slow the human-rights abuses of Serbia's Slobodan Milosevic, who was menacing the Muslim population of Kosovo, a part of Serbia. To Russia, Milosevic was a partner and Serbia a friend. The human-rights abuses did not preoccupy Moscow, but NATO's posture in the region did. NATO was imposing its preferred political and military blueprints, setting the tone not just for its existing members but for Europe as a whole. Moscow dismissed Western claims about humanitarian assistance to Kosovar Muslims as cover for claims about American primacy in Europe. For Yeltsin, US military moves in the southeast of Europe impinged on Russian interests in the Balkans.

Yeltsin lost the battle in Serbia, and he lost the war of principle against NATO. Kosovo mattered enough for Russia to send some 200 troops to Pristina airport. They narrowly avoided a direct confrontation with NATO soldiers in 1999, a phantom collision, some twenty-three years before Russia and the West would find themselves close to war in Ukraine. Russia and NATO were flagrantly traveling in opposite directions, courting disaster, though Russia was hardly in a position to wage a war against NATO in the Balkans. Because Russia was not yet free from economic dependence on the West in 1999, from loans and other kinds of aid, Yeltsin's hands were largely tied. For Moscow, two developments drove home the political, and not just the military, nature of the NATO operations in Serbia. One was the redrawing of Serbia's borders and the sudden creation of a separate Kosovo, which would declare its independence from Serbia in February 2008. NATO could remake the map of Europe at will, meaning, Moscow worried, that Europe was what Washington wanted it to be. In the second development, Milosevic fell from power in October 2000. In a display of Western soft power, Milosevic was then brought to justice in the Hague. Europe was truly what Washington wanted it to be, and not just geographically. For Moscow, this was a double embarrassment, the loss of Russia's man in Belgrade and of the pretense that Russia would have any decisive say in European affairs. In 1999, Poland, Hungary, and the Czech Republic had joined NATO. Not entirely coincidentally, 1999 was also the year in which Vladimir Putin was promoted to prime minister and on the very last day of the year to acting president of the Russian Federation. Yeltsin's disgrace, which replicated Gorbachev's disgrace in 1989, was Putin's entrée. In Russian foreign policy and in Russian domestic politics, Putin was tasked with the avoidance of such disgrace.

Putin's response to the prospect of a NATO-dominated Europe was Yeltsinesque. It was tied to the Commonwealth of Independent States—to a regional vision for Russia. In the 1990s, globalization was driven by the United States, by Western Europe, by Japan and by China. Russia might profit from globalization in 2000, but it was not at all on par with the world's biggest economies. What it could attempt was influence through trade, commerce, coercion, and versions of confederation involving Russia's neighbors. Closest at hand were neo-Soviet Belarus, which was politically, culturally, and linguistically intertwined with Russia; Kazakhstan, an oil-rich former Soviet Socialist Republic with a sizable ethnic Russian population; and Armenia, which appreciated Russian backing amid its conflicts with Azerbaijan and Turkey. Many in Central Asia and in the south Caucasus appreciated the chance to work in Russia and to send home remittances. As the Russian economy steamed forward, Moscow and Saint Petersburg became boom towns in the 2000s, attracting labor forces from across the former Soviet Union, not least from Ukraine. This power of attraction was a built-in asset for Russia as far as Russia's regional influence was concerned, but Putin was often heavy-handed about his project of integration and union. As a model, Russia had less to offer than the United States or Europe, and in Eastern Europe Russia had a toxic history of imperialism. The easiest partners for Russia—by virtue of language, proximity, and infrastructure—were the post-Soviet countries. Yet each of these countries had an intricate relationship with the Soviet and the imperial Russian past. This could and did translate into wariness about a Russian-led future.

Wariness about Russia's regional role led to the second US-Russian collision after the Cold War. Georgia was the native country of Joseph Stalin and of Eduard Shevardnadze, Soviet foreign minister from 1985 to 1990; Georgia had been lodged in the Russian empire before 1917. After the three Baltic republics, Georgia was the post-Soviet country that tried most energetically to break away from the Soviet mold after 1991 and to will itself into the West. Georgia experienced the Rose Revolution of 2003, when Mikhail Saakashvili, a charismatic reformer, entered the scene—the youthful personification of George W. Bush's Freedom Agenda. Elected president in 2004, Saakashvili had mastered the phraseology of reform and anti-corruption. He was media savvy and positioned himself as the voice of a new generation: he had been born in 1967, well before the collapse of the Soviet Union, but he was the product of Georgia's twelve years of independence, the culmination perhaps of this independence. Saakashvili aligned himself with Europe, with the United States—with the West, though geographically Georgia was closer to Iran and to Russia than it was to Germany or France. He aligned himself with the spirit of the West, winning Washington's support. To Putin, it might seem a case of Serbia redux, though Russia and Georgia shared a border, making it closer to Russia than Serbia was. In Serbia, the United States had removed a Russian partner (in Moscow's interpretation). In Georgia, the United States had installed a Russian enemy (again in Moscow's interpretation). Having shown that it could alter the map of Europe, the United States might be on the verge of showing that it could alter the map of the south Caucasus as well.

Russia's war in Georgia post-dated the promise of NATO membership for Georgia by about two months. The chimera of NATO membership was less the cause of war than the last straw in Moscow.[20] Impatient and erratic, Saakashvili had no qualms about needling Russia, walking up to the edge of war on the false assumption that he had Washington behind him. He had Washington's best wishes, but the US military would not be coming to the rescue. In its first daring move against the West, his August 2008 invasion of Georgia, the Kremlin was clearly probing to see just how far he could go. The risk undertaken was daunting. Had the United States chosen to support Georgia militarily, Medvedev (and Putin behind him) could not have easily backed down, and Russia might well have lost the war. For this and surely for other reasons, Russia held back from taking Georgia's capital city, Tbilisi. Although the Russian military committed human-rights abuses in Georgia, they were not on the scale of Milosovic's rampages, which had instilled in Washington the "responsibility to protect" as a possible justification for going to war. Having complained loudly and for years about the travesty of Kosovo's NATO-led separation from Serbia, Russia separated south Ossetia and Abkhazia from Georgia, stylizing itself the protector of their minority populations from an aggressive Tbilisi. Having redrawn an international border, Russia was sending a message—to Georgia, to Europe, to the United States—that was not esoteric. When it chose, Russia would wage war and set the terms of international order, using artificially created statelets as bargaining chips. Russian foreign policy inevitably has to be of an independent and assertive nature.[21]

Medvedev tinkered with Russian foreign policy between 2008 and 2012. He did not consider ending Russia's "frozen conflict" in Georgia for the sake of good relations with the West. He did not consider ending the entrenched "frozen conflict" in Moldova. Medvedev would not have become president had he meaningfully differed with Putin or with Yeltsin before him about Europe. (His one great concession to NATO and the West was not in Europe but in the Middle East, and it was, according to Putin at least, a career-ending concession.) In 2009, Medvedev handed Europe a proposal for redoing European security, for Europe as a joint Western-Russian condominium, which in practice meant that Russia would have certain veto- and decision-making powers within Europe. Medvedev's proposal garnered no interest outside of Russia. Versed in the precedents of Moldova, Georgia, and the Chechen wars, Russia's European neighbors were unenthusiastic about cooperating with Russia on European security. NATO's open-door policy was set in stone. It could not be undone without changing NATO's own DNA, and the open-door policy made European security a matter of NATO on the one hand and of individual countries on the other. Medvedev's proposal that Russia should have certain powers within Europe—and powers that did not necessarily begin with Europe's individual nation states—was consistent with Yeltsin's and Putin's thinking. As Medvedev blandly stated on Russian television in 2008, "There are regions in which Russia has privileged interests."[22] Putin would be less sanguine than Medvedev about what this privilege entailed.

* * *

Ukraine occupied a unique place in the regions where Russia claimed to have privileged interests. Russia had many run-of-the-mill interests in Ukraine. The economies of Russia and Ukraine overlapped. The transit of Russian gas to Europe went through Ukraine, not all of it but a significant amount. Of the many reasons Russia had "privileged interests" in some places, in Medvedev's parlance, an emotional one was the presence of Russian speakers or of ethnic Russians, an imprecise term for those who felt themselves to be of Russian descent through family more than just through language or culture. Ukraine might have seen all its citizens simply as citizens, and so might Washington—the United States being a country in which language and ethnicity are not supposed to determine citizenship. Russia tended to take a different view. There were Russian speakers and ethnic Russians all over the former Soviet Union, perhaps as many as 30 million of them, a shaping fact of Russian foreign policy in the 1990s and thereafter.[23] Nowhere was the number of these "stranded" Russians greater than in Ukraine. If czarist Russia had considered itself the guardian of Orthodox Christian Slavs in the Balkans, then Yeltsin's and Putin's Russia took an interest in the ethnic Russians in the Baltic Republics, in Kazakhstan, and especially in Ukraine. In the fluid culture of post-Soviet Ukraine, ethnic Russians might feel at home; they might think of themselves as Ukrainian citizens; or they might feel like second-class citizens; the overall situation was not free of problems. Moscow was perpetually on the lookout for these problems.[24]

Another interest Russia had in Ukraine was military or strategic. In the abstract, Russia might describe Ukraine as a buffer zone, mandating either direct Russian control of Ukrainian territory or the necessity of a compliant Ukraine. This viewpoint was common enough in military and elite political circles in Moscow, but there was no Western invasion to fear and no Ukrainian invasion to fear. A non-abstract problem for Moscow was what to do about Crimea, one of the region's historical oddities. Crimea had been drawn into the Russian empire in the eighteenth century, Catherine the Great having wrested it from the Ottoman Empire. Sevastopol, home to Russia's Black Sea Fleet, was a city of "military glory," a site of Soviet sacrifice in World War II and before that in the Crimean War. Until 1954, Crimea had been part of Soviet Russia. In this year, Nikita Khrushchev gave it as a gift to the Ukrainian Soviet Socialist Republic: 1954 was the 300th anniversary of the Pereyaslav Agreement, through which Ukrainians and Russians had joined forces against the Polish-Lithuanian Commonwealth, a marriage of convenience in the eyes of some and a knitting together of Ukraine and Russia in the eyes of others. In the 1990s, there had been an impulse to Crimean separatism. Home to many retirees from the Russian military, Crimea had a population that was heavily ethnic Russian. It could have sympathies for Moscow over Kyiv, but an actual will to separate was small to non-existent, and adept diplomacy mitigated the whole issue. Ukraine's and Russia's friendship treaty of 1997 secured their common border and set the terms for Russia's leasing of a naval base in Sevastopol.[25]

To these economic and military interests around Ukraine Putin added a civilizational touch that was not second nature to either Yeltsin or Medvedev.

The Russian Orthodox Church had growing stature in Russia's domestic and foreign policy under Putin. The church had been integral to life in czarist Russia and to czarist foreign policy. Kyiv could figure in Russia as the foundational city of Slavic Orthodoxy and Moscow as the third Rome, the inheritor of Kyiv's and Constantinople's piety and of imperial Rome's power. It was not that the Russian Orthodox Church clarified everything in Russian foreign policy. Russian affection for Serbia had something to do with Orthodox Christianity and its revival in the 1980s and 1990s, but Georgia was a predominantly Orthodox Christian country, and that did not prevent a war between Russia and Georgia in 2008.[26] Putin, an increasingly conservative, increasingly reactionary modernizer, used the church to position Russia as a repository of traditional values. In Ukraine he envisioned a natural Ukrainian-Russian convergence on the plain of civilization. The historical argument began in the distant past: Kievan Rus' was the transmission point for Orthodox Christianity from Byzantium via Chersonesos, in Crimea; Ukrainian land was thus the civilizational cradle for Muscovy and for what would become modern Russia. Ukraine was the place where the seed had been planted. Having grown from the same seed, Russia and Ukraine were organically united. Russian involvement in Ukrainian life—whatever that might entail—was not meddling and not interference in this historical scheme. It was the natural conjoining of two fraternal peoples, two brothers bound to the same past and to the same destiny.

Putin could synthesize interests and cultural affection into an aspirational union between Russia and Ukraine, one more important to him than Russia's commercial dealings in Central Asia or its security concerns in the south Caucasus. Let Ukraine slip into Europe and Russia is bifurcated—because Russia and Ukraine are one. Bring these two countries close together, and the entire region falls into place. In terms of practical cooperation, Ukraine had a lot to offer Putin's Russia: a market of some 40 million people and a neo-Soviet military industrial complex ready-made for supplying the Russian military, which it did (until 2014). Putin and Medvedev both favored the elaboration of a Eurasian Customs Union (ECU), first proposed by Putin in an article in the newspaper *Izvestiya*, which he published in October 2011. At its inception was the trio of Belarus, Kazakhstan, and Russia, but what it needed to matter and to flourish was Ukraine. Rather than a union more Asian than European (without Ukraine) there would be a union more European than Asian (with Ukraine).[27] The ECU could finally fuse together the three mostly Orthodox Christian countries of Russia, Belarus, and Ukraine. They could also be characterized as the three east Slavic nations by language affinity and the three descendants of Kievan Rus'. Backward-looking in part, Putin's vision for the ECU was the height of modernity in his own eyes. "The Eurasian Union is a project for maintaining the identity of nations in the historical Eurasian space in a new century and in a new world," he explained in 2013, referring to the bloc created in 2010.[28] New century, new world on the one hand, and on the other, the maintenance of an ancient civilization in a historically significant Eurasian space. Such culturally and historically inflected modernization was typical of Putin's political purview and hardly atypical for Eastern Europe in general. It set the tone for Putin's foreign policy.

* * *

After 2003 and the start of the Iraq War, Putin appeared to grow more confident about Russia's modernization. It was a modernization that integrated the state, the military, and an economy that was closely tied to the Russian state and the Russian military. Money making might seem to be front and center, as the Yeltsin-era chaos died down, as Russia became more globally integrated, and as high oil prices lubricated the Russian economy between 2000 and 2008. Unlike Medvedev, though, Putin was not a market-oriented leader: he was not one to swoon over Silicon Valley. Putin was a traditionalist Russian leader, whose aim for economic modernization was to stave off military defeat (at the hands of a technologically superior and congenitally hostile West) and to create the conditions for military victory (measured at times in territorial expansion).[29] Putin's modernization suited a foreign policy in which offense and defense continuously mingled and in which the best defense was offense of one kind or another. A country's wealth could be enjoyable per se, but for the Russian state the function of wealth was also strategic, as it is for most states. Putin poured Russia's oil wealth into military modernization, the purpose of which was to build up the might of the state. Peter the Great, avatar of Russia's modernization who created the Russian navy and who engineered Russia's eventual great-power status, was a role model for Yeltsin and for Putin alike.[30] Russia's miserable military performance in the Georgia War did not convince Putin to change course and to modernize for the sake of democracy, as the West might have recommended. To the contrary, it convinced Putin that more and better military modernization was in order, though not at the expense of other budgetary priorities.

After 2003, as the Iraq and Afghanistan wars began to bog down the United States, Putin became less respectful toward western-style modernization. Perhaps he had contemplated embracing it in 2000 or 2001, making Russia more politically open and more of a free-market economy. Perhaps he was not speaking his mind in these years, when he did not define Russia against the United States; but over time the western model faded from Putin's outlook until at some point it disappeared entirely. In the years when a September 11 patriotism infused American life, Putin was not critical of domestic American politics. Counterterrorism and patriotism made sense to him. What Putin increasingly rejected—and not just for propaganda purposes—was American foreign policy. He explained his thinking at the 2007 Munich Security Conference: American pretensions to hegemony, in Putin's mind, were undeserved. If countries, including Russia, had to bow to the reality of American power, so be it. It was regrettable, but it was the way of the world. If these same countries had to applaud the liberal international order while bowing to the reality of American power, that was quite another thing. Putin interpreted NATO's open-door policy as emblematic American behavior: luring with money; manipulating through US government institutions disguised as think tanks and the organs of civil society; and, once the ground had been readied, exerting the gravitational pull of the American military. NATO expansion, say, to Latvia had not been done to benefit Latvia or to honor democratic ideas. Washington had done it to bring American power to Latvia, meaning that countries like Latvia were American puppets. Though Russia could not reverse past decisions about Europe, Putin described himself (at the 2007 Munich Security Conference) as on the losing side of a rigged and hypocritical system. All Washington, no Moscow. This was no way to conceptualize or to modernize Europe. By 2007, Russia was ready to say no to the United States.

If US foreign policy left a lot to be desired in Europe, in Putin's eyes, it was not much better outside of Europe. Perhaps it was worse. Putin's disdain for the Iraq War was common enough in 2003. Germany and France had refused to follow the United States into Iraq, although in France and Germany the critique of the United States accented the dishonesty of the Bush administration, of its complaints about non-existent weapons of mass destruction, and of the ulterior motives the United States had for the war. These motives were often alleged to be economic and tied to the flow of Middle Eastern oil. Europeans also disliked the toll the war took on Iraqi civilians, not to mention the human-rights abuses at Abu Ghraib prison and elsewhere. Putin's objection was more severe. Russia had its own economic interests in Iraq, and these were devastated by the war. That bothered Putin, who was also bothered by what he regarded as the war's destabilizing logic. A functioning autocrat had been eliminated; the Iraqi state had withered away; and the entire region had become less predictable, less orderly, less coherent than it had been before the war. As in Europe, many in Washington labeled the war a case of strategic incompetence, a blunder. Never inclined to give the United States the benefit of the doubt, Putin thought the war a kind of madness. The United States was a global hegemon with insufficient appreciation for its own hegemony. A true hegemon would have hewn more to the status quo. The United States was hegemonic and revolutionary at the same time, in Putin's calculus, a terrible combination as such and a terrible combination for Russia, which was quite far from being a hegemon and which feared instability, especially instability that was not of its own making.

The war in Afghanistan was more mixed for Putin than the Iraq War. Russia had some contact with the Taliban, the fanatical government that had harbored

Osama bin-Laden before September 11. Russian had no desire to see Islamist violence harden into solid political formations and for these formations to serve as the conduits for Saudi or Iranian or Pakistani mischief in Central Asia, or for these formations to become the cause of extremism within Russia. The United States was not doing Russia's work in Afghanistan, but neither was it out to undermine Russia in Central Asia. After all, any great power would have responded forcefully to September 11. Yet as a careful observer of US foreign policy, Putin could see the wide disparity between American rhetoric and the situation on the ground in Afghanistan. Washington said it was engaged in nation building in Afghanistan, ensuring human rights for Afghans, and ushering poor, wartorn country into the modern world. Meanwhile, the Afghanistan under American rule was politically divisive, riddled with violence and corruption, and painfully unliberated from religious extremism. Afghanistan revealed the underside of superpower status. Reality might be malleable. It might appear to correspond to Pentagon press statements and upbeat cable news reporting, but reality was not entirely malleable. In places like Afghanistan, reality could change a superpower more than this superpower could change reality. Precisely that had happened to the Soviet Union in the 1980s. Moscow had been humbled in Afghanistan, as Putin was well aware. The twenty-first-century war in Afghanistan might be doing the same to the United States.

Putin's barnstorming speech in Munich restated his preexisting complaints about US foreign policy and about global trends he disliked. These were his complaints against "colored revolutions." Each had its own name: Georgia's Rose Revolution of 2003, Ukraine's Orange Revolution of 2004, Kyrgyzstan's Tulip Revolution of 2005. These were three post-Soviet countries embroiled in generational and political change. Though their revolutions had little to do with the Iraq War, Putin could fold many events into his indictment of colored revolutions, beginning the narrative (for Russian audiences) in 1989 with the United States having induced the Soviet Union's untimely death. It was one process, one continuum, leading up to George W. Bush's Freedom Agenda. The United States waxed lyrical about democracy, employed its all-powerful CIA and related institutions to generate unrest, and then harvested the rewards of a predetermined regime change: it installed clients and partners, called the shots behind the scenes, and magically ensured that the "reformers" who came to power just happened to be enamored of the European Union, well-connected in Washington, and eager for their countries to join NATO. Georgia and Ukraine did not go the full revolutionary distance in 2003 and 2004, respectively, because of the West's reluctance about Georgia and because of internal divisions in Ukraine; but the worry about colored revolutions continued to suffuse the Kremlin's rhetoric. As if to flatter Putin's paranoia, NATO had at its 2008 Bucharest summit affirmed Ukraine's and Georgia's place in NATO in some hazy, American-led future. It was all just a revolution away.[31]

Putin never shared Medvedev's public optimism about the Arab Spring. If modernization empowered the state and the order it imposed, then something close to modernization's opposite was at issue when young people took to the streets, brought political leaders down, and gummed up the machinery of the state with their anarchism. What was modernization without firm leadership? What was modernization without national autonomy? And what was modernization for Russia without autonomy from the West? To a much greater extent than Medvedev did, Putin identified with "strong" leaders, with autocrats like Turkey's Recep Tayyip Erdogan (Turkey's prime minister as of 2003 and president since 2014), China's Xi Jinping (who came to power in 2013), or Syria's Bashar al-Assad (president of Syria since 2000). Putin did not dismiss them as throwbacks to the 1930s, destined to be marooned in some sea of global democracy. He embraced them as agents of progress or at the very least as providers of order. After World War II, the United States, Europe, and Japan had traveled a different path, having rejected the figure of the strong man, except for countries like Hungary, where Viktor Orban became a less than democratically inclined prime minister in 2010, or Italy, where Silvio Berlusconi, Putin's friend, at least acted the part of a strong man. (No meeting of the minds ever occurred between an increasingly un-democratic Poland and Putin's Russia.) Russia had more to gain by affiliating itself with like-minded strong men or with strong men who could keep the peace. To think otherwise, Putin was sure, was to indulge in the kind of political innocence that could destroy Russia. It was to think like Gorbachev.

* * *

Stage managed as Medvedev's presidency was, something went off script in 2011. A double turning point set the United States and Russia on a collision course in Libya—indisputably, if not yet irrevocably. In and of itself, Libya did nothing to harm US-Russian relations: what to do about Libya was a question on which Medvedev and Obama appeared to agree. The problem was Putin's reaction to Libya. Putin upbraided Medvedev for signing onto, of all things, a kind of colored revolution in Libya. "My main concern," Putin said about Medvedev's caving in to US pressure on Libya, "is the light-mindedness with which decisions to use force are taken in international affairs these days."[32] Putin was openly dismissive of the deal Medvedev had struck with the American devil. The bumpiness of the Medvedev-Putin relationship in 2011 followed by the shock of Putin's return a year later threw the entire US-Russian relationship out of joint. The United States was not crestfallen to lose Medvedev. Washington was perturbed to realize that Russian democracy was a switch Putin could turn on, when convenient, and turn off, when inconvenient. American skepticism about Putin's return deepened Putin's conviction that the highway of colored revolutions had Moscow as its final destination, nothing less than the dismantling of the Russian state. Putin's resumption of his presidential duties in 2012 was far more agitated than his assumption of power in late 1999.

In Putin's 2011 paraphrase, Medvedev's foreign-policy errors had a domestic political echo. If demand for Russia's autonomy in the world emanated from the will of the people, Medvedev had let the Russian people down; he had allowed American pressure to betray Russian interests. For the nervous Putin of 2011, Medvedev may have been more in tune with Russia's business elite, which cared about access to Western markets and investments, and more in tune with the Moscow intelligentsia, which cared about Russia's being in the good graces of the West, than he was with "real" Russians, who wanted the country to be combative or at least uncompromising in the name of Russia's interests—and the West be damned. Putin made this point at the September 2011 rally in which he announced his bid for the presidency: "Sometimes it seems to me that America does not need allies; it needs vassals. People are tired of the dictates of one country," exactly what he had said in Munich in 2007.[33] (The election was held on March 4, 2012.) By people, Putin may have meant an assortment of countries: international public opinion and not just Russian public opinion. Given that he was at a political rally, he must surely have meant that the Russian people were tired of American arrogance, tired of the American hunger for vassals, tired of the American manipulation of its so-called allies, allies that were in fact vassals. In his political speech and style, Putin had always had a populist touch. He was happy to be seen as a man of the people. In this comment, he was groping his way toward a populist foreign policy.[34]

By December 2011, protest movements were roiling the streets of Moscow and other Russian cities. If Washington had had illusions about Medvedev's Russia, so too had Russian liberals. They had the non-trivial freedoms of the Medvedev era to enjoy and their own newfound activism; they had the new Russian urbanism, the new cosmopolitanism of Russia's cities; and they had what was even more thrilling—the expectation that life and politics in Russia would get better by becoming more free, more urban, and more cosmopolitan. Before September 2011, the Medvedev moment could be construed as a transition. A less than liberal leader, a man in Putin's shadow, Medvedev might still be the precursor to a post-Putin Russia. Another leader could solidify Russia's relationship with the West and give Russia what it had never had historically, a lasting order that guaranteed political rights and a multi-party system. (Russia had a working constitution under Yeltisn.) Putin dashed these expectations in the fall of 2011. Medvedev had indeed been transitional, but it was a transition that boomeranged from Putin to Putin. That Russian society—at least in the big cities—had liberalized in the four years of Medvedev's presidency was not an illusion or a dream. Two opposition politicians, Boris Nemtsov and Alexei Navalny, were not slated to run against

Putin in 2012, though Navalny ran for the Moscow mayoralty in 2013. They did not hold office or have anything resembling real decision-making power in Russian politics. Yet they were waiting in the wings, omens of the Russia that was not Putinist, of a Russia more liberal than Medvedev ever aspired to be and of a Russia that, to be realized, would have to be clawed back from the security services. In the name of this Russia, people took to the streets in late 2011.[35]

Angered by the protests themselves, Putin was furious about the American response to them. Always suspicious where the United States was concerned, Putin interpreted State Department comments about the value of free and fair elections as meddling in Russian politics. Putin's ire would focused on the US secretary of state in 2011 and 2012, Hillary Clinton, one of the cabinet members who had prodded a hesitant Obama to bomb Libya.[36] For Putin, Clinton's State Department was responsible for the "dictates" that issued from Washington, the lofty speeches about human rights, the infatuation with military power, the romance of colored revolutions, the contempt for countries like Russia. On December 5, 2011, Senator John McCain, a friend of Hillary Clinton's, tweeted the following message: "Dear Vlad, the Arab Spring is coming to a neighborhood near you."[37] A darling of the Washington foreign-policy establishment, McCain had been a presidential candidate in 2008, though his hope for revolution in Russia was not exactly an official statement. It was not something President Obama would have said—or Secretary Clinton for that matter. From Putin, McCain's tweet elicited a rude response about the senator having lost his mind in Vietnamese captivity. Surely it confirmed everything Putin thought he knew about the United States and its addiction to regime change. So calculated and premeditated were these colored revolutions that an American senator could confidently predict where the next one was going to occur. Putin was not going to let a few protests get in the way of the Russian people, the real people, and he was not going to let an assembly of anti-Russian stooges topple the mighty Russian state.

Putin won his election in March 2012. The Arab Spring had not come to a neighborhood near Putin, despite the protests that had flared in Moscow's Bolotnaya Square and across the country in November and December 2011, lasting into the spring of 2012, and despite the people's clamoring for a Russia freed from the thieves who occupied the Kremlin, a "Russia without Putin." Libya receded into the past, though the debilitating aftereffects of NATO's military campaign there lingered on. By 2012, the Arab Spring was backfiring everywhere except for Tunisia. Europe was calm, and the United States was entering a campaign season of its own. In this election, Mitt Romney would point to Russia as an overweening threat to the United States. For Romney, Russia was a challenge because of Putin, though at a televised debate Obama demurred when he heard Romney sound the alarm. "The 1980s are now calling to ask for their foreign policy back because the Cold War's been over for twenty years," Obama quipped.[38] Nevertheless, after he won the 2012 election, Obama appointed Michael McFaul ambassador to Russia in January of 2012, an emphatic diplomatic signal at a precarious moment: the United States would not forget about democracy while Putin moved back into the Kremlin. On December 24, 2011, as many as 100,000 protestors had gathered to protest Kremlin overreach.[39] Putin was on edge in the spring of 2012. Everything he had said about the United States in Munich in 2007 was still true, in his eyes, and everything he had complained about then had gotten worse. The United States had moved on from Iraq to Libya. Colored revolutions were breaking out globally with worrisome regularity. Whether it was John McCain the Republican or Hillary Clinton the Democrat, the United States had Russia on its map of regimes that needed to be changed. Marching in lockstep, the American political elite would not let Russia be. Conflict, not conciliation, was on the horizon.

* * *

Fortunately for Putin, Ukraine and Belarus were calm in 2012. Next door to Ukraine, Putin had an erratic but subservient partner in Alexander Lukashenko, the leader of Belarus. Putin could look at Ukraine and reflect on all that he had accomplished there since 2004. Its paradigmatic colored revolution—themed orange—had petered out. In Kyiv, Putin had a subservient and not at all erratic partner in Viktor Yanukovych. Russia was leasing the port in Sevastopol for its Black Sea Fleet, a deal Yanukoyvch had extended to 2042. Gas was flowing in immense quantities from Russia into Europe through Ukraine, generating a corruption in Ukraine that served Russian interests. Yanukovych had muffled the prospect of NATO membership for Ukraine. He did not take it entirely off the table, which might have inflamed opposition, yet he was unmoved by the West's promise that one day Ukraine would join NATO. Ukraine's many millions of Russian speakers were speaking Russian in 2012. Many millions of parishioners in the Ukrainian Orthodox Church (Moscow Patriarchate) were attending services, praying at every liturgy to the Moscow Patriarch. There was one unfinished task, about which Putin could feel decently optimistic in 2012 and 2013, and that was to sell Ukraine on Russia's version of modernity, not that Putin wanted a strong Ukrainian state buttressed by a strong military, a "Russian-style" Ukraine: to the contrary. He believed in a Ukraine that would accept the guidance and protection of a strong *Russian* state, a Little Russian partner to Great Russia in nineteenth-century Russian parlance, endorsing the course set for politics and for foreign policy in Moscow. Ultimate success would be to persuade Yanukovych not to sign an Association Agreement with the foreign European Union and to switch over to the native Eurasian Customs Union with Russia, ensuring a shared future for these two fraternal countries and ensuring that regionally Russia would be in the saddle.[40]

Hovering behind his aspirations for Ukraine was the more marked conservatism Putin brought to the Kremlin in 2012. This style encompassed foreign policy and domestic politics. Figures like Alexander Dugin acquired more political prominence after Medvedev's Silicon Valley dreams came to dust. Born in 1962, Dugin had passed through Moscow's bohemian underground, mingling with the far-right circles that were coalescing in the 1980s. A bit like the bohemian Munich neighborhoods that Adolf Hitler frequented in the 1920s, bohemian or counter-cultural milieus rarely belong to the political Left alone—whatever the Left might mean in 1980s Moscow (or in the Munich of the 1910s and 1920s).[41] Dugin took up ideas from disparate sources: from Russian propagators of Eurasianism, an anti-Western strain of Russian imperialist thought that flourished after the 1917 Revolution; from far-right European intellectuals such as Baron Julius Evola, Carl Schmitt, and Alain de Benoist, who tended to celebrate antagonism and even violence over compromise and deliberation; and from practitioners of "geopolitics" like Halford Mackinder, a British academic popular at the beginning of the twentieth century who contrasted territorial with maritime empires and contended that the two were bound to clash. Skeptical of Boris Yeltsin and his amicable posture toward the West, Dugin thrilled to the first Chechen War and to Serbia's resistance to NATO in the late 1990s. In 1997, Dugin published a book, *The Foundations of Geopolitics: The Geopolitical Future of Russia*, in which he proposed that Russia annex Ukraine.[42] It became a bestseller in Russia and was widely read in government circles. In 2007, Dugin was deported and then banned from Ukraine for dabbling in Crimean protest movements (against the Orange Revolution) and for defacing a Ukrainian national symbol.[43] Dugin was an ideologue who built his reputation by being shocking. With his media savvy, he was anything but a bureaucrat or a policymaker. His ideas were less prescriptive than impressionistic, synthesizing an admiration for Soviet power, a nostalgia for the Russian empire, and an admiration for Putin's efforts to project Russian power in places like Ukraine. Dugin endorsed anything that might hinder Western pretensions to primacy in Europe or elsewhere. When useful, the Putin regime could appeal to Dugin's right-wing advocacy.

In late July 2013, Putin traveled to Kyiv for an evocative ceremony. It was to commemorate the 1,025th anniversary of Christianity coming to Kievan Rus'. He was accompanied by Patriarch Kyrill, head of the Russian Orthodox Church, and the trip took Putin to one of Kyiv's historic treasures, the Monastery of the Caves, in which many saints were entombed underground. Putin was reinforcing his preferred historical narrative in Kyiv. Both Putin and his father were named Vladimir: Vladimir the prince (in Ukraine he is Prince Volodymyr) who had, by getting baptized, brought Christianity to the eastern Slavic lands. That was Putin's Ukrainian pedigree, in his eyes, and by coming to Kyiv as Russia's president he was affirming Ukraine's Russian pedigree, the seamless bond between the two countries, which had created and would continue to create one another. It was not tourism for Putin, and it was not exactly a religious pilgrimage. It was cultural diplomacy. What completed it was the welcome Putin got from Ukraine's president. The two of them, Putin and Yanukovych, stood before the television cameras. They participated in a religious service. In Kyiv, Putin also attended a conference titled "Orthodox-Slavic Values: The Foundation of Ukraine's Civilizational Choice," and he celebrated Russian and Ukrainian Navy Days.[44] Away from Moscow, in Ukraine, Putin was at home. He was not lashing out as he had at Munich's Bayerischer Hof in 2007. He was being acknowledged for the modern Russian leader and for the friend of Ukraine that he claimed to be. For the vast majority of Russians or Ukrainians, Putin's 2013 visit was not memorable, but for Putin it was better than memorable. It was normal. Twenty-two years after the collapse of the Soviet Union and the abrupt divorce of Russia and Ukraine, Putin and Yanukovych were there shoulder to shoulder at the ancient Monastery of the Caves.[45] On this particular summer day in Kyiv, Russia and Ukraine were, according to Yanukovych and to Putin, twin protagonists of the same story.

PART II
PARTING WAYS, 2013–2021

4

Revolution Comes to Kyiv

News of these preparations alarmed the Corcyreans. They had no exclusive treaty with any other Greek state, and had not enrolled themselves in either the Athenian or the Spartan alliance. They decided therefore to approach the Athenians, to join their alliance and to try to secure some assistance from Athens.

Thucydides, *The Peloponnesian War*, Book 1:31

Revolution came unexpectedly to Ukraine. Sporadic protests had greeted Putin's visit to Kyiv in July 2013. Some objected to its implied narrative of Ukrainian-Russian brotherhood. Yet there was no sustained display of anti-Russian or Ukrainian national sentiment that July. Issues other than national identity took precedence. Ukraine was poor by European standards. Its government and society had long wrestled with corruption—as was the case for many post-Soviet countries—and Ukraine had its regional and linguistic differences. Ukraine was not Switzerland, a multi-ethnic, multi-linguistic state unaligned with NATO and with the European Union yet at ease with what it was and where it was. Not insulated by mountains and not surrounded by benevolent neighbors, Ukraine faced headwinds. President Yanukovych also had his dark side, which Ukraine's unruly media kept uncovering, though Ukraine had been at peace since gaining its independence in 1991. A large, diverse country, it was not more obviously polarized than most democracies. It was by no means Weimar Germany, stumbling from crisis to crisis and on the verge of collapse in 2013. Its people were hardly radicalized by politics, by religion, or by their linguistic diversity. In 2012, Ukraine had hosted the UEFA European Championship together with Poland, showing off its globalized normalcy and its modern infrastructure. That was the association most Europeans might have had for Ukraine in 2013 and for cities like Donetsk and Luhansk in eastern Ukraine. Five of the championship's matches were played in Donetsk, in its "superb, even beautiful modern soccer stadium," in the words of the journalist Tim Judah.[1] Ukraine could play host to Europe's rowdy soccer fans one year and to a pious Vladimir Putin the next. It was not trapped between Europe and Russia in 2012 or early 2013. It was open to both and seemingly untroubled by the stirrings of revolution.

Each revolution has its own logic, its own proximate causes, and its own deep history. Ukraine's came about because of unresolved questions in Ukrainian politics and foreign policy, not because economic conditions were unbearable in 2013 or because the Ukrainian government was so repressive (until November–December 2013) that revolution was the only way forward. Three factors had to intersect for a revolution to sweep Ukraine: one was Yanukovych's thuggish character and lack of political agility; another was a Russian will to exert control over Ukraine, which could elicit strong emotions from the Ukrainian population; and a third was the European will, not to exert control over Ukraine, but to draw Ukraine closer to Europe. Ukraine's revolution, which broke out spontaneously between November 2013 and February 2014, was affected by the outside world. It was—like most revolutions—as much a matter of the external as the internal direction of Ukrainian politics, a referendum on the state of the Ukrainian polity and on Ukraine's place in Europe, two inseparable issues. More than the French Revolution, Ukraine's revolution resembled the American Revolution, which was driven by the political situation internal to the thirteen British colonies and was at the same time shaped by struggle among various European powers—France, Britain, Spain, Prussia—a continuation of their European wars and a contest for imperial advantage in North America that long predated the American Revolution. Contemporary Ukraine is anything but an island. It is a country at the very heart of Europe. As much as European configurations matter to Ukraine, Ukraine's configuration matters to Europe. Ukraine's configuration has greatly mattered to Europe for centuries. The twenty-first century would be no different.[2]

The crack-up of Viktor Yanukovych's government changed everything for Vladimir Putin. Apart from revolution inside Russia, a revolution in Ukraine was the worst of all possible colored revolutions for the Kremlin. It was too close to home, and especially too close to home for Putin's vision of Russia's "neighborhood," confirming Putin's notion that the West was instigating revolutions across the post-Soviet domain. Russian red lines meant nothing in Washington or in Brussels. Whether with NATO or with the European Union, the West was moving forward as it wished. Putin would have to sacrifice some of Russia's working relationship with the West to achieve his aims in Ukraine, which were either preserving Ukraine's (Yanukovych-era) orientation toward Russia or imposing costs on a Ukraine eager to detach itself from Russia. For Putin, the precarity of Ukraine's status and the possibility that Ukraine might partner with Europe against Russia may have validated his decision to fashion a modern Russia independent of the West. Russia's autonomy, its freedom of action in Ukraine, rested on its capacity to oppose the West—militarily, if necessary. In an enduring asymmetry, the West tended to understand Ukrainian problems as Ukrainian problems, to which there were Ukrainian solutions, while Russia tended to understand Ukrainian problems as Russian problems, to which there could only be Russian or regional or Europe-wide solutions. For this reason, a crucial question for Putin was the posture of Europe's leading military power toward Ukraine, the posture of the United States: his inclination was to attribute any non-Russian or anti-Russian impulse in Ukrainian foreign policy to Washington's backstage whispering. Because the United States loomed so large in Putin's eyes, Putin tended to denigrate Ukrainian agency and to exaggerate the agency of the United States.

The prospect of a European nation trying to make itself more democratic was well received in Washington. It fit a familiar paradigm for Americans: the rising up of the Greeks against the Ottoman Empire in 1821, which Americans saw (somewhat imaginatively) as a rerun of their own recent revolution; the European uprisings of 1848, which could be interpreted as a pan-European turn to democracy and to politics in the American vein; the liberation of the Poles and the Czechoslovaks and the Baltic nations after World War I, not least because they employed Woodrow Wilson's idea of ethnic self-determination to redress Europe's imperial imbalances and constant wars; the American outrage at Moscow's annexation of the Baltic Republics after 1945 and later at the Soviet Union's invasion of Hungary in 1956 and of Czechoslovakia in 1968; and, most memorably of all, the jubilation of Americans in 1989, when Europe finally came to its senses, threw off the Soviet yolk and organized itself into a peaceful union of self-governing nation states, almost as if in 1989 Europe was making good on all that had been hoped for in 1776, embracing at long last the heritage of Jeffersonian liberty.[3] For the Obama administration, a Ukrainian political movement that lauded the European Union demonstrated the legitimacy—and the magnetism—of the liberal international order. Revolution in Ukraine had arisen from Ukrainian citizens, young and online and excited about greater rule of law for Ukraine. The United States did not advocate the toppling of Yanukovych's government; it played no role in his decision-making. The United States did not advocate revolution in Ukraine, but at every stage it was clear which side Washington was on. A Ukraine adjacent to the European Union, adopting its principles and ideals, would be a vastly better Ukraine than the one Yanukovych had mired in his corruption and in his undignified self-subordination to Vladimir Putin. Without seeking or wishing for an anti-Russian Ukraine, the United States pressed for a Ukraine separate from Russia, in part because Putin had displaced Medvedev in 2012, distancing Russia ever more openly from democracy and from the liberal international order.

Europe's response to upheaval and then to revolution in Ukraine was muted. As the Kyiv-based writer Andrey Kurkov put it in a diary entry dated March 18, 2014, "Events are progressing very quickly in Crimea, and very slowly in Europe."[4] Some European countries, especially in southern Europe, did not see themselves as involved. Ukraine was not in NATO. It was not in the EU. It was a foreign country, rather like Belarus, out there to the east of recognizable Europe. Other countries in Europe were highly exercised by the thought of revolution in Ukraine. For Poland and the Baltic states, Ukraine was following in familiar footsteps. It was following in their footsteps, expunging the Soviet demons and charting a course that would thankfully not be set in Moscow. For unforgotten centuries, western Ukraine had been in the Polish-Lithuanian commonwealth. After World War I, Poland, Czechoslovakia, and Romania had controlled the territory of western Ukraine. There were still bonds of memory, language, religion, and affection—and in the case of Poland of enmity (due to ethnic violence between Ukrainians and Poles in the 1940s).[5] For Poland and the Baltic Republics, Ukraine might be Europe's avant-garde and Europe's bellwether. In Western Europe, other priorities could assert themselves vis-à-vis Ukraine. Revolution fit in poorly with the gradualist, institutionalist frameworks of the European Union. The Eastern Partnership program of 2009 was never supposed to spark a revolution; it was meant to be the modest turn of a procedural screw. Though France and Germany did not root against revolution in Ukraine, they also had significant diplomatic and economic relationships with Russia, relationships they understood as preconditions for European security and European prosperity. Never exactly a friend, Russia had the potential to be a very unpleasant enemy: it was a nuclear power with a large conventional military; it supplied increasing amounts of gas and oil to Europe; it had meaningful relationships with China and in the Middle East with Iran, Turkey, and many other countries. France and Germany had to balance an ambient revolution in Ukraine and a recast relationship with Russia against the many blessings of the European status quo.

* * *

Not entirely unlike post-Soviet Russia, stability had been the holy grail of Ukrainian politics in the 1990s. The magnitude of the transition from Soviet to post-Soviet patterns of politics and living spurred the desire for stability. In the December 1991 referendum on separating from the Soviet Union, 92.3 percent of Ukrainians had voted for independence.[6] Once a Soviet politician, Leonid Kravchuk led Ukraine out from captivity and into the post-Soviet promised land. The joy of escaping from the Soviet Union was not fleeting, but it could get overshadowed by economic woes, a common feature for all fifteen post-Soviet countries that emerged in the 1990s, Russia very much included. Ukrainians could no longer rely on the familiar Soviet crutches and safety nets, and Ukraine had to compete in the global economy, while lacking in capital, rule of law, and the lived experience of private property and entrepreneurship. In 1993, miners from Eastern Ukraine went to Independence Square in Kyiv, to the Maidan, to express their (non-revolutionary) displeasure with Kravchuk's governance and to voice a sense not just of discontent but of neglect. These were the urgent Ukrainian problems in the 1990s, most of them economic in nature. What to do with Ukraine's nuclear weapons, the issue that preoccupied George H. W. Bush in 1992 and Bill Clinton after that, was secondary at best. Ukraine had no enemies from which to defend itself in 1993, and to get up off the ground it needed help from the United States and Western Europe. The nuclear weapons left in Ukraine after 1991 were worth less than the goodwill that could be purchased by giving them up.[7]

The second president of independent Ukraine was Leonid Kuchma. He did more than Kravchuk, the man of transitions, to shore up Ukraine's political system. Kuchma got 52 percent of the vote against Kravchuk's 45 percent in the 1994 presidential election, and he brought with him a group of cronies, his "Dnipropetrovsk clan," to Kyiv.[8] (Dnipropetrovsk would later get renamed Dnipro.) Ukraine was famous for the excellence of its soil, its agriculture, and for many of its industries. There was mining, steelworks, rocket production, the airline industry, and much else, but in the dislocations of 1991, the bottom of the Ukrainian economy fell out, as it did across the former Soviet Union. Kravchuk could have a gangster-ish quality to him. If he wanted to curtail some of Ukraine's corruption or if he wanted to be seen as a foe of corruption, he also wanted to profit from it. With more and more gas flowing from Russia into Europe, Ukraine could be the middle man. Out of neighborliness and for the sake of leverage, Russia supplied Ukraine with subsidized gas in the 1990s, while some Ukrainian elites benefited from rents delivered by gas sales and by gas transit. The prolif- eration of rent-seeking had many, many drawbacks for Ukraine. It encouraged corruption in the private sector and within the government, which were often overlapping entities, as they were in post-Soviet Russia, linked less by entrepre- neurial wherewithal than by bribery and kickbacks. Profiting from Russian gas also encouraged Ukrainian dependence on Russia, and even Yeltsin's Russia, which was not ill disposed toward Ukraine, cherished the idea of a dependent Ukraine. Worst of all, rent seeking and recycled petro dollars inhibited legal reform and the evolution of value-creating businesses, the creation of wealth through innovation. The fall of the iron curtain had brought Ukraine "closer" to Germany, and as time passed this proximity revealed the distance between Germany's world-beating economy and a very different set-up in Ukraine.

While turning a blind eye to corruption, Kuchma could cultivate the aura of a post-Soviet modernizer. He appointed Viktor Yushchenko prime minister in 1999 on Vice President Al Gore's recommendation. Gore esteemed Yushchenko as a reformer, as someone who would battle against corruption, bringing matu- rity to Ukrainian democracy.[9] In 1999, Kuchma was reelected, and a rocky period for Ukraine ensued. The bane of corruption touched Kuchma and opposition politicians like Yulia Tymoshenko, whose money and status derived in part from

Russian gas. The journalist Georgi Gongadze disappeared in September 2000. He had founded *Ukrainskaya Pravda*, an independent newspaper, and had been writing articles critical of Kuchma's government in its pages. In November 2000, Gongadze's decapitated body was discovered near Kyiv, after which a recording surfaced of Kuchma seeming to wish for or to order or to condone his execution, damaging his government's reputation in Washington, in European capitals, and in Ukraine.[10] Yushchenko had left the government in 2001 for personal and political reasons, and in November 2002, parliament approved Viktor Yanukovych as Kuchma's prime minister. Nobody in Washington or elsewhere would have confused Yanukovych and his known criminal record with the credentials of a reformer. To Kuchma's "Dnipropetrovsk clan," Yanukovych added his "Donetsk clan," a gang of associates from his native eastern Ukraine. In these years, Ukraine also made a hash of its relations with the United States by selling air defense systems to Iraq (before September 11) and then trying to cover this up (after September 11). Kyiv compensated for its misstep by sending more than a thousand of its soldiers to Iraq after the US invasion of 2003.[11] Kuchma governed with an unsteady hand.

Kuchma did not centralize authority in Kyiv as Putin had after he became president of Russia in 2000. Ukrainian politics under Kuchma was Janus-faced, an unlovely scrum of personalities and parties through which the country achieved and held onto a vibrant political pluralism. Ukraine did not have the checks and balance of a full-blown democracy. It did not have an independent judiciary, but it did have a democratic political culture. Because the Ukrainian government did not dominate Kyiv and because Kyiv did not dominate the country, ample space was open to civil society, for the free-wheeling initiatives of activists and journalists across Ukraine's many regions: Gongadze's death in 2000 in no way equaled the death of independent journalism in Ukraine. How far these initiatives sometimes went in challenging Ukraine's government and how much of a problem they could be for the government was clear from Kuchma's behavior; he surely wanted a more authoritarian Ukraine than he actually had. Positive as Ukraine's pluralism could be, the political terrain beyond the government's control was also inviting to Ukraine's many oligarchs, who established fiefdoms within the country, trading in their wealth for political influence and their political influence for wealth. Oligarchs controlled large swaths of the Ukrainian media landscape, meaning that Kuchma and other Ukrainian leaders could be pressured and at times pushed around by oligarchs. These same oligarchs might take advantage of divisions within society or splits in the government for personal gain. The architects and enforcers of Ukraine's poverty, oligarchs slowed down economic growth with their lawless impunity, their predatory approach to business, and their zeal for rent seeking.[12]

Unrelieved corruption and the ugly in-fighting of oligarchs, politicians and opposition figures anticipated the Orange Revolution of 2004. With Kuchma exiting the scene, the two candidates in 2004 were Yushchenko and Yanukovych. Yushchenko the reformer had his Western enthusiasts and his political party, Nasha Ukraina. (Two later Ukrainian leaders were affiliates of Nasha Ukraina circa 2004, Arseniy Yatsenyuk, the future prime minister, and Petro Poroshenko, the future president.) In September 2004, Yushchenko suffered dioxin poisoning, quite possibly at the hands of Russian intelligence, whereas Putin traveled to Ukraine to campaign for Yanukovych in 2004. The first round of voting, which favored Yanukovych was widely considered rigged, tipping Ukraine into crisis. Civic action gave this moment its revolutionary hue—some 500,000 people gathered in Kyiv at the height of the protests—though revolution may be too definite a word for the events on the ground.[13] The protestors did not gather to change the system in the Orange Revolution of 2004; they wanted a fair outcome to the election. The European Union and Russia both mediated the crisis, and a second election was held without incident. Yushchenko was the winner. The Orange Revolution left Vladimir Putin in a rage: "They are stealing Ukraine from under me," he was quoted as saying.[14] First, he had been outmaneuvered by a Ukrainian population that refused to accept a less than honest election. Then, he had been outmaneuvered by the election itself, which deprived Putin of the candidate he had publicly endorsed. Putin's "they" was not so much protestors in Ukraine or those who had voted for Yushchenko as it was Europe and the United States. The election presented the United States and Europe with yet another of their cherished reformers. The United States was content with Yushchenko's victory. For Washington, though, center stage was the Middle East and not Ukraine in 2004. Yushchenko's advance was simply a welcome sign that Eastern Europe was making its way—haltingly—toward the sunny uplands of global democracy.[15]

Putin may not have been militarily ready to invade Ukraine in 2004. He may not have been that enraged by Yushchenko's election.[16] Putin may also have judged—accurately, if this was his judgment—that Yushchenko's hold on power would be impermanent. Yanukovych was still waiting in the wings, and Yushchenko had to reckon with Yulia Tymoshenko, one of the country's dominant political personalities and no friend of Yushchenko's. The two of them were openly dueling after 2004. Nor did Yushchenko do a brilliant job of freeing Ukraine from corruption or of "Europeanizing" Ukraine as Europe and the United States had wanted him to do. The executive branch did not stop manipulating the legislature and the judiciary. Yushchenko's appeal as the darling of the Orange Revolution shaded into the long slog of his presidency, which was burdened by the same oligarch-heavy system that had taken root in the 1990s. Corruption was one of Russia's best levers of influence in Ukraine, and by that measurement Russia was not losing influence in Ukraine between 2004 and 2010—even without Yanukovych in the president's office. Russia may have been gaining certain kinds of influence, while Ukraine was not getting demonstrably closer to Europe. The ultimate reversal of the Orange Revolution came in 2010, when Yanukovych was fairly elected (by all accounts). Fascinated by Ukrainian history and especially by ancient Ukrainian history, Yushchenko made Stepan Bandera a hero of Ukraine before leaving office. Bandera was a controversial Ukrainian nationalist who had welcomed Nazi Germany's attack on the Soviet Union, though he was later imprisoned in Germany where he was assassinated by Soviet intelligence; he was someone whom Vladimir Putin and many Russians viscerally hated. It was a curious coda to Yushchenko's presidency.[17]

* * *

Up to 2014, Ukraine's foreign policy was indeterminate. The country Europeanized less rapidly than the three Baltic Republics had after 1991. Already in the 1990s, Latvia, Lithuania, and Estonia had no-nonsense paths to European Union and NATO membership, which they realized in 2004. In Western Europe and the United States, they counted as Europe, not as peripheral Europe, and they regarded themselves in the same light. Latvia and Estonia had large ethnic Russian and Russian-speaking populations, but in none of the three Baltic Republics was there any doubt about what the leading monoculture was. Each of the three Baltic Republics was relatively small in population: the biggest of them, Lithuania, was a country of some 3 million people. In 2004, Ukraine had a population of a bit less than 40 million. It was the size of Texas, and it had the regional variations of a big country, a heterogeneous homogeneity. Some of Ukraine's leading politicians were not native Ukrainian speakers, and several of its major cities had Russian-speaking majorities. Ukraine's economy was hard to extricate from Russia's, and eliminating Russian influence was not Kyiv's goal in the 1990s and early 2000s, when the political and economic activity around gas transmission knitted Russia and Ukraine together and when Russia was a big market for Ukrainian goods. Russian consumers buoyed the candy business of the Ukrainian oligarch, Petro Poroshenko, who was a political player before 2014 and who had some of his factories in Russia.[18] After 1991, Russia was no longer able to exert its will in the Baltic Republics, where Russian influence existed in patches but was very often a cause for worry. In Ukraine, Russia was exerting its will through many channels, as it had for centuries on Ukrainian territory. Europe did not end at Ukraine's border, and neither did Russia.

Leonid Kuchma's preferred phrase for Ukrainian foreign policy was "multi-vector." In practice, it was a foreign policy that extended out in two directions. Invested in a European Ukraine, Kuchma thought it would be helpful for Ukraine to join the European Union. In the rhetorical question of his deputy foreign minister, Oleksandr Makarenko, "where, in the final analysis, should Ukraine be moving—to the East, back to the past, or to the West, toward the future?"[19] Ukraine borders Moldova and Belarus, two countries for which EU membership was the most distant of prospects in the 1990s. It also borders Poland, Slovakia, Hungary and Romania, four countries that happily entered the European Union and the NATO alliance either before or in 2004. For Western Ukraine in particular, Ukraine's economic integration into Europe was the height of common sense. Kuchma cultivated good relations with the United States as well, a country integral to the West and to the future of Europe. The other direction for Ukrainian foreign policy led toward Russia. The border between Russia and Ukraine runs for 1,426 miles. (If one factors in Belarus, a country between a Russian ally and a Russian satrapy, the border is longer still.) Because of rents on gas and because of Russian subsidies on gas for Ukraine, the economic bond between Kuchma's Ukraine and Russia was near existential for Ukraine. The Russian language and Orthodox Christianity were cultural ties to Russia. Countless Ukrainian families were intermarried with Russian families. To develop and to prosper, a decent relationship with Russia was the height of common sense for Ukraine, especially as Russia was not creating severe difficulties for Ukraine while Kuchma was president. Whatever Boris Yeltsin thought about Ukraine in private, Yeltsin did not actively complicate Kuchma's "multi-vector" efforts to tether Ukraine to European neighbors in the West and to Russia in the East. Neither did Vladimir Putin in the early years of his presidency.

Once Ukraine's nuclear weapons had been handed over to Russia, US interest in Ukraine dwindled. Ukraine was not a source of regional problems, and for Washington its place in the world was up to Ukrainians. The European Union was interested in Ukraine but uncommitted either because it wished to postpone questions about Ukraine's future indefinitely or because it assumed that Europe was methodically Europeanizing its periphery in the 1990s and thereafter, ensuring that Ukraine's future would be European. Europe was expanding, drawing in new partners. It was an intoxicating success story, despite the disheartening example of Turkey, which had sought and never received membership in the EU. Turkey was officially recognized as an applicant for EU membership in 1999; but even if it was outside the institutional EU, Turkey was a dynamic country in the 1990s, engaged in trade and commerce with Europe, and a high-profile NATO member. For the European Union, as for the United States, the important thing was to keep options open and to respect Ukraine's right to choose where it wished to go. The EU eschewed an either-or approach to Ukraine, either European or Russian, believing instead in an and-and approach: solid working relations with Ukraine *and* solid working relations with Russia. In 2005, the European Parliament considered EU membership for Ukraine. Five years after the Gongadze murder and all it implied about executive power in Ukraine, the objections to EU membership for Ukraine had little to do with Russia or with geopolitics. They concerned rule of law and democracy within Ukraine.

The EU's low-key courting fostered rising expectations within Ukraine. In 1998, Ukraine's foreign minister, Boris Tarasiuk, could say point blank that "the European idea has become Ukraine's national idea," an interesting choice of words at a time when the European idea was itself post-national or as with the EU, transnational.[20] Tarasiuk's was one version of Ukrainian foreign policy, not multi-vector but forthrightly European: Ukraine as synonymous with Europe. In July 2004, however, Kuchma dropped the goal of having Ukraine join NATO. In December, the candidate Moscow did not prefer, Viktor Yushchenko, declared that "we aren't going to choose only one side—Europe or Russia."[21] If that was the boilerplate sentiment of a reformist and of a politician admired in Western capitals, then either Ukraine's national idea was malleable or the European idea did not require the choosing of one side over another. Yet at a 2005 meeting of NATO members, Yushchenko said that "we are a country located in the center of Europe. And we would like to see Ukraine integrated into the European Union and into the North Atlantic Alliance."[22] Here he was suggesting that Ukraine had chosen Europe. Kyiv could not make up its mind about accepting the EU membership that the EU could not make up its mind about offering, a symbiotic relationship of sorts. Appointed prime minister in 2006, Yanukovych was advised by the American political consultant, Paul Manafort, to endorse EU integration, while Yulya Tymoshenko, avatar of the political opposition to Yushchenko, went in 2006 to Moscow to meet with Putin and Medvedev, exploring other kinds of integration. Personal feuds and the churn of domestic politics complicated the conundrum of Ukraine's eventual choice, if it would ever have to make one, between Europe and Russia.

Starting in 2008, Ukrainian politics slid toward chaos. Domestic politics and foreign policy, relations with Europe and relations with Russia, were dangerously entangled, while Yushchenko, Yanukovych, and Timoshenko were battling one another for political and for petty reasons. In 2008, Yushchenko expressed an interest in joining NATO, and his government approached NATO for a Membership Action Plan (MAP), a tangible step toward entering the alliance. It was a step for which NATO was ill prepared, since Germany, France, and the United Kingdom were against a MAP for Ukraine, while the US government was divided on this question. Vice President Cheney was robustly in favor, and Secretary of Defense Robert Gates did not like the idea.[23] The absurd compromise—at NATO's Bucharest summit, which Putin attended—was to refuse Ukraine a MAP but to announce that one day Ukraine and Georgia would be NATO members. (Interestingly, Croatia and Albania were invited to enter NATO at the Bucharest summit.) The response of Russia's foreign minister, Sergey Lavrov, was that "Russia will do everything it can to prevent the admission of Ukraine and Georgia to NATO," and these were not empty words.[24] In 2009, Russia cut off gas to Ukraine for a while, and Dmitry Medvedev sent an angry letter to Ukraine, a warning shot regarding its potential Western orientation. Meanwhile, corruption and government mismanagement in Ukraine led the International Monetary Fund to withdraw from the country in 2009. The overall turbulence spooked many NATO member states. NATO did not withdraw its promise of eventual membership to Ukraine, but given the direction of Ukrainian politics there must have been relief in European capitals and perhaps even in the White House about the withholding of a MAP at Bucharest. By January 2009, Dick Cheney was no longer vice president, whereas his more cautious counterpart, Robert Gates, stayed on as President Obama's secretary of defense.

As President of Ukraine, Yanukovych looked back to Kuchma's foreign policy. In his 2010 inauguration speech, Yanukovych traced a variation on the theme of a multi-vector foreign policy. Ukraine, he affirmed, should be "a bridge between East and West, an integral part of Europe and the former Soviet Union at the same time."[25] He stuck by Manafort's advice to be pro-EU, though he seemed more overtly interested in cooperating with Putin, who had wanted Yanukovych to win in 2004 and in 2010 and with whom Yanukovych had more personal affinities than he did with the Eurocrats in Brussels.[26] A Foreign Ministry spokesperson tried—amusingly—to thread the East-West needle: "We want to move towards the West. But the best way of doing so is to get gas from the East."[27] Yanukovych got Putin to lower gas prices for Ukraine, and with Putin he made a deal on the Black Sea Fleet, which Russia was permitted to lease until 2042. In 2012, in a notable gesture, Yanukovych got through a new language law, granting Ukrainian and Russian status as official Ukrainian languages. This was domestic politics for Yanukovych, a gift to Ukraine's Russian speakers, many of whom served as his political base, and it was foreign policy at the same time, a gift to the Kremlin that had appointed itself the protector of ethnic Russians and of Russian speakers in Ukraine (and in other post-Soviet countries).

Yanukovych had something in common with a political leader to Ukraine's north. In Belarus, Alexander Lukashenko was not exactly Putin's puppet. He could be wily, playing Russia off the West and the West off Russia. All three "east Slavic" leaders—Putin, Yanukovych, and Lukashenko—were Orthodox Christians and all three had recognizably Soviet traits. From Putin's perspective, the arrangement was neo-Soviet or neo-imperial: national independence was not an impossibility for Belarus or Ukraine, but this independence needed to coexist with deference to Moscow. (In the Soviet Union, Belarus and Ukraine had had a degree of "national" autonomy, not least because this gave them votes at the United Nations, meaning that Moscow got multiple votes.) The Russian military was present within Belarus, as it was within Crimea. Alumni ties from the

KGB and the Red Army informally criss-crossed these three countries. Though it belonged to this non-equilateral triangle, Ukraine was far apart from Belarus. More than Belarus, it had a distinctive Ukrainian identity, not in every part of the country to be sure and not in every layer of society, but throughout Ukraine there were pronounced linguistic and cultural differences from Russia. Ukraine also had a democracy, which got less democratic the higher one went in the government but was vibrant and real at the grassroots level: Ukraine's presidents did not or could not operate as autocrats in Ukraine. Finally, Ukraine had European prospects that Belarus and Russia did not have. Belarus was commonly and a bit optimistically described as Europe's "last dictatorship." The map of Europe may have ended at the Belorussian border, whereas the EU and NATO, the reality and the mirage of Europe, flickered tantalizingly on the horizon of Ukraine's future.

* * *

In 2009, in the midst of a troubled and troubling year in Ukrainian politics, the European Union settled on a solution to the problem of un-affiliated states like Belarus and Ukraine. In 1994, Lukashenko had signed a Union Treaty with Russia. Under Lukashenko's thumb, Belarus was perilously close to Russia in 2009. Ukraine was far more independent, but it was politically unsteady in 2009, everything having been shaken up by the financial crisis of 2008. International institutions were demanding that Kyiv do something about the kleptocratic undertow of Ukraine's economy. Some two months after NATO's 2008 Bucharest summit, Russia had gone to war against Georgia, which, if Georgia was Europe, was the first European war of the twenty-first century. Russia's war also demolished Georgia's chances of entering NATO. (A requirement for NATO membership is that the applicant country not have border disputes.) Internally if not publicly, NATO and the EU had to accept that Ukraine, Belarus, and Georgia would not be entering either NATO or the EU any time soon. The same was true for Moldova, Armenia, and Azerbaijan, the three other "in between" countries from the former Soviet Union. Quite possibly they would never enter. Russia was growing more assertive in the affairs of these "in between" countries. Georgia and Moldova each played host to a "frozen conflict" by 2008, while Armenia was Russia's ally. The European Union was not always relevant in this unfinished region beyond its immediate jurisdiction, where so many of the trend lines were bad. There was so much that would fall into place if rule of law and democracy could be ingrained in these six post-Soviet countries—if they could be made more European, that is.

With the US financial crisis of 2008 rumbling ever closer to Europe, the number one challenge for Europe in 2009 was the integrity of the EU and not the destiny of Ukraine or Belarus. Nevertheless, an enterprising group of northern and eastern European diplomats pushed for EU action on the countries between

REVOLUTION COMES TO KYIV   109

Russia and institutional Europe. Poland's foreign minister, Radek Sikorsky, and Sweden's foreign minister, Carl Bildt, were especially vigorous advocates for doing something in this part of Europe—rather than constantly reacting to Russia's self-centered and corruption-driven initiative. They came up with the Eastern Partnership Program (EaP), which reflected contradictory aspirations. One was negative: the acknowledgment that actual membership in NATO or the EU did not necessarily await Belarus, Ukraine, Moldova, Georgia, Armenia, and Azerbaijan, though the EaP was not articulated in these terms. Another aspiration was positive, the charting of a roadmap for the EU in relation to six very different countries. The EaP would not be one speed or one-size-fits-all. It would not approach a Belarus stranded in not-Europe in the same way that it would approach Ukraine, which was not stranded at all in 2009 but was mired in choosing between Europe and Russia or at least in configuring its East-West orientation. If Armenia preferred to be in a union with Russia, the Eurasian Economic Union, its eventual choice, so be it—that was Armenia's decision to make. If Ukraine preferred to be in a union with the EU—although not in the EU, for which the EU was not ready—so be it. That was Ukraine's choice to make. The EU could afford to have a light touch. Non-negotiable for the EU, however, was the sovereignty of any country's choice, a principle with which Barack Obama entirely agreed. Such sovereignty was sacrosanct. Europe had had enough of empires, and no country can close the door on the choices of its neighbor without conducting itself as an empire. That stipulation was the heart and soul of the liberal international order.

The Eastern Partnership Program took shape slowly. It was Yanukovych's Ukraine that began working on an Association Agreement and on its accompanying Deep and Comprehensive Free Trade Agreement (DCFTA), which had one set of virtues for the EU and another for Ukraine. For Ukraine, the Association Agreement and the DCFTA were icons of progress. Yanukovych was not delivering prosperity to most Ukrainians; he was enriching himself at the country's expense; but with the EaP he still had the opportunity to deliver "Europe" or "more Europe." The DCFTA was potentially lucrative for Ukraine, where labor costs were cheaper than in the EU. Should travel and work in the EU become easier, remittances would flow back into Ukraine from Europe. The DCFTA would open the doors of trade between Ukraine and the EU, which was both an enormous market for Ukraine and an excellent source of outside invest-ment.[28] The EU did not stand to benefit all that much from the DCFTA with Ukraine. Its motives were more political or geopolitical: to ensure greater rule of law in Ukraine at a time when rule of law was deteriorating; to allow European norms to spread more rapidly in Ukraine, the good European habits of democracy and peaceful cooperation; and to provide an alternative to Russia, which was the European Union's regional Doppelgänger. Even so, an optimistic reading of Medvedev's "pro-Western" policies pre-2011 could align the EaP with Russia's phased integration into Europe: where Ukraine would go, Russia might follow. Despite its open-ended rhetoric, the EU's actions were not free from a zero-sum logic, and neither were Russia's. Behind Medvedev was Putin, whose rhetoric was stringently zero-sum, and in 2011 Putin was reclaiming the presidency. Negotiations over the AA finished in October 2011, and in July 2012 a draft DCFTA was initialed—moments that were anything but political high drama. To the extent that anyone pored over the details of these deals, the AA and the DCFTA were not especially controversial. Ukrainians favored an AA with the European Union over the Eurasian Economic Union in 2013, but by a modest margin. According to a Razumkov Center poll, it was 42 percent for "Europe" and 31 percent for "Eurasia."[29] There was not a clear majority on either side. The whole question could seem too bureaucratic to be polarizing.

Despite the effort expended on the Eastern Partnership Program, Europe's attitude toward Ukraine was tepid. For a while, the whole arrangement threatened to fall apart because Yanukovych had jailed the opposition politician Yulya Timoshenko in 2011 and because Ukraine's political system left so much to be desired. As many precedents attested, both the EU and NATO were at their most powerful when a country was applying for membership (or in this case for association status). The time to push for reform was when Europe had leverage. After Ukraine's Orange Revolution, Yushchenko's political career had congealed into disappointment, and the unreformed alternative to Yushchenko in 2004, Yanukovych, was even worse. He did whatever he could to evade the EU's conditions for reform, which he saw as obstacles to evade. True to his reputation as a man with at least one foot in the world of organized crime, Yanukovych knew that keeping Ukraine "in between" had its advantages. He could take each offer of support from one side and present it to the other as the reason for greater support. It was not a game that the EU was eager to play with Ukraine. The whole point of the Association Agreement was its spirit of legality, which was hardly a Russian precondition for doing business in Ukraine. Though the discrepancies in outlook between Kyiv and Brussels were glaring, the Association Agreement moved inexorably forward. In the end, the EU was so eager to see the AA with Ukraine signed that it did not demand Tymoshenko's release from jail, where she had been since 2011, something of a wink to Yanukovych and a clue perhaps to the Eastern Partnership Program's essentially geopolitical thrust.

Putin appeared to notice Ukraine's journey into Europe belatedly. Yanukovych's Russophilia may have clouded Putin's vision—the deals they had cut together; the language law favorable to Russian; and the respectful treatment of Putin when he visited Kyiv in 2013, two inter-related leaders commemorating the arrival of Orthodox Christianity in medieval Rus'. Not an anti-westernizer, Yanukovych was not a westernizer either. He had emphasized Ukraine's "non-aligned" status and its lack of interest in NATO membership. He put Ukrainian neutrality into legislation in June 2010.[30] The gradual procedural motions of an Association Agreement or of a Deep and Comprehensive Free Trade Agreement, their very names a plea for inattention, could be imperceptible day by day. Though Yanukovych had signed a memorandum in May 2013 making Ukraine an observer of the Eurasian Economic Union (EEU), Putin was aware that his EEU might not include Ukraine. When he realized that a path into the EU might be opening for Ukraine, he snapped into action. The EU might have devised the Eastern Partnership Program as compensation for not allowing its Eastern partners into the EU and for NATO's not letting them in. If this was the case, such inversions and subtleties did not necessarily register as inversions and subtleties in Moscow. Delicacy of attitude had not brought Western institutions so far to the East after 1991, in Putin's judgment. At the heart of Europe's eastward enlargement was not politesse. To the contrary: the closer the EU came to the Russian border, the closer NATO might come and with it the United States. These at least were the official Russian arguments. Unmentioned by the Kremlin but not less relevant was the Association Agreement as a blow to Putin's ego. NATO and Ukraine were impossibly far apart in 2013. Yet the symbolism of a Ukraine in the West, even if the reality was far more complicated than the symbolism, militated against Putin's cherished image of Ukraine. This was Ukraine as Russia's little brother.[31]

Putin prodded and cajoled Yanukovych not to sign the Association Agreement, including at a November 9, 2013, visit of Yanukovych's to Sochi, where Putin had one of his private residences.

The drama's sudden climax came later in November. The indecision had lasted for years. Not choosing had been the crux of Kuchma's and Yanukovych's "multi-vector" foreign policy, of their serial feints toward Europe and their serial feints toward Moscow. On November 21, 2013, Yanukovych pulled out from the Association Agreement several days before he was slated to travel to Vilnius to sign it. His garbled communication and the lateness of his decision point to the agony of his having to make it at all.[32] Even after November 21 he did not cancel his trip to Vilnius. He postponed the last word on the Association Agreement just a little bit longer. Having arrived in Vilnius for meetings on November 28 and 29, he described his predicament with emotion to Germany's chancellor, Angela Merkel, and to Lithuania's president, Dalia Grybauskaite. "I'd like you to listen to me," he said. "For three and a half years I've been alone. I've been face-to-face with a very strong Russia on a very unlevel playing field."[33] The pivotal word here is "alone." It captures the folly of the Eastern Partnership Program, a venture that offered just enough "Europe" to be enticing to countries that had no guarantees of European support and no commitment of European security assistance. Ukraine was indeed alone on a very uneven playing field. More reasonable might have been NATO membership first and then the Association Agreement, though NATO membership was out of reach for Ukraine in 2013, as France and Germany had ensured back at the Bucharest Summit in 2008. Instead, Europe stood aloof, under no obligation to do anything on Ukraine's behalf, while Yanukovych navigated what he knew to be less a political playing field than a geopolitical minefield. Part of the crisis unfolding in Vilnius in November 2013 was that leaders like Merkel and Grybauskaite did not know that there was a crisis brewing.

In the end, Yanukovych said "no" to Europe. He had turned his back on the European Union—to the great surprise of the Europeans in Vilnius—having decided in favor of Russia. In the third week of November 2013, before heading to Vilnius, Yanukovych had met secretly with Putin. No doubt they made some kind of deal, and Vilnius was merely a matter of finalizing their agreed-upon choice. As a reward, Putin floated a $15 billion loan without any of the cumbersome strings that the Europeans would have attached—no anti-corruption measures, no promises to revive Ukraine's beleaguered judiciary or not to jail political opponents. On December 17, not long after departing Vilnius for Kyiv, Yanukovych made his way to Moscow, the visit itself an expression of fealty. Moscow was calling the shots. Europe had been outflanked. Yanukovych had not liberated himself by choosing; he had tied himself to Putin. In January of 2014, Yanukovych was bringing Ukraine closer to the Eurasian Economic Union, which was to be Vladimir Putin's coup de grace. Putin had many levers to pull in Kyiv, and with Ukraine in the Eurasian Economic Union, the regional momentum would at last favor Russia, the EU having been blocked once and for all. Belarus was already in the bag. Georgia and Moldova were pinned down by frozen conflicts. Armenia was on board with Moscow. Azerbaijan was the furthest from Europe of the six countries encompassed by the EU's Eastern Partnership Program, impossibly far from NATO's embrace and a country with which Russia could do business. By not signing the Association Agreement, Yanukovych in November 2013 had delivered something of exceptional value to his friend in Moscow.

* * *

Mustafa Nayyem was born in Kabul in 1981. His father had been the minister of education in Afghanistan prior to the Soviet invasion in 1979. In 1987, Nayyem's father went to study in Moscow, where he met a Ukrainian woman. They brought their family to live in Kyiv. Mustafa Nayyem studied aerospace engineering, played drums in a band, and around 2004 started to dabble in journalism. He moved between print and internet journalism, inhabiting different spaces in Ukraine's civil society, which, if anything, was activated and expanded by the misfortune of Yushchenko's presidency and the thuggish self-dealing of Yanukovych's presidency. (In 2014, Nayyem would travel to Palo Alto, California, where he studied "the structures of democracy" with Francis Fukuyama; and at Fukuyama's recommendation, Nayyem would later become a member of parliament in Ukraine.) The Association Agreement mattered to young Ukrainians like Nayyem, but in the lead-up to November 2013, the Agreement could seem either a legalistic nicety or simply the next inevitable step in Ukraine's integration into European institutions. When Yanukovych pulled back from the Association Agreement on November 21, 2013, it shocked Nayyem, who turned to Facebook and enjoined his fellow Ukrainians to wake up. "Come on guys," he wrote, "let's be serious, don't just 'like' this post. Write that you are ready and we can try to start something."[34] When people started to trickle onto the Maidan Square, as Nayyem had prodded them to do on social media, Yanukovych was on his way to Vilnius, his mind not entirely made up, it could still seem. By November 24, some 100,000 protestors were gathering on the Maidan. Four days later, Yanukovych arrived in Vilnius, and only on November 29 was "Europe" categorically rejected, though the story of the Association Agreement was not coming to an end. Something had certainly been started.

Nothing in politics is quite so mysterious as the onset of revolutionary fervor. In the early winter of 2013, four factors help to explain the coming of revolution to Ukraine. One was disappointment over the Association Agreement, which for everyone involved—for Putin, for Yanukovych, for many Ukrainians—had more emotional than practical meaning. The AA did not just provoke questions about the Ukrainian economy. It provoked the question of Ukraine's true nature, of its core identity, a question fully capable of generating political passion. A second reason, and one that extended beyond pro-European circles in Kyiv (beyond people like Mustafa Nayyem) was Yanukovych's personal corruption and a legacy of violence and criminality in the cadres close to him. This Yanukovych-directed anger was three years in the making by 2013, and anger about corruption in Ukraine had its origins in the 1990s. A third reason was the oligarchic system behind the formal political order in Ukraine, within which Yanukovych had many enemies. One of them was Petro Poroshenko, who had supported Kuchma in the 1990s and the Orange Revolution in 2004. He had been minister of trade and economic development under Yanukovych until he resigned in 2012. In the Maidan protests, Poroshenko and other oligarchs saw the chance to outmaneuver Yanukovych. Finally, because it emerged from the question of whither Ukraine, the protest on the Maidan was a national awakening. This awakening was not without its far-right element. "Stirring the nationalist pot was working well for those on the Maidan," writes the US diplomat Christopher M. Smith, an eyewitness to the revolution and someone sympathetic to the Maidan for personal and professional reasons; but far-right nationalism was not the driver of this national awakening.[35] The Maidan's galvanizing ideal was a more European Ukraine, its European-ness lying in the eye of the beholder. Not necessarily anti-Russian, a more European Ukraine would necessarily be less inclined toward Russia.

On November 30, Yanukovych cracked down on the Maidan protests. In classic revolutionary fashion, the state's resort to violence exacerbated the crisis the state was trying to control. Yanukovych's turn to violence implied that he could no longer persuade the Ukrainian population—not that he had ever invested much in the arts of persuasion. He had to quell dissent by force, a difficult job for Yanukovych given Ukraine's unpoliced political culture and given the fact that the oligarchs assessing his weakness had media and political clout of their own (something with which Putin no longer had to reckon in 2013). Yanukovych's turn to violence elicited widespread sympathy for the protestors. Outside of Kyiv, outside of more educated and more well-traveled constituencies, millions upon millions of Ukrainians were not going to take to the streets for the sake of the Association Agreement alone. In his diary of the Maidan, Andrey Kurkov puts outrage with Yanukovych and his corrupt government on par with the "refusal to bury the European dream" as a catalyst of revolution.[36] To intimidate protestors, the government relied on the Berkut, ominously dressed riot police, and so-called *titushki*, plainclothes enforcers and agents provocateurs. The excesses of an unpopular government, coupled with a twenty-first-century Europhilic Ukrainian-ness that had come willy-nilly to characterize the Maidan, transformed a local and somewhat abstract protest, a discreet protest, into a movement. Its inspiration was the dream of taming corruption, of fashioning a Ukraine that was not a Russian appendage, and of marching west rather than east. This dream mirrored the Eastern Partnership Program itself, which was more about the spread of European norms (and influence) than it was about the spread of European institutions per se. On stimulating interest in European norms, the EaP had overfulfilled the plan.

In November and December 2013, the United States had more than one position on Ukraine. Washington's preference would have been for new presidential elections in 2014. If Yanukovych was so unpopular, someone else would get elected, and life would go on. Popular sovereignty within Ukraine should determine the course of Ukraine's government. In his 2014 State of the Union address, given on January 18, President Obama addressed Ukraine, stating that "we stand for the principle that all people have the right to express themselves freely and peacefully, and have a say in their country's future." At issue was procedural fairness for Obama, who did not weigh in on Ukraine's future direction, affirming instead the importance of choice itself.[37] That did not prevent Victoria Nuland, the State Department's assistant secretary for European Affairs, from appearing on the Maidan on December 10, 2013, and with Geoffrey Pyatt, US ambassador to Ukraine, passing out baked goods to the Maidan protestors, going beyond support for the right to protest and openly siding with the cause of the protestors, which was a Ukraine that leaned West. (EU representative Catherine Ashton was also in Kyiv at the time.) Assistant Secretary Nuland and Ambassador Pyatt also gave baked goods to the Berkut, but where their sympathies lay was hardly a secret, and it was not with the Berkut. In his memoirs, Secretary of State Kerry refers to the Maidan as "a Tahrir Square moment unfolding in Europe," a step toward liberty.[38] Senator John McCain, who had already taunted Putin on Twitter about an Arab Spring coming to Moscow, spoke at the Maidan on December 15, 2013. His words were revealing: "We are here to support your just cause, the sovereign right of Ukraine to determine its own destiny freely and independently. And the destiny you seek lies in Europe."[39] McCain did not limit himself to process and choice. Either he presumed that all Ukrainians were pro-Europe, which was not the case, or he felt that a Ukraine in Europe was in the national interest of the United States, which was not what the White House was saying. McCain was openly asking for an end to Ukraine's multi-vector foreign policy.

Such multiplicity of positions is hardly a-typical of US foreign policy. A co-equal branch of government, Congress has a constitutional mandate to set the course of US foreign policy. It is not a rubber stamp for the White House or the State Department. Senator McCain had the right to air his opinions on the Maidan, one that he was thrilled to exercise. Assistant Secretary Nuland's photo op on the Maidan was a bit more unusual given the president's conscious neutrality on Ukraine. She was not there only to protest the government-sponsored violence in late November. Like McCain, she preferred a European destiny for Ukraine, as did US Embassy staff in Kyiv. Nuland was in Kyiv in part because Yanukovych's decision not to sign the Association Agreement bothered her. At the more reticent White House, President Obama could not forestall the propaganda Russia would spin from McCain's comment and especially from an assistant secretary of state nourishing pro-Europe protestors on the Maidan. If the Kremlin believed or said it believed that the Maidan was a CIA plot, there would be no dissuading the Kremlin. Nevertheless, Obama and many in the US government may have underestimated the importance Libya held for Putin, the resentment he felt at NATO's "elimination" of Gaddafi, and his fear that NATO had a similar program in the works for Ukraine and Russia. The White House may have underestimated the investment Putin had made in Yanukovych, in his hopes for a Eurasian Economic Union with Ukraine. If so, it underestimated the collision course the United States and Russia had been on since the Orange Revolution. In 2013, Putin had a lot to lose in Ukraine, incalculably more than Medvedev did in Libya in 2011.

Having hosted Yanukovych in Sochi on December 6, 2013, Putin was in an unusual bind. The Maidan was a nightmare for him. As a young KGB officer, he had watched Soviet power slip away in East Germany, popular protests coinciding with well-placed pushes from the West. The analogy could not have escaped him some twenty-four years later: street protests in Ukraine were undermining an ally of Moscow and garnering approval in the West. Whether or not Putin believed that the CIA was behind these protests, he surely associated these protests with the promotion of American-style democracy, sometimes directly and sometimes through government-funded NGO's like the National Endowment for Democracy or the International Republican Institute. Whatever instruments of power the United States had in Ukraine—whether it was the power of example, the power of persuasion, or something harder like money or covert support—Putin was convinced that the United States was pulling Ukraine into its sphere of influence. Putin may have assumed that the United States was handling Ukraine as Russia handled Ukraine, which is to say roughly and with ulterior motives. Yet Putin's only option was to ask Yanukovych to clear up the protests and to hope for the best. Russia was getting ready to host the Olympics in Sochi in February 2014, the stage-managed culmination of Russia's arrival as a twenty-first-century superpower. The winter of 2013–2014 was the worst possible moment for Ukraine to go off the rails.

Yanukovych dug himself into a deeper hole in January 2014. The Maidan was a political movement with its focal point in Kyiv, and iterations of the movement broke out across Ukraine. As the Arab Spring had already shown, the dissemination of information was much faster and wider in an age of social media than it had previously been. Of this new era, Nayyem's Facebook post was iconic. Born in protest and in government violence, the Maidan quickly evolved beyond its singular cause—the rejection of the Association Agreement. Ukrainian and EU flags proliferated in downtown Kyiv and in other Ukrainian cities, recalling the 1989 uprisings in Eastern Europe, which invoked a larger Europe in order to outrun the past and usher in the future. The Maidan was an affirmation of nationhood much like the 1848 revolutions that had spread throughout Central Europe, and the Maidan could have a carnival feeling, a turning of public life upside down. It was, as all real revolutions are, a revolution of the senses. Instead of the dour, heavy-set Yanukovych locking Ukraine in a post-Soviet holding pattern, in harmony with Putin's wishes, the Maidan prized youthful self-sacrifice and novelty, and the quixotic happiness of declaring independence. It would come to be known as the "revolution of dignity" in contrast to the indignities of Ukrainian governance under Yanukovych. Knowing that he was the revolution's enemy, Yanukovych had no purely peaceful way of scaling back the protests. He was trapped not just by what he did but by who he was, and every time he resorted to the use of force the revolution grew in size, strength, and scope. Yanukovych had the political instincts of a George III or a Louis XVI.

When violence backfired, Yanukovych came to think that the revolution could be extinguished if the government had greater powers of control, unwittingly solving one of the revolution's biggest problems. Everyone could recall the Orange Revolution of only ten years before, which had come about because of a rigged election. The Maidan was not the Orange Revolution redux in

2013: its Achilles' heel was that in 2010 Yanukovych had been democratically elected. To oppose him was not to defend democracy as such; and by passing on the Association Agreement, Yanukovych had not violated Ukrainian public opinion.[40] Approximately one third of Ukrainians would have wanted Yanukovych to sign an agreement with Putin's Eurasian Economic Union. Marginally more Ukrainians preferred the European Union. The decision about the Association Agreement was legally and politically his to make. Back in November 2013, the Maidan protesters had a disagreement with Yanukovych over a single decision, though from the beginning some may have fantasized about unseating him. Yanukovych did the Maidan a great service on January 16 when he finalized the "dictatorship laws," as they were called in the language of the Maidan.[41] About two years earlier, Ukrainians had watched the orchestrated demotion of Dmitry Medvedev and then the Russian state's crushing of protest in Moscow's Bolotnaya Square and elsewhere. Laws intended to impede Ukrainian civil society resonated within this regional context. Once Yanukovych tied himself to the dictatorship laws, while continuing to employ violence, the Maidan had a new purpose, one that had nothing to do with EU regulations. This was a preservation of Ukrainian democracy co-terminous with the choice of "Europe," bringing the revolution full circle. Whatever the shortcomings of Ukraine's oligarch-heavy political system and however many politicians under Yanukovych had been on the take since 2010, there was a Ukrainian democracy to be preserved in January 2014.

The revolution climaxed in February 2014. After November 2013, Yanukovych could not retrace his steps and supply the signature that would Europeanize Ukraine. Nor could protesters realistically ask him to set back the clock. Yanukovych's dictatorship laws gave an open-ended protest movement a simpler and less retrospective job to do: to push for the repeal of the dictatorship laws. Meanwhile, having made himself increasingly dependent on Putin, Yanukovych was less and less able to ignore Putin's advice, which was to do in Kyiv what Putin had done—under less strenuous circumstances—in Moscow in 2012. Putin wanted Yanukovych to end the revolution, while protestors marched on the Ukrainian parliament on February 18, 2014, in part to forestall Kyiv's "becoming" Moscow. They set fire to the headquarters of Yanukovych's political party, demanding a return to Ukraine's 2004 constitution. The protestors wanted to tame the prince who wanted to subdue them through fear. Yanukovych got the message. The Maidan is a public place and since the miners' protest there in the 1990s it had been a common site for public demonstrations in Ukraine. A parliament building and political headquarters are something else entirely. Enough protesters could shut parliament down, in which case the government might not be able to function; and an attack on a party building might develop into an attack on politicians themselves. Even if the intent of the protestors on February 18 was to pressure Yanukovych and thus to win specific concessions, Yanukovych understandably worried that his government could fall, that he personally was losing his grip on power, and that he was in physical danger.

These days in Kyiv would shake the foundations of Europe. Shortly before the earthquake, European and Russian diplomats rushed to Kyiv. German foreign minister, Frank-Walter Steinmeier; French foreign minister, Laurent Fabius; and Polish foreign minister, Radek Sikorsky, had come to meet with Yanukovych.[42] As partnership was fading from Europe's East, the Eastern Partnership Program Sikorsky had helped to invent was honoring the law of unintended consequences. Rather than wanting Yanukovych to leave office, the European diplomats wanted him to negotiate with the protestors and to broker a compromise; they wanted him to stay in office. Yet on February 20, the revolution experienced its darkest hour and its turning point. Protestors not far from the Ukrainian parliament were fired on—possibly by Ukrainian security services, possibly by other entities. The facts have ever since been hard to establish. Dozens of people were killed, and together with some who had been killed earlier they were designated the "heavenly hundred." On January 16, the revolution had gotten its most palpable cause when Yanukovych overreached politically. (The dictatorship laws, a provocative exercise in futility, were reversed on January 28.) On February 20, the revolution had gotten not its first martyrs but its best-known martyrs. In addition to restoring the 2004 constitution, the protestors had the "heavenly hundred" to avenge or at least to remember. The revolution had found its emotional center.

Between February 20 and February 21, the diplomatic wheel spinning furiously, Russia's Vladimir Lukin joined his European counterparts to see if Yanukovych's government could be salvaged. The diplomats went back and forth between the opposition and Yanukovych, and they pulled a rabbit out of a hat. Yanukovych had already agreed to a restoration of the 2004 constitution. He then accepted the formation of a unity government that would include opposition figures, which was to be followed by early elections (scheduled for December 2014). Though Lukin had participated in the negotiations and though Yanukovych was supposed to stay in power until the next round of elections, Russia did not sign the agreement. Either Lukin knew something that the other negotiators did not, or he did not wish to be a party to such an extensive array of concessions and to the gathering sense that the revolution was carrying the day. Boxing champion and opposition politician Vitaly Klitschko went to the Maidan to announce the result of these negotiations, which the crowd there greeted with consternation. Prior to February 21, there were credible reports of security-service personnel changing sides, the consequence of the government's self-defeating order to fire on the protestors. Yet on February 21 it was possible to believe that the worst of the disorder was over, that the protestors had gotten what they had been asking for, and that Yanukovych, who was unlikely to win any further elections, had nevertheless found a safe and reasonable way to retire from public life.

* * *

At some point, Yanukovych decided that fleeing Ukraine was more prudent than staying. His active plans to leave can be dated to February 19, before the deaths of the "heavenly hundred" and before his sweeping concessions to the Maidan protestors. Perhaps he made these concessions because he would no longer be responsible for honoring them; they would be the headache of Ukraine's next leader. If he feared for his personal safety on February 19, with sufficient urgency to start packing his bags, his anxiety must have worsened after February 20, the revolution's bloodiest day. The loyalty of his bodyguards and security services, never put to the test before 2013, could by no means be taken for granted, and on the Maidan he was the villain of the story. What would the ten months look like between February and the election in December? What would the government of Ukraine look like with opposition figures embedded within it, with their newfound power and their preening self-confidence? What would relations with Russia look like now that Yanukovych was being tugged, via an EU-themed revolution, to the West and to Europe rather than to the East and to Russia? Yanukovych fled to save his own hide. That much was not uncertain at all. He also fled a political and geopolitical riddle that had become insoluble—by him and quite possibly by anyone. The ceaseless negotiations on February 19, February 20, and February 21 belied the emerging zero-sum calculus of Ukraine's position in Europe. Though it was not of his own making, Yanukovych had grievously mismanaged this calculus. In the spirit of poetic justice, he was its first victim.[43]

Ukraine did not fall apart on February 21, when Yanukovych fled in a blaze of cowardice. Yanukovych had not escaped to Dubai or to Geneva or to London. He had fled to Russia. This was unsurprising, but it still spoke volumes. Without Russia's backing, without Russia's protection, Yanukovych was at sea, a petty criminal at risk. This implied less an unbroken bond between Ukraine and Russia, which was Putin's view, than a bond of manipulation and artifice, upon which Yanukovych had built his political career. Putin's tendency to manipulate Ukraine came at great cost to Russia. Challenged on a policy question by public opinion, tripped up by a spot of protest, Yanukovych's house of government was not much more than a house of cards. His actual house, on the outskirts of Kyiv, was the perfect metaphor for his three inglorious years as president. It commemorated the inventive theft that was the lifeblood of Ukrainian politics under Yanukovych, the piling up of useless luxuries and the gangster's love of gilded opulence, tucked behind walls and gates—beyond the reach of public scrutiny. After his flight, Ukrainians promenaded around Yanukovych's property, gazing in amusement and disgust at the zoo animals and the terrible art and the unchecked self-indulgence. It was a vulgarian's Versailles and the ideal counterpoint to the stoical ethical codes of the revolutionaries, who had stood outside in the cold for their country before they had bled for it. Yanukovych, hiding behind Putin, had stolen all he could and run away—to Russia.

In Yanukovych's absence, Oleksandr Turchynov was appointed acting president of Ukraine on February 23. A plan was put in place for presidential elections on May 25. Petro Poroshenko won them and formed a new government. In many respects, life carried on as before—blissfully without Yanukovych for many, though not for all. Had Ukraine been Australia, its revolution might have ended with an auditioning autocrat's request for political exile, with the smooth transfer of power and with the new era that began when Poroshenko became president. Yanukovych's flight did not undermine Ukraine's economy or its constitutional order. As of January 2014, a key goal of the revolutionaries was the *restoration* of the Ukrainian constitution. It was an un-Bolshevik revolution, conservative in a sense and therefore limited, but Ukraine was not a continent unto itself. Beyond Ukraine, the revolution's meaning lay in the gulf it opened between Russia and the West, and in the gulf it opened between Russia and Ukraine. Putin spent the final days of the Maidan-Yanukovych drama hosting the Winter Olympics in Sochi, smiling for the camaras and doing what he could to enjoy the games he had set before the world. The Sochi Olympics illustrated the distance Russia had traveled since 1991, when poverty and imperial loss had unmoored Russian life and when the United States had crowned itself the winner of the Cold War. February 2014 was supposed to be the month in which that narrative would be retired, and as if on cue the Russian Olympic team received the most medals in Sochi. February 2014 was the time when the revolution in Ukraine ended, ending in success for the revolutionaries. It was also the month in which the fervor and festival of revolution yielded to the brute exigencies of war.

5

War in Ukraine, Round 1

> The Spartans grew apprehensive of the enterprising and revolu-
> tionary spirit of the Athenians.
>
> Thucydides, *The Peloponnesian War*, Book 1:102

After not choosing Europe in 2013, Ukraine chose it the next year. A revolution had moved Ukraine from one position to the other. Yanukovych's fall also
precipitated a war in Ukraine or a combination of wars—one in Crimea, a peninsula extending out into the Black Sea, and another in eastern Ukraine, where a
degree of spontaneous civil unrest, out of cycle with the Maidan protests, became
the pretext for a separate Russian invasion. Revolutions typically coincide with
wars: wars lead to revolutions and revolutions to wars. Set in motion by the Seven
Years' War before it, the American Revolution had been a war against the British
Empire. Also set in motion by the globe-spanning Seven Years' War, the French
Revolution led to two decades of war in Europe, known as the Napoleonic wars.
Caused in part by World War I, the Russian Revolution of 1917 unleashed four
years of civil war and the Soviet invasion of Poland in 1920. The Nazi Revolution
of 1933, a response to World War I, was the cause of World War II. The collapse
of the Soviet Union was akin to a revolution. If it was a revolution, though, it
occurred—shockingly—at a time of relative peace. Nor did the Soviet Union's
collapse issue immediately in war, except in former Yugoslavia, which for local
and historical reasons succumbed to war in the 1990s. The wars of Soviet succession were slow to intensify. They began in earnest in Georgia in 2008 and continued with a vengeance in Ukraine in 2014.

Although Russia's annexation of Crimea and incursion into eastern
Ukraine were global turning points, many of the arguments Putin used to justify his actions were regional. A Ukraine overtaken by neo-fascist nationalism
was turning its back on Russia and seeking to ally with the West, the Kremlin
contended. Ukraine was about to fall victim to NATO's ruthless expansion after
1991, an imperial project sponsored by the United States and furthered, when
necessary, by the colored revolutions at which Washington was so expert and
which had been inflicted on Ukraine in 2013. Putin emphasized his responsibility to protect Russian speakers or ethnic Russians in a Ukraine hostile to
their interests, in a Ukraine that would forcibly try to Ukrainianize them and

somehow to crush them. Less vivid in Putin's speeches was the global dimension to Russia's actions, a countering of US influence in Ukraine that was also a pushing back against US power outside of Ukraine and outside of Europe. Still in the coils of the financial crisis in 2014 and then entangled in a migrant crisis in 2015, Europe had vulnerabilities that Russia might exploit. The United States was less obviously unstable, but it too had its vulnerabilities. The best way to achieve global objectives vis-à-vis the United States might be to destabilize the United States from within, which is what Russia would attempt to do in 2016, a global project par excellence and at the same time a response to the Maidan Revolution (for Putin). Russia's 2016 reach into the American body politic would bear fruit of a most unexpected kind, uniting Russia, Ukraine, and the United States into an unholy trinity of cause and effect, of action and reaction, all the way down to Russia's 2022 invasion.

Ukraine's task in 2014 was national, not global. When Ukraine gave up its nuclear weapons in 1994, nobody in Ukraine or in Russia envisioned a war between Russia and Ukraine. In the Budapest Memorandum, Russia had pledged to protect Ukrainian sovereignty from outside invasion, rendering Russian invasion a theoretical absurdity. Not long after the Budapest Memorandum was signed, Russia and Ukraine agreed to a friendship pact. Yet the new government that formed in May of 2014 had to fight a war against Russia, a war that Russia was better equipped to fight. The war had begun with decisions made in Moscow and was carried out by Europe's largest conventional military; Russia was a nuclear power to boot. Another of Kyiv's wartime challenges was to make good on the Maidan. Ridding Ukraine of Yanukovych had happened at the behest of oligarchs as well as at the will of the Maidan protestors: the revolution had not put an end to corruption or to oligarchs' involvement in Ukrainian politics. Reducing corruption, especially when that corruption has a home in government, is among the hardest things any government can attempt. Doing so while fighting a war is drastically harder. After the Maidan, Ukraine had to elaborate a new foreign policy. Yanukovych's multi-vector balancing act was a relic of the past, but until he rebuffed Europe in Vilnius, Yanukovych's foreign policy was in line with that of previous Ukrainian presidents. Not committing was the tradition. With Ukraine and Russia at war in 2014, there was no longer an act to balance. Ukraine had to figure out its status as a European country separate from Russia, which is the status Yanukovych's escape and Russia's turn to war had both solidified.

As Russia's war in Ukraine reverberated throughout Europe, each European country registered the novelty in its own way. Even NATO membership was cold comfort for Poland and the Baltic republics in the brave new Europe of 2014. All four countries had been invaded by Russia (or by the Soviet Union) in the past, which created an instant sympathy for Ukraine: as went Ukraine, so would

Eastern Europe go. Southern Europe, from Portugal to Greece, had much less of a connection to Ukraine. From a southern vantage point, this might be another Georgia war, far away and not viscerally Europe's problem. The United Kingdom saw important principles at stake—Ukrainian sovereignty, peace in Europe—and did not doubt that Russia was at fault or that Russia's military adventurism needed to be punished. France agreed with Britain about the crisis but was more inclined to see 2014 as a moment for European diplomacy underpinned by French leadership. If Russia had started intruding on European peace, unbuilding Europe, then France would be instrumental to the construction of a Europe that might restore the peace, ideally with Russian compliance, if European diplomacy would be sufficiently skillful. Germany did not actively disagree with either Britain or France. More Portugal than Poland vis-à-vis Ukraine, Germany found itself the leader of those European countries that wanted to maintain the European status quo, to preserve all the cooperation and prosperity that had been gained after 1945 and still more after 1991. War was not the solution to any of the problems in German foreign policy. Punitive measures plus negotiation would have to convince Russia of the truth Germany had pulled from its twentieth century, the truth that never again could Europe descend into war.

Post-Yanukovych Ukraine elucidated the differences between Russia and the West. Entirely consistent with its thinking about the world, the Obama administration approached Ukraine as a case study in the liberal international order. Ukraine had an absolute right to its sovereignty. It had a right to make its own choices. It had a right to peace. It had a right to as much Europe as Europe might wish to give and as Ukraine might wish to take. Ukraine was a country in duress in 2014, and on its behalf the United States pioneered a sanctions regime, which the European Union eventually joined. One way or another, Ukraine would be precedent setting in Washington's view, and Russia could not be allowed to rewrite the unwritten bylaws of the liberal international order. Like China, Russia had profited from this order before 2014, from the relative peace in Europe and Asia, from the integrity of their own borders and from the wealth and technology transfer that globalization afforded. It would be insanity for Russia—not to mention calamity for Ukraine—if Putin were to tear everything down and to impose a might-makes-right ethos on Europe. Putin would have to see the light; he would have to come to his senses. The events of 2014 and 2015 revealed punishing discrepancies between Russia and the West. Putin had crossed the Rubicon, whereas his Western antagonists wanted to undo his war without going to war themselves, not psychologically accepting the fact that war had come to Europe in February 2014. Before the Maidan, Ukraine had been drawn to Europe through Europe's sheer magnetism and not at all at the barrel of a gun. It had been Ukraine's business, but Putin's Russia acknowledged no such independence for Ukraine. That was the whole point of the 2014 invasion of Ukraine and of

Russia's jubilant annexation of Ukrainian territory. Who had agreed to make the United States the legislator of international affairs, Putin had asked in Munich in 2007 and then again in 2014. Nobody had, he was sure, and in Ukraine he would prove the point.

*　*　*

The annexation of Crimea was a coup for Putin, and in Russia its popularity was not just a top-down phenomenon. Even many, like Alexei Navalny, who were in the political opposition applauded Putin's gambit. In this, grievances and historical demons played a role. Moscow's long retreat from Europe, its voluntary withdrawal of troops, its need to accept limits imposed by others, to live by their preferences and their dictates: this recessional of Russian power and influence and control could be reversed in Crimea. To have experienced the collapse of the Soviet Union as a loss, a sentiment not at all uncommon in Russia, could frame the annexation of Crimea not as a violation of international law or as the theft of Ukrainian territory but as a balancing of the books, as justice being done (at long last) on Russian terms. Crimea's annexation was also popular as an index of Russia's future. It was not primarily a retrospective act, though it was often interpreted as such. More to the point, Russia was realizing in Crimea its destiny as a post-Soviet and as a properly modern country. It was pursuing its aims autonomously, a pursuit that did not mandate conflict with Europe or with the United States. Autonomy could be the choice to cooperate, as in certain areas Russia had cooperated with the United States after September 11, but autonomy would brook no deference; deference was the opposite of autonomy. In addition to a set of military and political moves, annexing Crimea was a refusal to defer to the West and its pronouncements about what Russia was and what Russia could do. It was as if Russia had been waiting for decades to defy the West. In 2014, it could do so in a part of the world that many Russians considered their neighborhood far more organically and justifiably than it was the neighborhood of the United States or of Western Europe.[1]

The manner and timing of the annexation intertwined. In the West, Russia's tactics, its style of war, would acquire the name "hybrid war." The combination of military force with information, disinformation, and propaganda was sometimes presented as an extraordinary invention of the Kremlin. (A better argument is that all wars are hybrid.) Russian military thinking was surely simpler. Where the United States was concerned, the annexation of Crimea was designed to stay beneath a certain threshold. Russia's 2008 war in Georgia had been similarly designed: the optics of invasion had been played down and the humanitarian costs of the war had been kept relatively low. The Russian military did not bomb or march into Tbilisi. In Crimea, Russia sent in soldiers not wearing uniforms. The "little green men" could be mistaken for pro-Russian Ukrainians, which they were not. Local actors, sympathetic to the prospect of annexation, helped them to infiltrate government buildings, and the operation was conducted with such speed that Kyiv had little time to react. The annexation had no shortage of military menace to speed it along, but neither did the Russian soldiers have to beat the local populations into submission. These populations were either too taken aback to resist, or they did not wish to resist. The Obama administration, which had to decide on the spot what to do about the "little green men," was in an unenviable position. It had to contemplate military action in a war that did not have the hallmarks of a war and against a country that was vociferously denying its willingness to wage war in Crimea or anywhere else in Ukraine. Thus did Putin facilitate the Obama administration's understandable desire not to get embroiled in a war with Russia.

The timing of the annexation was not less pivotal to the Kremlin's success. A somewhat aloof party to the negotiations in Kyiv, the meetings on February 20 and 21 meant to defuse the protests throughout the capital city, Russia had all along been making its plans to annex Crimea. Yanukovych was packing his bags on February 19, though he could have told Putin earlier that he intended to run away. The closing ceremony of the Winter Olympics in Sochi was February 23, and the Crimean parliament in Simferopol was seized on February 27, six days after Yanukovych departed Kyiv by night. Thematized as a response to Western aggression, to its intrusive colored revolutions, and to NATO expansion, as if NATO or the CIA were running the show in Kyiv, Russia's annexation of Crimea capitalized on a moment of weakness within Ukraine, the "Revolution of Dignity" still in progress, an acting president trying to pick up the pieces, and the Ukrainian government and military paralyzed by the double helix of revolution and war. At a politically delicate moment, the Ukrainian parliament's passage of a language law that privileged Ukrainian also stirred the passions of some Russian speakers in Ukraine.[2] Whether innovatively hybrid or standard-issue military conduct, Putin's tactics confused outside observers. To compound the confusion, the Russian military was not exactly invading Crimea in 2014. It had been in Crimea all along—on its leased naval base. The annexation of Crimea could be staged as a comic opera, as a Gilbert and Sullivan production set on the Black Sea, as a farce. Yet it and its consequences were deadly serious.

March 2014 was the month of annexation. Putin opted not for the rituals of war—battle, surrender, peace treaty—but for the rituals of pseudo-legality. With Crimea under Russian military control, a referendum was scheduled for March 16. It did not grant respondents the option of rejecting annexation. The referendum was obviously a sham, acceptable as spectacle for those who deemed Russia in the right (in Crimea and in Russia) and an amalgam of insult and political theater for everyone else. It mocked Kyiv, which could not win back Crimea in March. It mocked Europe, which had so decorously trumpeted its Eastern

Partnership Program in 2009 and then had to stand by and watch as a piece of this partnership was extracted from Ukraine and grafted onto Russia; it mocked Washington, the self-declared guarantor of the liberal international order and the keeper of the peace in Europe. In the liberal international order, the rearrangement of borders had no place: territorial annexation inverted Europe's rules-based order. On March 17, an early raft of US sanctions was applied to Russia, but this was in lieu of a military counter-response to annexation. On March 18, a treaty of accession was signed in the Kremlin, according to which Crimea was Russia. On that same day, Putin gave an address on annexation. Russia was back, he argued in his speech. For Putin, it affirmed modern Russia's autonomy better than the Winter Olympics in Sochi, on which he had lavished so much money. Any big country could put on the Olympics. Only Putin's Russia could have annexed Crimea.[3]

In Europe and the United States, bafflement mingled with anger. Everything had been going so well in Ukraine. After February 21, Ukraine was on track to get beyond the upheaval, the corruption, and the drift of the dismal Yanukovych era. The Maidan was sometimes called the Euromaidan. Europe was the Maidan's north star, representing democracy, human rights, wealth, the West, a civilization not Russian in tone and texture. This same Europe had been the north star in 1989, lifting East Germans over the Berlin Wall and bringing Poles, Czechs, and Hungarians back into the European family—after the long night of Soviet occupation. Given this historical backdrop, how could it be that the Euromaidan had culminated not in European cohesion or European togetherness (from East to West) but in territorial annexation and war? While the United States spearheaded sanctions on Russia, the Europeans held back. It was a conflict in Europe, an ill omen, but Europe had survived the frozen conflicts in Moldova and in Georgia. To a considerable degree, it had forgotten about them by 2014. Upset as France and Germany were about the annexation of Crimea, they were not going to destroy relations with Russia overnight. Europe had long dedicated itself to deliberation, discussion, diplomacy—not just as techniques but as emblems of the European way of life. It was through those conduits that some solution would have to be reached with Russia. Disinclined to use force, even to use its economic muscle in the spring of 2014, Europe was navigating new terrain with an old map and an old compass. It was not stuck in the twentieth century. It was stuck in the first decade of the twenty-first century.

The annexation of Crimea harmed and humiliated Ukraine. Putin might reference Soviet history and contend that Crimea was eternally Russian: that played well in Russia. In Ukraine, national independence dated back to 1991, and independence was independence *with* Crimea. Crimea determined the map of Ukraine. It had belonged to the Ukrainian economic order. Its Russian-leaning residents might at times have dabbled in separatism, but its Crimean Tatars and ethnic Ukrainians did not at all welcome annexation; nor was there anything resembling a separatist movement in Crimea before February 2014. After annexation, some 40,000 Crimean Tatars would leave Crimea for Ukrainian territory not under Russian occupation.[4] Those who stayed often suffered human-rights abuses. By declaring Crimea's residents Russian citizens, Putin meant to imply that Ukrainian citizenship was temporary and that it was adjustable. With the wave of a wand in Moscow, Ukrainians could be turned into Russians. Putin meant this to be insulting to Kyiv. More abstractly, the first job of any country is to defend its territory and to preserve its borders. The uncontested annexation of Crimea was a military debacle for Ukraine, one that might be followed by sincere or engineered separatism in other parts of the country, some of which were in a state of turmoil in February and in March 2014. At the same time, the loss of Crimea and its many pro-Putin residents made the rest of Ukraine more Ukrainian, not that any Ukrainian politician would have said this publicly. The detachment of Crimea from Ukraine streamlined national politics. Had Putin stopped with the annexation of Crimea, it would have tainted Ukraine's relationship with Russia for a long time to come. The West would never have accepted the annexation. It would have been a dark coda to the months of constructive revolution on the Maidan. It might also have remained a self-contained turn of events, loudly heralded in Russia, while slowly fading from consciousness elsewhere, even in many parts of Ukraine; but events were not self-contained in Ukraine in that unquiet March. There was trouble in the country's east.

* * *

The annexation of Crimea had coherence. It had a beginning and an end, something that in the spring of 2014 was missing from eastern Ukraine, which is not a precise term of art. Neither is the Donbas, a name for a region in eastern Ukraine, which borders Russia and has a high density of Russian speakers. It is also heavily industrial and more urban than many of the country's other regions. Kharkiv, Donetsk, Luhansk, and Mariupol are the cities in or near the Donbas. Western Ukraine moved in the pathways of Central European history, while eastern Ukraine or the Donbas had belonged to the Soviet Union for as long as there was a Soviet Union. Prior to that, it had for centuries been a part of the Russian Empire. In the Donbas, non-trivial Soviet ties expressed themselves in Lenin statues and in Soviet monuments. Many of the Soviet monuments were to the Red Army that had seen heavy fighting in this area, the army that had liberated the local population from German occupation. Families that were Ukrainian-Russian or Russian-Ukrainian were common in the Donbas, unsurprisingly, given its proximity to Russia. In Soviet times and in independent Ukraine, the Donbas was also notable for a hard-edged political culture, for protests and for strikes. In February 2014, the Donbas had one of its own in Kyiv, Viktor Yanukovych, a son of Donetsk. Some from the Donbas supported the Maidan, and some did not, fearing a kind of disenfranchisement, an unwilled westernization or an unwilled Ukrainianization. The Maidan could have disturbing overtones in Ukraine's east (and south) that it did not necessarily have in Kyiv or in western Ukraine.[5]

A wave of spontaneous anti-Maidan sentiment did ignite across some of eastern and southern Ukraine in February 2014. Corrupt and wrong-headed and provincial as Yanukovych was, he had been democratically elected, and he had constituencies other than oligarchs and other than the gangsters with whom he grew up. Many of those constituencies were in the east, and some were ethnic Russians or Russian speakers who believed that Ukraine should have the de-centralized cultural and language policies of a Canada or a Switzerland. They worried about a mono-cultural Ukraine—not that this is what more than a minority of Maidan protestors were advocating.[6] As for many in Ukraine, the whole European Union-Eurasian Economic Union tug-of-war was not purely an emotional issue in the east, not purely a matter of identity. The Association Agreement with the European Union was destined to benefit some in Ukraine more than others. In the east, Yanukovych might have gained in popularity by leading Ukraine into the Eurasian Economic Union, which would have expedited trade between Ukraine and Russia; the area's machine-building factories were particularly well oriented toward the Russian market. Anti-Maidan rallies in the Donbas in early 2014 were acts of protest that could given a separatist accent. Wags in Moscow spoke of a "Russian spring," likening events in the Donbas to the "Arab Spring" of 2011, poetic justice for a United States enamored of anarchy.

Non-artificial anti-Maidan sentiment (such as it was) delighted Putin. His an-nexation of Crimea must have come off some shelf in the Ministry of Defense, so quickly and so smoothly did it go. Crimea as Russian—*krim nash*, Crimea is ours, a phrase often repeated by Russians in 2014—had consensus support across Russia. It had currency before Putin himself came to power. By contrast, Putin's actions in the Donbas, a region with less romantic hold on Russians than Crimea, were clearly unplanned. In March, an eccentric nationalist, Igor Girkin, whose nom de guerre was "Strelkov," was doing what he could to incite local populations against Kyiv in the Donbas, a low-comedy Lawrence of Arabia.[7] Putin may have considered an outright invasion of the Donbas in the spring of 2014. If so, he decided against it, staying within the mold of the Georgia War, which he justified as the protection of minority populations. Six years later, the Kremlin's pretext for invasion or for cross-border interference was once again the plight of a minority population. Putin did not completely invent the "separatists" of Ukraine's east, separatists being the language the Russian government pre-ferred for *all* the residents of the Donbas, the vast majority of whom had nothing to do with separatism or with violent opposition to the post-Yanukovych gov-ernment in Kyiv. Putin used the spontaneous disgruntlement about the Maidan as a means to reverse his defeat in February 2014. Who lost Ukraine? one might have asked in Moscow after Yanukovych ran away from Kyiv. Putin wanted the answer to be that Ukraine was *not* lost. Ukraine was being won and won back for Russia. Russian influence acquired in the Donbas might compensate for Russian influence lost in Kyiv. What interested Putin in the Donbas was regaining the political ground in Ukraine that he thought had been taken from him.

Russian backing of the Donbas irregulars was definite but also ad hoc and incremental. Given the injustice of Yanukovych's demise and the outsized Western role in Kyiv in the lead-up to the May 25 presidential elections (in Putin's view), any trouble that could be bestowed on Ukraine was good trouble. That was a clear-cut reason to inflate localized unrest in the Donbas, to fund it, to arm it, and to plug it into a "separatist" storyline on Russian media, which favored the motif of civil war: not Ukraine drawing together on the Maidan but Ukraine falling apart as a result of the Maidan. In March 2014, oppositional and separatist initiatives underperformed in Mariupol and Kharkiv, two cities with predominantly Russian speakers, though with residents who thought of themselves as Ukrainian, who had no desire not to be in Ukraine, and who did not aspire to radical political change of any kind. In Donetsk and Luhansk, two other Donbas cities, protestors either gained more local traction or got a more effective dose of Russian support; a Donetsk People's Republic was proclaimed on April 7. "Separatists" were able to take over government buildings and to block Kyiv from regaining control. Amid this turmoil, Russia obfuscated its intentions in a cloud of contradictory statements: Russia was not involved; it was not a party to the Ukrainian civil war; it was the protector of Russian speakers and ethnic Russians in Ukraine and elsewhere; of course it was on the side of the "separatists." In April, a declaration of independence for the "people's republics" materialized, while Putin started to speak about "Novorossiya," an eighteenth-century turn of phrase, which implied an imperial program on Russia's part, the Crimea-style incorporation of southern Ukraine into Russia, from Mariupol to Odessa.[8] On May 11, more sham referendums were held. Putin was sowing confusion at every turn.

In April 2014, representatives from the United States, the United Kingdom, and the European Union met in Geneva to see what could be done about the Donbas. An available mediating institution was the Organization for Security and Cooperation in Europe (OSCE), which on paper had the tools to resolve this crisis of invented and instrumentalized separatism. The OSCE dated back to the 1970s and to the Helsinki Final Act, that breakthrough diplomatic agreement. The act had secured Europe's borders and initiated a new stage of cooperation between the West and the Soviet Union in Europe, though outside of Europe the Cold War raged on as it had before. After the fall of the Soviet Union, the OSCE was an institution unlike the NATO alliance. It was not a military structure with its key decision-makers in Washington, DC. It was more open: Russia and Ukraine were both members. It was there for problem solving across Europe's many borders, a venue for Russians, Ukrainian, Europeans, and Americans to talk through their differences. The OSCE was less diffuse than the United Nations, which never played a substantive role in Ukraine. However well suited it was (theoretically) to ending the crisis, though, OSCE mediation was rejected by Russia and its Donbas minions. The OSCE would continue to monitor the tensions in the Donbas, a phantom arbiter of events. Russia did not want the crisis to be resolved by the OSCE and still less by the United States. It had another agenda entirely.

On May 2, a tragedy with cascading implications for Russia occurred in Odessa, a city in southern Ukraine and not in the Donbas. The details of this tragedy have never been satisfactorily ironed out. A group of anti-Maidan protestors had gathered in Odessa. Encountering opposition, they went into the city's Trade Union Building, where according to one narrative the building caught fire and where according to another some forty-two people were intentionally killed. The people certainly died, as did a few others in Odessa on that day, but at whose direction (if the narrative of murder was correct) was unknown.[9] The story of the May 2 deaths saturated Russian news media, whereas May 2 never really registered in the West. For a sizable stretch of Russian public opinion, still euphoric about the annexation of Crimea, it was a turning point: the revolution in Ukraine was not simply about corruption in Ukraine or about a commitment to one customs union or another. It was, as the Russian government had been repeating over and over again, a matter of far-right Ukrainian nationalism, a fascist turn in Ukraine, whatever that might mean. The enemy of these rabid nationalists was anyone who was Russian or Russian-speaking or anyone who wished to see a more Russian-leaning Ukraine. The terrible events of May 2 most likely did not alter Putin's approach to the Donbas. Instead, they lent a public justification to a series of operations far more ambiguous than the annexation of Crimea. A far-reaching problem for Putin, which he may never have clearly discerned, was the singularity of Crimea. It boosted his domestic popularity, giving him a reputation for strategic foresight, but there was no pro-Russian peninsula in the Donbas or anywhere else in Ukraine. In the Donbas, there was an undefined landmass between Ukraine and Russia, and by May 2014 it was a sprawling para-military mess.[10]

* * *

Amid this uncalm, Petro Poroshenko was elected Ukraine's president. He had a mandate to abandon Yanukovych's foreign policy. No longer would Ukraine adhere to "non-bloc status." With renewed energy, it would adopt the goals of joining the European Union and of joining NATO. The March annexation of Crimea had transformed Ukrainian public opinion, downsizing support for

Russia. Russia had come and taken Ukrainian territory, with the enthusiastic support of Crimea's people (in Moscow's telling of the tale) and with a lawless display of force in the eyes of many Ukrainians. Russia was thus at war with Ukraine, rendering Ukrainian neutrality an impossibility. The May 11 referenda had been held not in the complete administrative regions of Donetsk and Luhansk, since only parts of these regions were under "separatist" control, but in concocted political units—the Donetsk People's Republic and the Luhansk People's Republic. These republics existed on Ukrainian soil. Technically, they were not being drawn into Russia, which would have outraged Kyiv and which would have had profound legal and political consequences for Russia. The Crimea-style annexation of Donbas territory might have provoked a sharp Western response. These republics were easier for Russia to maintain as fictional entities. Throughout the spring, many of their non-fictional residents fled in droves into other parts of Ukraine or into Russia. The made-up referendum created for Crimea anticipated the essence of these people's republics: fabricated leadership, fabricated politics, fabricated legal and diplomatic status. Their very artificiality was an asset for Moscow. Were Kyiv to head in the right direction, they could be returned to their legitimate owner—to Ukraine. Were Kyiv to head in the wrong direction, they could be used for punitive disruption.

As soon as he won the election on May 25, 2014, Poroshenko was a wartime president. Ukraine's strategy had an unimpeachable end state, the restoration of the country's territorial integrity. By no means did Poroshenko accept the annexation of Crimea, but in May and June he prioritized the Donbas over Crimea. The Donbas was the crisis at hand and the crisis in which the Ukrainian military could make more headway. Having an elected president was a plus. Although a war with Russia was not what the Ukrainian military had been expecting before February 2014, the Ukrainian military mounted stiff resistance against the larger and better-funded Russian military. A fierce battle took place around Donetsk airport, during which the Ukrainian soldiers were presented in the Ukrainian media as "cyborgs," as superhumanly brave. The airport changed hands several times. It was destroyed in the process, an early image of the horror that was befalling Ukraine. An international public might have associated the Donetsk airport with the 2012 Euro Cup, back when Donetsk was just another corner of Europe—much as Sarajevo had been during the 1984 Winter Olympics, when the Cold War had moderated and a decade before the city was shelled by Serbia. During these 2014 Donbas battles, Russia was blatantly supporting the "separatist" soldiers. Arms were flowing across the border, but the Kremlin maintained a veneer of plausible deniability, shedding crocodile tears at the sight of a neighboring country strangely at war with itself.

The Russian narrative of civil war encountered two setbacks in June. The Ukrainian army started to make real progress on the battlefield. The "separatists" were a fighting force formed with little political legitimacy. There were not enough bona fide separatists for a political movement and still less for a triumphant army. An army staffed as much by mercenaries as by insurgents or separatists was slowly losing to Ukraine's military in the early summer of 2014. (On June 26, Ukraine signed the Association Agreement with the European Union, which Yanukovych must have ruefully observed from his Russian exile.) The second setback for Moscow, an international episode, occurred on July 17. Malaysian Airlines flight MH17, from Amsterdam to Kuala Lumpur, was shot down with a Russian-made BUK missile.[11] Separatist operatives had been identified in the area from which the missile was fired, and the combination of a deadly missile and operational incompetence corresponded to the reality of un-trained, non-professional soldiers doing the bidding of a world-class military power. The Kremlin responded with a blizzard of deflections and lies, inserting into the bloodstream of the international media a host of extravagant conspiracy theories. The Ukrainians had done it. The CIA had done it. The whole shoot-down had been staged. It was somebody else's conspiratorial plot to defame Russia. It never happened. To state the truth would have been awkward for Moscow. Not only would it have required the Kremlin to take responsibility for this tragedy. It would have proven that Russia was at war with Ukraine.

The downing of MH17 altered the nature of the conflict. Before July 17, the goings-on in eastern Ukraine could be downplayed or dismissed as a minor disturbance. The Russians may have been exaggerating their distance from it all. They were not bystanders, but perhaps it was a low-grade civil war in which Russia had taken sides, or perhaps it was some esoteric settling of scores. European countries had diverged from the United States after the annexation of Crimea by not sanctioning Russia, an important signal. For Holland, the loss of life from MH17 was especially traumatic, as the Dutch citizens had not been killed in a natural disaster. The firing of a missile at a civilian airliner certainly looked like an act of terrorism or war, and it was not Ukraine's war alone, some local Russian-Ukrainian squabble, in which justice and injustice were beside the point. It was Europe's conflict too, a fact that should have been apparent in November 2013, when war was not in the air. The whole drama had begun with the question of Ukraine's place in Europe, with the Eastern Partnership Program that was proffered to Ukraine, with the Association Agreement that had so rudely interrupted Yanukovych's idyll of corruption and thievery. The Maidan had been a mass referendum on Europe, which was not peripheral to Ukrainian life. Nor was it peripheral to Moscow's perceptions of Ukraine or to Moscow's strategic attitude toward Ukraine. Because it was integral to Ukraine, Europe could not help being integral to a war in Ukraine. Reacting to the outrage over MH17 and to the death of European citizens, the European Union changed course. It signed on with the United States, expanding the sanctions regime first implemented to punish Russia for its annexation of Crimea.

After the MH17 episode, Russia changed course as well. To prevent further such disasters and to forestall a Ukrainian victory in eastern Ukraine, Putin decided in August to dispense with the charade of civil war and of independent separatists valiantly struggling to secede from Ukraine. He put the Russian military directly into the war. Russia was already being sanctioned by the United States and by Europe, and there was no telling when these sanctions might be lifted. Moscow had no plans for returning Crimea to Ukraine or for apologizing for the shooting down of MH17. A Ukrainian triumph in the east and an end to the conflict on Ukrainian terms would play very poorly for Putin at home. Once again it could be asked—who lost Ukraine? That was a question Putin would do a great deal to avoid. Winning may have been nebulous in August 2014. Losing was not at all nebulous, and it was at hand. Humanitarian aid convoys started running from Russia into eastern Ukraine in August. According to the Kremlin, they were just bringing food and medical supplies, something very few believed. By September 1, Russian regular forces, having been brought into the fight, had defeated Ukraine in the battle of Ilovaisk, a World War II–style clash that took place between August 24 and 26—nothing hybrid about it. Ilovaisk was a meaningful battle. It stopped Ukraine's momentum. It gave a ragtag anti-Kyiv army, led by bumbling figureheads, the sense of being invincible, securing greater control over the conflict for Russia. No commercial airliners were shot down during or after the battle of Ilovaisk. This time the setback was on the Ukrainian side.[12]

Ilovaisk had a demoralizing effect on the Ukrainian government. The Maidan's promise had been to refresh Ukrainian politics, to turn away from the troubled past and to forge a better future, the promise of all revolutions. None of this would happen if Ukraine would have to mobilize for a long war. Russia held a lot of military advantages on its side and Ukraine was a country with friends but without allies. The more prudent course was to sue for peace. Mariupol and Kharkiv, two important eastern cities, were only lightly touched by the war. They could be kept untouched with an end to war. To sue for peace would be to consign Donetsk and Luhansk to their tragi-comic republics. Crimea would be lost as would a slice of eastern Ukraine, but peace would pay its own dividends, and who could say what the future would bring—maybe a stronger Ukrainian military, maybe another leader in Russia, maybe a Ukraine in NATO. Politically, the trick was to sue for peace without explicitly suing for peace, to end the hostilities without giving away too much, and not to yield to a compromised version of Ukrainian sovereignty. Ideally, the sued-for peace would be qualified and contingent and vague enough to be a cessation of hostilities and not much more than that. Though Putin had won a battle, he should not be allowed to win the peace. With an uncompromising peace, Poroshenko could salvage his honor and not get labeled weak by his Ukrainian opponents and critics. Had the battle of Ilovaisk been a Ukrainian and not a Russian victory, it would have been easier to continue the war rather than grudgingly to accept a negotiated settlement.

* * *

The battle of Ilovaisk led to the second major diplomatic summit of 2014. In February, international diplomats had met in Kyiv until their harried last-minute efforts were unkindly overtaken by events. Seven months later, Ilovaisk imposed several bitter lessons on the Ukrainian government. Military assistance from the West would not be forthcoming. It had not yet come from the United States, which vacillated on this point, and it would not come from the European Union, which did not itself have much meaningful military assistance to offer. The European countries that did have military assets followed the lead of the United States. Another lesson was that Russia was trying to coerce outcomes without stating what these outcomes were. Russian officials would not negotiate in the name of what they genuinely wanted: what Putin likely wanted (dominion over Ukraine) he could not get with negotiations. Poroshenko was learning what Yanukovych had learned earlier—what it feels like to be "face-to-face with a very strong Russia on a very unlevel playing field," though this time with war instead of the threat of war as the problem. Britain, France, Ukraine, and Russia had all gathered in June 2014 in Normandy, which inspired the "Normandy format" label for their negotiations. A Normandy-format meeting after Ilovaisk took place in Minsk, the capital of Belarus, an intermediary of sorts between Ukraine and Russia, although an intermediary immeasurably closer to Moscow than to Kyiv. Lukashenko, the Belarusian president, played the host in Minsk, welcoming Angela Merkel, Francois Holland, Petro Poroshenko, and Vladimir Putin as guests. Not physically present in Minsk, United States was a diplomatic presence nevertheless. It was represented by Britain and France, its NATO allies. The "Normandy format" was supposed to improve on the US-led diplomacy in the Balkans back in the 1990s. The fall of 2014 was to be the hour of Europe.

Leaders from the four Normandy powers, together with representatives of the OSCE and the leaders of the two Donbas people's republics, converged on Minsk on September 5. In the early hours of the morning, they hammered out an agreement. It would be known forever after as "Minsk" or more precisely as Minsk I, since a Minsk II would be negotiated in February 2015. Minsk I had the abstruse complexity of a Kafka short story or novel, possessing meanings within meanings, paradoxes within paradoxes, contradictions within contradictions. In its opaque language, a seemingly rational façade concealed the sharp divergence of interests between Putin's Russia and Poroshenko's Ukraine. A rational inter-pretation of Minsk goes as follows: in Minsk, on September 5, 2014, when the Minsk protocols were signed, Ukraine and Russia agreed to stop the fighting and to accept a new status for the Donbas, which is to say for those Ukrainian territories (other than Crimea) under the control of the Russian military.[13] Co-terminus with this new status would be the withdrawal of Russian troops and the holding of "free and fair" elections—not a sham referendum, that is, as had been the case in Crimea. The Donbas would remain Ukraine and its residents Ukrainian citizens, but its greater degree of autonomy would give it a political tenor different from that of central or western Ukraine. Superficially, Minsk was not a defeat for Ukraine. Whether this was a tweak to the Ukrainian political system, which had long been decentralized, or a fundamental remake was hard to say. To hasten the "implementation" of Minsk—in the lingo of Minsk diplomacy—the Europeans tied their sanctions on Russia to Minsk, and so did the United States, giving the transatlantic relationship a shared goal. In theory, Minsk was the way for everyone to exit the crisis. Everyone got something. Everyone gave something. The sanctions would be lifted when Russian soldiers left eastern Ukraine and the elections were carried out. When this happened, the entire crisis would be over.

Though the rational interpretation of Minsk made sense to many diplomats and journalists, it was far from the Kafkaesque truth of Minsk. The Minsk protocols were fantastically unclear, not that this is unusual in the annals of diplomacy, but the lack of clarity carried many inherent risks. First, President Obama was well intentioned to call this the hour of Europe; but the absence of the United States, Europe's primary security guarantor and the regional bugbear for Russia, was only one aspect of Minsk's oddness. Russia cared about Ukraine not least because of its potential relationship to the United States, whether through NATO or through Ukraine's military ties to the United States. The United States was very diplomatically active in Ukraine and had been since the Maidan Revolution, keeping in touch with France and Germany, and what Hollande and Merkel said in Minsk reflected in part the thinking of the United States. Yet Kyiv could read what it wanted into the American absence in Minsk. Perhaps the United States was the bad cop to Europe's good cop, in which case Kyiv would not have to yield quite so much.[14] The American absence might be similarly regarded in Moscow, as an indication that the Europeans were there in their pin-striped suits, but if things went badly the American cavalry might be summoned, and so Moscow should not yield quite so much. Maybe Minsk was just a piece of paper, to which the United States was the mysterious non-signatory, the shadow superpower in an already confused and confusing set of negotiations.[15]

So began the intricate dance of Minsk diplomacy. Ukraine insisted that Minsk had a particular sequence. First, the Russian soldiers would be withdrawn from eastern Ukraine, after which international monitors could run a free and fair election. Once the election was held, eastern Ukraine would be a normal part of the country as it had been prior to February 2014. The text of the Minsk agreement did not invalidate the Ukrainian reading of it. It could be so interpreted, and on balance the Europeans and the United States endorsed the Ukrainian take on Minsk; or they chose not to contradict it. Yet the Ukrainian reading of Minsk pointed to a larger dilemma. The West would not alter the on-the-ground military arrangement in Ukraine. It believed, as Chancellor Merkel was fond of saying, that there was no military solution to the crisis, but without greater military power on its side Ukraine would be unable to impose its reading of Minsk on a recalcitrant Russia: Poroshenko had gone to Minsk after a Ukrainian defeat. Only a few months in power, Poroshenko knew well how unpopular Minsk would be in Ukraine. Had he been less vigilant about maintaining the Ukrainian reading of Minsk, he might have had to deal with very vocal protest from Ukrainians, who had just demonstrated the efficacy of protest and who had just witnessed the sudden loss of Crimea. Poroshenko did not have the political room to make a deal that reflected Russia's military superiority circa 2014 and that would have allowed him to remain the president of Ukraine.

Russia insisted on its preferred sequencing of Minsk. It thought that elections should come first, reminiscent of the Crimea referendum carried out in the presence of Russian soldiers. Once these elections were concluded and autonomous status for the Donbas was secured, presumably establishing a Russian-led statelet in Ukraine, Russia would withdraw its forces from the Donbas. Because of the difference in sequencing, discussions about Minsk went in circles, but it was not the technicalities of Minsk that were slowing Moscow down. Russia's invasion of the Donbas, following from Russia's "loss" of Yanukovych, was the key, the means of controlling political outcomes in a Ukraine no longer governed by Yanukovych. The Donetsk and Luhansk People's Republics were crime ridden and expensive for Moscow, and some of their criminality spilled over into Russia. These people's republics were also the object of Western sanctions, a drag on the Russian economy. For Moscow, they were levers of geopolitical influence. If Russia were to give them up, then Ukraine might well go all the way over to the West. Russia could complain about the NATO and the United States at international fora; it could try to bribe people in Poroshenko's government; it could make political mischief inside Ukraine; but this did not add up to much. With Russian troops in the Donbas—and with the two clownish republics as a festering wound within post-Maidan Ukraine, inhibiting foreign investment and making Poroshenko look helpless—Ukraine might get tripped up. At any point, Russia could pull the lever and make everything worse, or it could pull the lever and make everything better. Back at home, with parts of the Donbas in its grip, the Kremlin could imagine that it was dictating Ukraine's future.

Minsk's many inadequacies foreshadowed its non-implementation. The fighting did not stop in the fall of 2014. It exploded once again in January and February 2015. At Debaltseve, the Russian military scored another victory, a repeat of Ilovaisk. By this point, the war had caused 14,000 casualties on the

Ukrainian side as well as millions upon millions of internally displaced people.[16] For the second time, the "Normandy" group meandered its way through to a written text—Minsk II—which was finalized on February 15, 2015.[17] It reworded Minsk I, without addressing any of its underlying flaws, a fiendishly unstable state of affairs.[18] To a degree that Moscow could not quite see or accept, Russia's actual political influence in Ukraine was slipping away. Russia's military actions, coupled with its prior support for Yanukovych, were political debits in the Ukraine repurposed by the Euromaidan. By its own criteria, which were the pursuit of greater influence in Ukraine, Russian foreign policy was counterproductive. Too much coercion and too little persuasion equaled too little influence. Of this, Minsk was symptomatic. Ukraine had a very different challenge with Minsk. Ukraine was at war with Russia, whose troops were still occupying Ukrainian territory, and Kyiv did not have military strength adequate to its needs. The silence about Crimea in Minsk diplomacy illustrated this unspoken dilemma of Ukrainian sovereignty. The fighting died down considerably after the battle of Debaltseve, enabling a degree of normalcy in Ukraine, a big country in which many lived far away from Crimea and the Donbas. Yet the more political independence Ukraine gained from Russia after 2015, the less it could escape this punishing balance of military power, whereas the more Russia lost its political leverage in Ukraine after 2015, the more it would resort to the leverage it did have, which was not political and not diplomatic. It was military. The seeds of the 2022 war were planted in these Russo-Ukrainian disparities of intention and capability.

* * *

In 2007, Putin had complained to the Munich Security Conference about the excesses of US foreign policy. How much Putin truly blamed the United States for the fall of Yanukovych and for the formation of a pro-Western government in Ukraine is hard to say. He did give speech after speech to this effect, though he had to know the weakness of this contention. Putin lamented the overreach of American power, to which he eventually added a critique of the West as decadent, as having jettisoned its cultural traditions and Christian heritage. This too was highly rhetorical, but the mentions of decadence were as important as were the indictments of Western or American power. In 2014, Putin felt he had reason to confront the West, and confront the West he did. Russia had much more military power at its disposal in 2014 than it had at the time of the war with Georgia, while the record of the Iraq and Afghanistan wars spoke for itself by 2014: two massive wars fought by the United States and its allies for practical and for idealistic reasons, neither of which was an American victory. The distance between the stated aims of American foreign policy and the reality behind them was striking. Decadence implies fragility—and an ignorance of one's own fragility. It was the fragility of the West (real and imagined) that Putin was eager to explore and exploit once a major Russia-West confrontation had finally come. Ground zero of the confrontation between Russia and the West, Ukraine was pivotal in every respect. The scope of the confrontation, however, was global. It ranged from the Middle East to the hearts and minds of the American electorate. After 2014, Putin would be proactive in all of these domains.

The global contours of Russia's more confrontational posture first became visible in Syria. Syria and the Soviet Union had had a close relationship, and the Russian Federation had a naval base in Latakia in Syria, a legacy of Soviet times. Beginning in 2011, Bashar al-Assad's Syria had felt the effects of the Arab Spring, on which the position of the United States was not fully certain. The Obama administration thought it was time for Assad to go, though it did not stipulate how he should go and wavered about getting directly involved. On August 20, 2012, the president mentioned a "red line" on chemical-weapons use, but when al-Assad crossed this line nothing was done. Obama had the example of Libya behind him in 2012, of his own rush to military action there and of the disaster zone the country had become. Syria was agony for Obama and a bleak commentary on American power in the Middle East. Syria's civil war was a gross repudiation of international order. ISIS, a militant terrorist insurgency, swept across Iraq and eastern Syria in 2014. Iran, Turkey, and Israel each had rival military agendas inside of Syria, and al-Assad, who had subjected Syrian citizens to massive bombing and to chemical warfare, was in every respect a part of the problem. A massive US invasion of Syria remained out of the question, echoing too closely the wars in Iraq and Afghanistan. It would have clashed with the mood of a war-weary US population in 2014 and 2015. Obama had other things he hoped to accomplish in his second term. The widening Syrian catastrophe presented countless dangers and no opportunities.

As was so often the case, Obama and Putin looked at the world through entirely different lenses. They spoke different strategic languages. Where Obama saw a quagmire, Putin saw an opening for Russia. Despite having the Latakia port and despite having a strong working relationship with Iran, post-Soviet Russia had had nowhere near the clout and visibility in the Middle East that the Soviet Union had once enjoyed. One aspect of the opportunity Putin intuited in Syria was a Russian "return" to the region, which for Russia was an escape from its anomalous post–Cold War isolationism. Syria was a foothold or a platform for ambitions not limited to Syria. Once again, the idea of autonomy motivated Putin: the image and reality of a Russia not subordinate to the West, not subordinate to anyone. Backing al-Assad in practice, which Russia already did in theory, would disrupt European and US hopes for Syria, hopes predicated on a resolution to the fighting and on the democracy that was supposed to replace al-Assad's dictatorship. US policy had coalesced around al-Assad's eventual departure. Were al-Assad to stay, and to stay because of Russia's support, Russia would have a grateful client in the Middle East. Simultaneously, the notion of Europe and the United States as the trendsetters, as the tacit masters of Europe and the Middle East, as the co-sponsors of their vaunted liberal international order, would be exposed as hollow. Al-Assad's survival would be an addendum to the Arab Spring, to the whole run of colored revolutions, and to the travails of twenty-first century American power. Al-Assad's survival would therefore be relevant to Ukraine. The fall of leaders like Yanukovych was not inevitable. It was not the international trend but a regrettable exception to the trend of strong (read: autocratic) leaders. If this was the prevailing trend, Putin's Russia, not Obama's United States, was the ascendant power.

Russia's move into Syria was captured in surveillance photographs in August 2015, six months after the battle of Debaltseve. Al-Assad was delighted to partner with a leading military power. Quite possibly, Putin saved him from getting overthrown or killed in the Syrian civil war, which had become a multi-theater war involving Iran, Israel, Turkey, and the United States (because of the ISIS presence in Iraq and Syria). Russia's commitment centered on air power. Putin wanted to avoid the loss of Russian soldiers in Syria, though at the same time he wanted Russian officers to get the experience of combat. The United States did not contest a Russian role in Syria, something Putin could not have known in advance but something which he must have assumed. Contesting Russia there was judged too risky and too remote from core US interests. Russia proceeded to control the Syrian air space in tandem with the Syrian military. This compelled Israel, which was fighting Iranian and Iranian-backed forces from the air in Syria, to pay heed to Russia and to redirect its diplomatic relationship with Russia, showing Putin the kind of deference that mattered greatly to him domestically and on the international stage. Across the Middle East, Russia benefited from its decision to join the war in Syria. It benefited through increased arms sales and through increased prominence. Russia was in no hurry to end the civil war in Syria, which went on and on and on. Russia's newfound leverage derived from its partnership with al-Assad but most of all from its application of military force, much like the kind of leverage it had given itself in Ukraine and especially in eastern Ukraine, where in 2015 Russian troops were digging in.[19]

In Putin's self-assessment, his move into Syria surely counted as a masterstroke. It reversed Russia's downward spiral in Eastern Europe and before that in Libya and Iraq. Putin could claim to have halted a colored revolution in Syria, though this oversimplified a kaleidoscopically complicated civil war: Yanukovych and al-Assad had very little in common, and neither did Ukraine and Syria. Putin particularly relished his newfound prestige in the Middle East at a moment when the United States was officially trying to stigmatize and isolate Russia—because of its annexation of Crimea and non-compliance with Minsk. The Russian military performed its tasks well in Syria, and at relatively low cost to Moscow. Most meaningfully perhaps, the Syria intervention was well executed foreign policy for Putin. It was—stylistically—the foreign policy of a superpower, bold, targeted, and global in scope. Back in Washington, the Obama administration was appalled by Russia's return to the Middle East. Al-Assad and Putin let their militaries operate in ways that caused terrible loss of civilian life, spurring the outflow of millions of migrants into Turkey and through Turkey into the European Union. Russian advances in Syria also confirmed a narrative of US decline projected by Russian and Chinese media—of the United States looking for the exits in the Middle East and elsewhere, which was not at all the impression the White House wanted to foster. Long accustomed to having Russia react to its decisions, the United States had been forced to react to Russian decisions in the Middle East. The United States and Russia had a rush of diplomatic conversation about Syria in the summer of 2016 until everything collapsed into mutual recriminations in the fall—after Russian forces bombed a UN convoy. As in Ukraine, Russia stood on one side of the conflict in Syria, and the United States stood on the other. They were symmetrically opposed, a harbinger of things to come.

Had Yanukovych stayed in power through 2016, Russia might never have ventured into Syria. Putin's "loss" of Ukraine—and, as he saw it, the areas not under Russian military control had been lost to the United States in 2014—had increased his appetite for confronting the United States outside of Europe. By going into Syria, Putin was flirting with a direct confrontation between the United States and Russia. Whatever Putin said about American decline, he could not ignore US military might. Russia did not have the military technology that the United States had; it did not have the logistical capabilities; it did not have the same degree of naval or air power; it did not have the global reach of the US military. In Europe, Russia had many conventional military advantages. That was not the case in the Middle East, where Turkey was a NATO ally, where Israel was a close ally of the United States, where the United States had a serious presence in Iraq and military ties to Egypt, to Jordan, and to many of the Gulf Arab states. In the Middle East, Russia was the David to the American Goliath. Putin studied US vulnerabilities as well as US strengths, and in Syria he could capitalize on the fact that Syria was not a top US priority. Having said a great deal about Syria, as if Washington were in charge of the situation—an occupational hazard of American diplomacy—the Obama administration was ultimately reluctant to act. Making the most of this reluctance, Putin could deal a blow to US power and standing in the region, and this is what he accomplished. Syria was not the only pressure point Putin associated with a United States that still towered over Russia in Europe and the Middle East. It was in fact the lesser of two vulnerabilities.

* * *

Political interference had been a Cold War pastime. Both sides did it. The Soviet Union sent its spies to the United States. It funded certain radical organizations and peace movements in Western Europe. It engaged in active measures, elaborate efforts at deception that sometimes hit home: the dissemination, for example, of the false narrative about the CIA and the spread of the AIDS virus in Africa in 1980s.[20] Though this operation amplified negative perceptions of the United States internationally, it fell short of meddling in the domestic affairs of the United States. The United States also practiced active measures in the early years of the Cold War. The CIA assisted anti-Soviet partisans in Eastern Europe, and the espionage never ceased. From a Soviet point of view, with which the young Vladimir Putin had grown up, the United States had very effectively meddled in the domestic political affairs of the Soviet Union in the 1980s. It had stirred up discontent, amplified the anti-Soviet ministrations of a Polish Pope, stoked Eastern European nationalism as a means of weakening the Soviet Union, and abetted the Soviet Union's self-sabotage under Mikhail Gorbachev. Putin fit post-Soviet Ukraine and Russia into this same storyline. A bevy of Western NGOs and government-funded institutions existed to build "democracy" in Ukraine and Russia. Their real purpose was to undermine Russian statehood, to prevent the emergence of strong leaders like Putin, and to diminish Russian reach in Europe so that the United States could expand its bases of economic and military power. After the Soviet Union had fallen, the United States having pushed it over a cliff, NATO had been rapidly enlarged. That was the American formula, a mélange of espionage and political trickery. It had been the American formula during the Cold War, and it was the American formula after the Cold War.

In the 1990s, the United States had lulled itself into the belief that the Cold War was over. That led it to draw two widely shared conclusions. One was that democracy promotion—an enthusiasm of the Clinton, George W. Bush, and Obama administrations—was a neutral enterprise, almost an act of political philanthropy. Since political legitimacy derived from democracy, from the will of the people, to promote democracy in other countries was per se legitimate. For the many institutions that received funding from the US government, there was every reason to engage in democracy promotion in Ukraine and Russia. They were contributing to regional stability and to respect for human rights; they were helping the people of Ukraine or the people of Russia. The other widely shared conclusion was that post–Cold War Russia had lost its superpower status. It might harass its neighbors. Its intelligence services might murder former Russian spies on British or on German soil, but Russia would not—or could not—take on the United States directly. Two months after Assistant Secretary Victoria Nuland appeared on the Maidan in December 2013, Russian intelligence leaked a recording of her phone conversation with the US ambassador to Ukraine. To many Russians, the recording presented Nuland in a bad light. She sounded like the behind-the-scenes arbiter of Ukrainian politics; beyond that it had little demonstrable effect.[21] Yet it was a serious crossing of the line, a sign that Russia was stripping away inhibitions that had been in place in the 1990s and thereafter. To the extent that he was trying to embarrass Nuland *inside* the United States, Putin considered the internal politics of the United States fair game, and because he so much hated US-style democracy promotion, he thought that he was more than justified in bringing the fight to the United States. He was merely doing what in his view the United States had been doing continuously to Russia throughout the twentieth and the twenty-first centuries. With its generally low opinion of Russia, the US government ended up being too complacent about the release of Assistant Secretary Nuland's phone call. It did not yet see the pattern behind the incident.

A year or so after the Nuland phone call was made public, Putin placed a much more ambitious bet against the United States. Russian intelligence set about infiltrating various institutions of domestic American policies, several of which were related to the Democratic Party. Obama was not up for reelection in 2016, but his former secretary of state, Hillary Clinton, whom Putin reviled, was the obvious Democratic front-runner. She had left the State Department in 2013 to prepare for her presidential run. It was a common technique of post-Soviet Russian politics to assemble *kompromat*—compromising material—on a political adversary and to deploy it in the news media. Hillary Clinton had a long career behind her, and for politicians there is always *kompromat* of one kind or another. Putin's government set out to damage the prospects of Hillary Clinton and the Democratic Party in 2016. Another of the Kremlin's objectives was to foul up the electoral process, for which 2016 proved to be the perfect year. It was the first election that would be significantly determined by social media, and not just social media used to acquire lists of voters or to organize rallies. At issue was social media and the news cycle, social media and the texture of political discourse, social media and the reputation of public figures, social media and the soul of a political culture. The Kremlin hardly needed to employ active measures. Social media was a vast zone of low-cost, legal distortion, an invitation to foreign governments to manipulate the constant manipulation that was occurring online. By early 2015, just as the presidential season was beginning, Russian intelligence had found its way to certain opportunities. Then, on June 16, 2015, a world-famous celebrity announced his candidacy. He was a skeptic about Ukraine, a critic of democracy promotion, someone indifferent to NATO, someone dismissive of the European Union, and someone who was, of all things, after the mounting US-Russian tensions in Obama's second term, an unapologetic admirer of Vladimir Putin.

6

Russia, Russia, Russia

But they're so bad, so they come up with this Russia, Russia, Russia
hoax, and they know it's a hoax.
        Donald Trump, speech at 2023 CPAC conference, March 5, 2023[1]

The rivalry between the Soviet Union and the United States, succeeded by the
rivalry between the United States and post-Soviet Russia, is so historically entrenched that it has its own rituals and conventions, its own etiquette, its own
predictability. Harry Truman and Joseph Stalin set the original pattern: mutual
criticism, mutual competition, mutual suspicion, everything short of actual
war. The rivalry has had its built-in comedy—the car that Richard Nixon gave
to Leonid Brezhnev at Camp David and that Brezhnev almost drove into a tree.
The rivalry could be light-hearted: an Olympic hockey match or a chess game
that suddenly took on world-historical significance. It had more than its share of
tragic and near apocalyptic moments, such as the Cuban Missile Crisis of 1962.
When leadership changes hands in Washington and in Moscow, history implies
continuity: that the American side will emphasize democracy and the need for
a Europe living in liberty and that the Soviet or Russian side will emphasize security, stability, or some scheme of political and economic organization sharply
at odds with American norms. (This much Alexis de Tocqueville had lucidly
anticipated in the 1830s, in the last paragraph of *Democracy and America*, which
predicted a twentieth-century world divided between American democracy
and Russian authoritarianism.) A few figures on both sides have found it possible to get beyond the competition and the dissonance. Other leaders—the vast
majority—have embraced and thrived on the dissonance. From 1945 to 2016,
even during the convivial Bill and Boris show of the 1990s, the dissonance was
almost always the real story. It is the tradition, the roots of which are buried deep
in the twentieth century, if not in the nineteenth or eighteenth centuries.[2]

Though this tradition did not vanish in 2016, it got completely revised, taking
on a form it had never previously assumed. Much US-Russian dissonance
remained after 2016—without the usual trappings. Not much had changed in
Russia, where Vladimir Putin had regained the presidency in 2012 and was
rightly perceived as certain to win it back in 2018, an election year in Russia.
Putin did not revolutionize Russian foreign policy in 2016. Since the Maidan

Revolution of 2013–2014, enmity toward the United States had been in over-drive, one of the constants of Russian foreign policy. The times were changing in the United States, as it embarked on a four-year period that was among the most bizarre in its entire history. The anomalies of a President Trump were too many to count: the background in real estate, in casinos, in marketing and tel-evision; the president's addiction to social media and to spontaneous, often highly personalized bursts of communication; the perplexing coalitions that crystallized around the personality of the president much more than around a political party or movement; and the vulgarity not only of Trump the man but also of Trump's moment in the limelight, completing the merger of entertain-ment and politics that had always been an aspect of American politics and in 2016 became the heart and soul of American politics. The never-ending circus in the White House telegraphed surreal disarray at a center of global power. No anomaly would prove more unwieldy than Donald Trump's opinions about Russia and his relationship to Putin. Trump was the most extravagant and the most outspoken Russophile ever to occupy the White House.

Trump's fondness for Russia, luridly fascinating as it might be, never added up to much diplomatically. From the beginning, ties to Russia or alleged ties to Russia threatened to destroy Trump's presidency, as over time would ties to Ukraine or alleged ties to Ukraine. The political noise generated by these ties defined Trump's presidency, generating much of his media coverage in addition to his acute sense of embattlement. A nexus of paranoia connected Trump to his critics and his critics to Trump, and at the heart of the paranoia was almost always Russia—"Russia, Russia, Russia," as Trump was fond of saying. Yet it was not anything related to Russia that sapped Trump's popularity before the 2020 election. His defeat had much more to do with the COVID pandemic and its economic fallout. For Democrats and for Republicans, Trump's loss to Biden in the 2020 election did not have a Russian point of origin. Similarly, Trump's rhet-oric about Russia, his suggestion that Russia was somehow a superior country to Germany or to France or to other NATO partners of the United States, was far more extreme than his administration's actual policies toward Russia, which were fairly conventional. Trump did not pull the United States out of NATO. He did not accept the annexation of Crimea. He did not try to negotiate a grand bargain over the heads of the Ukrainians. If anything, Trump hardened the US posture toward Russia in his deeds, while his written and spoken words floated free in the poisoned media ether. The mood of the Trump presidency was so the-atrical precisely because the presidency itself (and the responses to it) could be so untethered to reality. With Russia, the reality of Trump administration policy was close to being boring.

Two aspects of Trump's America extended beyond the theater. Both illu-minate Russia's decision to wage war in 2022—some thirteen months after

Trump left office. One was drift in American foreign policy, a confusion Trump instilled at its core. To what was the United States committed? To democracy? To Europe? To free trade? To human rights? To the liberal international order? The cacophony of the Trump years exposed a perilous lack of consensus. The superpower that had excelled at continuity since 1945, that had largely spoken in one voice before 2016—a fixture of the international landscape, to the delight of some and the irritation of others—was no more. The United States had lost its way with Trump, as if it were (at least) two countries. A related problem, and the second non-theatrical aspect of Trump's America, was polarization or polarizations: Republican and Democrat, liberal and conservative, urban and rural, elite and populist, internationalist and isolationist, local and global, outward looking and inward looking, post-racial and racist, religious and secular, modern and anti-modern, homogeneous and heterogeneous. The high priest of polarization, Trump could not get enough of the political fury. It was not what Trump did that mattered vis-à-vis Russia and its foreign-policy deliberations. He tried for little and accomplished little. It was what the United States seemed to be becoming—its aura of dysfunction—that mattered. It mattered most of all to Vladimir Putin, who had unfinished business in Ukraine in 2016 as he did in 2020. To many patriotic Americans, the Trump-era United States appeared to be rudderless abroad and acidly ill at ease at home, mired in some mad-cap cycle of chronic decline. To Putin, no American patriot, it must have looked much, much worse.

* * *

Trump's foreign policy blended the personal, the self-indulgent, and the serious. Trump did not unwind his business interests when he became president. These interests ran through his family, and some family members ended up in the White House, a legal or semi-legal blurring of the lines between money making, nepotism, and policymaking. The temple of such influence peddling was the Trump International Hotel in Washington, DC, where foreign governments could spend money to brighten their reputation. Foreign governments might also be approached with some awareness of what they could do for the Trump family, if not while Trump was president then by and by. Trump had been striving to operate in Russia in 2016, which is one clue to his pro-Russian statements on the campaign trail. The search for financial gain via the White House was not Trump's only political bias. He was more comfortable with men than with women, with autocrats than with democrats, with non-Europeans than with Europeans, with brash populist adventurers than with well-educated technocrats. He responded warmly to those political leaders who lavished him with praise, and at times he exploited an episode of overseas comity or tension to adjust the news cycle at home. In general, politics was the means to personal ends for Trump, to profit where possible and to attention and status at all times. Other presidents have had Trump's personal flaws. His lust for money and media attention are the stuff of American political history. It was the magnitude of his animating flaws that was unusual.

Not everything in the Trump White House was media spectacle or the politics of personality. Amid the scandals and the tweets, the firings and the perfervid messaging, the lies and the posturing, the rudiments of a new foreign policy took shape. As had Barack Obama before him, Trump decried the ill-conceived and wasteful Iraq and Afghanistan wars, arguing (as had Obama) that a less militaristic foreign policy would be a better foreign policy. After the trillions that had been misspent on nation building abroad, Obama had emphasized a need for nation building at home. Trump did not credit Obama for this insight, but he shared it. Trump believed, as Obama did not, that for too long foreign policy had been the province of elites—of "globalists," as Trump's advisor Steve Bannon might have put it—and that these elites had rigged the system. They had profited from military spending, padding their resumes and their bank accounts, and for their personal gain alone the globalists had brayed for war. Interestingly, Trump latched onto the issue of terrorism and argued for vigorously opposing it. Yet he broke almost entirely from the counterterrorism strategies that the Republican Party had adopted after the September 11 attacks, especially the promotion of democracy. Cheered on by the complicit mainstream media, the Bushes were standard-issue globalist elites, who through free trade and forever wars had left common Americans impoverished. Trump was going to be different.[3]

Like Obama, Trump expressed discontent about economic inequality. In his assessment and prescriptions, however, Trump could not have been more at odds with Obama. The international order aligned with free trade, and trade had long been the engine of internationalism, thriving when there are agreed-upon rules. Free trade serves key US interests, the Obama administration contended, by bringing wealth to the United States and advancing US alliances, which is why in the last year of his second term President Obama was furiously trying to construct two trading blocs, one in Asia and one in Europe. By contrast, Trump considered free trade the ruse of anti-American elites. It had destroyed manufacturing in the United States, Trump said over and over again. China had stolen American jobs and American intellectual property, siphoning off from the United States the secrets of great-power status. The most memorable phrase from Trump's 2017 inaugural address was "American carnage." There he stood on the steps of the US Capitol, surveying a nation in ruins. The ruins were a function of globalization, a word that had been the shining light of Bill Clinton's two terms in the 1990s. Compromised a bit by the friend-foe binaries of fighting terrorism, globalization was not anything George W. Bush rejected. He celebrated cross-border commerce and trade no less than Ronald Reagan and Margaret Thatcher had. The Obama White House had not looked askance at the word *globalization*: it contained cosmopolitan multitudes. In Trump's verdict, a less globally active United States would be a more prosperous United States, and a comparable truth held for legal and illegal immigration in Trump's political view—the less of it the better. Trump evoked a fortress America that had political pedigree on the Left and on the Right but that had not been an important motif in American foreign policy since the late 1930s.[4]

Angered by the optics of overreach, Trump looked for places where the United States was stretched thin. Without ending the war in Afghanistan while he was president, Trump moved the United States much closer to the exit than President Obama had been willing to do. In the Middle East, Trump's goal was foreshortened involvement. Iran had to be harshly dealt with, whereas the Gulf Arab states could be embraced, whatever their human-rights records, and Trump was zealously pro-Israel. He saw Syria and Iraq as quagmires into which he did not want to be pulled. The most acute area of overcommitment, Trump complained, was in Europe, which was rich and at peace and basking in the protection the United States stupidly gave it, not because this was the will of the American people but because it was the whim of a few malicious elites. European and American elites colluded in institutions like NATO and the European Union, where they waved the banner of globalism, curbed the sovereignty of proud nation states, and wrote checks that had to be paid by the United States. Trump's dislike of NATO and the EU was stylistic. Not minding them for what they were, Trump hated them for what they represented, envisioning himself as on the cusp of a movement that would liquidate these out-of-touch transnational constructs.[5] Under the sun of a new nationalism, the United States could recover from the excess into which it had been lured by its overseas "partners." More than anything, Trump had been elected to put America first.

Trump lost many, perhaps most of his foreign-policy arguments. Either he could not really convince the public or he could not convince his own administration, parts of which thrived on defying him. Yet on China Trump won the day.[6] The Obama administration had vacillated, never quite willing to give up on China. Asia was the future, and at the heart of Asia was China, one of the keys to globalization. Beijing had not yet figured out what China would be, and younger people in China did not necessarily endorse the repressiveness, the blinkered nationalism, the zero-sum logic of China's one-party political leadership. When these young people grew older, new opportunities might come forward. The widespread protests staged in Hong Kong between 2019 and 2020 indicated the path China might one day take, just as Ukrainians had chosen the path away from authoritarianism in 2013. Such was Obama's long-term hope for China. Ever the anti-Obama, Trump was categorical about China. It had swallowed immense amounts of American capital and then turned around and tried to knock the United States from its geopolitical pedestal. The United States had been cheated by a China that troubled Trump not because it was un-democratic—that did not trouble Trump at all—but because Beijing wished to supplant the United States. It was also doing some of the things, like manufacturing on a massive scale, that the United States to its shame had forgotten how to do. There was no Chinese carnage. There was only the long horizon of China's competitive edge.

Russia never fit clearly into Trump's overall worldview. Trump was more precise about his preferred method of relating to Russia (in a friendly manner) than he was about Russia itself. A vast infrastructure of people and institutions in Washington, DC, was dedicated to democracy and human rights. They were Democrats, independents, and Republicans, and they commanded real resources and real influence inside and outside the government. Some of them remained in the government while Trump was president, and he treated them as the detritus of the Obama era. As he did with Saudi Arabia, Turkey, and the Philippines, Trump happily eliminated democracy and human rights from official US policy toward Russia. He would not criticize foreign leaders like Putin for their democratic deficits. He admired them for their democratic deficits, their strength, their freedom from legal restraint, their cunning. Trump did not criticize Putin for annexing Crimea. He suggested that the annexation had been cleverly aggressive on Russia's part, yet another sign of Putin's strategic genius. Trump did not criticize Putin for meddling in the 2016 election, the most fraught of subjects for Trump. Trump expressed no discernible interest in what Russia was politically or geopolitically. What he valorized with Russia—as he did with North Korea, to which Trump made several spectacular overtures—was the art of the deal. Previous American presidents had complained about Putin's autocratic tendencies, and Putin held them in contempt, Obama especially. Why not stop complaining, take the world as it is, and see what can be done through common interests and person-to-person negotiation? That was one of Trump's commonly articulated positions on Russia, which he emphasized while running for president. Partners in toughness, he and Putin could cut deals together. On the campaign trail such messaging worked well enough, or it did not bother Trump's constituency enough to make a difference.

In the White House, Trump was hemmed in by his absence of vision on Russia. He had it easier with China, toward which he could take the aggressive measures mandated by his theory of the case, his intuition of Chinese perfidy. He could impose tariffs; he could attack China verbally; he could bang the drum about a possible invasion of Taiwan. Once in office, Trump had no idea what deals he should make with Putin. With Russia, Trump shied away from any kind of attack. Seemingly, he had no agenda other than not damaging the US-Russian relationship, whereas the agenda Putin had was to make a deal on Ukraine.[7] Had Trump recognized the annexation of Crimea, he could have had Putin eating out of his hand. Had Trump given official heft to Ukrainian neutrality, had he argued that Ukraine should not be a member of NATO and that it should not be in NATO because its membership would violate Russia's *legitimate* security concerns, he would have had a mollified Putin. It would have been back to the post-September 11 partnership between Russia and the United States. Trump may not have had personal problems with these hypothetical concessions, but he had any number of political problems with them. Big concessions to Putin would have made him look weak, which he could not tolerate, and they would have turned many Republicans against him. Even if he had made these concessions, he would still have to answer the question—why did he want to have Putin eating out of his hand? For the sake of a US-Russian alliance against China? For the sake of bringing peace to Europe? For the sake of pulling American troops out of Europe? For the sake of avoiding nuclear war? Trump's inability to resolve or even to pose these questions left him with random impulses but without an analysis, without a direction, and without anything resembling a strategy toward Russia.

Over the course of four years, Trump enacted important changes in the US posture on Asia and the Middle East. These changes followed not just from his private business interests, from his will to get reelected in 2020, or from personal relations with foreign leaders. They followed from Trump's non-performative convictions about China, trade, and human rights, and about core US interests in these areas. On Russia and Europe, Trump's convictions amounted to much less than they did in Asia and the Middle East. He was a bomb thrower when he talked about Russia and Europe—and a mess of contradictions in his actions. Trump declared NATO "obsolete" on the campaign trail, and two new countries entered NATO on his watch. Trump railed against European free riding, while his administration increased its military spending in Europe. Trump could imply that the annexation of Crimea was Russia's subversive right, and he chose to send lethal military assistance to Ukraine. The US-Ukrainian military partnership deepened considerably on Trump's watch, either on the president's command or without his knowing it, something that could only enrage Vladimir Putin. As for the European Union, Trump had expected other countries to leave the European Union after Brexit.[8] His prediction was wrong, and Trump was obliged to deal with the European Union as other Americans presidents had. The EU carried on. Solemnly worded op-eds about the death of Atlanticism were a transatlantic preoccupation for the four years Trump was president. They were exercises in hyperbole. Frantically worded op-eds about Trump and Putin also abounded. They too were off the mark. Putin and Trump talked past each other. Russia got no gifts. Ukraine's military modernization proceeded apace, its extent apparent only in February 2022. (By 2022, Ukraine was spending 5.95 percent of its GDP on defense, an exceptionally high percentage for a European country.)[9] When it came to Russia, Trump was not the sui generis deal maker he was in his fantasies. He was a mildly hawkish Republican president.

* * *

The real Trump Russia story was of domestic vintage. For this Trump himself bore significant responsibility. His irresponsible and self-defeating behavior was a three-act drama that could be titled "Campaign, Transition, and Presidency." Trump could not be accused of dissident thinking about Russia. He may have been incoherent on the campaign trail, worrying that the United States was simultaneously too deferential to Russia and too confrontational. He may have been ignorant of Russian foreign policy. He may have been callous toward Ukraine, implying that he would cut a deal with Putin over the heads of the Ukrainians and frequently tarring Ukraine with blanket accusations of corruption. He may have been rude to the Europeans, striking a pose of impatient transactionalism and dismissing the appreciation of NATO that had previously been second nature to American presidents. Trump's "America first" mantra may have signified a return to the head-in-the-sand traditions of American isolationism, when Trump was campaigning in 2016; but it was his right to campaign as he wished. For those who voted for Trump, it was their right to vote for him, whether or not he was incoherent or callous or isolationist. On the campaign trail, Trump consistently advocated a "better" relationship with Russia. He did so even when it might have been more politically opportune to have done the opposite. The Republican Party's 2012 candidate, Mitt Romney, had identified Russia as a grave security threat to the United States. Many Republican voters, long accustomed to the etiquette of US-Russian competition, were expecting to hear a similar message in 2016. Trump never gave it to them, and yet he got elected.

The sins of Trump the campaigner were not intellectual. They entailed his campaign's choice of personnel. Especially in the domain of foreign policy, the Trump campaign attracted a motley crew of unknowns and grifters. In the spring of 2016, Trump's rapid ascent in the Republican primaries produced a chorus of "never Trump" Republicans, who refused to get anywhere near his campaign. At the same time, Trump's need for a foreign-policy team opened the door to experts and to "experts" who had never expected to walk the halls of power. Several of them had prior connections to Russia, connections that could vary from travel to consulting work to giving speeches. Several were approached by people with ties to the Russian government—exactly when Russian intelligence was actively interfering in the election (on Trump's behalf). Most likely, this motley crew did not harbor Russian agents, though Russian intelligence would undoubtedly have enjoyed planting paid agents or fellow travelers inside the Trump campaign. Everything happened too quickly for this to have been an easy option for Moscow. Instead, there were haphazard meetings, mysterious links, and low levels of professionalism and integrity on the Trump campaign. "If that's what you say I love it," Donald Trump Jr. wrote in response to a June 3, 2016, email, promising him damaging material on Hilary Clinton and making clear that the source of this material was the Russian government.[10] That was the reigning mentality on the campaign, and it was exceedingly dangerous.

Someone other than Trump could have defused this situation by looking into such shady behavior and holding campaign staffers to account. Someone other than Trump could have responded to the accusations of Russian interference in the election—which were credible, if not irrefutable by the summer of 2016— not by brusque denials but by working with the FBI or other US government authorities to root out the interference. In a sense, Trump did the opposite. He hid the fact of his ongoing business dealings in Russia during the campaign. Members of his campaign, like Roger Stone, had connections to WikiLeaks, the renegade distributor of classified information that laundered Russia's espionage and active-measures operations.[11] Trump's demonization of Hillary Clinton and of Democrats was so intense that Trump gave the impression of seeing Russia as helpful and the Democratic Party and Obama White House as conspiratorially aligned against him, the true foreign agents. It may have been more than an impression: it may have been Trump's point of view. This mindset, mixed with Trump's opportunism, led him to deploy information Russian intelligence had pilfered from the Clinton campaign. Meanwhile, many journalists were unable to distinguish between "real" campaign news and Russian interference in the campaign, making a bad situation worse. When the scandal should have been the Russian interference, news stories too often foregrounded the object of Russian interference—the allegations of impropriety on the part of Clinton and her staff. In a particularly unbelievable episode in July 2016, Trump ad-libbed a request for Russia to interfere in the election: "Russia, if you're listening," he said, "I hope you're able to find the 30,000 emails that are missing," words followed by Trump's standard justification that they were a joke.[12] By running a ridiculous campaign Trump time and time again got himself off the hook. His improbability as a candidate let him get away with murder.

Among Trump's most consequential mistakes was to appoint Paul Manafort his campaign director. An unscrupulous product of Washington lobbying, Manafort had ventured far afield from Washington, DC, in his never-ending search for money, and one of the many places where his dark arts were lucrative was Ukraine. Official Washington may have preferred Viktor Yushchenko over Viktor Yanukovych in 2004, siding with the protestors during the Orange Revolution of 2004. Paul Manafort saw that there was money to be made from working with Yanukovych, who paid Manafort to run an "American-style" campaign for him in 2010, to supply the right set of images and talking points and to get him more votes in an election than Yushchenko. Manafort did what he could to help Yanukovych across the finish line, and it never bothered Manafort that Yanukovych was obscenely corrupt or that Yanukovych had many friends and connections in Moscow. Manafort's deputy, Konstantin Kilimnik, was one such connection. Kilimnik had received a military education in the Soviet Union, worked for IRI, an American think tank (in Moscow), and was—accounts vary on this point—either a Russian intelligence agent himself or "linked" to Russian intelligence, whatever that might mean. Manafort and Kilimnik should have been nowhere near an American presidential campaign. Instead, they met in person during the campaign, in May and then again in August 2016, when Manafort supplied Kilimnik with sensitive campaign information.[13]

"Russiagate" followed directly from Trump's chaotic campaign. He had named Michael Flynn as his national security advisor in waiting. Flynn had long worked in the intelligence community, a gifted practitioner of counterterrorism, but he felt underappreciated and had a grudge against President Obama, who advised Trump not to hire him. After leaving government, Flynn had received $45,000 for a speech given in Moscow—at an event celebrating RT, a vehicle of government propaganda. Flynn was photographed next to Putin at a dinner. Either freelancing or at the behest of someone in the Trump orbit, Flynn reached out to the Russian ambassador to the United States, Sergey Kislyak, and in a telephone conversation intercepted by US counter-intelligence, Flynn was overheard requesting an unusual favor. The US government was going to expel a group of Russian diplomats, a response to Russia's recent meddling in the election. Over this Flynn had no control, but he asked Ambassador Kislyak to pass a message to the Kremlin. He asked the Kremlin not to retaliate, and the Kremlin did not retaliate, earning president-elect Trump's public admiration.[14] Trump's transition team was undercutting the Obama administration. Not illegal per se, this was shockingly audacious and strange. Whatever Flynn achieved or hoped to achieve with the Russian government, he ensnared himself in legal and political problems that were entirely of his own making.

Flynn's problems blew up the moment Trump was sworn in as president of the United States. President Trump, his paranoia aroused, responded to the FBI's interest in Flynn as if it were the departing Obama administration's secret plot to run him out of the White House. Trump disseminated a welter of contradictory, half-true, half-invented statements after Flynn was fired for lying to the FBI, smearing his opponents and defending his innocence and probity. On May 9, 2017, Trump fired James Comey, director of the FBI, further tightening the screws of government oversight on him and his campaign. "Russiagate" was *the* story of Trump's first year in office, and Trump's paranoia was only one of his many problems. By not admitting to small mistakes (hiring choices), Trump very often entangled himself in the appearance of having made big mistakes (colluding with Russia). Yet Trump was not a paranoiac without enemies, and "Russiagate" was two things simultaneously. It was Robert Mueller in the position of special prosecutor, meticulously sifting through the permissible evidence, avoiding the spotlight, and authoring a report (released publicly on April

18, 2019) that was even-handed and that, even if it did not exonerate Trump of wrongdoing, was clear about Trump's *not* being a Russian agent; no Trump fingerprints were found on the 2016 Russian meddling. Leaving final judgement to the Department of Justice, led by an attorney general (William Barr) willing to cover for Trump, Mueller had not established Trump's obstruction of justice as one might in a court of law—especially for a president still in office.[15] Legally speaking, it was the end of the story. Trump was not innocent. Neither was he guilty of the wilder accusations that trailed his presidency.[16]

The other side of "Russiagate" was the court of public opinion, as rough and unruly as the 2016 Trump campaign had been. In this court, evidence and accusation, fact and invention, "mainstream" media and tabloid journalism mingled together. The thrill of connecting the dots often sanctioned the thrill of making outlandish claims, as a great deal of "regular" journalism became indistinguishable from opinion journalism or from outright political advocacy. The social-media churn muddied all waters. Trump the non-stop entertainer fell victim to the non-stop entertainment of "Russiagate," to the Saturday Night Live skits that depicted him as the stooge of a shirtless Vladimir Putin, to the internet memes of his having fired Comey in an endless Night of the Long Knives, of being, if not an outright Russian asset, intangibly in the wrong and wrong because he was beholden somehow to the Kremlin. Trump had giddily unleashed this kind of media free-for-all on Hillary Clinton: he had brought new degrees of fury to American politics and new degrees of dishonesty. For several years, the American public digested the possibility—half manic worry, half joke—that Trump was indeed Putin's puppet and that there was a Russian spy in the Oval Office. Benedict Arnold had merely been a turncoat general, and centuries later his bad name was proverbial. If Trump really was a Russian asset, if the levers of American power really were in Konstantin Kilimnik's hands, then Benedict Arnold would be fated to fade into obscurity. Trump's treason would have been a "conspiracy so immense," as Senator Joseph McCarthy had characterized an earlier cycle of fear and recrimination in Washington, that it would have defied even Senator McCarthy's prodigious gift for exaggeration.

*　*　*

In the court of public opinion, "Russiagate" reached its denouement in Helsinki, Finland. Not until July 2018 did Trump and Putin find the occasion to meet directly. Given the dissonance in the US-Russia relationship, a state visit for Putin in Washington or for Trump in Moscow was out of the question. Helsinki was an inspired choice. It was the city in which the Soviet Union and the West had completed the Helsinki Final Act of 1975, a far-reaching agreement on borders and on human rights. In 1975 and in 2018, Finland was an independent country that bordered Russia but was not in NATO. Finland was the West, and it could represent the principle of European neutrality; for Russia it could be the good West, a geopolitical middle ground. Trump had campaigned and been elected on the assumption that he could accomplish something of value with Putin, which might mean discussing the rise of China or the course of the Syrian civil war. More ambitiously, Trump and Putin could, if they wished, share their thoughts on Ukraine, where low-grade fighting continued along the line of contact in the east and where the Minsk diplomatic process had for years been going nowhere. Before the Helsinki meeting, Trump was speaking openly about his wish to withdraw the United States from NATO.[17] The less vivid scandal of the Helsinki summit was the two-hour private conversation Trump and Putin had, breaking with the White House protocol that deputies be present. In Trump's case, these would have been the national security advisor (John Bolton at the time) or the secretary of state (Mike Pompeo). They write down what is said, and some record exists for those in government who need to know what came up. Only translators accompanied Trump and Putin for their two hours in Helsinki, ensconced in a provocative privacy.

The top-tier scandal in Helsinki was the press conference. Often enamored of playing the tough guy at his rallies and ever capable of attacking Republicans and Democrats alike, Trump was almost submissive to Putin in Helsinki. He seemed to be currying Putin's favor, as if Putin were the teacher and he the student or more disturbingly for Trump, with the Mueller investigation ongoing, as if Putin were the boss and Trump the subordinate. Trump's fawning touched on a sensitive matter of American national security. Asked whether he believed that Russia had meddled in the 2016 presidential election, Trump responded by acknowledging that the intelligence community back in Washington was sure that it had. Then Trump, standing next to Putin, distanced himself from his own government. Putin had told him that Russia was not involved, Trump explained, and without fully siding with Putin Trump implied that the Russian president had convinced him. Even Putin looked surprised, as if by going so far over to the Russian side Trump was doing Putin a disservice, which he was. Despite the outlandish things Trump had said before the Helsinki summit and despite being under investigation for colluding with the Russian government on his 2016 election, Trump's embrace of Putin at the summit made him the least credible interlocutor with Russia imaginable, not least in the eyes of many Republicans. In a political system in which the legislature is a co-equal branch of government on foreign policy, Trump was boxing himself in. He was depriving himself of the power to persuade Republicans of anything about Russia, though on other issues he was very much the leader of his party.[18]

On an international stage, Trump had let it be known that his real adversary was not overseas. It was the other party personified by Hillary Clinton. In the press conference, Trump recycled claims about erased emails that he had made incessantly on the campaign trail. Trump's advisor on Russia, Fiona Hill, who was with him in Helsinki, was so horrified by what she was hearing at the press conference—"a head-spinning, incoherent monologue," in her words—that she considered pulling a fire alarm or faking a medical emergency to get Trump to stop.[19] That the press conference reflected badly on Trump was self-evident. That it reflected badly on the state of American politics and foreign policy was not much less self-evident. So riven was the American political scene by the minutia of character assassination that nothing else was visible—even in venues far from the trenches of domestic American politics. By the time Trump returned to Washington, DC, he was not yet at the half-way point of his presidency, but diplomatically speaking he was finished with Russia. He had never demonstrated the discipline required to hammer out an agenda. Even if Trump had devised a path to negotiation with Russia, the Helsinki summit would have made it impossible to traverse. Together with his most vociferous critics, whose obsession with Russian malevolence knew few limits, Trump had tied an albatross around his neck. In the three years between the Helsinki summit and the inauguration of Joe Biden in January 2021, US-Russian relations were neither promising nor overtly terrible. They were empty, and in these three years of wasted time Vladimir Putin came up with the idea of reinvading Ukraine.

* * *

As Russia receded somewhat after the Helsinki debacle, it was Ukraine's turn to enter the thickets of American politics. Trump broke with a taboo of the Obama administration by approving $250 million of "lethal" military assistance to Ukraine—Javelin anti-tank missiles in particular.[20] In Washington, Trump was not going against the grain by giving lethal military aid to Ukraine. When this decision was quietly announced in December 2017, it was the opposite of a scandal. With the provision of lethal aid to Ukraine, Trump also had something more personal in mind. Before there was a scandal involving Ukraine and Trump, Ukrainians went to the polls and chose a new leader. Petro Poroshenko had become Ukraine's president in May of 2014, and he had not been stellar.[21] Though he devoted himself to Ukraine's military modernization, he could not erase the fact that he was an oligarch,.[22] Whatever his achievements and whatever his shortcomings, Poroshenko was a democrat. He let the election of 2019 run its course, and the winner of this election, Volodymyr Zelensky, could enjoy the legitimacy that came with genuine electoral victory; Zelensky got 73 percent of the vote in the final round. His 2019 campaign had been focused on peace in the country's east. Born in 1978, Zelensky was some thirteen years younger than Poroshenko, and in his youth resided a very important circumstance. If taken as a unit, Belarus, Ukraine, and Russia had all been ruled by Soviet or neo-Soviet or identifiably post-Soviet figures since 1991. Thirteen years old when Ukraine gained its independence from the Soviet Union, Zelensky was non-Soviet. His informality, his accessibility, his comfort with politics as entertainment or as mass-media communication gave him a profile very different from Lukashenko in Belarus or Putin in Russia—or Poroshenko in Ukraine, for that matter. More important, Zelensky was not a candidate of the country's east or the west, of the north or the south. He had political backing across the country. He was not the president of a divided country. Nor did he seek to divide the country as a campaigner. This was a crucial asset once he took power.[23]

Trump did not care about Ukraine. He believed that the annexation of Crimea and incursion of Russian soldiers elsewhere in Ukraine were of no consequence to the United States.[24] Trump could reference a conspiracy theory about the 2016 election, according to which the meddling had been the handiwork not of Russia but of Ukraine (in collusion with Hillary Clinton), and for Trump the liberal international order was the silly obsession of the previous administration. President Trump, who invested nothing in diplomacy related to Ukraine, did not visit the country or invite its leaders to visit Washington. Ukraine was not robbing the United States blind like China or taking advantage of the United States like Germany. It was not a great power like Russia, and Zelensky was too moderate and too modest to garner Trump's personal approval.[25] Ukraine came onto Trump's radar for an accidental set of reasons, all of them stemming from Trump's desperation to get reelected in 2020. Trump rightly assessed the probable Democratic front runner to be Joe Biden, who while vice president had held the Ukraine portfolio. Vice President Biden had thrown himself into anti-corruption work. One of his goals—shared by many different government agencies in Washington, by many European governments, and by many Ukrainian reformers—was the removal of Prosecutor General Shokhin, who was seen as an impediment to judicial reform. Poroshenko took some time to comply with this request from Washington. In the end he came through, not necessarily because he was convinced about the need for judicial reform but because Poroshenko wanted to stay in Washington's good graces. For most Americans, these would have been esoteric matters during Obama's second term, distant rumblings from a distant land.

Sensing an opportunity, people around Trump linked Biden's prior anti-corruption actions in Ukraine with work that Biden's son, Hunter, did in Ukraine while his father was vice president. Hunter Biden had been welcomed onto corporate boards in Ukraine and had received money for consulting—no doubt because of his family name. A tentacle from the Trump campaign led back to Ukraine in the person of Paul Manafort. Former New York mayor and close Trump associate, Rudy Giuliani, joined forces with government officials— Gordon Sondland (US ambassador to the EU), Kurt Volker (special envoy to Ukraine), and Rick Perry (energy secretary), who dubbed themselves the three amigos—to dig up dirt on Hunter Biden in the spring of 2019. Since there was no real dirt to be dug up, Hunter Biden's work in Ukraine having been unseemly but not illegal, a pressure campaign was mounted for the invention of information or for the insinuation of guilt without information. For non-compliance with the shenanigans of Giuliani and others in Trump's orbit, the US ambassador to Ukraine, Marie Yovanovitch, was subjected to public defamation, starting in April 2019.[26] (She had been appointed ambassador to Ukraine in the last year of the Obama administration.) It was not that she was asked to join the plot and refused. She was not on the Trump Team, and her personal integrity and her efforts to counter corruption in Ukraine made her an impediment to the plotters. She would be fired for no reason at all on April 24.

Yovanovitch's forced exit coincided with the inauguration of Volodymyr Zelensky. Zelensky gradually realized that Ukraine might not receive lethal military assistance from the United States unless something was provided in return. Simply by announcing an inquiry into Hunter Biden's business activities in Ukraine Zelensky could damage Joe Biden's reputation. He could suggest that the drive to get Prosecutor General Shokhin fired was a cover for protecting Hunter Biden, which it was not. Zelensky held this key to the 2020 American election in his hand. President Trump had deputies such as Gordon Sondland barter over an Oval Office visit for Zelensky in July, dangling the promised aid to Ukraine before Zelensky. Trump exerted more direct pressure on Zelensky in a July 25 phone call. Zelensky, who could not be sure that Trump would win reelection in 2020 and who had much more to lose than to gain from Trump's scheming, demurred. (He did endorse Trump's negative opinion of Ambassador Yovanovitch in the phone call.) The phone call was flagged by a whistleblower, who filed a complaint on August 12. The complaint grew into an investigation and then, after the *Washington Post* broke the story on September 20, into impeachment hearings on Capitol Hill.[27]

Trump was eventually impeached, from which three contradictory lessons about the state of the union could be drawn. First was the vigor of American democracy. Even without getting convicted, Trump did not emerge unscathed from his impeachment trial. Risking the ire of the president, several officials who worked for Trump came forward to describe in excruciating detail Trump's criminal intent and the ease with which Trump folded life-and-death questions of national security (US military assistance to Ukraine) into a scurrilous attempt to undermine a political opponent. Had Trump gotten away with it, Biden's political career might have been terminated at the behest of a sitting president, a poignant counter-factual given that Biden did indeed win the 2020 election and would go on to be one of the pivotal wartime actors in 2022. The second lesson contained in Trump's impeachment was the high degree of polarization in American politics, the biggest cliché of the Trump era. Not just the congressional voting but the public discussion divided along party lines. Trump's opponents were thoroughly, irreversibly convinced of his guilt. Trump's supporters were thoroughly, irreversibly convinced that impeachment was just more of Russia, Russia, Russia. Between February 5, 2020, when the Senate acquitted Trump, and January 6, 2021, when the US Capitol was stormed at Trump's instigation, Trump was at his most uninhibited and the pandemic-addled country at its most polarized.

The third lesson of Trump's impeachment was the sorry state of American foreign policy. A refrain of the Trump years was that of America in decline, and the impeachment proceedings did not make this refrain any less believable. With the face of a Roman senator, Trump was an American Nero, fiddling with Twitter while Rome burned or while Rome was about to catch fire. One can only guess about the impression the impeachment trial made on Vladimir Putin. The lesson about the vigor of American democracy would have left Putin cold. Looking at the United States, he surely felt grateful for the Russian system, in which checks and balances meant little and in which the press had not been entirely cowed into submission (yet) but was vastly less autonomous than the American press. The high degree of polarization in 2019 and 2020 got Putin's notice. He would invoke this point frequently when describing the United States, and Putin was glad to equate polarization under Trump with the decrepitude of democracy per se: the Trump commotion as the purest form of democracy. The prospect of American decline would have been most enticing of all to Putin. How the mighty had fallen! The mastermind of the Soviet Union's downfall, the crafty practitioner of colored revolutions was bogged down in Iraq and Afghanistan. It was falling behind China economically, and in Europe it was tied in knots, antagonizing Germany and confused about NATO and the European Union. And what did the United States want from Ukraine? To cut it loose or to give it weapons? Washington had come to specialize in confusion.

The decadence of American foreign policy was so far advanced in 2019, Putin might have surmised, that an inward-looking United States, a superpower run by a mafia boss, would not remain a superpower for long. Perhaps, with the assistance of countries like Ukraine, Trump aspired to be America's Yanukovych, another oligarch protégé of Paul Manafort, who cooked the books and stole what he could, while other countries went about advancing their interests. That for Putin would have been the opposite of an American tragedy. It would have been a step in the right direction.

* * *

In Eastern Europe and elsewhere, Trump had disavowed regime change and colored revolutions. A Putinist to this degree, Trump had no patience for human rights. He condemned the street protests that coursed through the United States in the summer of 2020 after the murder of George Floyd, which had occurred on May 25. Trump agreed with Putin that many past American experiments in supporting dissent and protest—in Egypt, in Ukraine—had been ill advised. Trump did appreciate some insurgencies, if that is how Brexit can be described or the tenure of Brazil's Jair Bolsonaro or the Philippines' Rodrigo Duterte, and depending on the country, so too did Vladimir Putin. On these points, Trump and Putin saw eye to eye, which made it ironic that a kind of colored revolution broke out when Trump was president, one that could not have been much closer to home for Putin. Ukraine's revolution had come about in the winter of 2013-2014. In the summer of 2020, revolution hovered over Belarus. Had a Democrat been in the White House or a Republican other than Trump, Putin would surely have blamed the United States for what was happening in Belarus, so closely did the events there imply the familiar progression: aging autocrat, tainted election, street protests, political uprising, regime change. This is what Putin had already witnessed (with variations) in Georgia, Kirghizstan, Ukraine, Tunisia, and Libya. It was the last thing he wanted to see in Belarus, where everything for so long had been so blissfully quiet.

Lukashenko had been up for reelection in August 2020. He was a Soviet-style dictator, and the election was worthless. The opposition movement's leader was Svietlana Tsikhanouskaya, who was born 1982, four years after Volodymyr Zelensky. She had stood for election in 2020 after her husband was arrested in May of that year. Tsikhanouskaya was certain that she had won the election, while protests and demonstrations against Lukashenko roiled Belarus. Another Maidan might be in the offing, but Lukashenko had studied Yanukovych's response to protests in Ukraine, and his approach was more hard line than Yanukovych's. Yanukovych had used violence, but he could not deny the protestors freedom of assembly. So he ended up in a political netherworld between democracy and dictatorship, which is inhospitable to dictatorship. Lukashenko admitted no room for democracy, subjecting protesters to mass arrest and intimidation. It mattered of course that Belarus was a consolidated dictatorship in 2020, whereas Ukraine in 2013 and early 2014 was a democracy at risk of becoming a dictatorship. Lukashenko coordinated his actions with Moscow, which did not have to intervene but which could reward Lukashenko with support and with resources. Having crushed the protest movement, Lukashenko lost some of his independence. In the winter of 2022, Putin would invade Ukraine from Russia's south and east—and from Belarus in the north, a counter-intuitive consequence of the upheaval in summer 2020.

The Trump administration did nothing about Belarus. Several months before the contested election—on February 1, 2020—Secretary of State Pompeo had visited the country. He had been curious to see whether Lukashenko, who cherished the idea of his independence, might be looking to slink away from Moscow. Pompeo's visit was inconclusive.[28] Without a knowable agenda for

Ukraine, for Russia, or for Belarus, Washington was a bystander to the back and forth of protest and crackdown in Minsk. The Trump administration was far too distracted by domestic politics in the summer of 2020—by impeachment, by the upcoming election, by the pandemic, by civil unrest in the United States— to take a stand on the situation in Belarus. Belarus was nevertheless a turning point, outlining the newly zero-sum nature not just of Russia's relationship with the United States but of Russia's relationship with Europe and of Europe's with Russia. Having gone into exile in the European Union—in Lithuania— Tsikhanouskaya became Europe's darling, a courageous democrat who had taken on Europe's last dictatorship and an icon of feminist activism.[29] In Europe and to a degree in the United States, Tsikhanouskaya was recognized as the legitimate leader of Belarus. She was not just invited to speak at universities. She was invited to address parliaments across Europe, to address the European Union and the US Congress (after Joe Biden was elected), as if she were the Belorussian head of state. The EU and the European nations that lionized Tsikhanouskaya did not directly apply the presumed illegitimacy of Lukashenko to the presumed illegitimacy of Putin; but it was a matter of one plus one equaling two. In the Eastern Partnership Program of 2009, Belarus and Ukraine were both supposed to assimilate European norms. The process was to be peaceful and open-ended, and by the summer of 2020 that aspiration was ancient history. By the summer of 2020, what had once been open-ended had become either-or. Either Lukashenko or Tsikhanouskaya would prevail, which is to say that in Belarus, either Russia or Europe would win. By the same token, in Belarus either Russia or Europe would lose.

Putin would do whatever he could to forestall a repetition of the Maidan in Lukashenko's Minsk. Many European countries championed Tsikhanouskaya even if the Trump White House did not. They did so, Putin might have surmised, because the West's aim was still to encroach on Russia and ultimately to remove him from power. What had happened after the Maidan? Pro-Western politicians had taken over in Kyiv and immediately pushed Ukraine toward NATO. Ukraine was working hand in glove with Western militaries, enabling the expansion of Western military sway through the Trojan horses of "democracy" and "reform." Despite the annoyance caused by a pig-headed Lukashenko, Putin had what he needed to beat back the West in Belarus. But what of Ukraine, where everything was trending in the wrong direction? Trump had delivered nothing for Russia, whereas to Ukraine he had delivered lethal military assistance. Vis-à-vis Ukraine, Trump was more than useless for Putin. He was an unpredictable question mark, though in a second term the president who wanted to withdraw the United States from the NATO alliance might begin to be helpful. That was Putin's dilemma in the summer of 2020—in addition to the protests in Minsk and in addition to the Belarussian government-in-exile forming with the assistance of the usual transatlantic suspects. There was also an election upcoming in the United States. If Joe Biden won, the orgy of polarization might end and with it the serious discussion of ludicrous ideas and the self-immolation of a once-proud superpower. A new phase of concentrated support for Ukraine might begin. Biden had experience with Ukraine. With Obama, he had applauded the Maidan back in 2013, and like lemmings, the Europeans would fall in line behind him. For Putin, keeping Belarus on board might not be enough. It might be necessary to do something about Ukraine.

PART III
COLLISION, 2021–2023

7

The Search for Guardrails

> The bottom line is, I told President Putin that we need to have some
> basic rules of the road that we can all abide by. I also said there are
> areas where there's a mutual interest for us to cooperate—Russian
> and American people—but also for the benefit of the world and the
> security of the world. One of those areas is strategic stability.
>
> President Joe Biden, press conference held June 16, 2021,
> Geneva Switzerland[1]

The governments of Russia and China are not less unstable than the government of the United States. Putin has periodically faced the eruption of protest within Russia. He has a long record of strife with the oligarchs, with the political figures and with the journalists who have gotten in his way. Alexei Navalny, an opposition activist whom Putin has had poisoned and jailed, has employed social media to argue that Putin is not who he says he is—that he and his cronies are a crime syndicate.[2] Putin's 2022 war against Ukraine has revealed how badly Russia is governed, how much internal trickery and lies have fouled up Putin's military modernization, and how poor Russian decision-making can be. Behind the edifice of China's one-party system is a welter of competing interests, and China has had to subdue dissent in Hong Kong, in Tibet, and in other places where Beijing's rule is resented. China's mismanagement of the COVID pandemic was striking: government dishonesty, excessively stringent lockdowns, bursts of civic unrest, and then the country's quick opening up, though without sufficient rates of vaccination to quell the pandemic. Russia and China are not necessarily worse at governance than the United States, but neither are they demonstrably better. All three countries—China, Russia, and the United States—struggle with their bigness, with their regional and political heterogeneity, and with their vaunted international ambitions. Of this trio, however, only the United States puts its problems out there in full view, broadcasting them, debating them, investigating them, mocking them, hating them, falling in love with them, diagnosing them, and belaboring them for all the world to see.

For the four years that Donald Trump was president, the problems of the United States were given obsessive media attention in the United States and internationally. It was a captivating story: the world's most powerful country in the hands of an erratic man and the world's most historically solid democracy humbled by a president uninvested in democracy. It was impossible not to watch the American soap opera under Trump, who tended to bring his opponents down to his level and who stoked the fires of racial discord throughout his presidency—most vividly in the summer of 2020, when the United States seemed to be edging toward civil war. Trump's botched handling of the pandemic contributed to hundreds of thousands of excess deaths. (To very little media fanfare, Putin also botched the pandemic; nobody knows the Russian death toll.) Washington, DC, is a global media hub. The scope of media access to government and to the record of government mismanagement in the United States would not be tolerated in Beijing or Moscow. The travails of the Trump White House enhanced this national and international media presence in Washington, enhanced it by monetizing it. "We shall be as a city upon a hill," John Winthrop had written about colonial Massachusetts in 1630, when there was no United States yet and when the Massachusetts Bay Colony was a mere blip on the American continent, "the eyes of all people are upon us." Winthrop had a high opinion of the Massachusetts Bay Colony. Trump's Washington was no city on a hill. It was a city in trouble and the eyes of many, many people were upon it.

The nadir of the Trump presidency came on January 6, 2021, the day on which the United States came close to losing its elected government. But for a few accidents of policing and crowd flow, the mob that entered the US Capitol, where the vice president had joined both houses of Congress to confirm the results of the presidential election, might have murdered the vice president and members of Congress. Most likely Trump would not have had the wherewithal to assume dictatorial power, if that was his intent on January 6, but preventing Biden's inauguration could have ended the American political experiment and with it the role the United States plays internationally. Every detail of this national nightmare—from Trump's incendiary speech in the late morning of January 6, to the ferocity of the insurrectionists, to the terrified members of Congress, to the Confederate flag carried through the Capitol, to the mock gallows erected outside the building—could be found on film and photograph. Media coverage with endless social-media amplification was nonstop, and by no means did it end in the early morning of January 7, when Biden was confirmed as the next president of the United States and some semblance of normal life returned. The inquiry into January 6 has been extensive, as have the efforts at journalistic analysis and public commemoration. In a suite of hearings, the US Congress has ensured that still more details have been gathered and subjected to public scrutiny. Not only did this event define the Trump presidency, its final and most terrible chapter, but it would do a great deal to define Joe Biden's presidency as well.

Joe Biden came to the White House in search of guardrails. This could apply to his own ailing country, for which guardrails had multiple meanings. One was the White House absenting itself from the social-media outrage that had fueled the Trump presidency and stirred up the January 6 insurrection. Biden would have social-media accounts but would use them for the distribution of talking points and official messaging, much the way Woodrow Wilson had used the first modern press conference in the early twentieth century. Biden would do what he could do to cool down American politics. He consciously minimized Trump's personality, avoiding the name of Trump in his speeches and public statements. Biden did not demonize Trump the man. In a sense, Biden minimized his own personality as well, something that came naturally to him. The oldest man ever to win the presidency, a politician to his fingertips, Biden opted for low-key charm rather than high-octane charisma. He did not mind being dull. Biden also came to the White House from decades in the Senate, where he had Republican friends and colleagues. He did not mind making American politics dull.[3] With a reputation for political moderation, Biden could establish guardrails for American politics by not unduly antagonizing Republicans. It would all work imperfectly. In his first years in office, Biden scored legislative achievements but won no big bi-partisan victories. Even without having found the magic middle of American politics, he could be proud of the midterm election results in 2022. The Democrats held onto the Senate. The election itself was calm, its results undisputed. On balance, it rewarded the more moderate candidates in both parties. The seditious spirit of January 6 had to a degree subsided.

The search for guardrails animated Biden's foreign policy as well. Erecting guardrails was not the same as staging another reset with Russia. Dmitry Medvedev and the allure of a modern Russia were both gone with the wind by 2021, the word "reset" a synonym for self-defeat or at the very least for disappointment. Whereas a reset would have been naïve, finding guardrails did not depend on improved relations with Russia. Nor did it imply that the Kremlin should be given carte blanche, bygones be forgotten, and a new page politely turned. In his foreign policy, Biden was on balance less optimistic than Obama, either by temperament or because of the four years of Trumpian misrule that separated Obama's 2017 departure from Biden's 2021 arrival. Biden did not expect much of Putin, and his overriding foreign-policy concerns were not Russia-focused. They were the denial of advantage to China, the sole "peer competitor" to the United States and one that was challenging American interests across the globe; the reigning in of the pandemic, which was far from over when Biden took the oath of office in January 2021; the drawdown of a US military presence in Afghanistan; and the combating of climate change, a crushing challenge that Trump had cheerfully ignored. These concerns were global in nature, and for the Biden White House each depended on the revival of the liberal international order. Though Putin's Russia would not help the United States to deal with China, it might have contributions to make on public health or on climate change or on nuclear non-proliferation. Ideally, Russia could be neutralized and blocked from interfering with the Biden administration's larger concerns. Hence the need for guardrails, which translated in practice into tempering conflict with Russia.

A US-Russian relationship moderated by guardrails implied a static Russia. This was a legitimate possibility in 2021, Putin having been in office for two decades. Close to seventy years old, he had elaborated a flawed but highly sustainable formula for ruling his country. Russians had personal freedoms so long as they did not intrude on the Kremlin's business; they were freer than they had been in the Soviet Union. Though Putin's Russia lacked a bona fide constitution and legal system, personal freedoms were widespread, giving the Kremlin legitimacy in the absence of competitive elections and for the most part draining the spirit of protest from society. Corruption and graft kept the wheels of the regime and the economy moving, and so did legitimate businesses. A petrostate, Russia had the means to act internationally, but it tended to act on the margins of international politics—in disaster zones like Syria or in border disputes along its own periphery. The country infatuated with frozen conflicts could itself appear frozen and immobile. Another aspect of this seemingly static setup was Putin's cultural conservatism, his veneration for the past as he espoused it, and his supposed fear of democracy, change, and modernity. Putin could appear to be a late-stage authoritarian in 2021, a conservative figure desperate to hold onto his power and privileges. He could not be changed by actions in Washington, but perhaps he could be cordoned off and left alone. The problem with this allegedly static Russia was Russia itself. Not static at all in 2021, Russia was a radical country under the leadership of a radical president, everything in fearsome motion. This is why the guardrails between Moscow and Washington, sincerely sought by the Biden administration, never materialized.

* * *

In 2021, Europe was not static either. The twelve years from 2009, when the Eastern Partnership Program (EaP) was introduced, and 2021, when the Trump era came to an end, had been eventful. Europe withstood serial financial crises. The center held, and the euro did not collapse as a currency. The migrant crisis of 2015 did not break Europe, and the European Union survived Brexit with aplomb. Brexit wound up harming Great Britain more than it did the European Union. Nor did the European Union opt out of the sanctions regime it had imposed on Russia in 2014—in the name of "Minsk" diplomacy. After 2014, Ukraine and Europe drew closer together in many respects, making good on the Europhilic promise of the Maidan. The movement of businesses and people across borders, the integrations of daily life brought ever more Ukraine into Europe and ever more Europe into Ukraine. Ukraine was not at any point poised to enter NATO or to enter the EU, but after 2014 it had many opportunities to cooperate with

NATO, both at NATO gatherings and through training exercises. The trajectory of further integration along these various lines, such integration having been the impetus for the EaP in the first place, was a steadily rising line. As if to complete this rosy picture, a portion of Belarusian society indicated hopes for *its* European future in the summer of 2020, seemingly retracing the steps Ukraine had taken in 2013 and 2014. Europe's most potent power, undimmed in 2020 and 2021, was the power of attraction.

Europe's magnetic power informed what could be termed a European foreign policy. In 2014, France and Germany and with them the EU had nominally stepped into the lead on Ukraine. They skirted the question of Crimea, the most dramatic revision to Europe's borders since 1945, Crimea being roughly the size of Massachusetts. Tackling the question of the Donbas, Europe's position was resolute on paper. Europe knew exactly what it wanted in Ukraine after Russia's 2014 invasion: because Russia's military presence in eastern Ukraine was illegitimate, an illegal act, fundamentally un-European, it could not be accepted, and Europe did not accept it. "Minsk" diplomacy would allow Russia to save face, European diplomats hoped, facilitating Russia's eventual exit from Ukraine. Minsk would grant an amnesty to the "separatists" and some kind of autonomous status to Donetsk and Luhansk, provided the Russian military units were withdrawn. At that point, sanctions could be lifted, bringing manifold benefits to Russia—a return to partnership with Europe coupled with silence about Crimea. Russia's sustained occupation of Crimea would not prevent a normalizing of relations between Russia and Europe, if only Moscow would withdraw its soldiers from eastern Ukraine, an unspoken but important element of Minsk diplomacy. Europe's version of Minsk was not a bad deal for Russia, but it assumed that Russia wanted to be in Europe's good graces and that for the sake of being in Europe's good graces it would be willing to leave Ukraine.

The Kremlin never came close to complying with the European version of Minsk. After February 2015, when the heavy fighting stopped, the Russian occupation of eastern Ukraine became indefinite, and Russia was not pulling back. It made a military move into Syria in the summer of 2015, not that Europe was in a position to stop Russia. Yet Russia's backing of Bashar al-Assad contributed to a migrant crisis that unsettled Europe, a factor in Britain's vote to leave the European Union in 2016. Russia proceeded to meddle directly in the 2016 US presidential election with the intention, among others, of damaging the transatlantic relationship. Russia also interfered in the domestic political affairs of many European nations, including Germany.[4] In March 2018, Russian intelligence officers used Novichok, a chemical agent, to poison a British subject (and former double agent), Sergei Skripal, in the south of England, operating with impunity on British soil.[5] In summer 2020, Russia was instrumental in the suppression of a pro-European protest in Belarus, lending economic and political support to the Belarussian government and thereby helping Lukashenko to stay in power. Russia did what it could to complicate NATO's and the EU's activities in the Balkans. From Syria to Belarus to Ukraine, Moscow's actions were an expanding problem set for European security after 2015. As soon as the ink was dry on the Minsk agreements, Putin had applied himself to building a Europe less whole, less free, and less at peace. Europe's efforts with Minsk had been more than irrelevant. They had done nothing to forestall the emergence of a more confrontational Russia.

These problems did not fully register in Europe or at least in Western Europe, where the impulse to soothe relations with Russia was entrenched. Nowhere was this impulse more robust than in Germany, which proceeded with the Nord Stream 2 pipeline against the objections of many Eastern European countries and against the objections of the Trump White House. (Trump's objections, given his unpopularity in Germany, may have made it harder for Berlin to jettison Nord Stream 2.) In its own eyes, Germany had good intentions. To enmesh Russia in the European economy was a way of bringing European influence to Russia and over time of grinding down Russia's un-European authoritarianism. To retain Germany as a bridge to Russia, after Germany had wreaked so much havoc in the Soviet Union during World War II, was an ethical responsibility to the past and to the future, but Berlin's position on the Nord Stream 2 pipeline also underscored the absurdities of Europe's Minsk diplomacy. In one register, Europe was criticizing Russia for having invaded a European country. In another, it was doing business with Russia for practical reasons and supposedly for the sake of a better European future, and Germany was hardly the only European country receiving Russian gas and oil or profiting from access to the Russian market.[6] Sanctions, which lose their effectiveness over time, were not augmented when Russia defied Europe's stated objectives by staying put in eastern Ukraine. The Nord Stream 2 pipeline sent a similarly conciliatory signal to Moscow. *Wandel durch Handel*, change through trade, a popular German aspiration for Russia, was closer to *Handel durch Handel*, trade through trade. The price Russia had paid for its actions in 2014 and 2015 was hardly exorbitant, while European countries did not seem all that concerned about their regional security. Their leaders talked as if an uncompromising set of rules applied to everyone—and certainly to Russia. They behaved as if these rules were soft and malleable.

Even when Trump became president, Europe did not change gears. This was an American president who regularly advertised his disrespect for Europe. Trump's resume bristled with strange connections to Russia. He was more at ease with Putin than with Merkel, and he bartered Ukraine's security in hopes of destroying a domestic political opponent. As if this were not ominous enough, Trump refused to accept his electoral defeat in November 2020, looking on with glee as a band of his supporters stormed the US Capitol on January 6. The

United States was problem-ridden and unreliable, but this self-evident truth did not compel European countries to increase their defense budgets or to rethink their dependence on NATO—to take matters into their own hands. Nor did it compel Europeans to modify their position on Ukraine, to reduce sanctions on Russia, to consider recognizing the annexation of Crimea, or to attempt a normalization of relations with Russia because the United States was no longer reliable. The world was shifting around Europe, with the United States off kilter and China manifestly on the rise, but Europe was not purchasing more military power for itself, and at the same time it was not pulling back from its old instinct to grow and expand—or to try to get Russia to follow the rules. Between 2016 and 2021, European influence in Ukraine was rising. Looked at from the Kremlin, Europe was a contradiction and quite possibly an inviting contradiction, unable to balance its strengths and its weaknesses. Though Trump did not create these European discrepancies, the cold light of his indifference did a lot to expose them.

Exacerbating Europe's season of discontent was a flurry of leadership changes. In Great Britain, Boris Johnson became prime minister in July 2019. His personal lack of discipline resembled Trump's, and Johnson was, like Trump, the creation of a media age, skilled at getting people's attention and eager to do so by being outrageous. Like Trump, Johnson loved political bluster, and like Trump, he was a faux populist, a man born to wealth and privilege with a knack for presenting himself as the tribune of the people. He was garishly unserious. Olaf Scholz replaced Angela Merkel in December 2021. A technocrat in spirit and serious to a flaw, he seemed small after sixteen years of Merkel's consequential chancellorship. Scholz did not reject any of Merkel's previous positions on Ukraine and Russia. He was not about to alter the sanctions regime or to reset relations with Putin. Hailing from the Social Democratic Party, which had pioneered *Ostpolitik* in the 1970s and which was softer on Russia than Merkel's CDU, Scholz was not going to attempt anything big with Russia. He dedicated himself to the careful curating of the status quo. Merkel had worked no miracles with France's Emmanuel Macron, who had come to power after Minsk had been negotiated. Like Merkel, Macron did not recognize Minsk for the deferral of problems that it was. Merkel, Macron, Johnson, and Scholz all assumed that Ukraine could occupy its gray zone forever, one foot in the European Union, one foot out, one foot in transatlantic security structures, one foot out. On this they were either foolish or unduly sanguine about what the future had in store. Unknowingly, they were the leaders of a Europe adrift.

* * *

Volodymyr Zelensky was not at all adrift in early 2021. With more emphasis than before, he was leading Ukraine toward the West. Zelensky was a native Russian speaker, and his entertainment career had taken him often enough to Russia, where he was popular as a comedian and TV star. When campaigning in 2019, he attributed malaise to Poroshenko, suggesting that such initiatives as the creation of a canonical Ukrainian Orthodox Church (Kyivan Patriarchate), which were dear to Poroshenko, were peripheral to Ukraine's real problems. Zelensky presented himself as the peace candidate and by implication as someone who could negotiate with Russia.[7] Minsk diplomacy was vague enough and its language plastic enough that it could—in the course of a political campaign—be made to mean many things. A bit of openness and a bit of creativity and perhaps progress could be made, and if progress could be made on Minsk, then the war itself might finally start to wind down, to Ukraine's benefit. The unresolved war was hurting Ukraine's economy. Investment and insurance had been complicated by the war with Russia and then by the uneasy peace. By 2019, with four years of costly stalemate in the background, a peace candidate had certain advantages over Poroshenko, who had shown Ukrainians how to avoid losing the war but not how to win it. In the forward-looking manner of a political candidate, Zelensky did not exactly promise victory in the war or the expulsion of Russian soldiers from Crimea and the Donbas, and he made no mention of capitulation to Russian demands. More elusively and more enticingly, he spoke about an end to the war.

In office, Zelensky had to balance two competing challenges. One could be described as the Trump challenge. This entailed not angering Trump, who was no friend of Ukraine. In the spring of 2019, Trump's minions were running amok in Ukraine, seeking information—or "information"—that might be damaging to Joe Biden. Beyond the need to placate Trump was the sheer mystery of Trumpism. What if the United States left the NATO alliance? What if US-German relations imploded and with them the transatlantic relationship? Zelensky had to hedge against a Democratic president in 2021 and at the same time to keep some distance from Trump, having to hedge as well against an unstable United States. Every European country had to in 2019 and 2020, two especially feverish years in American politics. The other challenge facing Zelensky was domestic. Ukrainians may have voted for a peace candidate in 2019, but they did not want an elected Ukrainian president to kowtow to Putin, while Russia drove a hard, intransigent bargain on everything related to Ukraine. Putin thought that Russia had prevailed on the battlefield in 2014 and 2015, and he was not wrong about this. Russia held many of the key military cards, and it considered itself a great power. If Moscow were to withdraw its soldiers from the Donbas, Putin would only expect something very substantial in return—like the international recognition of Crimea as Russian territory or the closing of NATO's open-door policy. Neither ceding Crimea to Russia nor affirming Ukrainian neutrality was an option for Zelensky. Even considering these possibilities might be the end of his presidency.

In late 2019, Zelensky could be seen walking this tightrope. In September, he negotiated a prisoner exchange with Putin.[8] On December 9, he traveled to Paris for a meeting of the Normandy Four, a quartet of countries (Ukraine, Russia, France, and Germany) that was supposed to manage the "Ukraine crisis." In previous months, Zelensky had endorsed the so-called Steinmeier formula, an interpretation of Minsk that was a bit weaker than what Poroshenko had been willing to accept, placing the withdrawal of Russian troops at the end of the process (as Russia had been arguing for) rather than at the beginning of the process (as Ukraine had been arguing for).[9] On December 8, 10,000 members of a "red Lines for Zelensky Chamber" gathered on the Maidan, while others assembled near the office of the president.[10] They were putting Zelensky on notice. He was not to yield to Putin as Yanukovych had some five years earlier in Vilnius. In Paris, Zelensky had a solo meeting with Putin during which no breakthrough was achieved, though neither Putin nor Zelensky walked out in anger; in Paris, Zelensky was able to negotiate another prisoner exchange with Putin. A further meeting of the Normandy Four was scheduled for March 2020. It was canceled, not because Zelensky and Putin had locked horns but because the pandemic had upended this kind of in-person diplomacy. In the spring of 2021, Zelensky proposed meeting with Putin in the Donbas, to which Putin's maddening response was that the "Donbas is an internal issue of the Ukrainian state," as if Russian soldiers were not sitting there in plain sight.[11] By the spring of 2021, the hour was already late.

Joe Biden's inauguration in the winter of 2021 eased Zelensky's political situation. Trump was gone, and a friend of Ukraine was in the White House. This Biden had tried to be as Obama's vice president. President Biden was eager to restore transatlantic relations, to strengthen NATO, and to ensure the independence of countries like Ukraine. Biden, who was not going to bring Ukraine into NATO, was not going to oppose Ukraine's aim of joining NATO, as Trump might have done, had Zelensky pressed the issue. As of January 2021, Zelensky could use Biden's victory in the United States to deal with some of his domestic political headaches. Ukraine's economy was far from stellar in 2021. Zelensky had few new ideas about fighting corruption, and those ideas he did have he was inexpert at implementing. Zelensky was at best a moderately popular president in 2021, his approval ratings in early 2021 hovering around 30 percent—not such a bad number by international standards.[12] His presidency was not going anywhere in particular, which may have prompted him to put some additional space between Ukraine and Russia. In February 2021, Zelensky approved the sanctioning of eight individuals, among them Viktor Medvedchuk, a friend of Vladimir Putin and a godfather to one of Putin's children. For years, Medvedchuk had been a go-between and a political figure in Ukraine aligned with "pro-Russian" voters and with the "pro-Russian" party once known as the Party of the Regions, Viktor

Yanukovych's party, of which Petro Poroshenko had been somewhat confusingly a founding member.[13] On February 2, 2021, Zelensky had three Russian-oriented television stations, each of them owned by Medvedchuk, shut down.[14] In May, Medvedchuk was placed under house arrest.

On February 26, 2021, Zelensky took up the subject of Crimea. He signed a text, "On Certain Measures Aimed at De-occupation and Reintegration of the Temporarily Occupied Territory of the Autonomous Republic of Crimea and the City of Sevastopol." The idea had been presented at the September 2020 UN General Assembly in New York: the formation of a "Crimean Platform," a diplomatic path to Crimea's de-occupation. The February 2021 text anticipated a conference that would be held in Kyiv seven months later, in August, which was the formal launch of the Crimean Platform. Representatives of forty-four countries attended together with heads of state, foreign ministers, and defense ministers. The countries of Europe were all present as was Secretary of Transportation Pete Buttigieg. That Crimea belonged to Ukraine was not a novel sentiment in 2021; there was no confusion about this in the Ukrainian government. That Crimea belonged to Ukraine was the position of Petro Poroshenko no less than of Volodymyr Zelensky. The Crimea Platform was meant to remind Russia that Crimea had not been forgotten and that its occupation of the peninsula had not been accepted, despite a widespread Russian conviction that Crimea's annexation was both a fait accompli and a correction of the historical record. Between 2016 and 2018 and at incredible expense, Russia had constructed Europe's longest bridge across the Kerch Strait, linking the Russia mainland with Crimea. While Crimea as Russia had been normalized in Russia, the Crimean Platform was striving—at a high level of international recognition—to normalize Crimea as Ukraine. Crimea's true status had not changed in 2014. Crimea is, was, and would be Ukraine, Zelensky was promising.

For Zelensky, Ukraine's future membership in NATO was by no means certain. Neither was it impossible. In March 2021, Zelensky had let Ukraine participate in NATO exercises, a gesture of defiance toward Russia.[15] On June 14, 2021, at the NATO summit in Brussels, it was once again affirmed that Ukraine and Georgia would one day join the NATO alliance, the claim first announced at the Bucharest summit in 2008. From June 28 to July 10, Ukrainians participated in the "Sea Breeze 2021" exercises with NATO member states in the Black Sea, and from September 22 to September 30, Ukrainians joined with NATO members for joint exercises on Ukrainian territory. Not much later, on October 17, Secretary of Defense Lloyd Austin III touched down in Kyiv, where he stated that the open-door policy for NATO was very much still in effect and that he hoped Ukraine would walk through it, a boost to Zelensky's goal of having Ukraine join NATO.[16] If Ukraine was still outside the Western club in 2021, the momentum was clearly on the side of greater integration with Europe, on the one hand, and greater transatlantic integration, on the other. The Biden administration's oft-stated aim for Ukraine was its Euro-Atlantic integration, as it had been for the Obama administration. Whereas Trump had his minions run amok in Ukraine while he was president, such that most American discussions about Ukraine were discussions about Trump and his impeachment, Zelensky and Biden would be working in tandem. Biden prized the pre-Trump status quo, giving Zelensky a political opening. Whatever Moscow might have hoped for from Trump or from Zelensky had not come to pass. Subtly, quietly yet irreversibly, the summer and fall of 2021 were the end of an era in Russia's attitude toward Ukraine and the West. There would be no more Normandy Four meetings, and not just because of the pandemic.

* * *

When he opted for war in February 2022, Putin was often depicted in the West as an out-of-touch tyrant. He had surrounded himself with sycophants. He did not understand the world he was living in. There he sat in the Kremlin admiring the architectural signifiers of Russian greatness, having deluded himself into thinking that he was a latter-day Peter the Great. By 2022, Putin's political vocabulary was so out of sync with the political vocabulary of most American and European politicians and pundits that it could best be explained by mysticism, a default attitude toward Russia, going back to the Marquis de Custine's travelogue, *Russia in 1839* or *Empire of the Czar*, in which de Custine equated Russian politics (and Russian life) with artifice and deception, with an un-European irrationalism.[17] In addition to Putin's talent for artifice and deception, which were real enough, there was an element of pragmatism in his march to war. What had been done was not working (in his terms). As he would not have accepted, Ukraine's westward drift was a problem very much of Putin's own making. The government in Kyiv, which turned to the West after the Maidan, might have eventually turned back toward Russia or turned in upon itself had Putin not resorted to force and had he not launched a destructive war in the Donbas. Without the 2014–2015 war, Ukraine's hybridity—its balancing and mixing of Ukrainian and Russian culture and of the Ukrainian and Russian languages—might have endured forever. Because of his militaristic approach, Putin had embraced a counterproductive logic, pushing Ukraine into the arms of the West while still wanting a Ukraine that was subordinate to Russia. The more Putin tried to coerce Ukraine, the more he alienated the people of Ukraine, pushing them away from Russia. This was irrational enough. Yet the Putin who recognized Ukraine's westward momentum after 2014 was not being irrational at all. On this point he was analytically correct.

Nor was Putin delusional about his record of foreign-policy success. He could have made the following case. He had inherited a humiliated land from Yeltsin.

It had to stand by and watch as NATO expanded territorially and as NATO transformed itself from a defensive to an expeditionary alliance—in the Balkans, in Afghanistan, and in Libya. Yeltsin's Russia could not even deal with such internal problems as Chechen separatism. By creating a strong executive, by restoring economic growth, by modernizing the Russian military, Putin could claim to have brought Russia forward: subduing Chechnya; stopping NATO's advance into Georgia in 2008; stopping NATO's advance into Ukraine in 2014; showing Georgia and Ukraine that there was a limit to how far they could venture away from Moscow; bringing back Crimea; planting the Russian flag in eastern Ukraine; restoring Russia's great-power status in the Middle East in 2015; building up a meaningful partnership with China, the superpower of the future; punishing the United States in 2016 for its meddling in Ukrainian affairs; and projecting Russian power deep into Africa and Latin America. The West had not achieved its goals for Crimea or for eastern Ukraine, Putin could contend, and by 2021 Western sanctions had become an afterthought, a formality. Russia continued to sell gas and oil all over Europe. Its economy had weathered the sanctions tied to "Minsk implementation" so well that by 2021 the United States and Europe had effectively stopped talking about Minsk implementation. In 2021, Putin very likely thought that he was on a roll, the virtuoso of Russia's twenty-first-century restoration.

Two changes could be detected in the self-confident Putin of 2021, and neither of them favored the creation of guardrails. Both were intensifications of traits he and his regime had had for a long time, since 2000 perhaps, the year Putin came to power. The first was Putin's open disdain for democracy. The pretense that Putin led United Russia, a political party; that he stood for elections; that he was beholden to the Russian constitution had been maintained in earlier phases of his presidency. This image started to crumble in 2007 and 2008 until it fell apart in 2012. The evolving Russia-China partnership had openly anti-democratic connotations, and Putin attributed Russia's foreign-policy constancy to its not being a democracy, lamenting the disruption brought to other countries by elections, by street protests, and by political movements independent of the state. It helped that between 2008 and 2021, the years in which Russia slipped into dictatorship, democracy was experiencing a global recession, inverting the trend of the 1970s and 1980s, when democracy was on the rise internationally. In 2021, it was regularly asked whether the United States would remain a democracy, while several NATO member states (Poland, Hungary, Turkey) were becoming less and less democratic by the year. Here too Putin may have felt himself to be on a roll, and he could have cited Volodymyr Zelenksy's moderate approval ratings in Ukraine or Zelensky's announcement in December 2021 that one of the country's oligarchs, Rinat Akhmetov, had been preparing a coup d'etat in Ukraine.[18] After all, Zelensky had been democratically elected, and Ukraine's political woes in December 2021 (real or perceived) were the woes of a democracy.

The second change in Putin more directly foreshadowed war. A former law student, President Putin loved to read history. The conclusions he drew were entirely outside the mainstream of European and American intellectual life. A standard Western reading of European history, shared by most policymakers, was that the demons of nationalism were still alive, but they had been consigned to the "margins" of Europe—to Nagorno-Karabakh, a dispute between Armenia and Azerbaijan, or to the Balkans, which were the paradigmatic European outlier after the Cold War. The rest of Europe had moved on, and the glory of the 1990s, in this reading, was the independence of Europe's "small" countries, whose independence marked the end of empire within Europe. The other protagonist of the 1990s was the European Union, because it was transnational, legally minded, and deliberative; it was the exact opposite of fascist or Soviet domination. Many US and European policymakers were committed to this interpretation of European history, in which Russia did not figure very prominently. The key point, in this interpretation, was that Russia had *not* been harmed by the Soviet Union's collapse. Russia had been welcomed into Europe, and with Putin it had taken up some elements of the invitation and rejected others, a regrettable situation until 2014 and a worrisome situation after the annexation of Crimea and invasion of the Donbas. There was always the chance, though, that Russia would see the light, return to the European fold, and then, by staying within its borders, enjoy being both a European and a modern country. Had Mikhail Gorbachev not spoken warmly of a Europe stretching from Lisbon to Vladivostok, a Eurasian zone of peace and cooperation? Had Yeltsin not tried to hold on to the rudiments of this vision in the 1990s? Was this not what "the Russians" themselves wanted?

A hodgepodge, Putin's analysis of Russian history went in almost the exact opposite direction. He cherished Russia's pre-revolutionary past. In the nineteenth century, Russia had been an enormous empire—an Asian power, a Middle Eastern power and a European power. Putin identified at times with the modernizers of late-imperial Russia, those (like Pyotr Stolypin, a prime minister of Russia from 1906 to 1911) who had tried to strengthen the Russian state and to foster economic growth. On the Soviet period Putin tended to be contradictory. In April 2005, he had famously described the collapse of the Soviet Union as the "greatest geopolitical catastrophe of the twentieth century," and he had no qualms about celebrating Stalin's victory in World War II.[19] Putin made World War II into the cornerstone of a state-sponsored Russian identity—through holidays, processions, and popular culture.[20] At the same time, he had no affection for Vladimir Lenin or Mikhail Gorbachev. Lenin had succumbed to a romantic internationalism, giving semi-autonomous status, for example, to an invented political entity called Ukraine, and he had condemned the Soviet Union and Russia within it to the silliness of Marxism.[21] Stalin wrested geopolitical strength from the Leninist inheritance by sheer force of will, vaulting the Soviet Union over

Nazi Germany in 1945. Khrushchev and Brezhnev held onto the gains Stalin had won for the Soviet Union—namely, a European imperium. Gorbachev gambled it all away in demeaning displays of goodwill toward a West that wanted to expel Russia from the European garden. Gorbachev ended up a midwife of American, EU, and NATO primacy in Europe (East and West), throwing away the hard-won gains of both the Soviet Union and imperial Russia. Putin synthesized the radical striving of the Soviet Union and the reactionary striving of imperial Russia into what the historian Serhii Plokhy has astutely characterized as "the effort to revive a conservative utopia."[22]

Putin frequently appealed to history in the summer of 2021. He disagreed with those who saw in the Soviet Union's collapse an opportunity for Europe's long-suffering nation states, its "small" states.[23] The collapse of the Soviet Union had severed Ukraine from Russia. Had this involved only the western regions of Ukraine—the territory, say, around Lwiv, not far from the Polish border—it might have been tolerable. Instead, artificial borders drawn by Lenin had given an independent Ukraine its contours in 1991, cruelly separating a single people—Russians and Ukrainians. Kyiv, Odessa, Kharkiv, and Mariupol were Russian cities on Russian land, Putin argued. On this land lived Russians, who might have certain regional traits, traits that could be called Ukrainian or "little Russian" in nineteenth-century Russian parlance, quirks of speech or dress or cuisine, but these were not a separate people in either an ethnic or a political sense.[24] Progress would be achieved not by mindlessly affirming that every country was sovereign and independent: Russia needed to remove the artificial elisions and divisions to which an unjust history (and Western aggression) had subjected Russia. Putin was placing himself in the tradition of Russian leaders who had contested infringements on Russian land: the Mongols in the sixteenth century, the Polish-Lithuanian Commonwealth in the seventeenth century, Sweden in the eighteenth century, Napoleon's France in the nineteenth century, Nazi Germany and the twenty-first century West via the pro-Western "junta" it had established in Kyiv in 2014.[25] Dmitry Medvedev added a newspaper essay of his own in October, arguing that any further contact with the Ukrainian government was senseless. Putin's and Medvedev's ideas were extreme on their own terms, if one were to take them seriously as a roadmap for Russian foreign policy.[26] In the West, if his ideas made any sense at all, they were merely fumes from the imperial past, absurd and absurdly repellent.

Even in Russia, Putin's historical reasoning fell between the marginal and the eccentric in 2021. A dictator's ideas may be eccentric. They often are, but, if acted on, they are not marginal.

* * *

In his enthusiasm for guardrails, Joe Biden was never naive about Putin. He knew that Russia had come to mean too much in American life, that it could be a signifier of American decline, for evil in the world, for the anarchy eating away at international order. Biden had been very critical of Putin on the campaign trail, calling him a thug at one point. Yet as president he was intent on treating Russia as a country and not as a signifier. Putin was who he was, a thug in a world of thugs. With or without Putin, Russia had the potential to be a severe problem with Iran, its long-standing partner; with China, the Biden administration's overriding concern; with Turkey, a NATO ally of the United States that did an uncomfortable amount of business with Russia; with Israel, which depended on Russian permission to carry out military operations in Syria; and with Ukraine, where "Minsk" had never gotten off the ground and where Russian troops were stationed in Crimea and in the Donbas. The point of guardrails in the US-Russian relationship was not the expectation that they would make Russia friendlier or that they would inspire democratic change in Russia; the hope for a democratic Russia had died long ago. The point of guardrails was that Russia could cause a lot of harm. It could derail the Biden presidency. Preventive in nature, guardrails were less ambitious than the earlier metaphor of "offramps," the language of 2014, had been. To take an offramp is to change direction on an established grid. In 2021, avoiding accidents was the more prosaic intention.

Already in January 2021, at the outset of the Biden presidency, a victory for guardrails was notched. This was the signing of the START-2 treaty. Arms control had been the ballast of Cold War stability. It had been the form of cooperation possible while the United States and the Soviet Union fought multiple proxy wars against one another. In the late 1980s, arms control had brought President Reagan and General Secretary Gorbachev closer and closer together. Common action on non-proliferation continued on into the 1990s, similarly building bridges between Washington and Moscow. Somewhat recklessly, George W. Bush pulled the United States out of a few arms-control agreements with Russia, after which Obama and Medvedev brought arms control back to life. Russia assisted the Obama administration in Syria by joining with the United States to prevent Bashar al-Assad from using chemical weapons. (When al-Assad held onto his chemical weapons and continued to use them, Russian assistance proved to be superficial.) Arms control would fall victim to Putin's return in 2012 and to the mutual mistrust aroused in 2014. A self-styled deal maker fascinated by arms control, Trump could make little headway on this issue when he was president. Biden's and Putin's agreement to keep START-2 going looked like a step in the direction of probity and normalization. It took the temperature down by a few degrees.[27]

In early 2021, Ukraine was far from the headlines. Trump's first impeachment trial had been followed by a second impeachment trial—related to the January

6 riots, a domestic matter. Zelensky was not a political figure of international stature in 2021. If people outside Ukraine knew anything about him, it was that he was a former comedian or that he had been on the other end of the "perfect phone call" with Trump. The Biden administration's position toward Ukraine was to do no harm. Ukraine and Zelensky could be nudged toward greater anti-corruption activism, the painstaking work Vice President Biden had supervised between 2014 and 2016. President Biden did not prioritize Ukraine. There was no obvious gain for Biden in Ukraine, no political or diplomatic advantage in rethinking "Minsk" diplomacy, and within the United States there was minimal interest in Ukraine. The Russian soldiers showed no signs of leaving, and in any country anti-corruption ventures are a difficult slog. For Biden, the whole question of corruption in Ukraine had gotten tangled up in his son Hunter's public profile, the object of fantastic speculation concerning Hunter's laptop and the money he had earned in Ukraine while his father was vice president. Even though Hunter Biden had not been convicted of wrongdoing, Biden-Ukraine ties were not ones that the president wanted to highlight in the spring of 2021.

Much more in the headlines were China, Afghanistan, and the pandemic. A US-Chinese meeting in Alaska in March 2021, which featured a tense televised exchange of criticisms, suggested that China would be as thorny for Biden as it had been for Trump. Not unlike Putin, Xi Xinping was approaching dictatorial power in China, and he did not hide his hunger for Chinese greatness. For the United States, the two hot wars of the Cold War had both been in Asia (in Korea and Vietnam). Perhaps another such confrontation—this time over Taiwan—was brewing, a possibility on which the Biden administration was laser focused. Meanwhile, the war in Afghanistan was winding down for the United States. Twenty years in and the United States had not rewritten the code of Afghan politics. The Taliban had not been defeated, and the domestic political will to prosecute the war had steadily declined among Republicans and Democrats alike. Biden did not disagree with Trump about the need to end the war, plans for which were being drawn up as soon as Biden became president. And in the spring of 2021, the pandemic was still everywhere. For the past year, it had upended international politics, redefining the nature of state power, roiling supply chains, and massively increasing debt, not least for the United States and Europe. A responsible foreign policy would do much more to take public health into account than had been the case in the past. Two foreign-policy experts, Thomas Wright and Colin Kahl, both of whom would enter the Biden administration, co-authored a 2021 book about the pandemic, which they characterized as the end of the "old international order."[28] Such were the big-ticket problems at the start of the Biden administration.

Russia slowly wound its way back into the news in April 2021. Without explanation, it assembled a sizable buildup of troops and equipment on its border with

Ukraine. This was not accompanied by any recognizable diplomatic push. Russia was not setting terms and conditions. It was not offering anything, not objecting to anything. Whatever optimism had been felt in Moscow about the "peace candidate" in Ukraine's 2019 presidential election had come to dust by spring 2021. For this reason, it was hard to define the Russian military buildup as an effort to strongarm Volodymyr Zelensky, to get him to offer Russia concessions. It may, however, have been a response to Zelensky's "Crimea platform," to the arrest of Putin's friend, Viktor Medvedchuk, or to the uptick in enthusiasm for NATO membership that could be detected in Kyiv after Trump's retreat to Mar-a-Lago in January 2021. The Biden administration took note of the buildup and, interested in establishing guardrails, adopted an exploratory stance. It would be worth getting a clear sense of Putin's thinking and perhaps making a bit of a unilateral effort to move US-Russian relations toward "strategic stability," while taking competition and a clash of worldviews between Washington and Moscow as a given. Biden called Putin in April. In his public statements, he did not go out of his way to speak ill of Putin. His demeanor toward Putin was professional, and from the phone call came the idea of a summit meeting, not a rerun of the surreal Helsinki summit of 2018 and by no means a rerun of the amiable hamburger summit Obama and Medvedev had pulled off in the halcyon days of the reset.

Conciliatory gestures were apparent on both sides. Around Ukraine, Russia stood down in May. It did not withdraw all of the equipment it had amassed, and no Russian troops left the territory of Ukraine in 2021; Minsk was as unimplemented as it had ever been. Russia's moderation of tension could be explained in various ways: perhaps the buildup itself had been a feint, a means of instilling fear so that this fear could be employed for non-military purposes; or perhaps the buildup had been more menacing in nature but not menacing enough for Putin to forego a meeting with Biden. To get to Geneva he may have backed down in the late spring, or perhaps the spring buildup was a ruse, an effort to confuse onlookers when a second military initiative, the real one, would follow the first in the fall of 2021. In the spring, Putin's pull-back may have struck Washington as a small bit of positive momentum. Biden in turn held up $100 million of military aid that was destined for Ukraine.[29] By getting out of Berlin's way, he allowed Germany to go through with its cherished Nord Stream 2 pipeline project. Part of this gift to Germany was atonement for the Trump years, during which Germany in general and Angela Merkel in particular had been the frequent objects of White House wrath, but the approval of Nord Stream 2 was also a signal to Russia. Putin had not done much to earn a normalization with Europe. In Ukraine, he had certainly done nothing to accede to Europe's "Minsk" conditionality. Yet it was worth reminding him that a normalization with Europe was achievable. The United States was not so inflexible; it was not intent on weakening Russia. Bridges could still be built. If Russia were to begin good-faith negotiations over Ukraine and over European security, while scaling back its re-liance on military force, many more bridges could be built.

Before Biden and Putin would meet in person, Biden needed to put some ad-ditional space between himself and Trump. Trump had cozied up to Putin and needlessly alienated European countries. In this, Trump had been a presiden-tial anomaly. Never exactly the anti-Trump, Biden was temperate with Putin and moderate at the beginning of his presidential journey, but he was as warm in his embrace of Europe as Barack Obama had been in his second term. Nothing that Biden said about Europe was novel. Biden admired the European Union. He greatly valued the transatlantic relationship, and he went so far as to describe the US commitment to NATO as "sacred."[30] In the spring of 2021, shoring up the transatlantic relationship was a precondition to the search for guardrails with Russia. No warming of relations with Russia was to be achieved through the neglect of NATO or over the heads of the Europeans, very much including the government of Ukraine. Once Biden could show that he had won back the confidence of the Europeans, that as far as transatlantic relations were concerned everything was in place and that his word was good in Kyiv, he could meet with Putin. Biden planned his high-stakes Geneva meeting with Putin after a series of cordial conversations with European leaders. Pre-Trump these meetings would have been pro forma. Post-Trump they were newsworthy. Biden had a message for Europe, from which he would not be pivoting away, and it was a message to Moscow: the United States and its European allies stood in unison. America, as President Biden was fond of saying, was back. So too was the transatlantic relationship.

* * *

The Geneva summit came off nicely. It had an air of tradition to it, starting with the setting, the city of multiple Cold War summits—Eisenhower and Khrushchev in 1955, Reagan and Gorbachev in 1985. Biden and Putin spoke for several hours privately. No shoes were pounded on podiums, and the bickering into which Richard Nixon and Nikita Khrushchev descended—their "kitchen debate" of 1959—belonged to an acrimonious Cold War past. A striking detail of the Biden-Putin summit in Geneva was the respectful tone cultivated by both presidents. There was an absence of personal animus, something remarkable given the demonization of the United States in state-controlled Russian media, given Putin's loathing of Biden's previous boss, Barack Obama (and of Obama's secretary of state, Hillary Clinton), given Putin's long litany of grievances about US foreign policy and given Biden's prior descriptions of Putin as a killer and a thug. The congenial tone was remarkable after Putin's meddling in the 2016 election, after the outsized worries among many Americans that some secret Russian poison had entered the American body politic, and after the Russian media (and possibly Russian intelligence) had amplified narratives implicating Hunter Biden in international malfeasance. The Biden-Putin summit could so easily have failed. Instead, it was an exercise in diplomatic routine. The news from the summit was that there was no news, no personal fireworks, and no dramatic "deliverables." The small palace in which Putin and Biden met—in a library, with a globe between them, as if the two of them had just given a seminar on geopolitics—complemented the genteel tenor of the meeting itself. These were not two countries visibly heading over the precipice.

President Biden chose not to give a joint press conference with Putin. That had happened three years earlier in Helsinki, when Trump had served up the most vivid diplomatic embarrassment in American history. Putin gave his press conference indoors. He showed his competitive edge by presenting himself as an elder statesman, a man of experience and of stamina, who could withstand a barrage of tough questions from the international media. At times cogent, at times rambling, he drove home a well-worn narrative of unacceptable NATO expansion. Least acceptable of all, Putin argued, was a Western military presence moving east in its partnerships and training exercises and moving east via Ukraine. This part of Putin's press conference was a clue to his future actions. Biden, who was gaffe-prone at times and who could get tongue-tied, held his press conference outdoors, the silvers and greens of the Swiss summer as his background, and he put on an excellent performance. He outlined those areas in which he was critical of Putin and on which he had his disagreements—Russia's democratic deficits and its violations of its neighbors' sovereignty. Biden was entirely un-Trump-like in his sticking to preset talking points. He was not dismissive of Putin or of the meeting he had just had with the Russian president. Biden was rolling up his sleeves in Geneva, making it apparent that he could accomplish something with Vladimir Putin.[31]

Practically speaking, what came from Geneva was the establishment of various US-Russian working groups. One was devoted to cyber security on the correct premise that in 2021 cyber was a domain of inter-state anarchy. There were long annals of arms control: there were no annals of cyber control. The United States and Russia were two cyber superpowers that had already collided in cyberspace, and it made sense to look into mutually acceptable rules. Another working group was devoted to "strategic stability." It was an accurate and revealing term intended not to imply a reset. The 2008 reset had been about cooperation and, even in the eyes of those who most ardently believed in it, about the eventual convergence of Russia and the United States. Medvedev would bring Silicon Valley to Russia, and on that basis an architecture of similarity could be built, resolving the foreign-policy tensions between Moscow and Washington. Strategic stability required no such high hopes. It required no actual cooperation, and it anticipated no eventual convergence. Russia would presumably remain Russia while America was back, according to the president, it was itself again—as dedicated to Europe, to democracy, to NATO, and to Ukrainian sovereignty and independence as it had ever been. A technique for managing the necessary collisions, strategic stability would curb the unnecessary collisions, much as the Russian and US militaries had successfully practiced de-confliction in Syria (since 2015). Strategic stability was the construction of guardrails par excellence.

That autumn, the working groups followed up on the mandate set for them in Geneva. An eerie calm fell on US-Russian relations, which Putin described in October 2021 as "on the right track."[32] Did Vladimir Putin go to Geneva knowing that he would be waging a brutal war against Ukraine in February 2022? Or was Putin making up his mind, probing for concessions from the West so that *the West* could normalize its relations with Russia and thus begin to deal with its internal economic tribulations, its political polarization, its military misadventures in Afghanistan and the Middle East and with the punishingly large challenge presented by China? When did Putin make up his mind? It is a question in search of evidence. Less elusive was the split-screen quality to the fall of 2021. While working groups met and did the tedious work of day-to-day diplomacy, while the Biden administration could still believe that a few guardrails had been put in place after a strange episode of military posturing in the spring, preparations for war were intensifying in Moscow. Putin's summertime speeches and writing about Ukraine could seem a hostile footnote to the harmonious Swiss summit, the self-indulgence of an aging autocrat. In Geneva, Putin had been workmanlike and non-confrontational. In other settings that summer, Putin's alter ego, his other political self, had been speaking viciously about Ukraine. It was the Geneva summit—alas—that had been the footnote to Putin's summertime speeches and writing. In those speeches and essays, hiding in plain sight, was the key to the coming war.

8

Removing the Guardrails

At the same time, the idea of Ukrainian people as a nation separate from the Russians started to form and gain ground among the Polish elite and a part of the Malorussian intelligentsia. Since there was no historical basis—and could not have been any, conclusions were substantiated by all sorts of concoctions, which went as far as to claim that the Ukrainians are the true Slavs and the Russians, the Muscovites, are not—such "hypotheses" became increasingly used for political purposes as a tool of rivalry between European states.

Vladimir Putin, "On the Historical Unity of Russians and Ukrainians," an article published on July 12, 2021[1]

The Soviet Union had been heavily invested in the motif of American decline. A bold step forward, the Bolshevik Revolution defined itself against the decadence of capitalism and the carnage of World War I, which it blamed on the malice of the capitalist great powers. Nowhere was capitalist decadence more potent than in the United States, that land of inequality, exploitation, and racism, and the stock market crash of 1929 confirmed this hypothesis. The United States and the Soviet Union were allies from 1941 to 1945. It was hard to portray the world's preeminent superpower, which is what the United States became in the 1950s, as mired in decline, but the motif returned with the Vietnam War, which many Americans interpreted as the cause or the symptom of national decline. The intensity of political protest in the 1960s and 1970s and the persistence of racial inequality in the United States reinforced long-standing Soviet tropes of American decline. Watergate contributed its bit to the declinist narrative. So did the association of the word *malaise* with the presidency of Jimmy Carter. The Soviet Union began to struggle with the story of American decline when its own decline intruded—at some imperceptible point in the 1970s. Declining living standards merged with Leonid Brezhnev's advancing senility, and by 1985 the Soviet Union was openly admitting the need for reform, a less visible effort to restore vigor to Soviet life, and an unspoken effort to catch up with the West. Ronald Reagan organized his political career around the image of a declining Soviet Union and an ascendant United States, "morning in America" as he put it in his 1984 campaign. Back and forth the Cold War argument about rise and fall continued to go.

A man with one foot in the Soviet past, Putin had come of age with these twentieth-century ideological battles. In the regime he constructed over the course of two decades, he comfortably synthesized Soviet, pre-Soviet, and post-Soviet elements. The Russian government could rehabilitate the memory of Soviet heroes; it could burnish the posthumous reputation of the KGB; and it could promote the Russian Orthodox Church as a respected institution, as if traditional Russian and Soviet values were one and the same, products of the same heritage.[2] Working off this synthesis, Kremlin officials could lament NATO expansion, the record of US-sponsored colored revolutions and the overall en-circlement of Russia by the West, which had crossed a line by trying to include Ukraine in this encirclement in 2014. It could lament the pushiness of the West and the resources the "collective West" might marshal against Russia. At the same time, Kremlin officials could contend that an aggressive West was nevertheless weak, effete, polarized, and fragmenting, and that the West was in the grips of chronic decline. An advantage of the declinist narrative in post-Soviet Russia was its prior use. To those who had grown up in the Soviet Union, the prospect of American or Western decline—cultural decline, political decline, and above all geopolitical decline—had pedigree. To what extent Putin himself subscribed to this narrative is hard to know. It is probable, though, that for Putin the narrative of decline was not just a tool for manipulation. Having proclaimed it over the years, he may have come by 2022 to believe it, or he may have proclaimed it be-cause he believed it. Had he thought the West to be ascendant, he might not have dispensed with the guardrails seemingly being erected in 2021.[3]

The Kremlin's claims about Western cultural decline were conservative in tone. A self-indulgent secularism had detached the West from its Christian traditions, fostering a West that was sexually deranged. This claim harmonized with the Kremlin's own cultural leanings, especially after Putin's conserva-tive turn in 2012, and it was intended to speak to right-leaning constituencies within the West, which to a certain extent it did in the 2010s and 2020s.[4] The claim about the West's political decline heightened points that were conventional wisdom in the West after Brexit and after Trump's election: that the social con-tract was disintegrating into civic antagonisms.[5] Whether it referenced the *gilets jaunes* (yellow vests) in France, to disruptive violence from the Left or the Right in the United States or to the January 6 riots, the story of protest and division was easy enough to tell. Without any help from the Kremlin, Western media were preoccupied with this very story of unrest and dissension, which Russian diplomats, journalists and influencers had an easy time broadcasting for their own purposes. Yet Putin's own interpretation of this divide went beyond the con-ventional wisdom in the West. Putin did not fret about there being too little de-mocracy, too little rule of law, too little civic activism, too little constitutional patriotism in the United States or elsewhere. He blamed democracy itself for the ills that had befallen the West. Democracies were unstable and inconstant, Putin argued, though he did not really defend authoritarianism as such. He praised the solidity and strategic acumen of "unified" states like Russia and China, states that did not get distracted by democratic meandering, states in which the will of the leader and the will of people were organically fused and states that were therefore not in decline.

The Kremlin's theses about Western geopolitical decline silhouette the 2022 invasion of Ukraine. In the official Russian narrative, the two sides of the West, Europe and the United States, each had distinct flaws. Europe's decline was mirrored in its dependence on the United States, its lack of real decision-making power, and its general fecklessness. The United States had decision-making power, it had economic and military assets that Russia did not have, but for all its wealth and for all its sophisticated technology the United States had no idea how to use its raw power. This, in part, had been Putin's point at the 2007 Munich Security Conference. By attacking Iraq, the United States had destabilized the Middle East. It had applied its power foolishly, a critique that echoed in Moscow after the 2011 NATO bombing campaign in Libya. Having abused its power, the United States did not stay the course. It had entered Iraq with the grandest ambitions, but when the going got tough it pulled back, and when the American population tired of the war, which by 2008 it had, voters elected a president who did not believe in the war, turning American foreign policy inside out. Trump the anti-internationalist was elected after Obama, turning everything inside out once again. As Putin told an audience of Duma leaders in July 2022 (four months into the war), what is happening is "the beginning of the cardinal breakdown of the American-style world order. . . . This is the beginning of the transition from liberal-globalist American egocentrism to a truly multipolar world."[6] The United States and Europe had both been adamant about Ukraine's sovereignty and independence in 2014. They had bragged about their sanctions and waited for Russia to come around, after which they did not do much about Ukraine or about "Minsk" diplomacy. The United States had a short attention span, Putin suggested. If it did not win as it had in the First Gulf War—quickly and absolutely—it was prone to slip free from its commitments and its stated principles.

To the extent that he was aware of such declinist narratives, Joe Biden did not put much stock in them. They were little more than the propaganda of a resentful country. Without a persuasive international vision of its own, Russia was reduced to taking potshots at the time-tested vision of the United States. Regardless of sour grapes in the Kremlin, though, Biden had to manage the perception of US decline in his first year as president. Biden had to acknowledge that the Trump presidency had been four years of self-inflicted and high-profile degradation. Belief in American decline was widespread internationally in ways that were hard for most Americans to accept, however critical they were of Trump. Biden knew that Trump had imposed lasting damage on American-led alliances, that Trump had pulled out of the agreement on nuclear non-proliferation with Iran, the "Iran deal," that Trump had pulled out of the Paris climate accords, that Trump had pulled the United States out from the World Health Organization during a global pandemic. Biden could not erase Trump's record of praise for autocracy and for autocrats. Nor could Biden promise that Trump would never return to power. Neither could the US Congress, which impeached Trump twice but refused to convict him either time. After staging a coup on January 6, Trump was free to run for reelection in 2024, and from Mar-a-Lago Trump continued to dominate the Republican Party, his popularity not much reduced. Biden had to prove that America was back, not just to allies but also to adversaries inclined to believe the worst of the United States; this in a way was Biden's most important audience. Always vigilant for evidence of American decline, Putin would subject the United States to a series of tests in the fall of 2021, removing guardrail after guardrail. Before he did so, he would witness two separate debacles for Washington: one in Afghanistan and the other related to Australia. Each happened to substantiate the appearance of American weakness and of a dysfunctional transatlantic relationship.

* * *

Withdrawal from Afghanistan had checked multiple boxes for the Trump administration. It was an end to the "stupidity" of American foreign policy under George W. Bush and Barack Obama, under foreign-policy elites who had inflicted their crusades on an beleaguered country, lining their pockets while problems festered at home. Stepping out from Afghanistan would show that the United States was not responsible for everything everywhere, that human rights had little to do with actual American interests, and that government spending could be redirected from Afghans to Americans. Vowing to pull out from Afghanistan was also a domestic political initiative for Trump. He was a president of courage, able to stand up to Washington's smug globalists. He could shunt them aside and drag the country in another direction, acting on the "America first" theme of his 2016 campaign. By slipping into nation building in Afghanistan, no less than in Iraq, George W. Bush and Barack Obama had put America second, Trump was saying, explaining not just the misery of these two "forever wars" but the ruined state of less affluent American communities, precisely the kinds of communities that had gotten Trump elected (in the Midwest and elsewhere) and to which, as president, he often addressed himself. Less specifically, curtailing the US military role in Afghanistan was popular among Republicans and Democrats. On Afghanistan, Trump did not just shape the national mood. He channeled it.

A curiosity of the Trump administration was that he did not himself withdraw the United States from Afghanistan. He set a timetable for withdrawal, and he started negotiations with the Taliban, going so far as to propose a Camp David meeting on the eighteenth anniversary of September 11. In February 2020, Trump worked out a deal with the Taliban for US withdrawal. Whether intentionally or not, he left quite a mess for the Biden administration, which was not less receptive to the national mood than the Trump administration had been. Biden could see the foreign-policy prudence of ending the US war in Afghanistan. Counterterrorism was far from the guiding principle of American foreign policy in 2021, and to deal with China, the United States would have to husband its resources carefully. The nation-building campaign had long ago foundered in Afghanistan, which had a president, an army, a capital city, and a sizable foreign presence pumping money into the economy. The situation facing the Western-leaning Afghan government was tenuous in a country long devastated by war and subject to cross-border influence from both Pakistan and a bevy of Middle Eastern states. Smashed to pieces by the United States in 2002, the Taliban had regrouped and was gradually winning back territory, putting it in the position to negotiate with the United States and, over time, to take the capital city of Kabul if not the entire country. For the United States to get out of Afghanistan, which Trump was eager to do, it would have to lose the war, which Trump did not at all want to do and which Obama before him had not wanted to do either.

The misfortune of being the president in charge when the twenty-year war in Afghanistan came to an end befell Joe Biden. His alternative was to send in tens of thousands of additional troops. In the spring of 2021, the Taliban was holding back because the United States was *not* widening the war. The war was terminating with a negotiated settlement not about the contours of Afghanistan's political future but about the departure of the United States and its allies. An increase in troops would have sparked direct confrontations with the Taliban, but that was not the worst of it for the Biden administration. An increase in troops would have been politically unpalatable at home, and it would have come with no guarantee of a better outcome in Afghanistan where US political objectives had failed well before Trump was elected. Afghanistan had not created a strong enough state or a strong enough army, and it had not created sufficient political legitimacy for either the state or the army. Billions and billions of dollars had disappeared into Afghanistan through inefficiency and corruption.[7] The horrors of a twenty-year war had made the United States unpopular in many parts of Afghanistan, something on which the Taliban had capitalized during its gradual military advance across the country. Ten thousand or twenty thousand additional US troops would do nothing to change a political project that may have been impossible to begin with. By 2021, Biden was well versed in the limitations that a twenty-year war had imposed on the United States.[8]

The Biden administration contributed to inherited woes by making mistakes of its own in Afghanistan. It inaccurately predicted the end phase of the war. The White House promised there would be no scenes of abrupt withdrawal from Kabul as there had been in Saigon in 1975, in the humiliating final days of the Vietnam War.[9] When Ashraf Ghani fled the country in August 2021, the United States was caught in a bind. There would be no well-run transition because there would be no transition at all. There would be a mad dash to get out, replete with endless images of panicked US officials and bedlam on the ground. Another mistake, a consequence of the first, was spotty communication with allies. Since the United States was the major military power in Afghanistan, the absence of the United States terrified Europeans stranded there—after the Taliban suddenly took Kabul. Their protection had vanished overnight, and European countries did not have the airlift capacity of the United States, making it hard for them to get their citizens out. In the wake of this dispiriting turn of events, the indictment of the United States ranged from incompetence to unreliability. Trump had conducted himself selfishly, unconcerned about insulting or injuring his European counterparts, brandishing his affection for America first. Biden had been gracious, even solicitous of US allies. He was polite and friendly, a man of acumen and experience elected to extract the United States from the madness of the Trump era. At this moment of truth, though, Biden too had shown what America first could mean. In an inversion of the anecdote, in which Putin sought guidance in 1989 and learned only that Moscow "was silent," in August 2021 it was Washington that was silent.

Afghanistan could be unkindly construed as typical of American foreign policy. When the Vietnam War had proven too exhausting, the United States pulled out, leaving its partner, South Vietnam, on its own. South Vietnam quickly collapsed, leaving North Vietnam in control of the whole country. In Iraq, the United States never entirely pulled out, but it only half accomplished what it set out to do, and over time it seemed to lose interest. In Libya, the United States and NATO had undertaken military strikes meant to prevent mass atrocities, honoring its self-declared responsibility to protect the vulnerable. The result was Libya's further political dissolution, and yet again Washington turned its attention elsewhere. Libya was far from the United States, and bringing order to Libya would have been immensely costly. Judged critically, the weakness of American foreign policy was its mixture of overconfidence, poor planning, and an impatience that stemmed from domestic American politics, from the desire for influence without cost and gain without sacrifice, from periods of frenetic action followed by long stretches of distraction and self-absorption.[10] Not a few Americans were sensitive to these critiques of American foreign policy. Putin embraced them—he had made these critiques often enough himself—to which he added his own overabundant envy and grievance vis-à-vis the United States.

Putin was personally invested in a United States that was unable to do what it said it would do.

Another scandal broke a month after the pullout from Afghanistan. Since the spring of 2021, the Biden administration had been quietly preparing for the sale of nuclear submarines to Australia, a means of strengthening Australia's hand against China. A third country in these discussions was the United Kingdom. Australia, the United Kingdom, and the United States (AUKUS) are very close allies, and their collaboration on Australia's naval development would have been uncontroversial, had Australia not had a preexisting contract with France and had this contract not stood in the way of finalizing a deal with Washington and London. France was informed of the AUKUS submarine deal only at the end of the negotiations, and it felt betrayed. The whole affair was not much more than the ruffling of diplomatic feathers, and by the winter it would be forgotten. The damage was to France's pride, not to any of its core interests, but coming on the heels of the mess in Afghanistan, which was *the* international news flash of the preceding period, the AUKUS story told itself: too clumsy to manage its alliances, America was not back. That September, a new wave of COVID infections washed over the United States, the Omicron variant, complicating the Biden administration's argument that vaccines had quelled the pandemic and that the post-pandemic safe haven had been reached. Biden's approval ratings took a sizable hit between August and September, from which they would never again recover. Between the foreign-policy and the public-health crises, the White House was struggling to project the expertise that had been Biden's selling point as a presidential candidate. For those who wished, Biden's age could be brought up against him at moments of difficulty. It could be used to bolster the sentiment that the United States was a superpower in decline. By trying to accentuate his own stamina in Geneva, Putin had highlighted this sentiment when he met with Biden before the Afghanistan pull-out and before AUKUS.

* * *

Only a few months after the Geneva summit, Putin once again gave himself the option of invading Ukraine. Three explanations can be put forward for Putin's decision-making in October 2021 and for his ultimate decision to wage war. They are not mutually exclusive, and very likely all three played a role in the decision. The first concerns timing and Putin's fear that Ukraine was slipping away. That was the essential problem, which derived from Yanukovych's decision to run away from Kyiv in February 2014, the moment Russia lost its informal influence over the Ukrainian government. The second explanation concerns perceived US and European disarray, while Ukraine, a mere puppet of the West after the Maidan, as Putin often said, had a former comedian as president: a lightweight in Kyiv, an array of lightweights in European capitals, and a less than intimidating

American president who had at best only one half of the country behind him. That was the opportunity. The third explanation for Putin's decision to invade is Russia-centric. Putin had faith in himself, in his military, and in the Russian people. Together they had been going from strength to strength since the annexation of Crimea. They were culturally and politically united, and they were willing to sacrifice for the common good in a way that the decadent West—postnational, post-religious, post-traditional, post-sacrifice—was not. Together, the Russian people and the Russian state, which were really the same thing, would win the war. That was surely the prediction.

While going from strength to strength in his own eyes, Putin was by his own admission losing Ukraine. Yanukovych and his likes were not coming back. Apart from go-betweens like Medvedchuk, who had been arrested in February 2021, and apart from the intelligence assets on Moscow's payroll, Russia had little sway in Ukraine. The Donetsk and Luhansk People's Republics were costly burdens to Moscow, consuming resources while providing no meaningful diplomatic leverage. Neither Kyiv nor the West was going to offer Russia concessions for the sake of bringing these territories back under Ukrainian control: Minsk diplomacy had been a road to nowhere for the West, for Ukraine, and for Russia, a finely worded non-solution to a grave set of problems. The annexation of Crimea had been a stroke of genius, Putin could assure himself, but Crimea's status was still uncertain; it was internationally unrecognized, even by China, and the Russian occupation of Crimea was not at all accepted by Ukraine. In a classic imperial dilemma, Putin had expanded his territorial possessions only to find that he now had more to worry about, more to defend, more to make secure. The protection of newly acquired territory fostered the need to acquire more territory. At the same time, the march to the West promised on the Maidan had continued under President Poroshenko. It was speeding up with Zelensky, not least because of the proudly pro-Ukraine government in Washington, the very opposite of what Putin would have enjoyed in a second Trump term. If by October 2021 Putin had not yet made up his mind to invade, he was steadily foreclosing his other options and almost forcing himself in the direction of war. He would continue foreclosing options through a bizarrely experimental diplomacy in December 2021 and January 2022.

Putin must have assumed that the invasion would succeed and that a triumphant invasion would at the very least decapitate Ukraine's leadership, if not its very statehood. For that reason, taking Kyiv would be pivotal to the invasion. It would solve multiple problems, enabling Russian control of eastern and southern Ukraine. Without a functioning government in Kyiv, Ukraine's military and state capacity would melt away. (Contemplating this scenario, Putin may have thought back to February and March of 2014, when a paralyzed Ukrainian state eased Russia's annexation of Crimea.) Control of eastern and southern Ukraine would ensure the security of Crimea, binding it to Russia, while a rump Ukraine, having lost much of its economic base, could be handed over to the West. If Poland and Hungary were to pursue territorial claims in this remnant of Ukraine, as they might be tempted to do, then all the better. In a neo-imperial Eastern European free for all, whatever had been said about sovereignty and about the independence of "small" countries in Europe would be consigned to the hazy American-led past. Russia would be at home and at ease in this brave new world of partition, annexation, cross-border interference, and erasable borders. Committed to very different rules, the United States would be lost, scrambling to catch up. In Putin's perception, Russia had been living in this age since 1991, as countries like Moldova, Georgia, Ukraine, and Syria could attest. A future of contestation might be bloody and full of risk, but for Moscow it was preferable to a future in which Ukraine would be a prospering member of the triumphalist Western club.

Anxiety about Ukraine's ties to the West may have mingled with Putin's low opinion of the West. To a degree, Putin's references to Western decadence were staged.[11] Though the image of Western decadence had its utility within and outside of Russia, as it had had for the Soviet Union, Putin had to know that Russia was not a hyper-religious, traditionalist society like Saudi Arabia or Iran or Afghanistan under the Taliban. Much of the lamented Western decadence was not at all foreign to Russia, where church attendance was low, abortion rates were high, and where young people claimed for themselves many of the personal and sexual freedoms that young people claimed in the West. (Putin was himself separated from his wife and reputed to have multiple mistresses and unacknowledged children.) Yet Putin's low opinion of the West—in the realm of foreign policy and war—was not just theatrics. It had formed in the years between 2003 and 2007, when Putin turned his back on the United States. It could have been based on perceptions of Western arrogance, a not uncommon perception in Russia. The West thought too much of itself. It overplayed its hand. It made claims in Ukraine that it could not back up, as it had in Libya, Syria, Afghanistan, and Iraq. The West lived in a cloud of self-flattery, in a foreign-policy la-la land, an eternal 1990s in which its enemies were always getting swept into the dustbin of history and the West was always winning the day. When reality intruded on this idealized self-image, the West turned and ran. Then it pretended its mistakes had never happened and moved on. The August 2021 exit from Afghanistan was tailor made to encourage Putin's low opinion of the United States and the West, for in Afghanistan the Europeans had not been able to correct the American mistakes; they had gone along with them. The summer events in Afghanistan mattered less than the twenty-year war in Afghanistan, which likely confirmed an understanding of American power conducive to Putin's crystallizing war aims.[12]

Other disparaging points about the West may have impressed themselves on Putin in 2021. The West had a leadership void. Angela Merkel left the chancellery in December 2021, and her absence was felt across Europe. A case could be made for Europe as tangled up in itself, divided into a half that championed the European Union and NATO, that believed in the mantras of European integration (including Ukraine's integration into Europe) and of the liberal international order. This was the Europe of the elites, while Europe's non-elite half longed for greater national belonging, for less cosmopolitanism and migration, for a return to borders and for more traditional values. This was the Europe of Viktor Orban, Silvio Berlusconi, and to a degree of Boris Johnson. It was the Europe of strengthening populist and right-wing movements, of the AfD in Germany, the alternative for Germany, which when it first became popular in 2015 was the alternative to Angela Merkel. If this polarized Europe was not just a caricature, then Russia could divide and conquer in Europe as it had tried to do before 2022 with issues like migration. Make the elites the owners of a costly commitment to Ukraine and see if the common folk would push in the other direction, splintering Europe and the transatlantic relationship alike. The West could wage war so long as the effects were not palpable, so long as it could feel good about its far-away efforts. The moment trials and tribulations arrived in the form of war or of its side effects, the West's celebrated democracy would give people the chance to air their complaints, to which the politicians would have to pay heed.

Back in the 1980s, the whole structure of Soviet power had been flimsier than it seemed. The Soviet leadership fell out of touch with the people, not in the glory days of World War II or amid postwar economic growth but in the later decades of the twentieth century. The West had intelligently capitalized on Soviet decay, and in places like Poland or the Baltic Republics there was a well of national sentiment to be tapped into—to dispossess Moscow of its empire. Mikhail Gorbachev had been the ultimate out-of-touch Soviet elite, and power had slipped through his uncalloused fingers. These were circumstances that could with some imagination be applied to the West in 2021. The United States was overextended globally. Its power was a thing of the past in ways that Washington did not recognize or accept. Perhaps the whole transatlantic setup was a sham, the project of a geriatric coterie of elites. Trump had taken a hammer to the edifice of NATO, and Britain had taken a hammer to the EU in the summer of 2016. An unexpected push might still bring it all down. If the promises given to Ukraine after 2014 could be proven hollow, the West would not only have betrayed Ukraine. The West's own elites might fall, and Putin could have the satisfaction of watching from Moscow while a populist 1989, a 1989 in reverse, made its way across Europe and the United States. There was only one precondition for the dream of a "Western Spring," if Putin were entertaining one in 2021. For it to come about, Russia's invasion of Ukraine would have to go according to plan.

The foil to a decadent West was a resurgent Russia. Barack Obama had denigrated Russia as a regional power. The West had a habit of condescending to Russia: an economic basket case, a stillborn democracy without Ukraine's love of freedom, a bully on the international stage but not even a very effective bully, "upper Volta with nukes," as some were fond of saying. Czarist Russia had declined into revolution in 1917. The Soviet Union had declined into non-existence in 1991, and post-Soviet Russia could not shake this indigenous curse of backwardness: Russia's progress was always behind the progress of the West.[13] Such condescension had enough truth to it to anger Putin, and he wanted to disprove or to turn this condescension against itself, as he did by opining on Western decline, but Putin had reasons other than sticking it to the West to think that Russia was resurgent. Putin's insulation from party politics and from elections, his long years in power and his gradual accumulation of a dictator's prerogatives, had to be relevant to his state of mind when he was deciding whether to invade Ukraine. Alexei Navalny had lamented—with data—that Putin was robbing Russia blind, that Russia's priorities should be domestic reform rather than foreign wars; and Navalny could be silenced. Putin was under no obligation to debate Navalny in public. Instead, Putin could manipulate the public through state-controlled media, which over and over again told the story of a post-Soviet Russia lost to misrule and despair until Vladimir Putin came to the rescue. At work and in his private life, Putin was surrounded by figures who had much to gain from convincing him of Russia's resurgence and of his own strategic intelligence. The information that flowed to the top of the Kremlin could be massaged in such a way as to reinforce what Putin wished to believe about himself, as underlings directed and responded to the needs of his ego. In their day-to-day functioning, all dictatorships are structured to justify and to flatter the cherished convictions of the dictator.

Within the vortex of Kremlin sycophancy, Putin could employ accurate and inaccurate information to describe Russia's resurgence. The accurate information was as follows: a dramatic economic expansion, starting in 2000 and owing quite a bit to higher oil prices; a victory in the second Chechen war, resulting in a hard stop to the conflict; a standoff with the United States over Georgia in 2008 in which Russia did not back down; the bloodless annexation of Crimea in 2014; the restoration of Russia's great-power status in the Middle East through an operation in Syria that was inexpensive for Russia; the carrying out of one of the world's most successful active measures in the United States in 2016, which caused genuine and lasting harm to the American political system; and the expansion of Russia's economic presence in Europe after 2014, despite what Americans and Europeans had said about no more "business as usual" with Russia. Inaccurate information swirled around Russia's military modernization, a project very dear to Putin's heart. This modernization made Russia's international resurgence possible, but a lot of it was heroic in the abstract and woeful in reality. Rampant corruption and cooking of the books were as endemic to Putinism as they are to most authoritarian systems. A lot of the money poured into the military poured out into the bank accounts of middlemen and of the military brass. Here the relative absence of investigative journalism or of parliamentary oversight was a drag on Putinism, a drag on what Putin wished to accomplish for Russia. What mattered in the fall of 2021, though, was not the military's real-life inadequacies; that would matter later. What mattered was the military Putin thought he had. On its supposed excellence, he would make his decisions about war and peace.[14]

Russia's military resurgence had dovetailed with its diplomatic resurgence. The Soviet Union had been a global power with the diplomatic infrastructure to match, and it had embraced what was known in the Cold War as the "third world," a raft of mostly post-colonial countries that were not wealthy enough to be the West in the way that Japan and Australia were the West and that did not necessarily back the Western side of the Cold War.[15] India was a paradigmatically non-aligned country during the Cold War, one with notable pro-Soviet leanings. The Soviet Union built networks of affiliation across Africa and the Middle East. It had partners in Cuba and North Vietnam, and until the Sino-Soviet split of the early 1960s, Mao's China and the Soviet Union walked hand in hand. This world vanished in 1991, when the Soviet Union itself vanished. Putin could not bring it back, but he could employ the muscle memory of his diplomatic corps to cultivate relationships beyond Europe and the United States. Russia's turn from the West in 2014 and the West's break with Russia accelerated the process. Arms sales, construction of nuclear power plants, gas and oil, Russian voting at the UN, the deployment of Russian media, the insertion of Russian mercenaries into conflict zones: Putin could use these tools to make friends and influence people, a long-term project that was by no means a failure for Russia. Across the globe, Russia was making significant inroads between 2014 and 2021.[16] They would pay dividends in 2022 and 2023.

Russia's preeminent partnership, pushed ahead by Putin after 2014, was with China. China was no substitute for the Europe Russia had labored to enter in the 1990s. It did not have the cultural or the lifestyle attraction that Europe did, but Russia did not "lose" Europe in 2014. Not that much had changed with the annexation of Crimea. Via the massive Chinese economy, Beijing had forms of leverage unavailable to Moscow, which was an in-built tension between the two countries, but asymmetrical as the China-Russia relationship was, it had its benefits for Russia. China could augment Russia's position by relieving worries about its eastern and southern borders, by providing Russia with markets unencumbered by Western sanctions, by expressing a disdain for American power or American "hegemony" similar to the Kremlin's, and by having a political system loosely compatible with Russia's. In Beijing, human rights and democracy were not the stumbling blocks for Russia that they were for the West. Xi Xinping, China's president since 2013, had a messianic view of China's destiny that matched Putin's aspirations for Russia. China's economic growth and military modernization, supervised by a leader who ruled his country with an iron fist, could signify that China was not decadent and dissolute, that its purchase on the geopolitical configurations of the twenty-first century was solid—far more solid than that of the faltering United States or the cosseted European Union. China and Russia did not speak of an alliance. They would not go to war together in Ukraine or in Taiwan. They would serve as a backstop to one another as the confrontations with the West mounted. Putin's working relationship with Xi Jinping was an arrow in his quiver. Russia was not to be isolated, Putin had declared, and the West's inability to understand this was a sign of its excessive self-regard, of its own mental isolation.[17]

* * *

In October 2021, Putin ordered a second military buildup. He had no way to hide it from prying eyes. The United States had superb capacities for satellite surveillance, and social media endangered many forms of secrecy. The movement of equipment and materiel was bound to show up on Russian social media, making it known to the world. The scale of the invasion Putin had in mind made the invasion's organization highly visible. (Some of the equipment that would be used in the February 2022 invasion had been left there in April 2021, when the troops were withdrawn from the border, ostensibly resolving this crisis.) To maintain the element of surprise under conditions of unavoidable transparency, Putin had to obscure his intentions. It helped that he had conducted a military buildup back in April and had not followed through to actual hostilities. Maybe the October movements were a repeat of the spring performance, a cat-and-mouse game in which the cat, without ever making a move, would always be on the verge of pouncing. It helped greatly that for so many people a large-scale invasion of Ukraine was unthinkable in 2021. That it was unthinkable for so many Russians was tacitly helpful for Putin as well. Russia was not at all on a wartime footing in October 2021. True, Putin had written some harsh words about Ukraine over the summer and he was moving around his armies, but did this really portend war? Until February 24, 2022, Putin's will to deceive would often hit the mark. A hard-to-read Kremlin allowed those who could not believe in a major European war not to believe that a major European war was coming.

One place where Putin's deceptions did not hit their intended mark was in President Biden's White House.

Twice in the recent past, the United States had gotten thrown off course by Russian obfuscation. In Crimea, Russian soldiers operated without insignia in 2014, the "little green men" who seemed to materialize from within Crimea. That these were Russian soldiers was not hard to tell, and everyone knew that the spring referendum was not real. Yet Moscow's obfuscation gave Western governments the excuse of having been confused. Crimea had not been invaded as Poland had been invaded by Nazi Germany in 1939 or Serbia had been invaded by Austria-Hungary in 1914. Something else had happened in Crimea, something indistinct. A West that did not want to consider war with Russia could file the annexation of Crimea under a label other than war—an illegal annexation or an example of "hybrid war," a series of maneuvers occurring somehow more in the media landscape than on the battlefield. Russia's second experiment in obfuscation came in 2016, when election meddling was conducted through layers of misdirection. It was not Russian intelligence handing information over to the American media. It was Wikileaks putting out newsworthy information. Abetted by a shameless presidential candidate, the American news media struggled and mostly failed to distinguish between inter-state meddling and everyday political news, which compromised the government's ability to explain what was happening. By the time the US government attributed the meddling to Russia, in October 2016, the damage had been done. Hiding the source of the meddling—to the extent that Russia could in 2016 and thereafter—drove political polarization in the United States. Even to call it meddling could imply a partisan affiliation, and all along Trump was engaged in obfuscations of his own making. From 2014 to 2021, misdirection had worked for Russia. It had worked exceptionally well.

Fortuitously, the White House was in a self-critical mood in the fall of 2021. The messy US pull-out from Afghanistan called into question two separate capabilities: harnessing intelligence and cooperating with allies. On the fall of the Ghani government in Kabul, the Biden administration had erred on the side of Ghani staying in power until 2022 or 2023. Too few questions had been asked about the likelihood of Ghani's government crumbling quickly. It was less an intelligence failure, since the future is impossible to predict, than a failure to use intelligence imaginatively, to game out all the possible scenarios. On alliance maintenance, the Biden administration had been too pleased with itself for not being the Trump administration. It had been too reliant on its gestures of esteem and respect toward Europe, on its verbal commitments to the liberal international order, on the administration's many personal bonds of career and friendship with European leaders and diplomats. Having not prodded the intelligence community to work through the darker eventualities in Afghanistan, the Biden administration had not worked through these eventualities in tandem with its NATO allies. In the rush to get out and not to lose too many American lives in the process, the United States left its European allies feeling shunted aside. The transatlantic goodwill that had amassed since Biden's inauguration in January dissipated in August 2021, and for France it dissipated further with the AUKUS scandal of the early fall.

While assessing the second Russian buildup in early October, the Biden administration took to heart several lessons from the past.[18] Many Biden administration officials had worked in the Obama administration: National Security Advisor Jake Sullivan, Deputy National Security Advisor Jon Finer, Secretary of State Antony Blinken, CIA Director William Burns, Director of National Intelligence Avril Haines, and President Biden himself. All of them remembered vividly the annexation of Crimea and the 2016 election meddling: from these hard knocks they had learned not be too slow or to be too reactive. Dealing with Russia as it gradually moved toward war demanded action and speed. It was equally necessary to contemplate assessments that were unpleasant and frightening and not to plug in comforting narratives simply because they were comforting. This was the salutary lesson of Ghani's flight from Kabul, for which the Biden administration had been psychologically unready. In general, governments tend to overestimate the durability of the status quo, especially when they have reasons not to wish for or to expect a sudden change. Yet the Biden administration did not bet on the status quo in the fall of 2021; it gradually accepted that war was on the horizon.[19] Another helpful conclusion drawn from Afghanistan and from the AUKUS dust-up was not to take alliances or coalitions for granted. They do not run themselves. They do not fall in line behind Washington's objectives unless they are made a part of a process, unless they are closely listened to, and unless they are consulted well in advance of crises.

The White House committed itself to preventing the war it knew Russia was planning. To do this, the United States did not threaten direct military action on behalf of Ukraine. President Biden threatened Russia with massive economic sanctions and with walling off Russia from Europe and the United States. Presumably with these messages in hand, CIA Director William Burns went to Moscow in early November 2021. (On January 12, 2022, Burns would travel to Kyiv to brief Zelensky on Russia's war plans.) The White House was lucky to have Burns, who is among the most respected foreign service officers in American history. President of the Carnegie Endowment for International Peace before being called back to government in 2021, Burns was a specialist on Russia. He had worked in the Russian embassy early in his career and had been ambassador to Russia from 2005 to 2008. Burns was soft-spoken, not without opinions but never weighed down by strong opinions. He was non-judgmental, which facilitated communication with the Russian political elite. Burns had a diplomat's gift for seeing the world through the eyes of others, and that may have been an incentive for his November trip to Moscow. His cautionary words and ultimatums, whatever they were, could not have surprised Putin, who was well versed in US sanctions and had surely come up with his own expectations about what Washington would do, were he to invade Ukraine. The information about

Russian decision making that Burns brought back from Moscow may have been the trip's real value for a White House struggling to read Putin's mind.[20]

With the prospect of war moving ever closer, the Biden administration had tasks other than deterrence. One was to prevent Russia from gaining the upper hand in the global public sphere. What had to be avoided, if possible, was Russia's creation of a pretext for invading—for the sake of pinning culpability on Ukraine. This pretext could be something akin to the little green men in Crimea, who had pretended to be peacekeepers assisting the local population rather than soldiers from one country who had crossed the border into another. A successful "false flag" operation might affect public opinion inside and outside Europe, in the United States, and in Ukraine. Even without Russian decoys and distractions, the United States would struggle to convey its interpretation of the situation to global audiences, some of which were more skeptical of the United States than they were of Russia. Another task was to prove that the United States had no desire for war in Ukraine and no wish to hurry Russia into war. To the contrary, the Biden administration had been seeking guardrails since coming into office. That was why Biden had met with Putin in the summer. It was why he would agree to a video meeting with Putin on December 7, 2021. It was why, for the United States, the four months before the war that began in February 2022 were months devoted to ceaseless diplomacy and to readying Ukraine to defend itself, not just to saying that war was coming. Those European countries that did not agree with the White House about Putin's bellicose intentions—and most did not—were heartened by Washington's willingness to talk. It was not the Iraq War redux. Never has there been more diplomatic activity between Washington and Moscow than there was in the frenetic weeks prior to February 24, 2022.

By February diplomatic conversation had run its course, and on February 12 the United States and Britain withdrew their embassy staffs from Kyiv, an unambiguous sign that war was imminent.[21]

* * *

Interpreted as brinksmanship, as going up to the edge, Putin's diplomatic overtures in the winter of 2021–2022 made a kind of sense. Had he not invaded in the end, this flurry of diplomacy might even have worked for him. It might have compelled the United States and its European allies to talk about first principles, and from this, Russia might have won real concessions, possibly including neutrality for Ukraine and limitations on troop and missile deployments in the European territory Putin claimed to be worried about. Putin's first military buildup in April 2021 had not left him empty-handed; his second military buildup could have been similar. Yet Putin's diplomatic approach was so off-putting that it is hard to classify as brinksmanship. Diplomatically, his maximalist demands were completely out of the ordinary. They were almost setting the terms of Western surrender, when neither Ukraine nor the West had lost a war or even a battle against Russia. Going over the heads of the Ukrainians, as he preferred, Putin asked that Ukraine be rendered neutral and de-militarized, an impossible demand. NATO membership had to be forever taken off the table, while NATO itself would have to be shrunk, walking back dozens of agreements that had been made since 1998. Putin was asking not just for the closing of the proverbial open door but for a restructuring of NATO by Russian fiat. Putin's diplomacy, hastily and sloppily carried out by a Ministry of Foreign Affairs that had no idea what it was doing, was more than impractical. It was insulting to Ukraine. It was insulting to NATO. It was insulting to Europe, and it was in-sulting to the United States. Designed to be insulting, designed to be categori-cally and rudely rejected, it was diplomacy less as brinksmanship than as theater of the absurd.

Putin's gonzo diplomacy may have been rooted in domestic politics. He had to be unsurprised when his diplomatic threats and ultimatums changed no hearts and no minds in the West. The crucial audience for Putin's diplomatic onslaught may have been Russian. In winter 2021–2022, Russians had little certainty about the prospect of war with Ukraine. On that topic Putin was inscrutable. What Russians could see, with the assistance of highly coordinated state media, was a West that was yet again saying no to Russia. Here Putin was building on a narra-tive that had traction and depth in Russia: the West had betrayed Russia after the Cold War, articulating superficial respect for Russian interests while dumping bad economic advice on Russia. Lording itself over a supine Russia, the West extended NATO and the European Union westward, a narrative that predates Putin's presidency. With his ultimatums, Putin was forcing the West to say no, not least because this "no" gave him real political currency at home. He was forth-rightly expressing the Russian position—Putin long ago having equated himself with Russia—and the West was as uncurious and aloof as it always was. Putin was orchestrating Western rejection. For the Kremlin, this was the final round of diplomacy in performative terms, a climax to the geopolitical drama that had begun in 1991, a narrative of shame turning to assertion, humiliation turning to pride, territorial loss turning to territorial expansion. It was a culmination, after which Russia would have to act in one way or another. In this manner, Putin may have been communicating the necessity of war to Russians without having to say anything about the war itself. He was merely a Russian statesman giving diplo-macy its due. If he had to opt for war in the end, he could not do otherwise.

Another function of Putin's diplomatic zealotry may have been emotional. He may have been indulging a revenge fantasy. He resented the exclusive clubs that were the European Union and the NATO alliance. They thought they spoke for Europe when they spoke for only a portion of Europe. They could never under-stand that Russia too was Europe, among other things, and they talked down to Russia. They believed they could rein in Russia, shove it onto some kind of offramp of their own making, discipline Russia with sanctions and get Russia to apologize for being Russia. The United States rhapsodized about a rules-based order and then broke whichever rule it wanted to break: tearing off Kosovo from Serbia; invading the sovereign nations of Iraq, Afghanistan, and Libya; and recognizing the Golan Heights in Israel, Syrian territory which Israel had acquired through means not much different from those Russia had used in the Donbas (through military force). Perhaps the pleasure of December 2021 and January 2022—for Putin—was the pleasure of instigating a global crisis around his personal grievances. He was stating Russia's terms for how Europe would be, for how it should function, and the Europeans and Americans were scrambling to respond. When Emmanuel Macron came to Moscow to meet with Putin and to hear him out, he was seated at the end of a long table, nominally because he refused to take a Russian COVID test. The visuals of the meeting spoke a language all their own, a European leader coming to Putin's court to ask for peace, a European supplicant in Moscow. In his pre-war diplomacy, Putin was on a dictator's joy ride, keeping the whole world waiting and the whole world guessing.

The essential purpose of Putin's unusual diplomacy was to distract. In 2022, Putin could not persuade the United States and other countries to believe that his intentions were peaceful. He was not staging a popularity contest. Nowhere was he trusted: his record of violence and of lying was too great.[22] The stark drama of what would happen was starting to remind observers not of the Cold War but of the late 1930s and of the conferences and crises that anticipated a world at war, of Hitler's demands and of Neville Chamberlain's umbrella. Putin needed to feed the media, the intelligence services, and the governments of foreign countries something other than war to report on, to talk about, and to think about. A never-ending blizzard of diplomatic statements, meetings, proposals, and press statements did the job. If Putin had made up his mind before December 2021, which is likely, the winter diplomacy had to have been intentionally pointless, saturating the airwaves with meaningless phrases, events, and scenarios. For those desperate for war not to come, Putin could avail himself of a magician's trick, which was to train his audience's attention on one object (the high-stakes diplomacy), which prevented it from focusing on another object (the imminence of war). Social media, with its intense concentration on present-tense happenings, its evisceration of context, and its constant production of memes, thickened this atmosphere of confusion, the same social media that for months had been revealing Russian military hardware moving toward Ukraine—in photograph and video. Until February 24, 2022, the magician kept his audiences suspended in disbelief, and to a great degree he succeeded. The war, when it came, would come to most as a surprise.

9

War in Ukraine, Round 2

So, Spartans, vote for war and the honor of Sparta. Do not allow the
Athenians to grow stronger.

Thucydides, *The Peloponnesian War*, Book 1:43

In late February and early March 2014, the Kremlin had been reluctant to comment on its actions publicly. According to the Russian government, Crimea was not being invaded. It was spontaneously moving toward a referendum, as if Crimea had been waiting for more than two decades to separate from Ukraine. The Russian soldiers fanning out across Crimea that March did not wear insignia. They appeared nameless and country-less, not the world spirit on horseback, as Hegel had described Napoleon passing through Europe in 1806, but the world spirit operating incognito, quietly altering borders, rearranging the map, remaking the rules. Likewise, the Kremlin had characterized the civil unrest in the Donbas as a civil war. It was arising from the people of the Donbas in April 2014 because of an obstreperous nationalism that had overtaken Kyiv. In the summer of 2014, the Russian military would move its hardware into the Donbas through convoys disguised as humanitarian assistance, a fictional touch. The story was that Russia was not at the center of the story. Putin was not driving events, he was trying to say; he was an onlooker. Civil unrest had broken out in Ukraine—regrettably—and in this civil war Russia may have picked a side, but Russia was in truth a benevolent neighbor. In actual fact, without Russian aid and encouragement the post-Maidan civil unrest in the Donbas, not all of which was manufactured from Moscow, would either have faded away or it would have been subdued by the Ukrainian military.

In February 2022, Putin was still working behind façades. Mounting an invasion that was not called an invasion in 2014 had hidden his true motives. It had made the situation in the Donbas seem provisional, and Russia's illusion of not invading had made the Minsk accords impossible to implement, confusing everything. For Kyiv to negotiate seriously with the Donetsk People's Republic (DNR) and Luhansk People's Republic (LNR), as the Kremlin consistently asked Ukraine to do, was to qualify the sovereignty of Ukraine. It was to bow to a non-existent civil war, when Russian military units were staffing and defending the DNR and LNR. Yet for Kyiv not to negotiate seriously with the People's Republics was to garner criticism internationally: Moscow blamed Kyiv for bypassing the DNR and LNR and thus for refusing to implement Minsk. Western diplomats and policymakers were confounded by a Russian government that systematically misrepresented the situation on the ground.[1] Russia's evasions had a paralyzing effect on the West, while the veneer of Russian innocence fostered an amnesia about Crimea and the Donbas in the West. For those wishing to move on with Russia, for the sake of business as usual and for the sake of business as such, Crimea and the Donbas could seem unclear to the point of hopelessness. When they were not touched by war, these territories were minimally important to the West, which suited Putin just fine. Perhaps Ukraine was simply one of the world's many intractable crisis zones. The posture of standing outside a crisis he had himself orchestrated gave Putin political latitude. Only he could put an end to the mayhem.

In the third week of February 2022, Putin tried to maintain this latitude under an entirely new set of circumstances. It was a clumsy effort. He had conducted enormous military buildups in the spring and fall of the previous year: nobody could ignore the Russian capacity to invade Ukraine in February 2022. Similarly, the Kremlin's go-for-broke diplomacy between December 2021 and February 2022 was meant to put Europe on edge. Putin was on the international stage, daring the West to capitulate to his vision of a neutral, de-militarized Ukraine and a truncated NATO alliance. These diplomatic statements and the meetings that occurred around them were presented as the avoidance of war: Putin said repeatedly that his goal was *not* to have a war over Ukraine. He was setting the terms for peace in Europe at the exact moment his government was cementing the inevitability of war. Since Ukraine had absolutely no intention of invading Russia in 2022, war could mean only one thing—a Russian invasion of Ukraine. Putin was moving far beyond the position he claimed to hold in 2014. No longer the passive observer of Crimean separatism or of a civil war between the Donbas and western Ukraine, he was in the eye of the storm. Russia had precipitated a diplomatic drama by placing its military forces around Ukraine and then by insisting that NATO's architecture be scaled back to what it had been in the late 1990s. There was no separatism and no civil unrest in Ukraine in the winter of 2021–2022, no crisis at all. There was only Putin upping the ante.

Putin tied himself in knots on the war. Quite possibly, he had been creating the tense environment in which a provocation could be staged, after which a Russian invasion could once again be couched as something other than an invasion—as a response to military and genocidal actions undertaken by the Ukrainian government. In January and February 2022, the US government was being incomparably more proactive than it had been in 2014 (vis-à-vis Russia's invasion of Ukraine) or in 2016 (vis-à-vis Russia's election meddling in the United States). The Ukrainian government was saying that there would not be war. It was not mobilizing its military—at least not officially. Most European governments were also agnostic about the war or convinced that it would not happen. Out there on its own, the US government was not just predicting that there would be war. President Biden was mentioning specific dates on which the war would begin, either forcing Putin to deal with misinformation from Washington (for a change) or getting these dates right and throwing Putin off balance. Deploying intelligence so publicly and so aggressively, risking the exposure of sources and methods, was hardly standard procedure in Washington, and for Russia it was only the visible part of a campaign to derail the coming war. Not less consequential was intelligence sharing between Washington and Kyiv, which would be a crucial element of the war's first days and weeks.

Putin's expectations for the war can be inferred from the war itself. It would be a massive invasion of Ukraine along multiple axes, stunning the Ukrainian military into submission; a quick conquest of Kyiv, resulting either in the flight or the imprisonment of President Zelensky and members of his government; and the large-scale going over to the Russian side by Ukrainians who were pro-Russian by conviction, by Ukrainians who had been bought off, and by Ukrainians who could see the writing on the wall—that Russia was soon to be in charge. These hopes rested on the on-paper superiority of the Russian military, which had not experienced a big setback since the first Chechen War in the mid-1990s, for which Yeltsin, not Putin, had been responsible. Putin's hopes rested on a low opinion of the Ukrainian government, which would presumably be unable to handle the Russian invasion, to keep the country together, and to muster sufficient international support fast enough to stay afloat. Putin's hopes also rested on the belief that Ukraine was a house divided, half Ukrainian and half Russian, half East and half West, half European and half not-European. The pressures of war would confirm these Ukrainian divisions, ending the war quickly on Russian terms, most likely with the country's partition and with Kyiv the capital of a Russian-controlled area, which would not function as a colony; it would be Russia becoming what Russia was. Putin was not so much declaring war on Ukraine as trying to expose its artificiality as a unified nation state. Moments after invading, Russia would pick up the fragments of Ukrainian statehood and assemble them into a structure that harmonized with Russian history and with Russian statehood.

What Putin launched on February 24, 2022, was in his own words a "special military operation." The immediate pretext was an accusation of genocide in the Donbas, a series of non-existent crimes attributed to the Ukrainian government. Putin announced the recognition of Donetsk and Luhansk as independent territories. Only parts of these administrative units had been occupied by Russia in 2014, the line of contact having been haphazardly set on the battlefield, when most of the fighting stopped in February 2015. Russia's special military operation of 2022 would finally "free" these territories. Putin outlined his objectives in a speech given on February 21, repeating familiar allegations of a dead end created by Ukrainian, US, and NATO intransigence.[2] That same day, in a grotesque spectacle, Putin forced his national-security staff to stand up and endorse the operation on television. Putin listened to his unsure staff looking bored, tapping his fingers on his desk. He was not taking in their ideas. He was making his government and the society behind it complicit in the coming war. The war was not his whim. It was the will of the parliament and the national security council, the will of the Russian nation. It was an oddly bureaucratic way to begin a war, or it was the right way to begin a special military operation, a mere surgical procedure. Putin's dry language signaled to Russians that what Ukrainians would experience as war would not be a war for Russia. The war would be something over there, something happening elsewhere, the preoccupation of technocrats, and no more difficult for Russia to administer than the annexation of Crimea or the administering of the people's republics in Donetsk and Luhansk. This downplaying of war would help Russians to transition from the normalcy of February 23, 2022, to whatever it was that was being started on February 24. Laced with hubris, Putin's public messaging before February 24 was a cocktail of evasion (for the outside world) and understatement (for Russians). Thus began the war that Putin was not willing to call a war.

* * *

A week or so after the invasion, the Russian military found itself fighting a war for which it was disastrously unprepared. Before the war, Putin had had the privilege of making all the significant decisions. He had ordered the military buildup. He could choose the terrain on which to fight. He could determine the timing— with some interference perhaps from the Biden White House. It was in every way his war, his reasoning, his planning, his strategy. The course of events was not entirely unfavorable to the Russian military. Russian units pushed up from Crimea, while others moved west from the Donbas. They covered huge amounts of territory, which in many cases were not under Russian control, though it could look this way on the newspaper maps of the war. In the south, the Russian advance was rapid. Elsewhere, what unfolded was failure after failure for Russia: the profligate expenditure of soldiers' lives and of materiel around Kharkiv, Chernihiv, and Kyiv, major Ukrainian cities in Ukraine's east and north that did not fall to Russia. Most dramatic was the failure to take Kyiv after Ukrainian soldiers repulsed an attack on Hostomel airport, some twenty-two miles from downtown Kyiv.[3] By mid-March, a poorly protected military convoy stalled north of the city, the victim of bad logistics, of shoddy planning, and of harassment from Ukrainian units that were showing none of the incompetence and disloyalty to their country that Moscow had expected of them. A knock-out blow to Kyiv might have given Putin what he wanted—an easy, quick, not very bloody victory and a country transformed overnight—but that was not at all what Putin got. The quagmire Russia had created for itself in the north and the east eclipsed whatever gains were made in the south. Much of Putin's prior thinking about the war had been delusional. Those in the Russian government who knew better, and surely there were many who did, had been unwilling or unable to point him in another direction.

Two inter-related circumstances rebounded against Putin. One was the country of Ukraine, where resistance to the invasion was fierce, and the other was the international support Ukraine received. Ukrainian resistance was not confined to the west of the country, as the notion of a divided country might have suggested. Resistance came from all segments of Ukrainian society, from those who were Russian speakers, from those who worshipped at the Ukrainian Orthodox Church (Moscow Patriarchate), from Ukrainians in the south and the east, from rural folk and from city dwellers. In those places where Ukrainians suddenly found themselves under Russia occupation, resistance was also intense, which is not to say that there were no collaborators and no people who welcomed Russia's invasion. Collaborators there were, though the number of people who welcomed the idea of invasion from without (and all that followed from it) was small.[4] The fighting against Russia, well led by Ukraine's military high command and boosted by civic action from Ukrainians not in uniform, translated first into the successful defense of cities, Kyiv most meaningfully, and then into the pushing back of Russian units around Kyiv and Chernihiv. In the fall, the Ukrainian military scored victories around Kharkiv and Kherson. By beating back the armies of a larger country, Ukraine deprived the Kremlin of one of its key assets. Ukraine demystified the Russian military, pulling back the curtain and exposing an institution that was poorly run, poorly equipped, and beholden to strategic concepts that had little bearing on reality, which in turn demystified a political leader who since 2008 had been trying to wrap himself in the mantle of a master strategist. Ukraine's civilians and soldiers cast a harsh light on Putin, who was no Peter the Great, no Alexander 1, and no Joseph Stalin. For a needless war of aggression, hastily planned and shambolically executed, Putin had put hundreds of thousands of Russians in harm's way.

Volodymyr Zelensky was the focal point of Ukraine's self-defense. Some of Zelensky's response to the war followed from his pre-political career. As an entertainer, an actor, and a producer, Zelensky had been a communicator immersed in twenty-first century media.[5] Here the contrast with Vladimir Putin could not have been greater, Putin whose communication style was some combination of staged Soviet formality and the staged informality of his annual call-in show, during which he would take choreographed questions from across Russia. Putin's pandemic-era isolation had been especially evident in the lead-up to the war, when he met with foreign dignitaries and with his own staff in socially distanced settings within the Kremlin; or when he spoke to the nation alone in his office. On February 24, Zelensky was a war president, forgoing a suit and tie and dressing in military green. An off-the-cuff style of speaking came naturally to him, and he used it to convey resolve and confidence, whether in his evening speeches to the nation or in photographed or filmed appearances that lent themselves perfectly to replication on social media. Zelensky had the Ukrainian people behind him because of the war and because of his media presence. He won the hearts of a global public because of the war, though for global audiences Zelensky's media presence was pivotal. He was the everyman who had become president, exactly as he had been in his television show, *Servant of the People*, and then this everyman was a brave wartime president. He helped people who may not have known much about Ukraine to relate to him and, more importantly, to relate to his country's cause. In many countries, public support for Ukraine enabled and at times forced governments to speed up their military assistance to Ukraine.

Zelensky showed physical courage. He was in a capital city under attack. Kyiv was not guaranteed to stay in Ukrainian hands, and the White House, no doubt recalling Ashraf Ghani's last-minute flight from Kabul in August 2021, six months before the start of the Russian invasion, offered Zelensky safe haven. "I need ammo," was Zelensky's terse response, "I don't need a ride."[6] Whether or not Zelensky actually said these words, the sentiment behind them was a turning point in the war. Zelensky's decision to stay in Kyiv demonstrated that Ukraine could survive the war and that Ukrainians would not be intimidated by the scale of the Russian invasion, by the reputation of Vladimir Putin, or by Russia's nuclear arsenal. Ukrainians thrilled to Zelensky's leadership, but it was hardly the sole factor in their willingness to soldier through: it reflected as much as it created their will to fight. Zelensky's leadership was decisive outside of Ukraine, preventing potential backers from hedging their bets. The United States and all the countries that wanted Russia to lose its war decided to support the Ukrainian government not with the certainty of victory but with the certainty that Ukraine would not give up, would not fall apart under the stresses of war, and would not disintegrate into regional blocs. US military support for Ukraine predated the war. US intelligence sharing had been salvific for Kyiv before the war; it had been stunning in its accuracy. Yet US military support for Ukraine took on new dimensions when Zelensky showed that he was the captain of the ship and that, like Winston Churchill in the catastrophic summer of 1940, he would carry on.

* * *

Before the war, Putin had been the master of suspense. An entire chapter of world history was turning on the decision he would make. Would he go to war or not? It was the most powerful Putin had ever been as Russia's president. This power slipped through his fingers in the first few days of the war. Putin remained a key decision-maker, the spider within an endless web of media coverage and speculation, and at no point out of options, but on the biggest decision of his life he had miscalculated. Russia had tethered its fortunes to a high-risk plan of attack, without having informed most of its soldiers that they would be fighting a war. A simple lesson of Russian military history is that geographic depth makes Russia hard to invade or hard to invade victoriously. Not as big as Russia, Ukraine is still a very big country; it too is hard to invade victoriously, hard to conquer. Astonishingly, Ukraine's geographic depth was somehow lost on the war's Russian planners, who threw their units into Ukraine without prior artillery bombardment. They then watched as the Russian soldiers never got far enough, as their supply lines grew overextended and as they subjected themselves to counter-attacks, not least because Russia had been unable to control Ukrainian airspace at the beginning of the war. Instead of donning their dress uniforms to march through Kyiv, as they had been told they would do, Russian soldiers were rapidly getting knocked off course and killed. They were dying in great numbers, subject to ambush in the forests and bogs of northern Ukraine.

Condemned to a near impossible plan, Russia's military suffered from the general ills of the Putin regime. Accountability in the Russian military was accountability to Putin. If money was stolen or numbers fudged because nobody wanted to disappoint the boss or because the boss was not looking, then money would be stolen and numbers fudged. Logistics were everywhere in disarray, which might not have mattered that much had Ukraine been defeated in a week or two but which very much mattered in the war Russia found itself waging by March 2022. The primordial error of the war was that Moscow had given it the green light in the first place. The military high command and the national security council were rubber-stamp bodies for a single individual, one who had been too long in power, who had in a sense read too much Russian history and who was too eager to write himself into its romanticized pages, enriching the empire through territorial expansion, when this was not the way of acquiring geopolitical power in the twenty-first century. (Twenty-first century geopolitical power is based less in territory than in political economy and technological capacity.)[7] Conversely, getting mired in long, draining, and unnecessary wars has been a way of losing geopolitical power at all times and in all ages. The odd ritual whereby Putin's national-security team went on television three days before the war and recited its pro-war catechism took on new meaning after the war had begun. It was not just a ritual of loyalty. It was a window into the regime's ill health.

When the Russian soldiers withdrew from Kyiv, they left in their wake a shocking record of brutality and crime. On March 31, Bucha and Irpin, two suburbs of Kyiv, were liberated, and shortly thereafter the story of their occupation was being photographed, recorded, and chronicled. The war crimes were so extensive that they could not be attributed to a few errant or overzealous soldiers. They were a concerted effort to intimidate and subdue the local population—through mass sexual violence and through mass executions.[8] Theft and the desecration of others' property were widespread. Two elements of the Russian war can be extrapolated from Bucha and Irpin and the many other places that were subjected to these horrors. The Kremlin's description of Ukrainians as "Nazis," its false accusations of genocide, its belittling of Ukraine and Ukrainians were dehumanizing, pitting Russian soldiers against the local population in a manner guaranteed to provoke atrocities. The opposite side of the same coin was the lack of any legal restraint within the Russian military. If Putin gave his approval or was thought to give his approval, it was legal. There were no institutions that could intervene and punish Russian soldiers and their officers for war crimes. There were no checks and balances, and instead of getting court-martialed, instead of there being an investigation, instead of Russian journalists being allowed to look into their past actions, the soldiers who had occupied Bucha were decorated by Putin on April 18, a signal to the Russian military as a whole.[9] Ilya Yashin, a prominent opposition politician in Russia, would be imprisoned for publicly mentioning Bucha, a signal to Russian society about what could and could not be said about the war.

Many other war crimes would follow. On April 8, just as the world was learning the words Bucha and Irpin for the first time, the Kramatorsk Railway Station was struck by a Russian missile, resulting in mass civilian casualties. Rather than the exception, this strike was the rule when it came to attacks on Ukraine's civilian infrastructure and residential communities, which were in the crosshairs of Russia's unhinged war. The 2014–2015 war had harmed many civilians, those in the war zones, those caught near the line of contact, and those who had been forced to leave their homes. This war had affected the lives of several million people. Still, in 2014–2015 there were many millions of Ukrainians—a majority—who were not living a war zone and for whom life was more or less normal. In the 2022 war, no person and no community was safe. Russia was prosecuting its war across the whole country, quite often with random missile attacks, driving people into their basements or into subway stations for hours or for days at a time. The war forced millions of Ukrainians into refugee status, most of them women and children, as men from the ages of eighteen to sixty were required to stay in Ukraine, and the war made for millions of internally displaced people, those driven from their homes or escaping Russian occupation or hoping for a greater degree of stability away from the fighting. The civilian suffering was beyond words.

News did get out from the territories Russia continued to hold, if not as comprehensively as it did from places like Bucha and Irpin. Filtration camps had been set up to reengineer Ukrainian society, separating those parts that would be loyal to the newly installed Russian administration from those that might be dis-loyal.[10] Under occupation, the Russian language would rule, and in schools and cultural institutions a Russian orientation would be enforced, the blueprint for all the territory Russia would occupy in the war. In the absence of a local popula-tion eager to be occupied, allegiance to Russia would have to be compelled. Those not with the program might find themselves deported to Russia. In an espe-cially cruel act of social control, thousands of Ukrainian children were deported to Russia (or held in Russian-occupied territories in Ukraine) and placed with Russian families.[11] Territorial occupation and social engineering were common enough in European history, especially in Eastern or Central Europe. They had been the tools of Nazi and Soviet rule, and in the 1930s and 1940s Ukrainians had suffered terribly under both of these regimes. The repetition of such state-sponsored criminality in Ukraine was shocking nevertheless, yet another reason to fight and an additional obstacle to negotiations with Russia. For Europeans, it was a very bitter revelation, a repudiation of progress in Europe, because Ukraine *was* Europe and massive human-rights violations were anything but European progress. To respond to this war by saying that Ukraine was on its own or that a settlement between occupier and occupied needed to be made at the expense of the occupied was not impossible. Some on the Left and on the Right thought that Russia had certain entitlements in Ukraine and that the West could ensure peace by granting Russia its entitlements; political figures like Victor Orban and Donald Trump could seem on board with this program. After Bucha and Irpin, though, many governments chose to back Ukraine for ethical as well as for stra-tegic reasons.

Russia's brutality and its fallibility on the battlefield changed the course of the war. The invasion revived every bad memory of Soviet occupation and before that of Russian imperialism in the Baltic Republics and in Poland, raising the ominous question of what Russian success might look like in Ukraine and across Europe. Who would be next? Putin had been emboldened enough on February 24, sure enough of his power, ambitious enough to do what he did, but what would happen if he were to become more emboldened and more ambitious? In Western Europe, though the fear of Russian invasion was small, the war was en-tirely unacceptable. It was turning back the clock of civilization to the darkest days of World War II. Even if Russia would not be marching into France, it had to be stopped in Ukraine—for Ukraine's and for Europe's sake. In the United States, the war was far away geographically. Although it generated little day-to-day fear, the Russian invasion hit the central nerve of American foreign policy, arraying authoritarianism and aggression against democracy and human rights. Joe Biden's visceral response to Putin's war, and his explanation of it as a war for de-mocracy, which was Zelensky's explanation of the war as well, would have been easily comprehended by Woodrow Wilson, Franklin Roosevelt, Harry Truman,

John F. Kennedy, and Ronald Reagan. The United States had fought two world wars in Europe, each characterized as a war to make the world safe for democracy. Helping to defend Ukraine against Russia, President Biden concluded, was within the best traditions of American foreign policy.

While the West shipped weapons and ammunition into Ukraine, an elaborate sanctions regime was erected. One of its agendas was to decouple the economies of Western and like-minded countries from Russia, a moral endeavor given how Russia was using the money it made abroad, and a practical endeavor, as European dependence on Russian gas and oil was a wartime liability. Another agenda was punitive. Even under the shadow of the 2022 invasion, Ukraine did not have treaty allies in the West: no outside country was obligated to defend Ukraine; no country was sending in its uniformed soldiers. A degree of separation would be there with the war, justified by the fact that Russia was a nuclear power and that outright war among nuclear powers would be suicidal. That was a consensus position. To live with this distance and this reticence—while watching daily the havoc Russia was wreaking in Ukraine—governments turned to sanctions, as they had in 2014. The aim of the 2022 sanctions was to impose costs and ideally to turn the Russian population against the war, to make it not worth Russia's while, or to sow division in the Kremlin. Finally, sanctions were intended to constrain the Russian war machine, which depended on microchips, on software, and on technological developments for which Russia needed access to the outside world. Over time, sanctions that impeded the construction of a high-tech, well-supplied Russian military might shorten the war. That was the aspiration.[12]

Gradually and then suddenly, the war brought Ukraine closer to European institutions. On the Maidan in 2013 and 2014, Ukrainians had waved EU flags.[13] It was sometimes said that the 130 people who died during the Revolution of Dignity were the first people to have died for the European Union. For this, Ukraine's reward had been an Association Agreement with the EU, the very thing Yanukovych had not signed onto in Vilnius in November 2013. Yet once the AA and the Deep and Comprehensive Free Trade Agreement with Ukraine had been finalized, the EU and NATO had no further agenda for Ukraine—other than wishing that at some point Russia might back out of the Donbas and Crimea. Ukraine had increasing contact with the EU but no real membership prospects after 2015, a combination of inertia within the EU and a less than stellar record of reform in Ukraine, not to mention the transatlantic havoc of the Trump years and the paralysis induced by a global pandemic in 2020 and 2021. As if in dialogue with the EU flags once waved on the Maidan, Ukrainian flags were everywhere to be seen in Europe in 2022—in people's houses, hanging from apartment windows, and on top of government buildings. Ukrainian flags had come to symbolize Europe as well as Ukraine, symbolizing a suffering all too familiar from European history and a set of European ideals, born in 1945, that the Russian invasion had once again impressed on European populations. On June 26, 2022, the European Commission began the process of Ukraine's EU membership, a much bigger step than the DCFTA and yet another way in which the European landscape had been altered on February 24.

* * *

When it came to support for Ukraine, the global picture was by no means simple. The coalition of countries that sanctioned Russia for its war and that lavished financial and military assistance on Ukraine went far beyond the transatlantic axis. Japan, South Korea, Singapore, Australia, and New Zealand were together with the United States, Canada, and the member states of the European Union and NATO. Outside of Russia, there was scant public support for Putin's war, though there were many who regarded the war either as an interminable conflict between Russia and Ukraine or an interminable conflict between Russia and the United States, for which culpability was American as well as Russian. Even among the countries that said they were Russian partners, China most prominently, sanctions on Russia were not to be overturned or ignored for Russia's sake. China complied with sanctions and did not send arms to Russia.[14] No country directly joined in Russia's fight. Although some foreign fighters went to help the Russian military, most foreign fighters were on Kyiv's side. Once the war lasted longer than had been anticipated in Moscow, the Kremlin had to scramble for materiel, turning for ammunition and for drones to Iran and North Korea, two countries that were already under massive Western sanctions. To a great degree, though, when it came to the fighting, financing, and provisioning of the war, Russia was on its own. This may have been unavoidable for Putin, and with the war, he wanted to demonstrate Russia's autonomy. Russia's relative isolation was also a function of his having premised the war on Ukraine's "de-nazification" and its rescue from "gay pride parades."[15]

Isolated in the prosecution of its war, Russia was not itself isolated by the war. While a wall arose between Russia and Europe, shutting down cross-border traffic and economic exchange, Russia's borders to the Caucasus, to Central Asia, and to Asia remained open, as did Russian access to most countries in Africa, Latin America, and the Middle East. Trade and travel continued in the south Caucasus and in Central Asia, intensifying as soon as Europe became hard to reach for Russians and for Russian businesses. More consequentially for the Russian war effort, many countries refused to join the sanctions regime and refused to support Ukraine militarily. Xi Jinpeng's China had vowed "no limits" partnership with Russia before the war, an overstatement, although China reaped economic advantage by not opposing Russia. Though war intruded on China's Belt and Road Initiative, infecting the center of the Eurasian continent with instability, it was clearly an opportunity for China—to build up Russian dependence on China and to watch the United States expend money and military resources in Europe that might otherwise have been directed toward Asia. Awkwardly for the Biden administration, with its conviction that democracy was on the line in Ukraine, such large and vibrant democracies as Brazil and India did not see the war in these terms. Without praising Putin's decision to invade, they said no to sanctioning Russia and to enhancing the Ukrainian military. The war was not really their business, they implied. Simply because the United States said the war was existential for the liberal international order was no reason for the war to be existential for them.[16] In 2022, the United States was at the center of a much bigger coalition than it had assembled for the 2003 Iraq War, the Second Gulf War, or for the war in Afghanistan. That said, the coalition behind Ukraine was smaller and less global than what the United States had arranged in 1991 during the First Gulf War.

Historical memory played a role in global attitudes. The Baltic Republics were grateful to the United States for its Cold War opposition to the Soviet Union and for ushering them into NATO in the first decade of the twenty-first century. They had their own reasons to rally behind Ukraine but doing so in the name of a US-led coalition also made intuitive sense. In Latin America, where the record of US interventions is long, the US position on the war in Ukraine could look hypocritical: the pure virtue of the United States could seem as improbable as the pure vice of Russia. In sub-Saharan Africa, many countries had prior connections to the Soviet Union, leaving bonds of affinity with Putin's Russia. As in Latin America, skepticism toward the good intentions of the United States was widespread in Africa, a consequence of Washington's hard-edged Cold War policies and of the global war on terror: France, the United States, and other Western powers had often run roughshod over the sovereignty of African countries. In the Middle East, the Iraq War could easily be referenced as a US violation of the rules-based order, the invasion of a sovereign country under false pretenses, which was exactly the crime Russia was being accused of committing in Ukraine. Underscoring such skepticism about the West was of course the worldwide legacy of European imperialism and colonialism, which compromised the position of Putin's Western critics. Russian media and Russian diplomats did what they could after February 24 to encourage such global disapproval and to popularize the image of a mendacious West.

While historical memory is abstract, the war's global economic impact was immediate, severe, and uneven. The United States experienced higher inflation because of the war, though by fall 2023, inflation was tapering off, unemployment was low, and economic growth was strong. Europe had a harder time of it. Millions of refugees flowed from Ukraine into Europe, where they were more graciously and widely received than Syrian refugees had been in 2015, though any influx of refugees comes with social and political tension. The war was wrenching for European economies, for Germany in particular, which had been unprepared to separate itself from Russian energy. High inflation and reduced economic growth were the price, sending Germany into recession. The costs of war were greater, however, outside of Europe and the United States. Famous for its black soil, Ukraine is an agricultural superpower, producing grain, corn, sunflower oil, and fertilizer. The war disrupted everything, whether it was agricultural production within Ukraine or the capacity to distribute agricultural goods beyond Ukraine's borders. At the start of the war, Russia had imposed a naval blockade, forcing Ukraine to shift to rail transport and trucking, which was no substitute for shipping. Although Turkey eventually brokered a "grain deal" between Russia and Ukraine, Russia could shut this deal off at any time, as it did in the summer of 2023. The price of foodstuffs shot up in Asia, Africa, and the Middle East, imposing costs from the war on populations that were poor and vulnerable. Wartime inflation made it harder for Latin American countries to revive their post-pandemic economies. The governments of the countries affected wished for the swiftest possible end to the war, which, whether by design or by accident, ended up being a form of global leverage for Russia and of global impatience with the West's support for Ukraine.

Some US allies were non-aligned on the war. Like China, Turkey derived opportunities from the new world of 2022 and 2023. Before the war, Turkey had been playing Russia and the United States off each other, getting different kinds of benefit from each country—a security guarantee from the United States through NATO, trade with Europe and air-defense systems from Russia. Because the war consumed so much of Russia's attention, while burning up its military resources, Turkey had more room to maneuver in Syria, where Russia was a partner of the al-Assad government and a check of sorts on Turkey's regional ambitions. Ankara had more leeway in the south Caucasus, advancing the interests of Azerbaijan against those of Russia's ally, Armenia. At the same time, Turkey manufactured the Bayraktar drone, which contributed so much to the Ukrainian war effort that Ukrainians started naming their children Bayraktar. All the while, Turkey avoided sanctioning or breaking off ties with Russia; Turkey was one of the countries from which sanctioned goods flowed into Russia. Israel, a close ally of the United States, was not sympathetic to Russia. Its population was sympathetic to Ukraine, but the Israeli government could not afford to anger Russia, which controlled Syria's airspace and had a partnership with Israel's archenemy, Iran. Israel sent humanitarian and non-lethal military aid to Ukraine. Otherwise, it stood aloof from the war, while maintaining diplomatic ties with Russia. Turkey and Israel did not set out to defy the United States on Ukraine, though Erdogan had little love for Washington. Nor did they follow Washington's lead. If the war opened doors for Turkey, improving its regional hand, it constrained Israel.

Keenly aware of its basic reliance on the United States, Israel could not ignore Russia's presence in the Middle East, which it had consolidated by moving into Syria in 2015. The war in Ukraine further unsettled an international scene that had not been particularly settled before the outbreak of this terrible war.

* * *

As summer turned to fall, the war did not subside. It took on new dimensions in the first two weeks of September, when Ukraine made a lightning strike on the region around Kharkiv, cutting through Russian lines and forcing additional retreats. Previously, Ukraine had exploited the advantages of defending territory and capitalizing on Russia's tactical and strategic mistakes.[17] In the second week of September, Ukraine went on the attack. Instead of conceding the advantages of defense to Russia, Ukraine showed its strategic skill, its ability to integrate so-phisticated Western weaponry, and its willingness to take intelligent risks. The Kharkiv offensive was prepared in close coordination with the United States and its NATO allies. Questions had lingered over the summer about providing weapons to Ukraine. Did it make sense to enable a war of attrition? Would a stalemated war not mean that time was on Russia's side? These questions were retired (for a while) by Ukraine's September offensive. The reason to aid Ukraine militarily was for it to win back territory. That was an answer to the depredations of Russian occupation, and it was a strategy that could divide into two scenarios. Either Ukraine might simply win back its freedom by winning back all of its territory, or it would put itself in the best possible position by reclaiming large swathes of its territory, giving it the option of containing Russia over the long haul or of negotiating with Russia from a position of strength. Ukraine's real and perceived position had improved immeasurably. Zelensky's reputation and that of his top military advisors acquired even greater luster.

The Ukrainian military did not stop around Kharkiv. It pressed Russian positions in the city of Kherson, in Ukraine's south. The confused relationship between Russia's political and military objectives reasserted itself in Kherson. The Russian advance in the south had been halted at Mykolaiv, though Moscow had dreamed of reaching Odessa and taking all of Ukraine's Black Sea coast. Kherson was hard to defend, and Ukrainian soldiers were inching closer to a city separated from Russian-held territory by the wide Dnipro River. Kherson was difficult for the Russian military to supply, and a quick retreat would have been the preferable military choice. Politically, Moscow was loath to do this. With hor-rific violence and destruction, Russia had taken Mariupol, a city on the Black Sea; Putin declared victory there on April 20.[18] A September withdrawal from Kherson would have left Mariupol as the only large city Russia had conquered and held, a dismal record for over six months of war. Kherson would remain in Russian hands until it was eventually (and inevitably) lost. The Ukrainians were fighting with vigor and purpose. Russian morale was obviously lower, though not non-existent: the Russian military executed a skillful retreat from Kherson. The strategic course of the Russian war was baffling, having become a war fought for the sake of not losing. Yet Putin was, by all appearances, still bent on winning the war, whatever that might mean after the Kremlin's initial war plan caved in on itself.

In late September, Putin proclaimed the annexation of four Ukrainian provinces. It was a turning point in the war. Putin's announced annexation rendered any negotiated settlement with Ukraine even more difficult, since Russia was declaring that Ukrainian territory was and would be Russian territory in perpetuity. For Putin to give up what he claimed was Russian territory would be almost impossible, and for Ukraine to accept the carving up of its territory would not be any easier. Whether or not Russia had been serious about negotiation in 2014 and 2015, it had kept alive various scenarios in the Donbas by not annexing Donetsk and Luhansk provinces. Putin ended this uncertainty in 2022. His on-the-fly annexation was one of the war's stranger episodes, because in none of the four provinces did Russia control all the territory. These were fictional annexations. At the same time that Putin was showing his long-term commitment to the war, he was showing how far he was of realizing his declared aims. Initial intentions to "denazify" and "de-militarize" Ukraine had been suitably vague. Being so precise in September and simultaneously revealing how incapable Russia was of defending its "annexed" territory was a shocking display of weakness on Putin's part. An unintentional admission, it outlined a Russian strategy for the war that had little bearing on the war Russia was actually fighting.[19]

To perpetuate the war, a reluctant Putin had no option other than to order a mass mobilization. The original invading army of some 200,000 could only have prevailed in a short war, in an invasion that engendered a quick Ukrainian surrender. Nothing of the sort happened. Of the 200,000 Russian soldiers who had been sent into Ukraine, very many had been killed or wounded, and even more had been exhausted. A contested occupation wore out the Russian soldiers. Putin was backed into ordering the mobilization of 300,000 new recruits, a messy process carried out in fall 2022. Announced on September 21, it inspired another wave of emigration from Russia, after the hundreds of thousands who had left at the beginning of the war. In September and October, the Kremlin may have held on to the idea of a special military operation, a war that was not a war. Terminology was increasingly beside the point when Russians could see their government girding for a major war. Mobilization diminished the space between the front and the home front, ending the summer idyll for those Russians who were not in uniform and for those who had trusted their government's presentation of the war as being far away and easy for a superpower like Russia to win. Social media in the West exaggerated the inefficiencies of mobilization, which in the end was carried out. After the Russian government had criminalized criticism of the war and any kind of protest, there was no movement to protest mobilization. Polling data showed a rising tide of fear in Russia. At the same time, it showed consistently high levels of support for Putin's war.[20]

Unable to move forward except in small increments in the Donbas, the Russian military struck Ukraine continuously from the air. It fired missiles and sent in swarms of drones, a few of which would evade Ukrainian air defenses and reach their targets. Kyiv, which had achieved a tenuous normalcy in the summer, was hit again and again, as were many Ukrainian towns and cities. Part of this was to instill terror, though these attacks did not dent Ukrainian morale, whereas the heedless aggression behind these attacks did much to enrage the Ukrainian population. Part of this campaign was meant to erode Ukraine's civilian infrastructure and especially its supply of electricity and water. The goal was to devastate the economic and social base of the Ukrainian polity and military, the same reason for the Russian naval blockade. By summer 2023 some 17 percent of Ukraine was under Russian occupation, and much of this territory had been rich in industrial and agricultural resources before the war. The war's effect on the Ukrainian economy was catastrophic. Air travel had ground to a halt. Millions had left the country or been displaced. War drove away investment and raised insurance costs, making Western economic aid instrumental to Ukraine's survival. Russia was subjecting Ukraine to attrition in part to prove its resolve, in part to pave the way for future offensives, and in part to exact revenge for its underperformance in the war. Each civilian casualty inflicted by Russia was construed by Ukraine and its supporters as an additional reason to end the war with a Ukrainian victory.

Because of rapid military advances, Ukraine was exposing vulnerabilities on the Russian side. Russia had to defend a vast perimeter against an army that knew how to fight and knew what it was fighting for. When not moving forward, Ukraine could still strike behind enemy lines, which it had been doing since the summer, blowing up fuel and ammunition depots and hitting carelessly concentrated groups of Russian soldiers. A few strikes were conducted on Russian territory. Instead of putting Kyiv under Russian control, the war had put Crimea, the jewel in Putin's political crown, within range of the Ukrainian military. Russia had also awakened a dormant West. The volume and quality of the assistance given Ukraine in 2022 and 2023 would have been unthinkable before the war. Even Germany, a country that prided itself on its pacifist ideals, crossed a threshold in January 2023, when Chancellor Scholz agreed to send Leopard tanks to Ukraine. For Germany, it was a grudging acceptance of war in Europe and of Germany's unmasked involvement in this war. For Russian media, the motif of German tanks "once again" appearing on Ukrainian soil was confirmation of the war as World War II redux, a narrative that the provision of weapons from the United States or the United Kingdom did less to underpin. A Russia contending with German tanks one year after invading Ukraine was not the war the Kremlin had been expecting back when the eyes of the world were on Putin and on what he might do with all the troops he had amassed on the Ukrainian border.

* * *

In December 2022, Volodymyr Zelensky came to Washington, DC. He met with Joe Biden at the White House and addressed the US Congress, where he was met with rapturous applause. Zelensky had justified the imperative of war to Ukrainians and to the world. One of the world's greatest military machines, which had defeated Ukraine at Ilovaisk in August 2014 and at Debaltseve in February 2015, had later been shredded on the battlefields of Ukraine. Democratically elected in 2019, Zelensky communicated to the US Congress the spirit of American foreign policy, going back to the nineteenth century, if not to the American Revolution itself. Placing his own humanist decency against Vladimir Putin's violent egotism, Zelensky spoke to the efficacy and worth of liberty and self-government. He was speaking an American language of foreign policy in Washington, knowingly or unknowingly evoking earlier European visitors to the US Congress: the Marquis de Lafayette's address to Congress in 1824, an ode to the liberty etched into the French and American revolutions; Hungary's Lajor Kossuth's address to a joint session of Congress in 1852, in which Kossuth, a hero of Europe's 1848 revolutions, linked his country's fight against empire to the example of American democracy; and Vaclav Havel's address to Congress in 1990, in which Havel praised a heritage of democracy shared by the United States and Czechoslovakia. In his 2022 address to Congress, Zelensky was thanking the US government for helping to save Ukrainian democracy.[21] Woodrow Wilson, whose vision of Europe as an array of democratic nation states had been rejected by Congress, would have felt vindicated, had he lived to hear Zelensky's speech to Congress in December 2022.

It could not have been lost on Zelensky that in this same building Donald Trump had been tried for his dirty dealings in Ukraine. To improve his political fortunes, Trump had held up the transmission of Javelin anti-tank missiles to Ukraine. Caught red handed, Trump did eventually release the weapons to Ukraine, where they proved extremely helpful in the 2022 war. Perhaps Zelensky, a man trained in the comic arts, savored the irony of his hero's welcome in Congress. Or perhaps the memory of Trump's scheming was troubling to Zelensky. The former president, whose impeachment had not led to his conviction, had declared his candidacy in November 2022, not long before Zelensky's visit to Washington. Trump was highly critical of Biden's support for Ukraine, as was his son, Donald Trump Jr., who regularly insulted Zelensky on social media, and as were such pro-Trump media personalities as Tucker Carlson, who asked why a deal could not be struck with Russia, why the United States was spending so much money on Ukraine, and why the United States was courting a nuclear war for the sake of a corrupt country thousands of miles from the American homeland. How much time did Zelensky have before Trump or someone like Trump returned to the White House? How much was the cheering in Congress to be believed? Where was the United States heading? Forward to victory with Ukraine? Or back to the unconsummated romance between Donald Trump and Vladimir Putin?

The Biden administration appreciated Zelensky's visit as a reward for its hard work on Ukraine. Irritation over the AUKUS submarine deal had evaporated. The embarrassing departure from Afghanistan had not been forgotten, but it was receding from public memory. Before and during the war, the United States had demonstrated the uniqueness of its power, despite years of speculation about China's rise, about new configurations of wealth and power, and about American decline. This singular power of the United States consisted of intelligence gathering, of financial sway, of military might, and of the ability to coordinate and convene. Had the United States not been there, Europe would have floundered in 2022. Europe's aggregate capacities were great, but they were not primarily military and they could not be concentrated in the way that American power could; Europe's national variety had its downsides. American power is especially effective when there is moral energy behind it, and in the case of Ukraine this energy came from the Ukrainian people's will to fight, from Zelensky's democracy-inflected heroism, and from the lawless war of aggression Putin had chosen to inflict on Ukraine. The path from Trump's first impeachment to Zelensky's wartime appearance in Congress was not just ironic, not just cause for concern. It was the path of Biden's double achievement. Civil unrest had ended in the United States on January 6, 2021. The 2022 mid-term congressional election had been peaceful, a vote of approval for the incumbent president. Only a nation at peace with itself could have done as much as the United States did for Ukraine and for Europe in 2022. The movement of formerly neutral countries like Sweden, Finland, and Switzerland either toward the NATO alliance or toward greater coordination with Washington (on Ukraine) indicated Europe's overall direction, a tremendous vindication of Biden's transatlantic convictions and ideals.

Yet even at this celebratory moment, there was no end in sight to the war. Anxieties other than domestic politics haunted Zelensky's American visit. To be won, wars usually depend on well-defined objectives: the unconditional surrender, say, of Germany and Japan in World War II. In Vietnam and Afghanistan—by contrast—the United States had military superiority, but it had lacked feasible objectives. As these wars dragged on, they gelled into military and a political liabilities and into wars that the United States wound up losing.

Washington had a very enthusiastic partner in Zelensky's Ukraine, for which the ideal objective was easy to describe: the complete restoration of Ukrainian sovereignty, from the Donbas to Crimea, and Russia's unconditional acceptance of Ukrainian independence and sovereignty. But how was this to be accomplished? Even after Ukraine's knock-out offensives around Kharkiv and in Kherson, Russia was not withdrawing its troops from Ukraine. It still held more territory than it did before February 24. An additional anxiety was how far Russia would go with its war. The military machine at Putin's disposal, battered though it was, was neither small nor incapable of adaptation, and Russia was still a nuclear power of course. An experienced autocrat presiding over what appeared in Russia to be a popular war, Putin was not subject to the vicissitudes of a free press and of elections. As the Taliban had in Afghanistan, he would attempt to wait out the West. He had gone to war out of fear of the West, or so he said. He had also gone to war out of contempt for the West. More than the fear, the contempt would surely encourage him to stick with the war.

By December 2022, the mutual contempt between Russia and the United States was so intense that it cast the fearsome Cold War in a strange light. When trying to install nuclear weapons in Cuba in 1962, Nikita Khrushchev had wandered into extreme danger. He and Kennedy found their way out of the labyrinth, prompting more communication between Moscow and Washington and several productive decades of arms control. The Cold War started to get its rules in 1962. As the 2022 war in Ukraine approached its first-year anniversary, arms control was one of its many casualties, suggesting that spending on nuclear weapons would go up and, more important, that Russia and the United States would have a much harder time advancing the principle of non-proliferation, an interest shared by the two countries (and the rest of the world). A simple lesson of the war in Ukraine was that it might not have happened, had Ukraine possessed nuclear weapons: Iran, North Korea, and many other countries had to be taking note. As for the war itself, it had an escalatory dynamic that distinguished it from the Cold War. In its second year, Washington and Moscow both believed the war would determine European and international order, making it a war that neither side could lose. If there were still limits and rules, it was impossible to say what they were. Russia's war against Ukraine had sparked collisions more potentially combustible than the Cold War, more so even than the Second World War. The new instability, European and global in nature, is the product of these collisions.

Conclusion

War is unpredictable.

Thucydides, *The Peloponnesian War*, Book 2:11

Wars' ends refer back to their beginnings. The conclusion of a war modifies the conundrum of its origins, and in war's aftermath the relevant history is not only written by the victor. After World War I, France, Britain, and the United States—the winners of the war—blamed everything on Germany. They structured their policies accordingly, requiring Germany to pay reparations and giving themselves the task of suppressing German militarism. Hence, the limits imposed on German rearmament; hence the occupation of the Rhineland; hence the efforts to construct a League of Nations, and with the Kellogg-Briand Pact of 1928 to outlaw war itself. If the problem of Europe was war and the cause of war was Germany, then the solution to the problem of Europe was to prevent war by subduing Germany. Yet many Germans did not accept that Germany was at fault for World War I or that some innately German malady had dragged Europe into the abyss in 1914. Adolf Hitler rose to power not as the man who would admit German culpability for the war but as the man who could explain the war to Germany and to the world. He argued that it was the fault of the Jews—both the war and Germany's defeat in the war, making World War II a battle over the interpretation of World War I. (In 1940, Hitler had the French surrender to him in the same train car in which Germany had surrendered to France in 1918.) Nazi Germany had come into being to relitigate World War I, while in 1939 the Allies were confronted once again with the demons of German militarism. Interestingly, the victorious Allies in World War II, the United States and Britain at least, changed their interpretation of World War I in the 1940s, having come to regard themselves more critically. Consequently, they made the post–World War II order in Europe much more a matter of securing European peace than of punishing Germany.[1]

The end of the Cold War elicited similar disagreements about its origins. A diversity of theories about the Cold War's origins had long proliferated in the United States. Of them, the most politically potent was the "triumphalist" argument associated with the historian John Gaddis, who happened to be one of the writers of George W. Bush's second inaugural address.[2] Gaddis argued that a starkly suspicious Joseph Stalin had provoked the Cold War.[3] This thesis could be woven into a validation of US policy: the United States succeeded in the Cold War because the United States had created a network of anti-Stalinist and democratic allies, the kernel over time of the liberal international order that inspired Barack Obama and his administration. In his 2005 inaugural address, President Bush spoke of "ending tyranny," not least because—in his view—the US investment in democracy circa 1945 had paid such handsome dividends. There was no single Russian view of the Cold War in the 1990s, but from Moscow it was easier to view the Cold War as a tragedy, as a long phase of unavoidable competition with the United States, which at the very least shared responsibility with the Soviet Union for the outbreak of the Cold War. (In its official position and in its historical scholarship, the Soviet Union had blamed the Cold War squarely on Harry Truman and the United States.) Yes, the United States had come out ahead by 1991. That much was beyond argument, but its good fortune was not the forward march of democracy and the elaboration of a lasting peace. It was Russia's defeat and Russia's humiliation. In his rise to power, Vladimir Putin would argue that Gorbachev had given up on the Cold War. In a fit of stupidity, Gorbachev had rescinded Moscow's control over half of Europe for absolutely nothing in return. For Putin, some kind of cold war between Russia and the United States was the state of nature: relations among great powers are characterized by their antagonisms not by their affinities. The test of a Russian leader was how well he navigated this never-ending battle of will.

Pinpointing the origins of Russia's war against Ukraine will matter in many ways. As with the origins of World War I and World War II, identifying the origins of this war will determine the apportioning of blame. It will shape the diplomacy that terminates the war, if the war will have a definite termination. The Treaty of Versailles rested on certain assessments of German war guilt. The terms of the treaty, coupled with the eventual German opposition to these terms, dominated the international landscape of the 1920s and 1930s. The origins of World War II were less ambiguous. Though neither the United States nor the Soviet Union disagreed with the claim that it was Hitler's war, they understood and acted on this claim in sharply divergent ways. On the American side, it was the German democratic deficit that, by enabling Hitlerism, had caused World War II. Postwar order would demand a democratic Germany, which is what the United States fostered in West Germany. In the Soviet reading, the Soviet Union needed a buffer zone, because it had been invaded from the West, a victim of Hitler's mania for *Lebensraum*. For this it needed a compliant Germany, which is what the Soviet Union fostered in East Germany. (Vis-à-vis twenty-first century Europe and Ukraine, Obama and Biden are clearly the sons of Harry Truman, and Putin is clearly the son of Joseph Stalin; in their way, they are all sons of the Second World War.) The mutual suspicion that emanated from these two incompatible German and European projects, each a response to the presumed origins of World War II, was a precondition for the next stage of conflict in Europe, which was the Cold War.

Countries invariably conceive their foreign policies in reaction to earlier conflicts. They are led by their sense of who was wrong and who was right, of what the core problem was and what the solution to that problem was, fighting the last war until it is no longer the last war. This preoccupation with the past can be the path to wisdom, to learning from history, or it can leave countries trapped in their interpretations of the past. To investigate the origins of an ongoing war, then, is not just to chart the present moment. It is to peer, however uncertainly, into the future.

Regarding the war in Ukraine, blame will run in different grooves. Ukraine, Europe, and the United States will place full responsibility for the war on Russia. It was Russia that invaded on February 24, 2022. Ukraine had no capacity and no will to invade Russia. NATO is a defensive alliance. Much like Stalin in the triumphalist view of the Cold War, Putin fell victim to his paranoia and his dictatorial power in 2022. He chose to subject Ukraine to a brutal invasion, to incentivize war crimes and not to negotiate a settlement in good faith. Whatever the outcome of the war, the West—meaning the governments of Western countries and mainstream public opinion within these countries—will likely adhere to this position.[4] The official Russian attitude, so long as Putin is in power, will be that this was a war of necessity. The West and Ukraine forced Putin into it by bringing Western military assets to the edge of Russia, by inciting a Russophobic Ukrainian nationalism, by refusing to negotiate anything substantial about European security after 1991, by masterminding regime change in Ukraine in 2004 and again (successfully) in 2014, and by altering Ukrainian politics for the sake of enacting regime change in Russia. When it comes to explaining the origins of the war in the court of international opinion, neither the West nor Russia will win. Russia will not persuade global audiences that its war is just, and the West will not persuade global audiences that Russia's unjust war is all that different from the wars fought for centuries by the European imperial powers, from the West's Cold War adventurism or from the wars of choice that the United States fought after September 11.

The relative power to blame will set the diplomatic configurations of the postwar period. A Russia that survives the war intact and can compel compromises from the West would be able to disseminate its idea that the war was necessary (and rational) for Russia, that Moscow had no other choice, and that in the end, a necessary war amounts to a just war. A Ukraine and a West that pushes Russia back to its borders or that could engineer a lasting deal on Ukrainian terms, not to mention a Ukraine and a West that could conclude the war with war-crimes tribunals and with Russia paying reparations to Ukraine, would be able to disseminate its theory of the case: that the war was profoundly unjust and that Russian setbacks and defeats bolstered European security, the security of Taiwan, and the security of all countries that face bullying neighbors. Most perplexing would be a war that results in stalemate or that simply does not end. The result of that would be a cacophony of arguments about the war's origins, a merry-go-round of blaming, of refusing blame, and of paralyzed diplomacy. The diplomatic situation would resemble the stalemating of the Korean War, in which there is no settlement but instead a long-term, semi-negotiated suppression of the more acute tensions. No side could ever really claim to have won the Korean War, and for that reason perhaps, the sense of its origins is still so murky, as if it were a war that somehow started itself. Such stalemates amount to waiting games, to a phase of calm before one or another actor decides to upend the status quo, as may still happen on the Korean peninsula. Blaming one another for an eternal war, Ukraine and Russia would be biding their time, the outcome too pivotal for either side to live forever with its irresolution, perpetually on the cusp of a new offensive.

Beyond the question of blame, which is as much political as analytical, scrutinizing a war's origins can illuminate commonly held assumptions. In the case of World War I, a widespread prewar assumption was that the West and progress walked hand in hand. Europe was advanced and civilized, having tamed much of the world with commerce. By advancing in education, in urban development, and in bureaucratic administration, the West had moved forward in the nineteenth century, and it had lost the primitive appetite for war. Not only was this assumption glaringly wrong—not least because it was so self-celebratory—but the adherence to progress blinded Europeans, Americans, and others to the technological changes that would make World War I so devastating. By the time atomic bombs fell on Hiroshima and Nagasaki, the earlier, optimistic assumption of progress had been reversed. Greater clarity about modern times framed a new assumption: that progress was possible but not inevitable and that technological progress in the military domain could be disastrous for civilians. By testing assumptions against events—by testing commonly held assumptions against the 2022 war in Ukraine, for example—the consequences of great events come into focus. The fog of war is familiar enough and real enough, but in their origins and their consequences, wars also clarify. They can cut through the intellectual fog.

* * *

Russia's 2022 invasion of Ukraine has shattered three prewar assumptions. The first was that peace in Europe is a given: that Europeans have learned from their past and eliminated the instinct for war or sublimated it into the battles fought on the soccer field; that the United States is an effective guarantor for the security of all of Europe, either through the NATO alliance or through its ability to block those who might interfere with or invade a European country; and that Europe does not have enemies willing to wage a conventional war against it. The second assumption was that Europe could manage its own affairs: that institutions such as the European Union or that some combination of France, Germany, and the United Kingdom could do what was necessary for Ukraine's security in 2014 or in 2022. Optimistic about European leadership, the Obama administration let France and Germany negotiate Ukraine's future in 2014 and 2015. "Minsk" diplomacy was supposed to have been the hour of Europe, and that hour has still not come. Third, Russia's choice of war in 2022 demolished the assumption that Russia could be easily or casually integrated into Europe, that integration was destined to happen at some point. Germany had tended to pin its hopes for Russian integration on commerce, and since 1991 Washington had tended to pin its hopes on an eventual Russian democracy (as well as on commerce). Russia was integrating more and more into Europe between 2014 and 2022, and hope for a quiescent Russia in Europe still carried weight before the 2022 war. The Biden administration's notion of a US-Russian relationship with guardrails may not have been one of outright cooperation and partnership; it was the hope for a relationship that would not go off the rails. At the same time, it inclined toward peaceful co-existence. With commercial ties between Russia and the West still intact in a relationship of pipelines as well as guardrails, a minimalist and tactical integration might not be impossible. That was still a working assumption in the spring of 2021.

The assumption of a permanently postwar Europe hid a hard truth. The history of Europe is the history of war, a truth that haunts Ukrainian history. For centuries, Ukraine had been carved up by invading empires: the Mongol Empire, the Swedish Empire, the Ottoman Empire, the Russian Empire, the Austro-Hungarian Empire, the Polish-Lithuanian Commonwealth. Denied a seat at the table in Versailles, though promised nationhood by Austria during the war, Ukraine enjoyed a brief moment of independence in 1918, after which it disappeared from the map—much as Poland had disappeared from the European map in the late eighteenth century. Nazi Germany ravaged Ukraine, starting with the invasion of Poland in 1939 and then in 1941 with Operation Barbarossa: Ukraine and its agricultural riches were at the center of Hitler's planning for the war, the *Raum* that was to give Germans *Leben*.[5] The Red Army stormed through Western Ukraine en route to Berlin, absorbing it into the Soviet Union, though fighting continued between Ukrainian partisans and Soviet forces well into the 1950s. Until 1991, Ukraine was ruled from Moscow. None of this wrenching history predetermined conflict in 2014 or 2022, and for twenty-three years an independent Ukraine was unharmed by war, not under assault from Russia, from Poland, or from Germany; but Ukrainian history amply illustrates the precarity of peace in Europe. The architects of the Eastern Partnership

Program (EaP) had only partnership in mind when devising their program for Ukraine in 2009—and for five other post-Soviet countries. The EaP therefore had no security component. Honorable as the intentions of its architects were, these architects overlooked the possibility of war in a region where for so long conquest and empire had been the norm. The West's folly from 2009 to 2022 was to have forgotten the history of Eastern Europe, to which Russia organically belongs. This history did not incline toward peace after 1945, and it has never been orderly. Admirably attuned to integration and cooperation, the twenty-first century West should have been ready in thought and deed for war.

It was during the Cold War that Europe started overestimating its genius for peace. Almost mythic was the achievement of Franco-German friendship in the late 1940s and 1950s, and not less impressive was the achievement of Anglo-German and Anglo-French comity. Centuries of violence fell away when these former lions agreed to live as lambs. Their reward was the fabulous prosperity of the postwar period, *les trentes glorieuses* as the French referred to the three decades after World War II. Eastern Europe's joyful return to Europe in 1989 confirmed Western Europe's faith in the European community as a political model. Confidence shaded into overconfidence when Europe's institutions expanded eastward after 1991. Europe is not a continent. It is a part of the Eurasian landmass, more idea than landmass, the name itself derived from Greek mythology, and the idea of Europe is no more precise than a myth. Europe is a literary figuration, and as such it can be endlessly debated, endlessly revised, endlessly reconfigured. Is Russia in Europe? Is Turkey in Europe? Is Tunisia in Europe? Is the United States an appendage of Europe? Is Latin America? Is Europe a culture or a civilization? Is Europe an empire or a set of empires? Is it a confederation? An alliance? Is it a racialized or racist idea? Is democracy intrinsically European? Is rule of law? The fact that these are and will ever be open questions was precisely what allowed protestors on Kyiv's Maidan Square to declare themselves European, and by declaring themselves Europeans to be Europeans, even if their country was not in the EU or in NATO. They dubbed their revolution the Euromaidan to underscore Ukraine's home in Europe, which the map of Europe very much affirms. As in 1989, a Europe that could change and grow was a part of Europe's chameleonic beauty in 2013.

Beautiful as this protean Europe might be, it was drifting away from a state of peace well before the Maidan Revolution. That which is hard to define is hard to defend. Georgia may have been Europe. It was regularly referred to as on a European path, but it was not European enough for the 2008 Russian invasion to disturb the motif of a Europe at peace. A year later, when representatives of the EU extended a hand to Ukraine, a country also on a European path, they had hoped that Viktor Yanukovych would extend his hand by signing an Association Agreement with the European Union. The EU finalized its Association

Agreement with Ukraine in 2015 and helped with anti-corruption efforts after that. Yet in March 2014, when Russia had annexed Crimea and when Russia invaded the Donbas, the EU did nothing for Ukraine other than to levy sanctions on Russia (months after the annexation of Crimea) and to request that Russia change course. Europe's most prominent leader, Angela Merkel, did not say that all options were on the table. There was no military solution to the crisis in Ukraine, she contended, which was code for saying that Europe would not send its soldiers and its military equipment to Ukraine. It was a preposterous response to a war, to which there are only military solutions. If the application of military force is publicly refused, then the party that is willing to use military force will decide when and how or whether to stop the fighting. In the Donbas, everything ended up revolving around Russia's decisions, which made France's and Germany's contributions to Minsk diplomacy empty to the point of cynicism. They were signing documents and stipulating terms that they no ability to enforce. Having agreed that Ukraine *was* Europe and having equated Europe with peace—a European country being one that was at peace by definition—France and Germany were revealing exactly how limited they were as European powers or how contradictory they were. They were not defending the Europe that they had never rigorously defined.

The United States was not much better. President Obama held back on Ukraine. At no point did he give an equivalent of his soaring "Cairo speech" in Kyiv. He did not seem convinced that the Maidan was the wave of the future as a few years earlier he had been convinced that the Arab Spring was the wave of the future. By 2014, Obama had already witnessed the unwinding of the Arab Spring. His giving in to calls for military action in Libya had been foolhardy by his own retrospective admission. After some internal debate, the Obama administration chose not to send "lethal" military assistance to Ukraine, because Obama did not want to rush into a war and because Germany and other European powers did not see a military option. The United States was in a place it had not been since 1991—in potential conflict with a nuclear power. Obama was not being pushed to intervene militarily in Ukraine; there was no domestic and little international pressure for him to do so. He could square the circle of Russia's annexation and invasion of Ukrainian territory by deputizing the Europeans to handle this European crisis and then by shoring up the NATO alliance, not as a factor within Ukraine but as a prophylactic against the war's spreading out beyond Ukraine's borders. Angela Merkel spoke Russian and could handle Putin directly; Putin himself spoke German. From overseas, the United States would make sure NATO members were secure. The Obama administration had arrived at a moderate position that accorded with its military resources, with the built-in limits of the nuclear age, and with public opinion inside the United States.

Unlike Angela Merkel's government, however, the Obama administration often spoke as if it were the guarantor of European security per se, not just the guarantor of the NATO alliance in Europe. Here the definitional problems of Europe were once again confounding. US officials repeated a phrase about Ukraine's "Euro-Atlantic" integration. Did that mean that Ukraine was already a part of the Euro-Atlantic world, which was not a given for a country on the Black Sea? Did it mean that Ukraine was bound for membership in the North Atlantic alliance? Signed in 1990, the Charter of Paris stated that European countries were sovereign and independent, and the Budapest Memorandum of 2004 had repeated this assurance for Ukraine. The United States objected to Russia's annexation of Crimea and incursion into the Donbas as violations of the sovereignty and independence of a European country, a reversal of the liberal international order that had grown from a Euro-American acorn into a global oak tree and that was at the center of Barack Obama's foreign policy. What did it mean, though, if these principles were voiced but not backed up? To unforgiving onlookers, it could mean that these principles were verbal exercises and that by extension the United States was more the rhetorical than the real guarantor of Europe's security. In actual fact, the United States was the guarantor only of those European countries that were already in NATO, an observation consistent with Obama's and Merkel's actions on the ground. The record of American foreign policy since September 11 was not just one of military overreach in Iraq, Afghanistan, and elsewhere. It was one of rhetorical overreach, the apogee of which was the embrace of Ukraine as European and even "Atlantic" after 2014, coupled with the refusal to accept any military commitments and sacrifices on Ukraine's behalf, as if Ukraine belonged to an imagined Europe but not to the Europe that actually mattered. Had Europe been at peace in 2014, this space between diplomatic utterance and military reality might have been irrelevant, but from 2014 on Europe was not at peace.

A line runs from the transatlantic evasions of 2014 to the 2022 war. For all the high-quality intelligence sharing before the war and for all that the United States would do for Ukraine once the war began, Russia's 2022 invasion of Ukraine was a failure of deterrence. It was a failure in Europe and in a country that the United States regarded as a partner, not least because it was in Europe and because it had, through struggle, put itself on the European path to democracy and human rights. Before the 2022 war, the United States had threatened Russia with earth-shattering sanctions, a threat Putin blithely ignored. Once it began, the United States reacted to Russia's war much more assertively than Russia must have expected. Had Putin factored the US role in, he might not have invaded or he might have waited to invade with a much bigger army, though Putin's most significant error of judgment was to underestimate the Ukrainian military. Putin's mistake was to do what he did when he did it. His self-made catastrophe in Ukraine proceeded from his own arrogance and from his overheated worldview. The invasion may have proceeded as well from his cold-eyed analysis of events in 2014 and 2015 and from the West's inability to define its commitments to Ukraine, which was both a part of Europe and too far from Europe to be vigorously defended. If in 2022 the West held back militarily, as it had in 2014, then Russia could establish facts on the ground and force the West to deal with them by diplomatic means, the arrangement that had hamstrung the West between 2014 and 2022. Until February 24, 2022, the West predicated its uncertain attitude toward Ukraine on the assumption that Europe was and would remain fundamentally at peace, that it had leeway, that a major war in Europe was unthinkable. This assumption turned out to be wrong.

The third assumption that disintegrated in February 2022 was that Russia was either peripheral to Europe or that it was a troubled but necessary partner in European affairs. Russia's marginality could be expressed in economic terms. Russia has a small economy compared to that of the United States or China or the EU. Russia's economy ran on fossil-fuel production, it was argued, overlooking the fact that Russia is among the world's largest food producers. Fossil fuel will become less lucrative when alternative sources of energy are secured. True, Russia had nibbled away at the edges of Europe in Transnistria, in Abkhazia and South Ossetia, in Crimea and in the Donbas, but this could be taken as proof of its middling stature. A genuine great power would be able to command the territory around it, if it so wished, or it would have the magnetism that the West had for Ukraine in 2013–14 and that Russia lacked. It would gain friends and allies by attracting them. The image of Russia as the new sick man of Europe could be conjoined to the figure of Vladimir Putin, a petty tyrant who resembled the "bored kid in the back of the classroom," in Barack Obama's words, an icon of masculine insecurity who hunted big game, had improbable deep-sea diving discoveries, and who rode a horse bare-chested.[6] Russia did not have governing institutions on par with the mighty Chinese Communist Party, and in the Kremlin was an aging regime populated by mediocrities. Russia's miserable handling of the COVID-19 pandemic could likewise be a sign of backwardness, of a waning and unpopular country locked in demographic decline. Relevance and irrelevance are in the eye of the beholder. For all the incompetence of Russia's 2022 war effort, the war demonstrated Russia's relevance for Europe, within Europe and on matters of energy, food supply, and inflation outside Europe.

A complementary assumption was that for there to be peace, Russia needed to be inside the European house, a welcome participant in European affairs. This assumption was humane and misleading at the same time. Here European history betrays a bitter pattern. In its various forms, Russia has been a contented member of the European political family for long stretches of time, when it has held an imperial position in Eastern Europe. Russia's participation in the Concert of Europe and the Holy Alliance was a precondition for Europe's proverbial "long century," the peaceful interlude between the Napoleonic wars and the First World War, and Russia participated with Latvia, Lithuania, and Estonia within the empire, with parts of Poland and parts of Finland under Russian control and with eastern Ukraine, central Asia, and the south Caucasus all ruled from Saint Petersburg. By contrast, the Soviet Union before 1945, the Soviet Union *without* Eastern Europe, had tense relations with the West. It was absent from the treaty making in Versailles in 1919, and it invaded Poland in 1920, a spoiler on Europe's periphery before it entered into a deal with the devil—with Nazi Germany—in 1939. After the end of the Second World War, tensions between the West and the Soviet Union, caused by frustrations over the division of Europe, led to the Cold War. Yet in 1975 the Soviet Union and the West struck a deal, the Helsinki Final Act, through which they agreed on the borders of Europe. A mostly peaceful interlude between 1975 and 1991 ensued in Europe. Not accidentally, this interlude coincided with Soviet control over even more territory than imperial Russia had subjugated before World War I. Modern European history has witnessed pendular swings between war and Soviet/Russian imperial control over Eastern Europe, with instability springing up at times from within the empire, as it did in the 1860s or in the 1980s (both times with the Poles rebelling against outside control) or from outside the empire, from Napoleon's invasion in 1812, and from Hitler's in 1941. The border between Russia and Europe—Russia and France, Russia and Germany, Russia and the European Union—is one of Europe's insoluble problems. This problem is by no means a figment of the past.

Russia's relations with the West will be conflictual for a long time to come. That must now be the governing assumption. The compromises that could make Russia a contented member of the European family are not those that the West will be willing to make. These compromises—the withdrawal of military support for Ukraine, the acceptance of Russian control over Crimea and the Donbas, the promise not to expand NATO into Ukraine or Belarus—were not plausible before the 2022 war. The radicalism of this war has made these compromises less plausible still. However much NATO and the EU can do for their members internally, they cannot eliminate the conflict between Russia and the West. They are on one side of the conflict and Russia is on the other, and so it will be. Russian leaders after Putin may try to diminish tensions with the West. They may have less extreme visions of Russian foreign policy than Putin does, and they may recognize that Russia has harmed itself, its culture, its economy, its ability to innovate by turning its back on the West. They will be hard-pressed, though, to tolerate a Ukraine in the EU and a Ukraine that is militarily co-extensive with the West. They will be hard-pressed either to stop the war, if it lasts past Putin's reign, or to accept culpability once the war is over, ceding Crimea back to Ukraine and agreeing to war-crimes tribunals and reparations, which will be the Western preconditions for any return to normalcy. The task is not to transcend conflict, an impossibility in this case. It is to manage a conflict of a kind that has never existed between among nuclear powers. In particular, the nature of the US-Russian collision in the third decade of the twenty-first century is more direct, more fluid, and less controllable than it was during the Cold War. Managing it will be a generational challenge.

* * *

Four consequences of Russia's war against Ukraine can be discerned through the mist of current events. The first is Ukraine's Western orientation. Russia has burned its bridges in Ukraine, something it had done partially with the annexation of Crimea and invasion of the Donbas and then comprehensively with its criminal attack in 2022. The West's wartime embrace of Ukraine is not less of a break with the past: it will reshape the contours of Europe. The second consequence is that war in Europe will not cease, even if the war in Ukraine simmers down, even if a cease-fire is reached, even if the war ends in a negotiated settlement: there is no road back to the tenuous peace of the 1990s and thereafter, not for a West that will have to worry about future Russian invasions and not for a Russia that has staked so much on opposing the West. The third consequence is that Russia, having de-coupled from the West and having been de-coupled from the West, will with China be pushing for a new international order, in which Western power and prestige is sidelined as much as possible. This Russian project is some two decades old, but after 2022 it will be pursued more ruthlessly, and it will encompass more blatant attempts not just to displace the West but to destabilize it, for which Russia has ample tools. The war's fourth consequence is that the United States will continue to play a uniquely large role in European and also in international affairs. The war in Ukraine has—after years of discussion about American decline—shown the United States to be a global actor unlike any other. Neither China nor Russia has the combined capabilities of the United States, and since 1917, conflict in Europe has consistently pulled the United States toward international engagement. This does not guarantee American success in Ukraine or anywhere else, but it is a development that will reverberate within and beyond Europe for a long time to come.

The war has rooted Ukraine in the West. When Volodymyr Zelensky ran for president in 2018–2019, he did so as a "peace candidate." Had he been able to find his way to peace, the tensions of the Donbas might have been resolved, and presumably a more genial relationship with Russia could have begun, for which there was political will in some parts of Ukraine and which in the scheme of things made economic sense for Ukraine. A definitive end to the war, had it been achieved, would have attracted outside investment to Ukraine, and commerce between Ukraine and Russia, two neighbors, would have expanded. Perhaps it was nothing more than a casual campaign promise, but Zelensky's gesture toward reconciliation with Russia shows that as late as 2019 the die was not yet cast. Ukraine had no realistic prospects of EU or NATO membership in 2019, and while Trump was in power, both Poroshenko and Zelensky had to be careful. The United States was an unsteady presence in Europe. Trump had declared NATO "obsolete." He could appear to side with Putin about the annexation of Crimea, and he spoke frequently of making deals with Russia. Trump's hatred of the European Union and Trump's unpopularity in Europe could be the harbingers of a transatlantic cleavage, in which case, the United States having turned inward and left Europe in the lurch, Ukraine might have found itself alone with Russia. Zelensky never doubted the merits of a Western orientation for Ukraine. Until Trump left the White House, however, there were significant limits to how far he could go in this direction. Biden's election did not immediately erase these limits.

In a flash, the war changed everything for Ukraine. EU and NATO membership may still prove elusive. They depend on the war coming to an end on Ukrainian terms and on some agreement on Crimea, both enormous challenges. If Crimea remains in Russian hands—without a negotiated settlement—then the EU and NATO would be accepting a member without secure borders, while also committing themselves to Crimea's liberation. If the war lasts indefinitely, then the war itself will impede Ukraine's incorporation into these institutions. Yet the EU and NATO may not be the sine qua non of Ukraine's Western orientation; they may not be necessary. It may be sufficient to bring Ukraine as far as possible into the European orbit during the war. The Ukrainian will to join Europe is unambiguous, and Europe's will to help Ukraine and to furnish it with a European path is unambiguous as well. These are the most meaningful drivers of change, even if Ukraine remains outside of "institutional Europe." Likewise, the high degree of Western military commitment to Ukraine has come about without Ukrainian membership in NATO. Even without an Article 5 commitment from NATO, the United States and other NATO members have rushed to assist Ukraine in its fight with Russia. Their contributions to the Ukrainian military are transforming it into one of Europe's most formidable fighting forces. There are affluent NATO members that have much less effective militaries. Ukraine has already become a Western ally, and this it will stay, the war's first and perhaps its most revolutionary consequence.

Its second consequence is a transformed Europe. A bit more than two decades after George H. W. Bush rhapsodized about a Europe whole and free, this dream has died. Bush surely underestimated the magnitude and the improbability of what he was hoping for. Not even the Roman Empire had forged a Europe whole, free, and at peace. The Roman Empire built walls in the north of England and along the Danube to protect its half of Europe and was constantly at war with the other Europe, which overran the Roman Empire in 476 CE, inaugurating centuries of turmoil, mass migration, and war. Wars within Europe were a constant of medieval history. Invented in the crucible of the Thirty Years' War, the absolutist states of early modern Europe reflected the need to fund and to staff modern armies.[7] Early-modern France, Britain, and Spain fought their wars throughout Europe and across the globe, from India to Africa to the Americas. In the twentieth century, two European wars became world wars, the Second World War bringing Europe to the brink of self-immolation. The resolution to World War II was not exactly peace and harmony in Europe. It was a terrifying forty-year Cold War, what the historian Stephen Kotkin, referencing the passing of the Cold War, has characterized as Armageddon averted.[8] Two well-worn generalizations can be spun from European history: that no single power has ever been able to control Europe and to rid it of war, not the Roman Empire, not the Soviet Union and not the United States; and that European wars have a dispiriting tendency to spill over into Asia, Africa, and the Middle East. Here the 2022 war in Ukraine has been no exception: its effects have been vehemently global, creating new fissures in the global economy, cutting Russia off from Europe, projecting different kinds of instability and unrest into the Middle East and Africa via higher prices for food or through the worldwide inflation caused by the war. After a few anomalous years of peace, Europe became in 2022 what it has always been, an epicenter of conflict, the fault line around which the biggest and worst geopolitical earthquakes tend to occur.

As for Russia, post-Putin leaders may be aggrieved about Russia's loss of influence in Europe, but they will most likely strive to build on Putin's basic war aim, which is Russian control of Ukraine. Crimea will be a flashpoint if Russia keeps it *and* if Russia loses it—its annexation having been welcomed in Russia in 2014 and many investments having been made to link it to mainland Russia. Russia and the West will remain on the verge of war or they will be at war. This will do much to influence Ukraine's destiny, much as Israel's destiny has been influenced by the permanent threat of war—and quite often by outright war. The threat and reality of war will not just influence Ukraine. Should Belarus go through another episode of protest, as it did in the summer of 2020, the entire region could be inflamed. The Belorussian opposition movement, granted asylum for the time being in places like Vilnius and Berlin, dreams of a European future for Belarus, which is not a less obviously European country than Ukraine. Given the extreme distrust between Russia and the West, Belarus finds itself in the zero-sum logic of the Ukraine war. It will be either Europe or Russia: it cannot be both. In a Belorussian state honeycombed with Russian military and on territory that served as a staging ground for Russia's 2022 invasion of Ukraine, Russia would almost certainly wage war not to "lose" Belarus. Through Belarus the war that began in Ukraine could easily spread into a wider war. The Southeast of Europe, where some countries are in NATO and some are not, is unlikely to descend into large-scale war, but there too the zero-sum competition between Russia and the West will play itself out. A fiery arc of instability, not a curtain of iron, has descended on Europe from the Baltic Sea to the Black Sea and from Belarus to Bosnia.

Having opted for war, Putin has secured Russia's lasting non-Western orientation. This third consequence of war is the confirmation of a trend as well as a rupture. Post-Soviet Russia never accepted the European order that came haphazardly into being in 1991, though for a while it lived with it.[9] Yeltsin spooked Russia's European neighbors with the first Chechen War (1993–95), and he resented NATO expansion, complaining as early as 1994 that "even before the legacy of the Cold War has been laid to rest, Europe risks encumbering itself with a Cold Peace."[10] By 1998, he was elevating to high office figures like Yevgeni Primakov and Vladimir Putin, both of whom had extensive security-services ties. If Putin thought it degrading for Russia to imitate the West, he did not reject capitalism or modern technology: his was a reactionary modernism familiar from the Europe of the 1920s and 1930s.[11] He gradually organized Russian foreign policy around revanche and around anti-Westernism, with the West symbolized by deviant and decadent lifestyles. Putin bet on the internal failure of the West between 2016 and 2021. His dream never came to pass. In 2021 or in early 2022, he decided on another bet against the West and its out-of-touch elites—his invasion of Ukraine. Russia's divorce from the West was not an opportunity cost of Putin's war. It was a conscious attempt to cordon off Russia from the influence of Western culture and Western politics and an attempt to minimize Russia's economic relationship with the West, which in the form of sanctions gave the West power over Russia. Russia's 2022 break with the West was on par with the Soviet Union's rejection of non-revolutionary Europe in the 1920s, and it was accompanied by the same mass exodus of more westernized Russians to the West.

Putin's rejection of the West will be hard for future Russian leaders to reverse. Globally speaking, Putin's war against Ukraine has worked for Russia. Democracies like Brazil and India have not rallied to Ukraine's defense. They have politely listened to Biden administration appeals to do more, while continuing to trade with Russia and to treat it like a normal country. Turkey has kept on playing the United States and Russia off each other, often more anti-American than it is anti-Russian. In Latin America, the Middle East, and Africa, Russia has been making inroads since 2022, as it had been since 2014 and as it had during the Cold War. Western sanctions and Western disapproval did not lessen Russia's international influence after 2014. This influence grew—sometimes through arms sales, sometimes through the construction of nuclear power plants, sometimes through the deployment of mercenaries, sometimes through cultural or historical or political affinity. These affinities describe (imperfectly) Russia's relationship with China. China and Russia will try to isolate the West over the war and to burden the West with its collateral damage. They will try to use a war that Russia wins or a "forever war" with no winner to argue that the West's power and influence are not what they were in the past. Less and less does the West have a global imprimatur for its endeavors: this is a shared Russian and Chinese conviction. The West's travails in Ukraine, whatever they turn out to be, can be incorporated into a narrative of Western decline, a narrative to which China and Russia were energetically committed before the 2022 war. If Russia and China cannot lead the world, they can be effective in splintering the very notion of global leadership, so that no one country or group of like-minded countries can lay claim to it.

The United States has long laid claim to the notion of global leadership, and to this claim Europe has always been pivotal. The United States has been a European power of sorts since the 1890s, when the US economy was too big for Europe to ignore and when the United States entered the superstructure of European dominion in the world. It was the Spanish-American War of 1898 that brought the United States into Asia, Spain's decline mirroring the ascendance of the United States. Though the United States came late to the First World War, it was among the three most important powers at Versailles. Woodrow Wilson left a lasting imprint on the political culture of Europe, encouraging the end of formal empire and the rise of democratic states. After all, the United States had become a democracy by separating itself from the British Empire, and at Versailles the United States welcomed independent nation states in Central and Eastern Europe, not that these states proved to be overwhelmingly democratic in the 1920s and 1930s and not that the United States was especially active in Eastern and Central Europe in the inter-war period. Washington could not halt the evolution of a Soviet Union that was anti-imperial in theory and robustly imperial in practice. Nor could it halt the evolution of a Nazi Germany, of a third Reich—an empire to succeed the Roman and the Holy Roman Empires—that was zealously imperial in theory and in practice. In the 1930s, the United States lamented the cost of imperialism in Central Europe, the dividing up of Poland and the Baltic Republics in the Molotov-Ribbentrop Pact, and the invasion of Poland that set off the worst war in human history. But not until the attack on Pearl Harbor and Germany's subsequent declaration of war, in December 1941, did the United States join the fight against the Third Reich.

European conflict in the 1940s ended up augmenting American power. The United States could mobilize industrial production even more capably than Nazi Germany did in the 1930s or than the Soviet Union did during the war. At their best, the public-private partnerships that drove wartime production in the United States linked private industry's talent for innovation with the government's talent for planning and organization—to awesome effect. Through the training of young minds, universities infused both private industry and the government with well-wrought talent. Internationally, the American way of war invited alliances, enduring alliances with the British Commonwealth and with the France represented by Charles de Gaulle and a less lasting, though no less necessary alliance with Stalin's Soviet Union. No World War II alliance, no defeat of Nazi Germany. The key American practitioner of alliance formation and maintenance, Dwight Eisenhower, became a two-term president in 1952, after having served as NATO's first Supreme Allied Commander. He and many others embedded the spirit of alliances in American foreign policy. The final ingredient of American power was more variable. It was the mobilization of the American public, which, when it happened, was a juggernaut, as it had been during World War II and at the beginning and the end of the Cold War. When public mobilization flagged, American foreign policy flagged with it, the best example of which was the Vietnam War. In World War II, industrial production, alliance building, and mobilization could not have been more effectively combined into the battering ram of American power.

After World War II, Europe was key to superpower status for Washington, which did not mean that Europe fell into the lap of the United States. The US commitment was to Western Europe. More was not possible in the late 1940s and thereafter, when the Red Army and the Soviet nuclear arsenal stood in the way. The United States met its commitment to Western Europe brilliantly— through NATO and through an alliance structure in which Western Europe and the United States were not exactly equals but in which NATO members all had a say and in which membership was voluntary. The attraction of membership was such that countries very much wanted to join and to stay in NATO. Western Europe was the showcase. Its freedoms and its prosperity were what the United States could promise—not always credibly—to countries outside of Europe, as they selected their partnerships and affiliations. The sprawling superpower status of the United States in the 1990s was confirmed by the rush of countries to join NATO and by countries from around the world that wanted to partner with the United States. A Pax Americana existed in post–Cold War Europe. In the eyes of American presidents and policymakers until Trump's election in 2016, it was the pillar of the liberal international order: deliberation rather than war, free trade according to agreed-upon rules, sovereignty and national independence as absolutes. This was not an order to be realized at the barrel of a gun. The liberal international order would be by invitation, though those countries that grossly violated it (like Saddam Hussein's Iraq or Muamar Gaddafi's Libya) might face the wrath of the US military. Rules are not rules unless they can be made to stick.

The four years of Trump's presidency raised worrisome questions about the United States and Europe. The immensity of the US economy and the vitality of public-private partnerships for the manufacturing of military power would not mean much, if the United States were to slide into civil war. Trump governed the United States by stoking outrage, filling his supporters and his enemies with fury and then putting himself forward as the only one who could handle the metastasizing chaos. His attempt to overthrow his own government on January 6, 2021, was not a footnote to his presidency; it was the keystone to his presidency. Trump did not stoke quite so much chaos internationally. He started no new war, and the four years in which he was president were relatively calm. Nevertheless, he threatened to destroy the transatlantic relationship, for which he had no respect. He wanted to invert US alliances into transactional, mafia-style hierarchies through which the United States would be paid for the protection it could offer. Trump also blocked the chances of mobilizing the US population behind any kind of foreign policy. He was too divisive in his domestic politics, and he did not share the perspective of a Woodrow Wilson, a Franklin Roosevelt, a Harry Truman, or a Ronald Reagan that internationalism was per se in the American national interest. Trump sought an American population captivated by his media antics. He wanted his critics to be excluded from political agency, while to the real Americans who were his backers he recommended selfishness, as if the point of American politics was to satisfy and to serve them personally. Had Trump been elected in 2020, American power in Europe and elsewhere might have waned without Russia or any other country having to do anything at all.

Trump's political career may not be over. Unless he does return to the White House in January 2025, though, the fourth consequence of the war in Ukraine will have been a restoration of American power in its traditional twentieth-century form. The war has revealed the importance of American military assets from intelligence gathering to stocks of ammunition to precision-guided missiles. Together with Ukrainian willpower and skill at strategy, the United States has given Ukraine technological and logistical prowess that no European country or combination of countries could give. American assistance is one of the major factors in the war, perpetuating a dynamic first set in motion in World War I, when American soldiers helped to turn the tide of the war, a dynamic that replicated itself in World War II and the Cold War. The Biden White House has excelled at alliance formation on Ukraine's behalf. Part of this is the work of American diplomats. Part of it is a White House that is comfortable with the give and take of alliances, not demanding too much, not going too fast, and not forgetting the flexibility that oils all alliances. If the United States did not itself mobilize for war in 2022 as it did in 1942 or in the first few years of the Cold War, it has emphatically stood behind Ukraine. In the 2022 midterm elections, anti-war Republicans did not surge forward. Bi-partisan support for Ukraine will not last forever, but it is a non-negligible circumstance. An outward facing, focused United States willing and able to convene dozens of allies and partners, not all of them in Europe, is both an unintended consequence of Russia's invasion and a force unto itself in international affairs.

* * *

The origins of war shadow the *Iliad*, the first major work of European literature, while its companion volume, the *Odyssey*, is a book about the consequences of war. Odysseus, the hero of the *Odyssey*, must journey for many years after fighting at Troy. He is not concerned with the political crisis that precipitated the war—the abduction of Helen and the initial counsels of war. He does not pretend to understand the war in which he fought and by which he was too much harmed to celebrate. For much of the *Odyssey*, for much of Odysseus's postwar life, he is silent about the past, though the past is not silent in him. He arrives in safety and finds himself at the court of Alcinous, king of the Phaecians, who promises to send him on his way home. Relaxing at the court of the hospitable Alcinous, Odysseus asks Demodocus, a bard, to sing to him about the war. Odysseus wants to hear about all that his comrades "did and suffered, all they soldiered through." Demodocus obliges. Memory and meaning converge for the first time in this book of forward motion, unspooling backward into metaphor. Known for his muscle and his cunning, Odysseus listens to Demodocus's song and weeps, his tears pointing us to the inner truth of his war or, rather, of all wars:

> tears,
> running down from his eyes to wet his cheeks . . .
> as a woman weeps, her arms flung round her darling husband,
> a man who fell in battle, fighting for town and townsmen,
> trying to beat the day of doom from home and children.
> Seeing the man go down, dying, gasping for breath,
> She clings for dear life, screams and shrills—
> but the victors, just behind her,
> digging spear-butts into her back and shoulders,
> drag her off in bondage, yoked to hard labor, pain
> and the most heartbreaking torment wastes her cheeks.
> So from Odysseus' eyes ran tears of heartbreak now.[12]

The truth of war is the tears of pain, even as the fight for town and townsmen is the stuff of heroism, not just in epic poetry but in the unsentimental terrain of real life.

In Russia's war against Ukraine, the tectonic plates of international relations are shifting. It is an event of global magnitude, as only a few wars ever are. The inner truth of this war is far more local, since the actual collisions of the war are not the collisions of abstract force, of geopolitics, or of international order as it is conceived in the Ministry of Foreign Affairs in Kyiv, in the State Department or in the Ministry of Foreign Affairs in Moscow. Wars are not experienced in the jargon of diplomats. The collisions of this war are the harrowing reality of Ukrainian civilians and soldiers. That this war is occurring in the same region where such terrible fighting took place after 1914, where Sovietization was so murderously violent and where so many of the crimes of the Second World War and the Holocaust were perpetrated is a further injustice, one that can be added to the injustice of the 2014–15 war fought on Ukraine's soil, round one of a much larger war. Taken together, the *Odyssey* and the *Iliad* remind us that what on its surface is military epic—the progression of world-historical events, the speeches, the strategies, the instances of valor—is beneath its surface tragedy. Even victory cannot ease the tragedy of war: "Every war," as Andrey Kurkov writes, "leaves a deep wound in the soul of a person."[13] Odysseus and his comrades won their war, which does not save them from their lasting grief. His hero's tears merge with the heartbreaking torment of the war's pictured victims. The tragedy of Russia's war against Ukraine is that it happened at all, and it is the tragedy of what has happened. The subjects of this tragedy, who bear no responsibility for the war itself, are the common people of Ukraine. It is a tragedy comprised of all they did and suffered, and all they soldiered through.

Notes

Abbreviations

AfD	Alternative für Deutschland
ABM	Anti-Ballistic Missile Treaty
AA	Association Agreement
AUKUS	Australia, the United Kingdom, and the United States
CDU	Christian Democrats
DCFTA	Deep and Comprehensive Free Trade Agreement
DNR	Donetsk People's Republic
EaP	Eastern Partnership Program
ECU	Eurasian Customs Union
EEU	Eurasian Economic Union
EU	European Union
FSB	Federal Security Service - Successor to Committee for State Security KGB
ISIS	Islamic State of Iraq and Syria, a militant terrorist insurgency
JCPOA	Joint Comprehensive Plan of Action
LNR	Luhansk People's Republics
MAP	Membership Action Plan
NATO	North Atlantic Treaty Organization
OSCE	Organization for Security and Cooperation in Europe

Preface

1. Of Leonid Kuchma and of the Ukrainian president who preceded him, Leonid Kravchuk, Olga Onuch, and Henry Hale write of them both having been "deeply embedded in former Communist Party networks." *The Zelensky Effect* (New York: Oxford University Press, 2023), 49.

2. On voluntary associations and the war, Ukrainian writer Andrey Kurkov writes that "in the Ukrainian language and in Ukrainian tradition the word *toloka* means 'community work done for the common good.' . . . Not so long ago, another word with a large number of meanings was added to the concept of *toloka*. It is the word 'volunteer.' This concept, which involves helping people whom you do not know, is relatively new to Ukraine. . . . Volunteers bring humanitarian aid to residents of front-line villages and cities left without supplies. Volunteers are even trying to evacuate residents from the occupied territories." Andrey Kurkov, *Diary of an Invasion* (Dallas, TX: Deep Vellum Publishing, 2022), 208.

3. Thucydides, translated by Martin Hammond, *The Peloponnesian War* (Oxford: Oxford University Press, 2009), 3, 13. Mark Galeotti asks whether Russia truly is "some new, 21st-century Sparta" and answers his own question with some skepticism: "If anything," he writes, "the Kremlin let itself be seduced by all this [militaristic] theater," meaning the public displays of military prowess typical of Putin's Russia. *Putin's Wars: From Chechnya to Ukraine* (New York: Osprey Publishing, 2022), 355.

Introduction

1. Alexis de Tocqueville, *Democracy in America*, vol. 1, translated by Henry Reeve (New York: Knopf, 1945), 434.
2. On the American tendency not to steer clear of international conflict, see Charles A. Kupchan, *Isolationism: A History of America's Efforts to Shield Itself from the World* (New York: Oxford University Press, 2020).
3. An amusing detail from Zelensky's career as a performer is from 2010, when he and his colleagues "were hired as the entertainment at President Viktor Yanukovych's 60th birthday party at the state dacha at Foros in Crimea," a meeting of two presidents. Owen Matthews, *Overreach: The Inside Story of Putin's War against Ukraine* (London: Mudlark, 2023), 138.
4. Published fifteen years after the collapse of the Soviet Union, Tony Judt's magisterial history of modern Europe is titled *Postwar*, as if war were never to return to Europe. See *Postwar: A History of Europe after 1945* (New York: Penguin, 2006).
5. For a study of 1989 as the birth of democracy in Eastern Europe and the creation of a new Europe, see Vladimir Tismaneanu, *Reinventing Politics: Eastern Europe from Stalin to Havel* (New York: Free Press, 1992).
6. Unequal as post-Soviet Russia turned out to be, inequality in Russia "was lower than among citizens in the United States, China, Brazil, and especially South Africa [circa 2017]," Kathryn Stoner points out. *Russia Resurrected: Its Power and Purpose in a New Global Order* (New York: Oxford University Press, 2021), 171.
7. On the history of US-Russian relations before the Cold War, see William Appleman Williams, *American-Russian Relations, 1782–1946* (New York: Octagon Books, 1971); and Norman E. Saul, *Distant Friends: The United States and Russia, 1763–1867* (Lawrence, KS: University of Kansas Press, 1991).
8. On wartime continuities with the Cold War past (circa 2022), see Stephen Kotkin, "The Cold War Never Ended: Ukraine, the China Challenge, and the Revival of the West," *Foreign Affairs* (May/June 2022), https://www.foreignaffairs.com/reviews/rev iew-essay/2022-04-06/cold-war-never-ended-russia-ukraine-war. For a different framing of the Cold War legacy, see Odd Arne Westad, "Has a New Cold War Really Begun? Why the Term Shouldn't Apply to Today's Great Power Tensions," *Foreign Affairs* (March 27, 2018), https://www.foreignaffairs.com/articles/china/2018-03-27/ has-new-cold-war-really-begun.

9. On Soviet efforts to Russify Ukraine after World War II, see chapter 24, "The Second Soviet Republic," in Serhii Plokhy, *The Gates of Europe: A History of Ukraine* (New York: Basic Books, 2015), 291–306.

10. Referring to its political leadership, Serhii Plokhy describes the Soviet Union in its last decades as "a Russo-Ukrainian condominium." *The Russo-Ukrainian War: The Return of History* (New York: Norton, 2023), 21.

11. See Leonid Kuchma, *Ukraine Is Not Russia*, translated by Tania Kantziou (Athens: Livanis, 2013). By distinguishing Ukraine from Russia, Kuchma did not intend to isolate Ukraine from Russia. Kathryn E. Stoner notes that "Russia [under Putin] was a strong financial backer and supporter of . . . Ukrainian president Leonid Kuchma." *Russia Resurrected*, 44. Likewise, in Serhii Plokhy's words, Kuchma "campaigned [in 1994] on a platform of rebuilding economic ties with Russia." *The Russo-Ukrainian War*, 45.

12. On the evolution of modern Ukraine, see Serhy Yekelchyk, *Ukraine: Birth of a Modern Nation* (Oxford: Oxford University Press, 2007); Paul Robert Magocsi, *A History of Ukraine: The Land and Its Peoples* (Toronto: University of Toronto Press, 2010); Andrew Wilson, *The Ukrainians: Unexpected Nation* (New Haven, CT: Yale University Press, 2015); Serhii Plokhy, *The Last Empire: The Final Days of the Soviet Union* (New York: Basic Books, 2015); Serhii Plokhy, *The Gates of Europe: A History of Ukraine* (New York: Basic Books, 2021); and Yaroslav Hrytsak, *A Brief History of Ukraine* (New York: Basic Books, 2024).

13. On the Helsinki Final Act, see Michael Cotey Morgan, *The Final Act: The Helsinki Accords and the Transformation of the Cold War* (Princeton, NJ: Princeton University Press, 2018).

14. For a history of the Putin regime, leading up to the 2022 invasion of Ukraine, with illuminating passages on the Russian-German relationship, see Michael Thumann, *Revanche: Wie Putin das bedrohlichste Regime der Welt geschaffen hat* (Munich: C. H. Beck, 2023). [*Revanche: How Putin Created the World's Most Threatening Regime*].

15. On (qualified) sympathy for Russia outside of Europe, amid its war in Ukraine, see Roger Cohen, "Putin Wants Fealty, and He's Found It in Africa," *New York Times* (December 24, 2022); and "Russia's War Could Make It India's World," *New York Times* (December 31, 2022).

16. On the technical aspects of US military support for Ukraine, see David Ignatius, "A 'Good' War Gave the Algorithm Its Opening, But Dangers Lurk," *Washington Post* (December 20, 2022), https://www.washingtonpost.com/opinions/2022/12/20/ukraine-war-russia-tech-battlefield/.

Chapter 1

1. On Barack Obama's immersion in the foundational texts of American politics, see James Kloppenburg, *Reading Obama: Dreams, Hope, and the American Political Tradition* (Princeton, NJ: Princeton University Press, 2012).

2. In his memoirs, Barack Obama describes his thinking on foreign policy as a cross between liberal internationalism and realism. He came to the White House believing that "the steady promotion of democracy, economic development, and human rights around the world served our long-term national security interests." He also embraced "the 'realist' school, an approach that valued restraint, assumed imperfect information and unintended consequences, and tempered a belief in American exceptionalism with a humility about our ability to remake the world in our image." Barack Obama, *A Promised Land* (New York: Crown, 2020), 217.

3. To put this argument in Barack Obama's words: "In the wake of World War II, with the rest of the world either impoverished or reduced to rubble, we had led the way in establishing an interlocking system of initiatives, treaties, and new institutions that effectively remade the international order and created a stable path forward." Obama, *A Promised Land*, 328.

4. For the Obama administration, an important theorist of the liberal international order was Princeton professor John Ikenberry, whose books and edited volumes include: *After Victory: Institutions, Strategic Restraint, and the Rebuilding of Order after Major Wars* (Princeton, NJ: Princeton University Press, 2001); *Forging a World of Liberty under Law: U.S. National Security in the 21st Century* (Princeton, NJ: Princeton Project on National Security, 2006); *The Crisis of American Foreign Policy: Wilsonianism in the Twenty-First Century* (Princeton, NJ: Princeton University Press, 2008); and *Liberal Leviathan: The Origins, Crisis, and Transformation of the American System* (Princeton, NJ: Princeton University Press, 2011). Another important international-affairs thinker for the Obama administration was Anne-Marie Slaughter, who was the State Department's director of policy planning from 2009 to 2011. Works of hers that informed the administration's approach to foreign policy were *A New World Order* (Princeton, NJ: Princeton University Press, 2004); and *The Idea that Is America: Keeping Faith with Our Values in a Dangerous World* (New York: Basic Books, 2007). For biographies of the key decision-makers in the Obama administration, see James Mann, *The Obamians: The Struggle inside the White House to Redefine American Power* (New York: Penguin Books, 2013).

5. The legacy of Harry Truman was especially important to the Obama administration, which in its personnel had many ties to the Truman National Security Project founded in 2005 in part to honor Truman and in part to foster national-security and foreign-policy positions that were "Trumanesque"—i.e., internationally engaged and amenable to alliances like NATO.

6. On the emergence of *Ostpolitik*, see Angela Stent, *From Embargo to Ostpolitik: The Political Economy of West Germany-Soviet Relations* (New York: Cambridge University Press, 1981); and Julia Von Dannberg, *The Foundations of Ostpolitik: The Making of the Moscow Treaty between West Germany and the USSR* (New York: Oxford University Press, 2008).

7. On Joschka Fischer's break with the United States over Iraq, see Paul Berman, *Power and the Idealists* (New York: Soft Scull Press, 2005). For a biography of Gerhard Schroeder, see Gregor Schoellgen, *Gerhard Schroeder: Die Biographie* (Munich: Deutsche Verlags-Anstalt, 2015).

8. Merkel's biographer, Ralph Bollmann, writes that "Merkel was never a heartfelt European, a circumstance to be explained by her socialization." [Eine Herzenseuropäerin was Merkel nie gewesen, das lag schon in ihre Sozialisation begründet.] Ralph Bollmann, *Angela Merkel: Die Kanzlerin und ihre Zeit* (Munich: Beck, 2021), 376. For an English-language biography of Angela Merkel, see Stefan Kornelius, *Angela Merkel: The Chancellor and Her World* (London: Alma Books, 2014).

9. On the legal complexities of the Obama administration's position on drone warfare, see Sam Moyne, *Humane: How the United States Abandoned Peace and Reinvented War* (New York: Farrar, Straus and Giroux, 2022).

10. Obama, *A Promised Land*, 530. For Europe as a centuries-old project combining human rights and peace, see Stella Ghervas, *Conquering Peace: From the Enlightenment to the European Union* (Cambridge, MA: Harvard University Press, 2021).

11. For landmark studies of post–Cold War German policy, see Angela E. Stent, *Russia and Germany Reborn: Unification, the Soviet Collapse, and the New Europe* (Princeton, NJ: Princeton University Press, 2000); and Mary Sarotte, *1989: The Struggle to Create Post-Cold War Europe* (Princeton, NJ: Princeton University Press, 2014).

12. The euro and other steps toward European integration were adopted by the European Community in December 1989, shortly after the fall of the Berlin Wall.

13. See Jeremy Rifkin, *The European Dream: How Europe's Vision of the Future Is Quietly Eclipsing the American Dream* (New York: Tarcher, 2004). Historian Tony Judt explored the other side of Rifkin's Euro-optimism in a pessimistic assessment of American politics (circa 2010) that was a tacit endorsement of Europe's future: *Ill Fares the Land* (New York: Penguin, 2010).

14. Merkel's biographer, Ralph Bollmann, describes the Obama-Merkel confrontation at Cannes in *Angela Merkel*, 416–417.

15. On the financial crisis of 2008 and its global implications, see Adam Tooze, *Crashed: How a Decade of Financial Crisis Changed the World* (New York: Penguin Books, 2018). See also Ben S. Bernanke, *The Federal Reserve and the Financial Crisis* (Princeton, NJ: Princeton University Press, 2015).

16. Two books by Obama administration officials that address the "pivot" to Asia are Jeffrey A. Bader, *Obama and China's Rise: An Insider's Account of America's Asia Strategy* (Washington, DC: Brookings Institution Press, 2013); and Kurt Campbell, *Pivot: The Future of American Statecraft in Asia* (New York: Twelve, 2016). See also Chi Wang, *Obama's Challenge to China: The Pivot to Asia* (Oxford: Routledge, 2017); and chapters 5–8 in Graham Allison, *Destined for War: Can America and China Escape the Thucydides Trap?* (New York: Mariner Books, 2018), 89–186.

17. For context on Robert Zoellick's 2005 speech, in which he identified China as potentially a "responsible stakeholder," see Amitai Etzioni, "Is China a Responsible Stakeholder?," *International Affairs* 87, no. 3 (May 2011): 539–553.

18. On neoconservative thought and the foreign policy of the George W. Bush administration, see Jacob Heilbrunn, *They Knew They Were Right: The Rise of the Neocons* (New York: Penguin, 2009); and Justin Vaisse, *Neoconservatism: The Biography of a Movement*, translated by Arthur Goldhammer (Cambridge, MA: Harvard University

Press, 2011). See also Francis Fukuyama, *America at the Crossroads: Democracy, Power and the Neoconservative Legacy* (New Haven, CT: Yale University Press, 2006).

19. Obama, *A Promised Land*, 365.

20. On the perceived connection between technological change and democratic prog-ress in the Middle East, see Jared Cohen, *Children of Jihad: A Young Man's Travels Among the Youth of the Middle East* (New York: Gotham Books, 2007). From 2006 to 2010, Jared Cohen served on the Policy Planning Staff of the US Department of State. On technological change, democratic progress and the 2008 Obama cam-paign, see Matt Bai, *The Argument: Inside the Battle to Remake Democratic Politics* (New York: Penguin, 2008).

21. As a general matter, recalls Samantha Power, who served on the National Security Council from 2009 to 2013 and whose "approach inside government . . . had a lot in common with activist strategies outside," many "of the US government's Middle East experts who attended our meetings argued that the political status quo in the region served US interests." *The Education of an Idealist: A Memoir* (New York: Day Street Books, 2019), 271, 286.

22. In his memoirs, Obama emphasized the leverage military aid gave the United States in Egypt. For that reason, among others, Mubarak's perpetration of "wanton violence on peaceful demonstrators, with all the world watching—that was a line I was un-willing to cross. It would do too much damage, I thought, to the idea of America. It would do too much damage to me." Obama, *A Promised Land*, 648.

23. Obama, *A Promised Land*, 639, 654. See Samantha Power, *A Problem from Hell: America and the Age of Genocide* (New York: HarperCollins, 2007). Before joining him at the White House, Samantha Power worked for Barack Obama when he was a senator. As a senator, as a candidate for the presidency in 2008 and as a presi-dent after that, Obama was anomalous in American politics, in Power's view. "Obama made diplomacy and engagement with adversaries a centerpiece of his candidacy [for the presidency]," she writes, noting at the same time "how few voices in high-level government discussions highlighted the nexus between human rights and US national security. . . . [T]he realist view . . . was dominant" [circa 2008]. In addition, "Obama's thinking departed in important ways from that of the foreign policy estab-lishment." Power, *The Education of an Idealist*, 172, 220, 222.

24. On Obama administration policy toward the Middle East, see Fawaz A. Gerges, *The End of America's Moment? Obama and the Middle East* (London: St. Martin's Press, 2012). On the Obama administration's decision to take military action in Libya, see Jo Becker and Scott Shane, "Clinton, 'Smart Power' and a Dictator's Fall," *New York Times* (February 28, 2016); and Scott Shane and Jo Becker, "After Revolt, a New Libya with 'Very Little Time Left,'" *New York Times* (February 29, 2016).

25. African history and politics are important themes in the book that helped to launch Barack Obama's political career: *Dreams of My Father: A Story of Race and Inheritance* (New York: Crown, 2004).

26. Mary Sarotte makes a persuasive argument for the enlargement of NATO having been zero-sum as well. Either American leaders "could enable the region of Central and Eastern Europe writ large—including post-Soviet states such as the Baltic and

Ukraine—to choose its own destiny at long last, regardless of the impact on Moscow; or they could promote cooperation with Russia's fragile new democracy [in the 1990s], particularly in the interest of nuclear disarmament." They could not necessarily do both. Mary Sarotte, *Not One Inch: America, Russia, and the Making of Post-Cold War Stalemate* (New Haven, CT: Yale University Press, 2021), 4.

27. For a comprehensive history of US Ukraine policy, see Eugene Fishel, *The Moscow Factor: U.S. Policy toward Sovereign Ukraine and the Kremlin* (Cambridge, MA: Harvard University Press, 2022). See also Sherman W. Garnett, *Keystone in the Arch: Ukraine in the Emerging Security Environment of Central and Eastern Europe* (Washington, DC: Carnegie Endowment for International Peace, 1997).

28. On the European transitions between 1989 and 1991, see chapter 17, "George H. W. Bush: Alliance Leader," in Robert B. Zoellick, *America in the World* (New York: Twelve, 2020), 418–442; and Susan Glasser and Peter Baker, chapter 20, "The Curtain Falls," in *The Man Who Ran Washington: The Life and Times of James A. Baker III* (New York: Anchor, 2021), 357–377.

29. Czechoslovakia, Hungary, and Poland set up the Visegrad cooperation in February 1991; it was meant to facilitate entry into the European Community (the precursor to the European Union) and NATO. Vaclav Havel was requesting some form of NATO membership for Czechoslovakia as early as 1991. See Sarotte, *Not One Inch*, 125. In April 1993, Vaclav Havel explained, during a visit to Washington, that "we are living in a vacuum. . . . [T]hat is why we want to join NATO." Vaclav Havel quoted in Sarotte, *Not One Inch*, 161. In Washington at the same time, Lech Walesa put the point more sharply: "We are all afraid of Russia. . . . [I]f Russia again adopts an aggressive foreign policy, that aggression will be directed toward Ukraine and Poland." Lech Walesa quoted in Sarotte, *Not One Inch*, 161.

30. On the history of NATO enlargement, see Ronald D. Asmus, Richard L. Kugler, and F. Stephen Larrabbee, "Building a New NATO," *Foreign Affairs* (September/October 1993); Strobe Talbott, "Why NATO Should Grow," *New York Review of Books* (August 10, 1995); James Goldgeier, *Not Whether But When: The U.S. Decision to Enlarge NATO* (Washington, DC: Brookings Institution Press, 1999); Strobe Talbott, *The Russia Hand* (New York: Random House, 2002); James Goldgeier and Michael McFaul, *Power and Purpose: U.S. Policy toward Russia after the Cold War* (Washington, DC: Brookings Institution Press, 2003); James Goldgeier with Derek Chollet, *America between the Wars: 11/9 to 9/11* (New York: Public Affairs, 2008); Ronald Asmus and George Robertson, *Opening NATO's Door: How the Alliance Remade Itself for a New Era* (New York: Council on Foreign Relations, 2014); Sarotte, *Not One Inch*; and James Goldgeier and Josh Shifrinson, editors, *Evaluating NATO Enlargement: From Cold War Victory to the Russia-Ukraine War* (New York: Palgrave Macmillan, 2023).

31. On the evolution and sheer complexity of state formation in Eastern Europe (from the seventeenth to the twenty-first century), see John Connelly, *From Peoples into Nations: A History of Eastern Europe* (Princeton, NJ: Princeton University Press, 2022). This monograph is as much a study of empires as it is of nation states.

32. For the text of the Budapest Memorandum, see https://policymemos.hks.harvard. edu/links/ukraine-budapest-memorandum-1994. A dissenting opinion on non-proliferation as the best frame for US policy toward Ukraine was John J. Mearsheimer, "The Case for a Ukrainian Nuclear Deterrent," *Foreign Affairs* 72, no. 3 (Summer 1993): 50–66, https://www.foreignaffairs.com/articles/ukraine/1993-06-01/case-ukrainian-nuclear-deterrent. Bill Clinton's national security advisor, Anthony Lake, argued in 1993 that if Ukraine was admitted "to NATO, the nuclear question would of course resolve itself." Anthony Lake quoted in Sarotte, *Not One Inch*, 160.

33. On the Budapest Memorandum, see chapter 2, "Dealing with Nuclear Weapons," of Steve Pifer's monograph, *The Eagle and the Trident: U.S-Ukraine Relations in Turbulent Times* (Washington, DC: Brookings Institution Press, 2017), 37–76. See also Yuri Kostenko, *Ukraine's Nuclear Disarmament* (Cambridge, MA: Harvard University Press, 2021); and Polina Sinovets, editor, *Ukraine's Nuclear History: A Non-Proliferation Perspective* (Cham, Switzerland: Springer, 2022).

34. On the pre-twentieth-century divisions of Europe into East and West, see Larry Wolff, *Inventing Eastern Europe: The Map of Civilization and the Mind of the Enlightenment* (Stanford, CA: Stanford University Press, 1994).

35. For a biography of Bill Clinton, see David Maraniss, *First in His Class: A Biography of Bill Clinton* (New York: Simon and Schuster, 1986).

36. On the foreign-policy priorities of the Bush administration after September 11, see James Mann, *Rise of the Vulcans: The History of Bush's War Cabinet* (New York: Penguin Books, 2004); George Packer, *The Assassins' Gate: America in Iraq* (New York: Farrar, Straus and Giroux, 2006); and Susan Glasser and Peter Baker, *Days of Fire: Bush and Cheney in the White House* (New York: Anchor, 2014).

37. In George W. Bush's description of the Bucharest summit, France and Germany were leery about Georgia and Ukraine entering NATO—because of Russia and because of corruption. "I thought the threat from Russia strengthened the case for extending MAP's to Georgia and Ukraine," Bush writes in his memoirs. "Russia would be less likely to engage in aggression if these countries were on a path into NATO. As for the governance issues, a step toward membership would encourage them to clean up corruption. . . . At the end of the debate, Prime Minister Gordon Brown of Great Britain leaned over to me and said, 'We didn't give them MAPs, but we may have just made them members!' " George W. Bush, *Decision Points* (New York: Crown, 2011), 431.

38. Interestingly, Chancellor Merkel, who had not favored a MAP for Georgia at the Bucharest Summit, traveled to Georgia on August 17, where she pronounced that "Georgia will become a member of NATO when it wishes, and this is what it wishes" [Georgien wird, wenn es das will, und das will es ja, Mitglied der NATO sein]. Angela Merkel, quoted in Bollmann, *Angela Merkel*, 305.]

39. Mary Sarotte argues for the Bucharest Summit as a turning point, not so much for European security as for Russian attitudes toward European security: "For Putin, that Bucharest summit [in 2008]—coming on top of Bush's 2003 invasion of Iraq and his 2007 decision to erect ballistic missile defenses (in the form of ten ground-based interceptors in Poland and a radar facility in the Czech Republic), all around the time

of 'color revolutions' in post-Soviet states—proved to be the breaking point." Sarotte, *Not One Inch*, 348.

40. Quoted in Paul D'Anieri, *Ukraine and Russia: From Civilized Divorce to Uncivil War* (Cambridge: Cambridge University Press, 2019), 152.

41. On post–Cold War German policy toward Russia and Eastern Europe, see Stephen F. Szabo, *Germany, Russia, and the Rise of Geo-Economics* (London: Bloomsbury Academic, 2015); Angela Stent, *Russia and Germany Reborn: Unification, the Soviet Collapse, and the New Europe* (Princeton, NJ: Princeton University Press, 1998); and Liana Fix, *Germany's Role in European Russia Policy* (London: Palgrave Macmillan, 2021).

42. Helmut Kohl, quoted in Timothy J. Colton, *Yeltsin: A Life*, 363. On Yeltsin's wavering about whether to hold a presidential election at all in 1996 see Timothy J. Colton, *Yeltsin: A Life* (New York: Basic Books, 2008), 356-357.

43. "Yeltsin as a reincarnation of the tsar was a recurrent motif in the discourse of the 1990s" and one that Yeltsin did not necessarily discourage, as Timothy Colton notes. Colton, *Yeltsin: A Life*, 323. Mary Sarotte eloquently describes US-Russian relations under Yeltsin's and Clinton's stewardship as "outward cooperation paired with darker undercurrents of national and personal weakness and need." Sarotte, *Not One Inch*, 158.

44. In his memoirs, George W. Bush describes the cross that was personally meaningful to Putin, whose "face and his voice softened as he explained that he had hung the cross in his dacha, which subsequently caught on fire. When the firefighters arrived, he told them all he cared about was the cross. He dramatically re-created the moment when a worker unfolded his hand and revealed the cross. It was, he said, 'as if it was meant to be.' 'Vladimir,' I said, 'that is the story of the cross. Things are meant to be.' I felt the tension drain from the meeting room." Bush, *Decision Points*, 196.

45. On counterterrorism as a bond between George W. Bush and Vladimir Putin, see chapter 3, "Bush and Putin in the Age of Terror," in Angela Stent, *The Limits of Partnership* (Princeton, NJ: Princeton University Press, 2015), 49–81.

46. On the effect of the Iraq War on US-Russian relations, see chapter 4, "The Iraq War," in Stent, *The Limits of Partnership*, 82–96.

47. "I viewed NATO expansion as a powerful tool to advance the freedom agenda," George W. Bush wrote in his memoir, *Decision Points*, 430.

48. On frozen conflicts in general, see Thomas de Waal and Nikolaus von Twickel, *Beyond Frozen Conflict: Scenarios for the Separatist Disputes of Eastern Europe*, edited by Michael Emerson (London: Rowman and Littlefield International, 2020).

49. Describing his initial impressions of Dmitry Medvedev, Michael McFaul, who served on Obama's National Security Council and as US ambassador to Russia, wrote that "Medvedev seemed like a pro-Western modernizer, albeit a cautious one." Relative to Putin, Medvedev "seemed more oriented to, or at least familiar with, Western ideas." *From Cold War to Hot Peace: An American Ambassador in Putin's Russia* (Boston, MA: Houghton Mifflin, 2018), viii, 73.

50. As Michael McFaul, one of the architects of the reset put it, "The word 'reset' described well what we aimed to do with Russia. . . . This [policy transition] felt new and

modern. It evoked changed." McFaul, *From Cold War to Hot Peace*, 85. For a comprehensive study of modernization as a trope and a theory in American foreign policy, see Nils Gilman, *Mandarins of the Future: Modernization Theory in Cold War America* (Baltimore, MD: Johns Hopkins University Press, 2007).

51. On this episode, see Mark Landler, "Lost in Translation: A U.S. Gift to Russia," *New York Times* (March 6, 2009), https://www.nytimes.com/2009/03/07/world/europe/07diplo.html.

Chapter 2

1. See "Interview to 'BBC Breakfast with Frost'" (March 5, 2000), http://en.kremlin.ru/events/president/transcripts/interviews/24194.
2. Lincoln Steffens's quote, "I have seen the future and it works," cited in Ella Winter, *Human Relationships and the New Russia* (New York: Harcourt, Brace, 1933), epigraph.
3. A fascinating book on progress, modernity, and terror in Soviet history is Barrington Moore Jr., *Terror and Progress—USSR: Some Sources of Change and Stability in Soviet Dictatorship* (Cambridge, MA: Harvard University Press, 1954).
4. On the economic dislocations of the late Soviet Union, which became the even more extreme economic dislocations of post-Soviet Russia, see Stephen Kotkin, *Armageddon Averted: The Soviet Collapse, 1970–2000* (New York: Oxford University Press, 2008).
5. On the literal breakup of the Soviet Union into fragments that were bought, sold, and preserved, see section 1, "Shards of Empire," in Karl Schloegel, *The Soviet Century: Archaeology of a Lost World* (Princeton, NJ: Princeton University Press, 2023), 7–74.
6. The paradigmatic text, reflecting 1990s-era optimism about globalization, is Thomas L. Friedman, *The Lexus and the Olive Tree* (New York: Farrar, Straus and Giroux, 1999). Another book in this vein is Thomas L. Friedman's *The World Is Flat: A Brief History of the Twenty-First Century* (New York: Farrar, Straus and Giroux, 2005).
7. On the relationship between Sobchak and Putin, see chapter 5, "Back in the USSR," of Philip Short, *Putin* (New York: Holt, 2023), 124–175.
8. For a detailed history of the KGB's financial dealings in the 1980s and their effect on state formation after the collapse of the Soviet Union, see Catherine Belton, *Putin's People: How the KGB Took Back Russia and Then Took on the West* (New York: Farrar, Straus and Giroux, 2022).
9. Masha Gessen calls the 1990s "perhaps the most contested decade in Russian history: some remember it as a time of liberation, while for others it represents chaos and pain." *The Future Is History: How Totalitarianism Reclaimed Russia* (New York: Riverhead Books, 2017), 3.

10. An excellent deep history of the "Washington consensus" is Gary Gerstle, *The Rise and Fall of the Neoliberal Order: America and the World in the Free Market Era* (New York: Oxford University Press, 2022).

11. A classic article on the complexities of medieval Russian politics is Edward Keenan, "Muscovite Political Folkways," *Russian Review* 45, no. 2 (April 1986). On the evolution of a "patrimonial state," which hindered the rule of law and the idea of private property in Russia, see Richard Pipes, *Russia under the Old Regime* (New York: Penguin Books, 1997).

12. On Russia's military modernization, see Dmitri Trenin, "The Revival of the Russian Military: How Moscow Reloaded," *Foreign Affairs* 95, no. 3 (May/June 2016): 23–29; and Keir Giles, *Russia's "New" Tools for Confronting the West: Continuity and Innovation in Moscow's Exercise of Power* (London: Chatham House, 2016). The prominence of military spending with the Russian budget was very high. By 2020, it was "absorbing an enormous 7 percent of Russia's GDP, compared with under 2 per cent for most NATO countries," Owen Matthews writes. *Overreach: The Inside Story of Putin and Russia's War against Ukraine* (London: Mudlark, 2023), 169.

13. A classic study of oligarchic power in 1990s Russia is Karen Dawisha, *Putin's Kleptocracy: Who Owns Russia?* (New York: Simon and Schuster, 2014). See also Bill Browder, *Red Notice: A True Story of High Finance, Murder, and One Man's Fight for Justice* (New York: Simon and Schuster, 2015).

14. Fiona Hill and Clifford G. Gaddy develop Putin's "statist" inclinations in chapter 3, "The Statist" of *Mr. Putin: Operative in the Kremlin* (Washington, DC: Brookings Institution Press, 2015), 38–62.

15. "Yeltsin wanted to join the West," writes Michael McFaul, and the economic side of this push was crucial. *From Cold War to Hot Peace: An American Ambassador in Putin's Russia* (Boston: Houghton Mifflin, 2018), 57. On the nexus of oil and politics in Russia, see Thane Gustafson's *Wheel of Fortune: The Battle for Oil and Power in Russia* (Cambridge, MA: Belknap Press, 2012).

16. Timothy Fry notes an "oil boom that doubled the size of the Russian economy from 1998 to 2008," adding that "Putin is popular for the same reason Yeltsin was not: the economy." *Weak Strongman: The Limits of Power in Putin's Russia* (Princeton, NJ: Princeton University Press, 2021), 41, 59.

17. For broad overviews of Russian foreign policy, see Jeffrey Mankoff, *Russian Foreign Policy: The Return of Great Power Politics* (New York: Rowman and Littlefield, 2011); and Andrei P. Tsygankov, *Russia's Foreign Policy: Change and Continuity in National Identity* (London: Rowman and Littlefield, 2022).

18. See Philip Zelikow and Condoleezza Rice, *Germany Unified and Europe Transformed: A Study in Statecraft* (Cambridge, MA: Harvard University Press, 1995).

19. On the possibility of Russia joining NATO, see Angela Stent, *The Limits of Partnership: U.S.-Russian Relations in the Twenty-First Century* (Princeton, NJ: Princeton University Press, 2015), 75.

20. In his memoirs, George W. Bush devotes one short paragraph to Russia's invasion of Georgia. He laments Russia's "unlawful military presence in South Ossetia and Abkhazia. Vladimir Putin called me during my last week in office to wish me

well, which was a thoughtful gesture. Still given what I'd hoped Putin and I could accomplish in moving past the Cold War, Russia stands out as a disappointment in the freedom agenda." *Decision Points*, 435. Michael McFaul writes persuasively that George W. Bush's "passion for pushing freedom and liberty around the globe . . . applied only episodically to Russia." McFaul, *From Cold War to Hot Peace*, 63.

21. Barack Obama, *A Promised Land* (New York: Crown, 2020), 337.

22. Obama, *A Promised Land*, 462–463.

23. On the presidency of Dmitry Medvedev, see J. L. Black, *The Russian Presidency of Dmitry Medvedev, 2008–2012: The Next Step Forward or Merely a Time Out* (London: Routledge, 2014).

24. On the Medvedev visit to Silicon Valley, see Andrew Clark, "Dmitry Medvedev Pick's Silicon Valley's Brains," *The Guardian* (June 23, 2010), https://www.theguardian.com/business/2010/jun/23/dmitry-medvedev-silicon-valley-visit.

25. On the hamburger summit, see Elisabeth Goodridge, "Just a Couple of Guys Grabbing Burgers," *New York Times* (June 24, 2010), https://archive.nytimes.com/thecaucus.blogs.nytimes.com/2010/06/24/just-a-couple-of-guys-grabbing-burgers/.

26. On the Obama-Medvedev reset, see chapter 9, "Reset or Overload? The Obama Initiative," in Stent, *The Limits of Partnership*, 211–234.

27. A detailed report on Skolkovo's successes and failures is "Skolkovo: A Case Study in Government-Supported Innovation," Wharton School of Business (December 20, 2013), https://knowledge.wharton.upenn.edu/article/skolkovo-case-study-government-supported-innovation/.

28. On Sergei Sobyanin's career as Moscow Mayor, see Evan Gershkovich, "Sergei Sobyanin, Moscow's High Priest of Urban Renewal, Is Biding His Time," *Moscow Times* (September 6, 2018), https://www.themoscowtimes.com/2018/09/06/moscow-high-priest-of-urban-renewal-sergei-sobyanin-is-biding-his-time-a62785.

29. On Samuel Huntington's first mention of "Davos man" in 2004, see Holly Ellyat, "Who Are 'Davos Man' and 'Davos Woman,'" *CNBC* (January 19, 2018), https://www.cnbc.com/2018/01/19/who-are-davos-man-and-davos-woman.html.

30. On Medvedev's visit to Davis, see Eric Pfanner, "At Forum, Medvedev Seeks to Reassure Foreign Investors," *New York Times* (January 26, 2011), https://archive.nytimes.com/dealbook.nytimes.com/2011/01/26/medvedev-defends-russias-modernization-efforts/.

31. Dmitry Medvedev quoted in Steven Lee Myers, *The New Tsar: The Rise and Reign of Vladimir Putin* (New York: Knopf, 2015), 382.

32. On this press conference, see Kathy Lally, "Medvedev Meets the Press," *Washington Post* (May 18, 2011), https://www.washingtonpost.com/world/europe/medvedev-meets-the-press/2011/05/18/AFQ6QX6G_story.html.

33. Dmitry Medvedev quoted in Myers, *The New Tsar*, 389.

34. "It was clear that Medvedev had serious reservations about any Western-led military action that could lead to regime change," Barack Obama wrote about him, "but he also wasn't inclined to run interference for Gaddafi." Obama, *A Promised Land*, 660.

35. Vladimir Putin quoted in Short, *Putin*, 526.

36. On Putin's reaction to the video of Gaddafi's killing, see Kim Ghattas, "What a Decade-Old Conflict Tells Us about Putin," *The Atlantic* (March 6, 2022), https://www.theatlantic.com/international/archive/2022/03/libya-russia-ukraine-putin/626571/.

37. In Obama's opinion, Medvedev's decisions about Libya were Putin's decisions. "It was inconceivable that Putin hadn't signed off on Medvedev's decision to have Russia abstain rather than veto our [UN] resolution, or that he'd failed to understand its scope at the time," Obama wrote, as if Putin were setting Medvedev up for failure. "In openly second-guessing Medvedev [after the vote], Putin seemed to deliberately make his hand-picked successor look bad." Obama, *A Promised Land*, 667–668. Samantha Power, who was at the National Security Council in 2011, shared Obama's assessment that Medvedev and Putin were operating in tandem on Syria, though she also notes that "Moscow had never been enthusiastic about licensing Western countries to use military force for ostensibly humanitarian purposes." See *The Education of an Idealist: A Memoir* (New York: Dey Street Books, 2021), 304, 305.

38. On the celebratory spirit of the 2018 World Cup in Russia, see Denis Sinyakov, "The World Cup Changed Russia, But for How Long?," *New York Times* (July 16, 2018), https://www.nytimes.com/2018/07/16/sports/world-cup/russia.html.

Chapter 3

1. Vladimir Putin quoted in Philip Short, *Putin* (New York: Holt, 2023), 223.

2. For the text of Putin's Munich Security Conference speech, which he gave on February 10, 2007, see http://en.kremlin.ru/events/president/transcripts/24034.

3. A classic study of the ethnic policies of the Soviet Union is Terry Martin, *The Affirmative Action Empire: Nations and Nationalism in the Soviet Union, 1923–1939* (Ithaca, NY: Cornell University Press, 2001). See also Richard Pipes, *The Formation of the Soviet Union: Communism and Nationalism, 1917–1923* (Cambridge, MA: Harvard University Press, 1997). Ronald Suny's rich study of changing patterns of ethnicity and nationalism in the Soviet Union and in the former Soviet space is *The Soviet Experiment: Russia, the USSR, and the Successor States* (New York: Oxford University Press, 1997).

4. "The first few years of Yeltsin's rule were a constant—and at times bloody—battle with reactionary nationalists and communists," Owen Matthews writes, "both of whom demanded the restoration of Soviet greatness." *Overreach: The Inside Story of Putin and Russia's War against Ukraine* (London: Mudlark, 2023), 65.

5. Writing about the popularity of Primakov's political ideas circa 1998, Timothy Colton notes that he "wanted a broad-based government, heightened state regulation of the market, and a more muscular foreign policy, all of which fit better with what parliament and the populace wanted than [former prime minister] Chernomyrdin and [candidate for prime minister] Kiriyenko had." Timothy Colton, *Yeltsin: A Life* (New York: Basic Books, 2008), 417. Serhii Plokhy writes that when Primakov was

foreign minister, from 1996 to 1998, he "had turned Russian foreign policy away from its Western orientation, seeing the enhancement of Russia's status in the 'near abroad' . . . as a requisite for its revival as a great power." *Lost Kingdom: The Quest for Empire and the Making of the Russian Nation* (New York: Basic Books, 2017), 318.

6. Masha Gessen describes Putin's 2000 ascent to the presidency as the "pretend election of a barely perceptible candidate who was the preordained winner." *The Future Is History: How Totalitarianism Reclaimed Russia* (New York: Riverhead, 2017), 211.

7. Party politics flourished in the Russia of the 1990s, but the political parties themselves were often too fluid and too weak to wield power. In the words of Timothy Colton, Yeltsin lacked "a key resource that leaders and aspiring leaders have in the retail politics of mature democracies: an effective party." Colton, *Yeltsin: A Life*, 347.

8. As Yeltsin wrote in his memoirs, *Presidential Marathon*, about his state of mind in 1998, when he was thinking about a successor, "I was already coming to feel that society needed some new quality in the state, a steel backbone that would strengthen the political structure of authority. We needed a person who was *thinking, democratic, and innovative yet steadfast in the military manner.*" Boris Yeltsin quoted in Colton, *Yeltsin: A Life*, 431.

9. On Russia's wars in Chechnya, see John B. Dunlop, *Russia Confronts Chechnya: Roots of a Separatist Conflict* (Cambridge: Cambridge University Press, 1998); Miriam Lanskoy and Ilyas Akhmadov, *The Chechen Struggle: Independence Won and Lost* (New York: Palgrave, 2010); James Hughes, *Chechnya: From Nationalism to Jihad* (Philadelphia, PA: University of Pennsylvania Press, 2011); and Olga Oliker, *Russia's Chechen Wars, 1994–2000: Lessons from Urban Combat* (Santa Monica, CA: Rand, 2000).

10. For a novel (first published in 2006) that offers a dystopian prediction about Putinism, see Vladimir Sorokin, *Day of the Oprichnik*, translated by Jamey Campbell (New York: Farrar, Straus and Giroux, 2012). Barack Obama described Putin circa 2008 as "a former KGB officer, two-term president and now the country's prime minister, and the leader of what resembled a criminal syndicate as much as it did a traditional government." Obama, *A Promised Land* (New York: Crown, 2020), 337.

11. The economic and political structure Putin created could be bureaucratic and rule-bound, but it was a vehicle of kleptocracy, rent seeking, and wealth transfer through political connections. Philip French notes that "by the end of Putin's second term, impunity had become one of the hallmarks of the regime." Short, *Putin*, 487. See also Lilia Shevtsova, *Putin's Russia* (Washington, DC: Carnegie Endowment for International Peace, 2003).

12. Mary Sarotte notes that while Germany's Chancellor Helmut Kohl was pushing for German unification and President George H. W. Bush was pushing to keep NATO the general frame for European security, "Gorbachev himself apparently did not yet know what he wanted [in 1990]." Sarotte, *Not One Inch: America, Russia and the Making of the Post-Cold War Stalemate* (New Haven, CT: Yale University Press, 2021), 45. "For Bush, the events of 1989–90 were apparently more about NATO than about Germany," Sarotte observes. Sarotte, *Not One Inch*, 105.

13. While Yeltsin shaped Russian public opinion on foreign policy, he was also shaped by Russian public opinion on foreign policy. Charles Clover cites a 2001 poll according to which 79 percent of Russians "felt the end of the USSR to have been a mistake, compared with 69 per cent in 1992; 56 percent saw NATO as a 'bloc of aggression' rather than a defensive alliance, an 18 percentage point rise since 1997. One of the largest subcategories to subscribe to this view included those with higher education (68 per cent)." *Black Wind, White Snow: The Rise of Russia's New Nationalism* (New Haven, CT: Yale University Press, 2016), 269.

14. Yeltsin respected Ukrainian sovereignty. When the Russian parliament gestured toward territorial claims on Sevastopol (in Crimea), Yeltsin responded by saying, "I am ashamed of parliament's decision. . . . We can't start a war with Ukraine, after all." Boris Yeltsin quoted in Serhii Plokhy, *The Russo-Ukrainian War: The Return of History* (New York: Norton, 2023), 69.

15. On Western policy toward Moldova, see William Hill, *Russia, the Near Abroad and the West: Lessons from the Moldova-Transdniestria Conflict* (Baltimore, MD: Johns Hopkins University Press, 2012).

16. Andrei Kozyrev, "The Lagging Partnership," *Foreign Affairs* (May/June 1994), https://www.foreignaffairs.com/articles/russian-federation/1994-05-01/lagging-partnership.

17. On US military and diplomatic action in the Balkans in the 1990s, see David Halberstam, *War in a Time of Peace: Bush, Clinton and the Generals* (New York: Scribner, 2002); and George Packer, *Our Man: Richard Holbrooke and the End of the American Century* (New York: Knopf, 2019). Richard Holbrooke's grandly titled memoir of his diplomatic efforts in the Balkans is *To End a War: The Conflict in Yugoslavia—America's Inside Story—Negotiating with Milosevic* (New York: Modern Library, 1999).

18. As early as 1993, Yevgeny Primakov "could convincingly argue that [Andrey] Kozyrev was deceiving himself and his nation about the truth of [NATO] expansion." Sarotte, *Not One Inch*, 166. On Primakov's tougher position on NATO helping him get him the job as Foreign Minister see Sarotte, *Not One Inch*, 202.

19. For the first use of the BRICS term, see Jim O'Neill, "Building Better Global Economic BRICs," *Goldman Investment Research* (November 2001), https://www.goldmansachs.com/intelligence/archive/building-better.html.

20. As Serhii Plokhy puts it, "There was no doubt that the war was directly linked to the outcome of the Bucharest [NATO] summit [in 2008]." Plokhy, *The Russo-Ukrainian War*, 89. Mark Galeotti argues that "already, from 2006, the decision had been made that something needed to be done about Saakashvili. From that year on, the North Caucasus Military District began staging increasingly elaborate and sizable military exercises that it would turn out were both wargaming invasion and also cover for the eventual troop build-up." Galeotti, *Putin's Wars: From Chechnya to Ukraine* (London: Osprey, 2022), 125.

21. On the Russia-Georgia war, see Svante E. Cornell and S. Frederick Starr, *The Guns of August 2008: Russia's War in Georgia* (London: Routledge, 2009); Ronald D. Asmus, *A Little War that Shook the World: Georgia, Russia and the Future of the West*

(New York: St. Martin's Press, 2010); Thomas de Waal, *Uncertain Ground: Engaging with Europe's De Facto States and Breakaway Territories* (Washington, DC: Carnegie Europe, 2018); and Mark Galeotti, *Russia's Five-Day War: The Invasion of Georgia, August 2008* (Oxford: Osprey, 2023).

22. Dmitry Medvedev quoted in D'Anieri, *Ukraine and Russia: From Civilized Divorce to Uncivil War* (New York: Cambridge University Press, 2019), 169. See also Gerard Toal, *Near Abroad: Putin, the West and the Contest over Ukraine and the Caucasus* (New York: Oxford University Press, 2017); and Vasif Huseynov and Nicholas Smith, *Geopolitical Rivalries in the 'Common Neighborhood': Russia's Conflict with the West, Soft Power, and Neoclassical Realism* (Stuttgart: Ibidem Press, 2019).

23. The estimate of 30 million ethnic Russians and Russian-speakers "who associated themselves first and foremost with Russia [and who] remained outside the borders of the Russian federation" is cited by Serhii Plokhy. *Lost Kingdom*, 315.

24. Speaking in April 2005, Putin characterized the Soviet Union's fall as "a genuine drama. Tens of millions of our co-citizens and compatriots found themselves out-side Russian territory." Vladimir Putin quoted in Tim Judah, *In Wartime: Stories from Ukraine* (New York: Tim Duggan Books, 2016), 8.

25. A standard work on the history and geopolitics of Crimea is Gwendolyn Sasse, *The Crimea Question: Identity, Transition, and Conflict* (Cambridge, MA: Harvard University Press, 2007).

26. For the role of Orthodox Christianity and the Russian Orthodox Church in Russian foreign policy, see Dima Adamsky, *Russian Nuclear Orthodoxy: Religion, Politics, and Strategy* (Palo Alto, CA: Stanford University Press, 2019). See also Alicja Curanovic, The Religious Factor in Russia's Foreign Policy (London: Routledge, 2012); and Nicolai Petro, "The Russian Orthodox Church," in Andrei Tsygankov, ed., *Routledge Handbook of Russian Foreign Policy* (London: Routledge, 2018), 217–232.

27. In an oft-quoted passage, Zbigniew Brzezinski observed that "Ukraine, a new and important space on the Eurasian chessboard, is a geopolitical pivot because its very existence as an independent state country helps to transform Russia. Without Ukraine, Russia ceases to be a Eurasian empire. Russia without Ukraine can still strive for imperial status, but it would then become a predominantly Asian impe-rial state." *The Grand Chessboard: American Primacy and Its Geostrategic Imperatives* (New York: Basic Books, 1997), 45.

28. Vladimir Putin quoted in D'Anieri, *Ukraine and Russia*, 193. Charles Clover has traced a long line of "Eurasianist" thinking in Russian and Soviet letters, thinking that crystallized around "the idea that Russia is not a nation but a civilization that has inherited the mantle of the Russian Empire and the Soviet Union, both of which were just transient permutations of some mystical unity that has possessed the inner [Eurasian] continent since deep antiquity." Clover, *Black Wind, White Snow*, 10.

29. Books on Russian foreign policy that contextualize Vladimir Putin's career histori-cally are William Fuller Jr., *Strategy and Power in Russia, 1600–1914* (New York: Free Press, 1992); John P. LeDonne, *The Russian Empire and the World, 1700–1917: The Geopolitics of Expansion and Containment* (New York: Oxford University Press, 1997); Dominic Lieven, *Empire: The Russian Empire and Its Rivals* (New Haven,

CT: Yale University Press, 1992); and Adam B. Ulam, *Expansion and Coexistence: The History of Soviet Foreign Policy, 1917–1967* (New York: Praeger, 1968).

30. On Yeltsin's admiration for Peter the Great, see Colton, *Yeltsin: A Life*, 41.

31. On Putin's reaction to "color revolutions" and on his use of "color revolutions" to frame his 2007 speech in Munich, see chapters 5 and 6 of Angela Stent, *The Limits of Partnership: U.S.-Russian Relations in the Twenty-First Century* (Princeton, NJ: Princeton University Press, 2015), 97–158.

32. Vladimir Putin quoted in D'Anieri, *Ukraine and Russia*, 188.

33. Vladimir Putin quoted in D'Anieri, *Ukraine and Russia*, 188–189.

34. For an English-language version of Putin's article on Eurasian integration ,see Vladimir Putin, "A New Integration Project for Eurasia: The Future in the Making" (October 3, 2011), https://russiaeu.ru/en/news/article-prime-minister-vladimir-putin-new-integration-project-eurasia-future-making-izvestia-3-.

35. On the career of Boris Nemtsov, see Andrey Makarychev, Alexandra Yatsyk, and Zhanna Nemtsova, editors, *Boris Nemtsov and Russian Politics: Power and Resistance* (Stuttgart: Ibidem Press, 2018). On the rise of Alexei Navalny, see Julia Ioffe, "Net Impact" *New Yorker* (March 28, 2011), https://www.newyorker.com/magazine/2011/04/04/net-impact.

36. See Jo Becker and Scott Shane, "Hillary Clinton, 'Smart Power' and a Dictator's Fall," *New York Times* (February 27, 2016); "A New Libya with 'Very Little Time Left,'" *New York Times* (February 27, 2016).

37. On the McCain Tweet, see Tim Mak, "Putin: McCain Has Blood on His Hands," *Politico* (December 15, 2011), https://www.politico.com/story/2011/12/putin-mccain-has-blood-on-his-hands-070488.

38. On this about quote, see Glenn Kessler, "Flashback: Obama's Debate Zinger on Romney's '1980s' Foreign Policy," *Washington Post* (March 20, 2014). https://www.washingtonpost.com/news/fact-checker/wp/2014/03/20/flashback-obamas-debate-zinger-on-romneys-1980s-foreign-policy/.

39. The number of 100,000 protestors on Bolotnaya Square is cited in Clover, *Black Wind, White Snow*, 314. Wide disparities exist between official and unofficial counting of the protestors.

40. In Putin's mind, the Association Agreement with the EU and NATO membership for Ukraine were intertwined. As he explained to Angela Merkel, "When I look at the membership of the EU and I look at the membership of NATO, I see basically the same thing. So when I hear about an Association Agreement for Ukraine, I know that NATO will follow." Vladimir Putin quoted in Short, *Putin*, 570.

41. On bohemian Munich as a seedbed of the National Socialist movement, see chapter 1, "Germany's Bohemia," in David Clay Large, *Where Ghosts Walked: Munich's Road to the Third Reich* (New York: Norton, 1997), 3–42.

42. For texts on the reconstitution of Russia during and after the Soviet period, see Ivan Ilyin, "Shto sulit miru raschlenie Rossii" ["What the Dismemberment of Russia Promises the World"], in *Nashi zadachi: Statii* (Paris: Russkii obshevoinskii soiuz, 1955), 245–257; and Alexander Solzhenitsyn, *Rebuilding Russia: Reflections and Tentative Proposals* (New York: Vintage, 1991). Timothy Snyder addresses the

thinking of Alexander Dugin and Ivan Ilyin in *The Road to Unfreedom: Russia, Europe, America* (New York: Crown, 2019). See also Marlene Laruelle, *Russian Eurasianism: The Ideology of Empire* (Baltimore, MD: Johns Hopkins University Press, 2012).

43. On Dugin and the West, see Charles Clover, who writes that "Dugin and other hardliners . . . contended that conflict with the West was a permanent condition for Russia." *Black Wind, White Snow*, 233. On Dugin's banishment from Ukraine see *White Snow, Black Wind*, 305. Serhii Plokhy proposes a tri-partite interpretation of Kremlin thinking about the outside world: Eurasianist and focused on geographic space; east Slavic and focused on a united Ukraine, Belarus, and Russia; and "Greater Russia" focused on populations or territory deemed historically Russian. See Plokhy, *The Russo-Ukrainian War*, 105.

44. On Putin's 2013 visit to Kyiv, see Sophia Kishlovsky, "Putin in Ukraine to Celebrate a Christian Anniversary," *New York Times* (July 27, 2013), https://www.nytimes.com/2013/07/28/world/europe/putin-in-ukraine-to-celebrate-a-christian-anniversary.html.

45. According to Owen Matthews, Putin spent "a total of fifteen minutes with Yanukovych [during his 2013 trip to Ukraine]. He spent the rest of his two-day visit with his old friend Viktor Medvedchuk at his luxurious Crimean dacha." Matthews, *Overreach*, 82.

Chapter 4

1. Tim Judah, *In Wartime: Stories from Ukraine* (New York: Tim Duggan Books, 2015), 129.

2. Speculating about the potential for conflict, Samuel P. Huntington addressed geopolitical tensions between Russia and Ukraine in *The Clash of Civilizations and the Remaking of World Order* (New York: Simon and Schuster, 2011), 165-168.

3. On Thomas Jefferson's legacy and the role of ideology in American foreign policy, see Peter S. Onuf, *Jefferson's Empire: The American Language of Nationhood* (Charlottesville: University Press of Virginia, 2000). On ideological patterns in American foreign policy, see Michael H. Hunt, *Ideology and U.S. Foreign Policy* (New Haven, CT: Yale University Press, 2009).

4. Andrey Kurkov, translated by Sam Taylor, *Ukraine Diaries: Dispatches from Kiev* (London: Harvill, 2015), 160.

5. For monographs on Ukraine's regional place and on questions of language, memory, and geography related to Ukraine, see Timothy Snyder, *The Reconstruction of Nations: Poland, Ukraine, Lithuania, Belarus, 1569-1999* (New Haven, CT: Yale University Press, 2004); Serhii Plokhy, *The Origins of the Slavic Nations: Premodern Identities in Russia, Ukraine and Belarus* (New York: Cambridge University Press, 2010); Steven Seegel, *Ukraine under Western Eyes: The Bohdan Nearila Kranciw Ucraina Map Collection* (Cambridge, MA: Harvard Ukrainian Research Institute,

2013); Steven Seegel, *Mapping Europe's Borderlands: Russian Cartographers in the Age of Empire* (Chicago: University of Chicago Press, 2012); and Steven Seegel, *Map Men: Transnational Lives and Deaths of Geographers in the Making of East Central Europe* (Chicago: University of Chicago Press, 2018).

6. Paul D'Anieri, *Ukraine and Russia: From Civilized Divorce to Uncivil War* (New York: Cambridge University Press, 2019), 34.

7. In the 1990s, Ukrainian foreign policy had Yeltsin's Russia as a reference point, and Yeltsin did not frighten Kyiv. As Timothy Colton writes, "Yeltsin dampened Russian revanchism, jingoism, and nostalgia for the Soviet Union. In the 'Near Abroad,' he reached understandings with the majority of the non-Russian fourteen, repatriated troops, did not employ ethnic Russians as a fifth column, and helped float their economies by supplying gas and oil at discounted prices." Colton, *Yeltsin: A Life* (New York: Basic Books, 2008), 266. Serhii Plokhy emphasizes the Ukrainian side of this normalizing equation: "By going out of its way to adopt a demonstratively tolerant attitude towards its Russian minority—the largest outside Russia—Ukraine made it much easier for Yeltsin to ignore pressures to protect the formerly dominant nationality in the peripheries of the empire." Plokhy, *The Russo-Ukrainian War: The Return of History* (New York: Norton, 2023), 33.

8. On Leonid Kuchma's political coming of age and career as president, see Taras Kuzio, "Oligarchs, Tapes and Oranges: 'Kuchmagate' to the Orange Revolution," *Journal of Communist Studies and Transition Politics* (March 16, 2007): 30–56. https://doi.org/10.1080/13523270701194839.

9. D'Anieri, *Ukraine and Russia*, 103.

10. On the murder of Georgi Gongadze, see Steven Lee Myers, "A Headless Body Haunts Ex-Leaders of Ukraine," *New York Times* (February 3, 2005), https://www.nytimes.com/2005/02/03/world/europe/a-headless-body-haunts-the-exleaders-of-ukraine.html.

11. See Michael Wines, "Report of Arms Sale by Ukraine to Iraq Causes Consternation," *New York Times* (November 7, 2002), https://www.nytimes.com/2002/11/07/world/report-of-arms-sale-by-ukraine-to-iraq-causes-consternation.html.

12. On the persistence of oligarchic power in Ukraine, see David Dalton, *The Ukrainian Oligarchy after the Euromaidan: How Ukraine's Political Economy Regime Survived the Crisis* (Stuttgart: Ibidem Press, 2023).

13. The number of 500,000 gathering to protest the 2004 election is cited in Gwendolyn Sasse, *Der Krieg gegen die Ukraine* (Munich: Beck Verlag, 2022), 51.

14. Vladimir Putin quoted in Philip Short, *Putin* (New York: Holt, 2023), 395.

15. On the Orange Revolution, see Andrew Wilson, *Ukraine's Orange Revolution* (New Haven, CT: Yale University Press, 2006). Behind the tumult of its high politics, Ukraine was doing well between 2001 and 2007, "a period of economic recovery," during which its GDP "grew by an average of 8 percent a year," as Tim Judah writes *In Wartime*, 139, 234. This period would come to an end with the global financial crisis of 2008.

16. Ukraine and Russia were not necessarily parting ways in 2004. Though Ukraine refused to join the Eurasian Economic Community into which Russia had drawn

Belarus, Kazakhstan, and other Central European countries, Ukraine's parliament approved Ukraine's entry into a Single Economic Space with Russia, Belarus, and Kazakhstan, another sign that the Orange Revolution was not fully revolutionary.

17. On Yushchenko's making Bandera a "Hero of Ukraine," see Clifford J. Levy, "'Hero of Ukraine' Splits Nation, Inside and Out," *New York Times* (March 1, 2010), https://www.nytimes.com/2010/03/02/world/europe/02history.html.   Serhii   Plokhy describes the Orange Revolution as decisive in the dividing lines it established, as an event that "put Ukraine and Russia and, subsequently, Russia and the West on a collision course that would eventually lead to war." Plokhy, *The Russo-Ukrainian War*, 36. "It was our 9/11," a Kremlin advisor, Gleb Pavlovsky, said of the Orange Revolution. Gleb Pavlovsky quoted in Plokhy, *The Russo-Ukrainian War*, 83.

18. On the cross-border complexities of Poroshenko's Roshen chocolate business before the Maidan, see Andrew E. Kramer, "Chocolate Factory, Trade War Victim," *New York Times* (October 29, 2013), https://www.nytimes.com/2013/10/30/business/international/ukrainian-chocolates-caught-in-trade-war-between-europe-and-russia.html.

19. Oleksandr Makarenko quoted in D'Anieri, *Ukraine and Russia*, 93. On the geopolitical orientation and foreign policy of Ukraine, see also Tatiana Zhurzhenko, *Borderlands into Bordered Lands: Geopolitics of Identity in Post-Soviet Ukraine* (Stuttgart: Ibidem Verlag, 2010); and Roman Wolczuk, *Ukraine's Foreign and Security Policy* (London: Routledge, 2002).

20. Boris Tarasiuk quoted in D'Anieri, *Ukraine and Russia*, 95.

21. Viktor Yushchenko quoted in D'Anieri, *Ukraine and Russia*, 134.

22. Viktor Yushchenko quoted in Plokhii, *The Russo-Ukrainian War*, 85.

23. Both Dick Cheney and Robert Gates have written memoirs of their time in government: Dick Cheney, *In My Time* (New York: Threshold Editions, 2012); and Robert Gates, *Duty: Memoirs of a Secretary at War* (New York: Vintage, 2015).

24. Sergey Lavrov quoted in D'Anieri, *Ukraine and Russia*, 163. Lavrov's position was paraphrased in a private communication between US ambassador to Russia, William Burns, and Secretary of State Condoleezza Rice, in which he wrote that "Ukrainian entry into NATO is the brightest of all red lines for the Russian elite (not just Putin). In my more than two-and-a-half years of conversations with key Russian players, from knuckle-draggers in the dark recesses of the Kremlin to Putin's sharpest liberal critics, I have yet to find anyone who views Ukraine in NATO as anything other than a direct challenge to Russia's interests. At this stage a MAP offer would not be seen as a technical step . . . but as throwing down the strategic gauntlet. Today's Russia will respond." For the full text of this cable, dated February 8, 2008, see the appendix to William J. Burns, *The Back Channel: A Memoir of American Diplomacy and the Case for Its Renewal* (New York: Random House, 2019), 459.

25. Viktor Yanukovych quoted in D'Anieri, *Ukraine and Russia*, 175.

26. As Olga Onuch and Henry Hale point out, "Signing an association agreement with the EU was part of his [Yanukovych's] electoral campaign [in 2010]." *The Zelensky Effect*, 101.

27. Quoted in D'Anieri, *Ukraine and Russia*, 184.

28. One of the attractions of the EU and of Europe to Ukraine was its sheer success, which Ukrainians could measure by comparing their country to neighboring Poland. "In 1990 the GDP per capita of both countries [Ukraine and Poland] was similar, as were life expectancy rates," writes Tim Judah. "Just before the war began [in 2014], Poland's GDP per capita was more than three times greater than that of Ukraine and Poles could expect to live almost six years longer than Ukrainians." Judah, *In Wartime*, xx.

29. On Razumkov polling data, see Leonid Peisakhin, "Why Are People Protesting in Ukraine? Providing Historical Context," *Washington Post* (December 19, 2013), https://www.washingtonpost.com/news/monkey-cage/wp/2013/12/19/why-are-peo ple-protesting-in-ukraine-providing-historical-context/. Differing somewhat from the Razumkov poll, the writer Andrey Kurkov noted in his diary (on November 22, 2013) that "the majority of our country's inhabitants know nothing about these two unsigned treaties and simply believe that an Association Agreement with the EU would lead Ukraine into Europe, while a treaty joining the Eurasian Economic Community would place us once again under the economic and political influence of the Russian Federation." Kurkov, *Ukraine Diaries*, 7.

30. On Yanukovych and NATO, see Eugene Rumer and Rajan Menon, *Conflict in Ukraine: The Unwinding of the Post-Cold War Order* (Cambridge, MA: MIT Press, 2015), 45.

31. On the competition between the EU and the EEU over Ukraine, see Samuel Charap and Timothy J. Colton, *Everyone Loses: The Ukraine Crisis and the Ruinous Contest for Post-Soviet Eurasia* (London: Routledge, 2016), 95–104.

32. According to the US diplomat, Christopher M. Smith, EU officials in Ukraine "were confident that the AA signing, scheduled for November [2013], was already a done deal." *Ukraine's Revolt, Russia's Revenge* (Washington, DC: Brookings Institution Press, 2022), 42. The writer Andrey Kurkov, who was in Vilnius for the summit, noted that the "Polish and Lithuanian politicians at the conference cautiously hypothesize that the Association Agreement will be signed in spite of everything." Kurkov, *Ukraine Diaries*, 7.

33. Viktor Yanukovych quoted in D'Anieri, *Ukraine and Russia*, 205. As if Yanukovych were not torn enough, his political homebase in the Donbas stood to gain greatly from metallurgic and other exports to the European Union if the Ukraine were to sign the AA. See Plokhy, *The Russo-Ukrainian War*, 93–94.

34. Mustafa Nayyem quoted in Joshua Yaffa, "Reforming Ukraine after the Revolutions," *New Yorker* (August 29, 2016), https://www.newyorker.com/magazine/2016/09/05/ reforming-ukraine-after-maidan.

35. Smith, *Ukraine's Revolt, Russia's Revenge*, 86. Histories of the Maidan Revolution include Juri Andruchowiytsch, *Euromaidan: Was in der Ukraine auf dem Spiel Steht* (Berlin: Suhrkamp Verlag, 2014); Marci Shore, *The Ukrainian Night: An Intimate History of Revolution* (New Haven, CT: Yale University Press, 2018); Olga Onuch, *Mapping Mass Mobilization: Understanding Revolutionary Moments in Argentina and Ukraine* (London: Palgrave Macmillan, 2014); Karl Schloegel, *Entscheidung in Kiew: Ukrainische Lektionen* (Munich: Carl Hanser Verlag, 2015). See also Taras

Kuzio, "Competing Nationalisms, Euromaidan, and the Russian-Ukrainian Conflict," *Studies in Ethnicity and Nationalism* 15, no. 1 (2015): 157–169.

36. Kurkov, *Ukraine Diaries*, 18.

37. For the full text of President Obama's 2014 State of the Union address, see https://obamawhitehouse.archives.gov/the-press-office/2014/01/28/president-barack-obamas-state-union-address.

38. John Kerry, *Every Day Is Extra* (New York: Simon and Schuster, 2018), 435.

39. John McCain quoted in "John McCain Tells Ukraine Protestors: 'We Are Here to Support Your Just Cause,'" *The Guardian* (December 15, 2013), https://www.theguardian.com/world/2013/dec/15/john-mccain-ukraine-protests-support-just-cause. McCain's message was consistent with the one being sent by the US Embassy in Kyiv. "While US envoys had consistently voiced our official approval of Ukraine's association with the EU," writes Christopher M. Smith, an embassy official in 2013, "I thought it would be advantageous in the home stretch to emphasize US support directly to the Ukrainian people . . . to assure [them] that the United States supported their aspirations to join Europe." Smith, *Ukraine's Revolt, Russia's Revenge*, 52.

40. It matters to the general course of the Maidan Revolution, from November 2013 to February 2014, that "the 2010–2013 period can only be described as one of steady, creeping democratic backsliding." Onuch and Hale, *The Zelensky Effect* (New York: Oxford University Press, 2023), 103.

41. The State Department couched these laws as anti-European. In the words of State Department spokesperson Jen Psaki, "If Ukraine truly aspires to a European future, it must defend and advance universal democratic principles and values that underpin a Europe whole, free, and at peace, and not allow them to be systematically dismantled." Jen Psaki quoted in Smith, *Ukraine's Revolt, Russia's Revenge*, 136.

42. Interestingly, US diplomat Christopher M. Smith writes in his memoirs of "a continuing frustration [in Washington] with the ineffectiveness of the EU in this situation [of negotiations with Kyiv]." Smith, *Ukraine's Revolt, Russia's Revenge*, 186.

43. On the pattern of events leading to Yanukovych's flight to Russia, see chapter 2, "Nobody Expected a Crisis," in Eugene Rumer and Rajan Menon, *Conflict in Ukraine: The Unwinding of the Post-Cold War Order* (Cambridge, MA: MIT Press, 2015), 53–86.

Chapter 5

1. On Crimea and its place between Russia and Ukraine, see Gwendolyn Sasse, *The Crimea Question: Identity, Transition and Conflict* (Cambridge, MA: Harvard University Press, 2007); Nataliya Gumenyuk, *Die Verlorene Insel: Geschichten von der besetzen Krim* (Stuttgart: Ibidem Verlag, 2020); Kerstin S. Jobst, *Geschichte der Krim: Iphigenie und Putin auf Tauris* (Berlin: Walter de Gruyter Verlag, 2020). See also Orlando Figes, *The Crimean War: A History* (New York: Metropolitan Books, 2011).

2. On the language law and unrest in Ukraine, see Serhii Plokhy, *The Russo-Ukrainian War*, 106.

3. On Russia's strategic response to the Maidan Revolution, see chapter 3, "Impact of the Crisis on Russia," in Eugene Rumer and Rajan Menon, *Conflict in Ukraine: The Unwinding of the Post-Cold War Order* (Cambridge, MA: MIT Press, 2015), 87–106.

4. The number of (at least) 40,000 Crimean Tatars who left Crimea after annexation is cited in Gwendolyn Sasse, *Der Krieg gegen die Ukraine* (Munich: Beck Verlag, 2022), 80.

5. See Gwendolyn Sasse and Alice Lackner, *Attitudes and Identities across the Donbas Front Line: What Has Changed from 2016 to 2019?* (Berlin: Center for East European and International Studies Report), Report 3 (2019).

6. After Yanukovych's flight, "large protests broke out in the cities Russian speakers called Lugansk, Kharkov, Odessa, and Dnipropetrovsk, as well as in Donetsk," writes Owen Matthews, *Overreach: The Inside Story of Putin and Russia's War against Ukraine* (London: Mudlark, 2023), 105.

7. On Igor Girkin's role in destabilizing the Donbas, not necessarily at Moscow's command, see Lawrence Freedman, *Command: The Politics of Military Operations from Korea to Ukraine* (New York: Oxford University Press, 2022), 366–389; and Anna Matveeva, *Through Times of Trouble: Conflict in Southeastern Ukraine Explained from Within* (Blue Ridge Summit, PA: Lexington Books, 2018). See also Benjamin Bidder, "Russian Far-Right Idol: The Man Who Started the War in Ukraine," *Spiegel Online International* (March 18, 2015), https://www.spiegel.de/international/europe/the-ukraine-war-from-perspective-of-russian-nationalists-a-1023801.html.

8. In an April 17, 2014, speech, Putin explained "Novorossiya" in the following terms: "What was called Novorossiya (New Russia) back in the tsarist days—Kharkov, Lugansk, Donetsk, Kherson, Nikolaev and Odessa—were not part of Ukraine back then. These territories were given to Ukraine in the 1920s by the Soviet government." Putin speech cited in Charles Clover, *Black Wind, White Snow: Russia's New Nationalism* (New Haven, CT: Yale University Press, 2022), 325. Notably, this exact area in Ukraine would be attacked in February 2022 and targeted for annexation by Russia, though the Russian military never made it to Odessa. It failed to capture Kharkiv and was driven out of Kherson by the Ukrainian military in November 2022.

9. On the May 2, 2014, events in Odessa, see Andrew E. Kramer, "Ukraine's Reins Weaken as Chaos Spreads," *New York Times* (May 4, 2014), https://www.nytimes.com/2014/05/05/world/europe/kievs-reins-weaken-as-chaos-spreads.html.

10. On Europe's response to the annexation of Crimea and the Russian invasion of the Donbas, see chapter 4, "Europe and the Crisis," in Rumer and Menon, *Conflict in Ukraine*, 107–144. See also chapter 3, "Breaking Point," in Samuel Charap and Timothy J. Colton, *Everyone Loses: The Ukraine Crisis and the Contest for Post-Soviet Eurasia* (New York: Routledge, 2016), 113–150.

11. The definitive study of the Russian weaponry used to shoot down MH17 is from Bellingcat. See "MH17: The Open Source Evidence," https://www.bellingcat.com/app/uploads/2015/10/MH17-The-Open-Source-Evidence-EN.pdf.

12. On the battle of Ilovaisk, see Viacheslav Shramovych, "Ukraine's Deadliest Day: The Battle of Ilovaisk, August 2014," *BBC* (August 29, 2019), https://www.bbc.com/news/world-europe-49426724.

13. For the text of "Minsk" 1, see https://www.peaceagreements.org/viewmasterdocument/1363.

14. According to Philip Short, "Poroshenko said later [after signing the Minsk agreements] he had agreed because it was the only way to stop the fighting, but he had known that it would never be implemented because neither the political establishment nor public opinion in Ukraine would accept it." Short, *Putin* (New York: Holt, 2023), 587. If true, Poroshenko was completely at odds with the Western take on Minsk, which was to take Minsk at face value.

15. As Gwendolyn Sasse correctly writes, "the annexation of Crimea, the war in the Donbas and finally the February 2022 invasion are three phases of the same war." Sasse, *Der Krieg gegen die Ukraine*, 121. ["Die Krim-Annexion, der Krieg in Donbas und schliesslich die Invasion seit Februar sind drei Phasen eines Krieges."]

16. The number of 14,000 casualties is cited in Serhii Plokhy's *The Russo-Ukrainian War*, 131.

17. For the text of "Minsk II," see "Protocol on the Results of Consultations of the Trilateral Contact Group," https://peacemaker.un.org/UA-ceasefire-2014.

18. In his memoirs, John Kerry notes his wish for greater US involvement in Minsk I and in Minsk II and complains of the United States getting shut out. "We needed to achieve a breakthrough on the diplomatic front," he writes. "Our initial approach was to let the Germans, French, Ukrainians and Russians take the lead. This approach had its upsides: it put responsibility on Europe to stay united on Ukraine, and it managed the risk of Putin seeing Ukraine even more conspiratorially through the lens of a US-Russian proxy fight. But those talks dragged on for months. . . . We attempted to insert ourselves in the process, but we were shut out by the participants time and again." Kerry, *Every Day Is Extra* (New York: Simon and Schuster, 2018), 437.

19. For studies of Russia's 2015 move into Syria, see Anna Borshchevskaya, *Putin's War in Syria: Russian Foreign Policy and the Price of America's Absence* (London: I. B. Tauris, 2021); and Dmitry Trenin, *What Is Russia Up To in the Middle East?* (London: Polity, 2017). For historical context, see Mark Katz, *Russia and Arabia: Soviet Foreign Policy toward the Arabian Peninsula* (Baltimore, MD: Johns Hopkins University Press, 1986).

20. On this particular active measure, see chapter 22, "AIDS Made in the USA," in Thomas Rid, *Active Measures: The Secret History of Disinformation and Political Warfare* (New York: Macmillan, 2020), 95–104.

21. On the leaked phone call, see Alison Smale, "Leaked Recordings Lay Bare E.U. and U.S. Divisions in Goals for Ukraine," *New York Times* (February 7, 2014), https://www.nytimes.com/2014/02/08/world/europe/ukraine.html.

Chapter 6

1. Donald Trump quoted in https://www.rev.com/blog/transcripts/trump-speaks-at-cpac-2023-transcript.

2. David Vogelsong, *The American Mission and the "Evil Empire"* (New York: Cambridge University Press, 2007).

3. Many of the best essays on Trump's foreign policy have been written by Thomas Wright. See "The Foreign Crises Awaiting Trump," *The Atlantic* (January 20, 2017), https://www.theatlantic.com/international/archive/2017/01/trump-russia-putin-north-korea-putin/513749/; "Trump Remains a NATO Skeptic," *The Atlantic* (May 27, 2017), https://www.theatlantic.com/international/archive/2017/05/trump-nato-article-five-israel-saudi-arabia/528393/; "Trump Is Choosing Eastern Europe," *The Atlantic* (June 6, 2018), https://www.theatlantic.com/international/archive/2018/06/trump-is-choosing-eastern-europe/562130/; "The Return to Great-Power Rivalry Was Inevitable," *The Atlantic* (September 12, 2018), https://www.theatlantic.com/international/archive/2018/09/liberal-international-order-free-world-trump-authoritarianism/569881/; and "Trump, Unchecked," *The Atlantic* (December 21, 2018), https://www.theatlantic.com/ideas/archive/2018/12/trump-administration-after-mattis/578890/.

4. On the turn toward greater ambition in American foreign policy (circa 1940), see Stephen Wertheim, *Tomorrow the World: The Birth of U.S. Global Supremacy* (Cambridge, MA: Belknap Press, 2020).

5. A photograph that summed up Trump's sense of himself as a transnational national revolutionary was the one taken with Nigel Farage, the outspoken Brexiteer, in Trump Tower on November 12, 2016. Fiona Hill links the figures of Farage, Trump, and Putin, observing that "Nigel Farage in the UK and Donald Trump in the U.S. Both Fit Putin's Populist Mold." *There Is Nothing for You Here: Finding Opportunity in the Twenty-First Century* (New York: Mariner, 2021), 172.

6. On the trade war with China, see Josh Rogin, *Chaos under Heaven: Trump, Xi, and the Battle for the Twenty-First Century* (New York: Harper Collins, 2021). See also Peter Navarro and Greg Autry, *Death by China: Confronting the Dragon—a Global Call to Action* (London: Pearson Press, 2011). From 2017 to 2021, Peter Navarro served in the Trump administration as director of the Office of Trade and Manufacturing Policy. On the expectation of mounting geopolitical conflict with China, see Elbridge A. Colby, *The Strategy of Denial: American Defense in an Age of Great Power Conflict* (New Haven, CT: Yale University Press, 2021). From 2017 to 2018, Elbridge Colby helped to write National Defense Strategy while serving at the Department of Defense.

7. On Russian attempts to strike a deal with the Trump administration on Ukraine, see Jim Rutenberg, "The Untold Story of 'Russiagate' and the Road to War in Ukraine," *New York Times Magazine* (November 2, 2022), https://www.nytimes.com/2022/11/02/magazine/russiagate-paul-manafort-ukraine-war.html.

8. Kim Darroch describes a meeting with President Trump, in which the president presented himself as "convinced that Brexit had been delivered by the same forces that had swept him [Donald Trump] to power, fueled by a flood of economic migrants from North Africa and the Near East, which had in turn been accelerated by chronic instability in those regions." Kim Darroch, *Collateral Damage: Britain, America, and Europe in the Age of Trump* (New York: Public Affairs, 2020), 45.

9. The number, 5.95 percent of GDP as allocated for defense spending for Ukraine, is cited by Mark Galeotti in *Putin's Wars*, 201.

10. Donald Trump Jr. quoted in Jo Becker, Adam Goldman, and Matt Apuzzo, "Russian Dirt on Clinton? 'I Love It,' Donald Trump Jr. Said," *New York Times* (July 11, 2017), https://www.nytimes.com/2017/07/11/us/politics/trump-russia-email-clinton.html.

11. On role of Wikileaks in Russia's meddling in the 2016 election, see Greg Miller, *The Apprentice: Trump, Russia and the Subversion of American Democracy* (New York: Custom House, 2018), 52–54.

12. Donald Trump quoted in Michael S. Schmidt, "Trump Invited the Russians to Hack Clinton. Were They Listening?," *New York Times* (July 13, 2018), https://www.nyti mes.com/2018/07/13/us/politics/trump-russia-clinton-emails.html.

13. As Peter Baker and Susan Glasser describe the interaction, Paul Manafort "secretly slipped internal campaign polling to Konstantin Kilimnik, an old business associate who happened to be a Russian spy and passed along the data to Russian intelligence." Peter Baker and Susan Glasser, *The Divider: Trump in the White House, 2017–2021* (New York: Doubleday, 2022), 83. On Konstantin Kilimnik, see also Miller, *The Apprentice*, 83, 84. On the "Steele dossier," see Glasser and Baker, *The Divider*, 214; and Miller, *The Apprentice*, 225–232.

14. On the details of the Flynn-Kislyak phone call, see Baker and Glasser, *The Divider*, 40–42.

15. As Peter Baker and Susan Glasser write about the Mueller report, Special Prosecutor Mueller had uncovered ten episodes that he considered "potentially obstruction [of justice] but felt he could not say so because of the Justice Department policy barring indictment of a sitting president." Baker and Glasser, *The Divider*, 318.

16. Of varied quality, many books have been published on Russian meddling in the 2016 presidential election and on Trump's (real and alleged) ties to Russia. They include Luke Harding, *Collusion: Secret Meetings, Dirty Money, and How Russia Helped Donald Trump Win* (New York: Vintage, 2017); Michael Wolff, *Fire and Fury: Inside the Trump White House* (New York: Henry Holt, 2018); Bob Woodward, *Fear: Trump in the White House* (New York: Simon and Schuster, 2018); Craig Unger, *House of Trump, House of Putin: The Untold Story of Donald Trump and the Russian Mafia* (New York: Dutton, 2018); Michael Isikoff and David Corn, *Russian Roulette: The Inside Story of Putin's War on America and the Election of Donald Trump* (New York: Twelve, 2018); Michael V. Hayden, *The Assault on Intelligence: American National Security in an Age of Lies* (New York: Penguin, 2018); Craig Unger, *American Kompromat: How the KGB Cultivated Donald Trump, and Related Tales of Sex, Greed, Power and Treachery* (New York: Dutton, 2021).

17. On Trump wishing to pull the United States out of NATO and discussing this with staff shortly before the Helsinki summit, see Baker and Glasser, *The Divider*, 205. John Bolton describes Trump as "prepared to get out of NATO" while president. John Bolton, *The Room Where It Happened* (New York: Simon and Schuster, 2020), 58. Kim Darroch, the British ambassador to the United States for much of the Trump administration, writes of President Trump telling the Swedish prime minister "openly that he would like to have the US to have the same posture as Sweden: outside NATO but cooperating when it chose." Darroch, *Collateral Damage*, 212.

18. Trump lost the trust of his own administration in Helsinki. As Peter Baker and Susan Glasser write of Dan Coats, Trump's director of National Intelligence, "Helsinki had been such an extraordinary event that it forever changed his view of the allegations about Trump and Russia," meaning that the president's director of national intelligence was concerned about Trump colluding or having colluded with Russia. Baker and Glasser, *The Divider*, 198. On the Helsinki summit, see also Bolton, *The Room Where It Happened*, 156–167.

19. Hill, *There Is Nothing for You Here*, 233. Hill analyzes the Helsinki summit in detail in her memoirs, *There Is Nothing for You Here*, 226–235.

20. On the 2017 US decision to provide lethal military assistance to Ukraine, see Tracy Wilkinson, "U.S. Decision to Provide Anti-Tank Missiles to Ukraine Angers Russian Leaders," *Los Angeles Times* (December 26, 2017), https://www.latimes.com/nation/la-fg-us-ukraine-20171226-story.html.

21. Olga Onuch and Henry Hale write of Poroshenko circa 2014 as a "consummate insider and oligarch . . . a member of every administration and regime coalition since Kuchma, including holding posts in Yanukovych's government—who had rebranded himself as a revolutionary figure [in 2013–2014] and co-opted the *maidan*'s radical ethos for his electoral victory." *The Zelensky Effect* (New York: Oxford University Press, 2023), 118.

22. When it came to military modernization, Poroshenko had a foundation on which to build. Between 2009 and 2013, Ukraine was "the eighth-largest arms exporter in the world, responsible for 3 percent of global sales, though a good proportion of this went to Russia." Tim Judah, *In Wartime: Stories from Ukraine* (New York: Penguin, 2016), 164. On Ukraine's military modernization before Zelensky came to power, see Bryan Bender and Wesley Morgan, "How U.S. Military Aid Became a Lifeline to Ukraine," *Politico* (September 30, 2019); and Mariya Omelicheva, "Washington's Security Assistance to Kyiv: Improving Long-Term Returns on Military Investments in Ukraine," PONARS (Program on New Approaches to Research and Security in Eurasia) Eurasia Policy Memo (September 2019), https://www.ponarseurasia.org/washington-s-security-assistance-to-kyiv-improving-long-term-returns-on-military-investments-in-ukraine/. In February 2019, "the Ukrainian parliament voted to formally enshrine Ukraine's commitment to join both NATO and the European Union in the country's constitution by a majority of 334 out of 385 votes," writes Owen Matthews, *Overreach: The Inside Story of Putin's War against Ukraine* (London: Mudlark, 2023), 185.

23. Zelensky's election, combined with the parliamentary election of 2019, in which Zelensky's "Servant of the People" party won an absolute majority, demonstrated that Ukrainian "society was more open in its identity and more unified in its backing of the Ukrainian state than political rhetoric often led people to believe," in the words of Gwendolyn Sasse. Gwendolyn Sasse, *Der Krieg gegen die Ukraine* (Munich: Beck Verlag, 2022), 42. ["Seine Wahl 2019 . . . zeigte . . . dass die Gesellschaft in ihrer Identitaet bereits offener und geinter hiter dem ukrainischen Staat stand, als es die politische Rhetorik oftmals vermuten liess.]"

24. As Peter Baker and Susan Glasser paraphrase remarks made in private to US allies at a 2018 G7 meeting, Trump stated "that Crimea was by rights Russian and that Ukraine was a corrupt state not worth defending." Baker and Glasser, *The Divider*, 189.

25. Trump's advisor Steve Bannon was probably speaking for the president when in 2017 he said to Germany's national security advisor, Christoph Heusgen, "You shouldn't care about Russia. You should care about China." Bannon quoted in Baker and Glasser, *The Divider*, 67.

26. The smear campaign was mounted by Fox News stars Sean Hannity and Laura Ingraham, the odd journalism, and a tweet from Donald Trump Jr. Interestingly, Poroshenko, had he stayed in power, might have colluded with the Trump White House. "Poroshenko, it has been reported," was ready to make the announcement [about Joe Biden] sought by Giuliani." *The Zelensky Effect*, 216.

27. Marie Yovanovich's memoir is *Lessons from the Edge: A Memoir* (New York: Mariner Books, 2022). On the treatment of Ambassador Yovanovich and the Trump administration activities that led to President Trump's first impeachment, see also Alexander Vindman, *Here, Right Matters: An American Story* (New York: Harper Collins, 2021).

28. On Secretary of State Pompeo's visit to Belarus, see Andrew Higgins, "Political Grip Shaky, Belarus Leader Blames Longtime Ally: Russia," *New York Times* (June 22, 2020), https://www.nytimes.com/2020/06/22/world/europe/belarus-lukashenko-russia.html.

29. On the 2020 protest movement in Belarus, see chapter 14, "The Revolution without a Name," in Andrew Wilson, *Belarus: The Last European Dictatorship* (New Haven, CT: Yale University Press, 2021). On the role of women in the protest movement against Lukashenko, see Alice Bota, *Die Frauen von Belarus: Von Revolution, Mut und Dem Drang nach Freiheit* (Berlin: Berlin Verlag, 2021).

Chapter 7

1. For the full text of President Biden's remarks, see https://www.whitehouse.gov/briefing-room/speeches-remarks/2021/06/16/remarks-by-president-biden-in-press-conference-4/.

2. On the arrest of Alexei Navalny, see Joshua Yaffa, "With Navalny Headed to Prison, Russia's Political Battle Enters a New Stage," *New Yorker* (February 3, 2021), https://www.newyorker.com/news/dispatch/with-navalny-headed-to-prison-russias-political-battle-enters-a-new-stage.

3. For a biography of Joe Biden, see Evan Osnos, *Joe Biden: The Life, the Run and What Matters Now* (New York: Scribner, 2020).

4. On the "Liza affair," a Russian attempt to stir unrest in Germany in January 2016, see Andreas Rinke and Paul Carrel, "German-Russian Ties Feel Cold War Chill over Rape Case," Reuters (February 1, 2016), https://www.reuters.com/article/us-germany-russia/german-russian-ties-feel-cold-war-style-chill-over-rape-case-idUSKCN0VA31O. On the murder of a Chechen man living in Berlin in summer 2019, see Christopher F. Schuetze, "Russian Is Convicted in Murder of Chechen Man in Berlin Park," *New York Times* (December 15, 2021), https://www.nytimes.com/2021/12/15/world/europe/germany-russia-berlin-murder.html.

5. For an excellent book on the Skripal and other such cases, see Andrei Soldatov and Irina Borogan, *The Compatriots: The Brutal and Chaotic History of Russia's Exiles, Emigres, and Agents Abroad* (New York: PublicAffairs, 2019).

6. "Even as Germany condemned Putin for Crimea," Owen Matthews writes, "it continued to ramp up its dependence on Russian gas." *Overreach: The Inside Story of Putin's War against Ukraine* (London: Mudlark, 2023), 128.

7. According to Olga Onuch and Henry Hale, "Unlike Poroshenko, Zelensky said [on the campaign trail in 2019] that he would even be willing to sit down with Putin to bring a halt to the killing, potentially making compromises with the enemy." *The Zelensky Effect* (New York: Oxford University Press, 2023), 176.

8. According to Owen Matthews, these negotiations changed Zelensky's mind about Putin, whose "last-minute bullying over the prisoner exchanges was 'the moment that [Zelensky] really understood at first hand what kind of people we were dealing with' in the Kremlin, recalled a senior Zelensky advisor who was directly involved in the prisoner-exchange negotiations. Matthews, *Overreach*, 147.

9. Whatever the nuances of Zelensky's position in 2019, Serhii Plokhy emphasizes continuity between Poroshenko and Zelensky on foreign policy, arguing that under Zelensky "there would be no change of Ukraine's commitment to join NATO, and the nation-building initiatives and cultural policies introduced by Poroshenko were maintained." *The Russo-Ukrainian War*, 139.

10. In the assessment of Owen Matthews, "The threat of a nationalist Maidan implacably destroyed Zelensky's attempt to bring peace in 2019—and would remain a major threat to any future negotiated peace in the endgame of the 2022 war." Matthews, *Overreach*, 148.

11. Vladimir Putin, quoted in Serhii Rudenko, *Zelensky: A Biography* (Cambridge: Polity, 2022), 53. On Zelensky and the 2019 "Normandy format" meeting in Paris, see Rudenko, *Zelensky*, 47–53.

12. Thirty percent approval ratings for Zelensky are cited in Gwendolyn Sasse, *Der Krieg egen die Ukraine* (Munich: Beck Verlag, 2022), 57.

13. Andrey Yermak, one of Zelensky's closest advisors and his chief of staff as of February 2020, also had ties to the Party of Regions. He was "a voluntary assistant to Elbrus Tadeev, a people's deputy" from this party from 2006 to 2014. See Rudenko, *Zelensky*, 143.

14. The United States approved of Zelensky's actions vis-à-vis Medvedchuk. On this, see Plokhy, *The Russo-Ukrainian War*, 141.

15. On Ukraine's 2021 participation in NATO exercises see Matthews, *Overreach*, 170. Matthews attributes this decision of Zelensky's to the "moment when the attack on Ukraine went from possible to probable." Matthews, *Overreach*, 170.

16. According to Don Jacobson, Secretary of Defense Austin "voiced support for Ukraine's aspirations to join NATO" during this visit to Kyiv. "Austin Visits Ukraine, Voices U.S. Support against Russian Aggression," *UPI* (October 19, 2021), https://www.upi.com/Defense-News/2021/10/19/ukraine-Austin-support-Russian-aggress ion/5011634675035/.

17. See Marquis de Custine, *Empire of the Czar: A Journey through Eternal Russia* (New York: Doubleday, 1989). See also George F. Kennan, *The Marquis de Custine and His Russia* (Princeton, NJ: Princeton University Press, 1971).

18. On Zelensky's announcement of a thwarted coup d'etat in Ukraine in December 2021, see Rudenko, *Zelensky*, 191.

19. Explaining this catastrophe, Putin observed that "tens of millions of our countrymen ended up outside our country's borders." Vladimir Putin quoted in Masha Gessen, *The Future Is History: How Totalitarianism Reclaimed Russia* (New York: Riverhead Books, 2018), 275. One did not have to be Russian to see the Soviet Union's fall as Russia's loss. US ambassador to the Soviet Union, Robert Strauss, claimed that "the Russians have never faced a reversal quite like the one they do now; the loss, without a contest of arms, of territories and populations that have been under Russian suzerainty since the early years of the Romanov dynasty." Robert Strauss quoted in Mary Sarotte, *Not One Inch: America, Russia and the Making of Post-Cold War Stalemate* (New Haven, CT: Yale University Press, 2022), 128. Owen Matthews links Putin's ideological outlook circa 2022 to his Soviet past, writing that the "ideology of late Putinism was the ideology of the institution that formed the men who led it—the Brezhnev-era KGB." Matthews, *Overreach*, 157.

20. May 9 Victory Day parades were brought to Red Square starting in 1999, when Yeltsin was still president.

21. "Lenin, never a strong believer in the all-Russian nation, was prepared to treat Russians, Ukrainians, and Belarusians as distinct peoples. According to him, the Great Russians were dominant, while the Ukrainians and Belarusians, former members of the privileged big Russian nation, were among the oppressed." Serhii Plokhy, *Lost Kingdom: The Quest for Empire and the Making of the Russian Nation from 1470 to the Present* (New York: Basic Books, 2017), 213.

22. Plokhy, *Lost Kingdom*, 346. An excellent overview of Putin's attitudes toward history, before his first invasion of Ukraine in 2014, is chapter 4, "The History Man," in Fiona Hill and Clifford G. Gaddy, *Mr. Putin: Operative in the Kremlin* (Washington, DC: Brookings Institution Press, 2015), 63–75.

23. For Putin's essay on the Second World War, published in the German magazine, *Die Zeit* in the summer of 2021, see Vladmir Putin, "Offen sein, trotz der Vergangenheit," *Die Zeit* (June 22, 2021). ["To Be Open, Despite the Past"], https://www.zeit.de/poli tik/ausland/2021-06/ueberfall-auf-die-sowjetunion-1941-europa-russland-geschic hte-wladimir-putin?utm_referrer=https%3A%2F%2Fwww.google.com%2F. For an English-language version of Putin's 2021 essay, "On the Historical Unity of Russians and Ukrainians," see http://en.kremlin.ru/events/president/news/66181.

24. On Kremlin rhetoric toward Ukraine, see also Dmitry Medvedev, "Pochemu bessmysleny kontakty s nyneshnym Ukrainskym rukovodstvom," *Kommersant* (October 11, 0221).

25. Yeltsin's attitudes toward the Russian past indicate that many of Putin's views are not unique to Putin. As Yeltsin said to a French academic, "I am a Russian . . . and I am not happy with the idea of the collapse of the [Soviet] empire. For me, it is Russia, it is Russian history. But I know it is the end. . . . The only way [forward] is to get rid of this empire as quickly as possible, or to accept the process." Boris Yeltsin quoted in Timothy Colton, *Yeltsin: A Life* (New York: Basic Books, 2008), 195. As Colton observes of Mikhail Gorbachev circa 1991, "He described the dismemberment of the

USSR as a mistake and a betrayal of a thousand years of Russian history, but accepted that he was unable to prevent it." Colton, *Yeltsin: A Life*, 207.

26. Putin's ideas were obviously extreme outside of Russia. Before the 2022 war, they may have been extreme within Russia as well. Timothy Frye cites a 2017 survey, according to which "56 percent of Russians favored a Russia with a higher standard of living, and 42 percent favored a Russia as a great power." Frye argues in his 2021 book that "Russian foreign policy elites may share a deep-seated desire for great-power status and strong anti-American views, but the Russian public is much more ambivalent." Frye, *Weak Strongman: The Limits of Power in Putin's Russia* (Princeton, NJ: Princeton University Press, 2021), 168, 170. For Owen Matthews, the radicalization of Russian foreign policy was a slow progression: "Between 2014 and 2020 the ideology of creating a Greater Russia by force," he writes, "travelled from the fringes into the political mainstream and eventually to the heart of official government policy." Matthews, *Overreach*, 115.

27. On the signing of START-2, see David E. Sanger and Anton Troianovski, "Biden and Putin Agree to Extend Nuclear Treaty," *New York Times* (January 26, 2021), https://www.nytimes.com/2021/01/26/world/europe/biden-putin-nuclear-treaty.html.

28. Thomas Wright and Colin Kahl, *Aftershocks: Pandemic Politics and the End of the Old International Order* (New York: St. Martin's Press, 2021).

29. On the hold-up in aid, see Plokhy, *The Russo-Ukrainian War*, 249. Not all US gestures toward Russia were conciliatory in the summer of 2021. Due to lobbying from Britain and the United States, "the question of returning to an 'open-door policy'—including MAPs for Ukraine and Georgia—was put on the agenda" for the 2021 NATO summit in Brussels. Matthews, *Overreach*, 186.

30. For one of President Biden's several references to the NATO alliance as "sacred," see https://www.whitehouse.gov/briefing-room/speeches-remarks/2022/03/26/remarks-by-president-biden-on-the-united-efforts-of-the-free-world-to-support-the-people-of-ukraine/.

31. On the Biden-Putin summit in Geneva, see Anton Troianovsky, Oleg Matsnev, and Ivan Nechepurenko, "Biden and Putin Say Talks Went Well, but Divisions Remain on Issues like Cyberattacks and Human Rights," *New York Times* (June 16, 2021), https://www.nytimes.com/2021/06/16/world/europe/biden-summit-putin.html.

32. Vladimir Putin quoted in Philip Short, *Putin* (New York: Holt, 2023), 648.

Chapter 8

1. Vladimir Putin, "On the Historical Unity of Russians and Ukrainians" (July 12, 2022), http://www.en.kremlin.ru/events/president/news/66181.

2. For a study of memory politics in post-Soviet Russia, see Jade McGlynn, *Memory Makers: The Politics of the Past in Putin's Russia* (London: Bloomsbury Academic, 2023).

3. Jade McGlynn argues that "confidence in the West's degeneracy was central to the Kremlin's calculations when invading Ukraine [in 2022]." *Russia's War* (Cambridge: Polity Books, 2023), 133. On the formation of Putin's attitudes toward the United States see chapter 12, "The American Education of Mr. Putin," in Fiona Hill and Clifford G. Gaddy, *Mr. Putin: Operative in the Kremlin* (Washington, DC: Brookings Institution Press, 2015), 285–311.

4. On Russian conservatism in general, see Richard Pipes, *Russian Conservatism and Its Critics: A Study in Political Culture* (New Haven, CT: Yale University Press, 2006). On Russian conservatism and its relationship to the Putin regime, see Mikhail Suslov and Dmitry Uzlaner, editors, *Contemporary Russian Conservatism: Problems, Paradoxes and Perspectives* (Leiden: Brill, 2019); and Paul Robinson, *Russian Conservatism* (DeKalb, IL: Northern Illinois University Press, 2021).

5. Of the many books on democracy in crisis or in decline published after 2016, the following are notable: Yascha Mounk, *The People vs. Democracy: Why Our Freedom Is in Danger and How to Save It* (Cambridge, MA: Harvard University Press, 2018); Steven Levitsky and Daniel Ziblatt, *How Democracies Die* (New York: Crown, 2018); Patrick Deneen, *Why Liberalism Failed* (New Haven, CT: Yale University Press, 2019); and Anne Applebaum, *Twilight of Democracy: The Seductive Lure of Authoritarianism* (New York: Knopf, 2021).

6. Vladimir Putin quoted in Owen Matthews, *Overreach: The Inside Story of Putin's War against Ukraine* (London: Mudlark, 2023), 355.

7. On corruption as one of the catalysts for US defeat in Afghanistan, see Sarah Chaves, "Afghanistan's Corruption Was Made in America," *Foreign Affairs* (September 3, 2021), https://www.foreignaffairs.com/articles/united-states/2021-09-03/afghanistans-corruption-was-made-in-america. Emma Sky's related set of claims about corruption and policy failure is developed in *The Unraveling: High Hopes and Missed Opportunities in Iraq* (New York: PublicAffairs, 2015).

8. According to Barack Obama, in his memoir, Biden had been skeptical of the US involvement in Afghanistan long before he became president, lamenting what he perceived as attempts "by an unrestrained military to drag the country deeper into a futile, wildly expensive nation-building exercise." *A Promised Land* (New York: Crown, 2020), 432–433.

9. "This is manifestly not Saigon," Secretary of State Antony Blinken stated on August 15, 2021. See Ed Pilkington, "'This Is Manifestly Not Saigon': Blinken Defends US Mission in Afghanistan," *The Guardian* (August 15, 2021), https://www.theguardian.com/us-news/2021/aug/15/antony-blinken-us-mission-afghanistan-saigon.

10. Two books that trace cycles of international engagement followed by retrenchment in American foreign policy are Peter Beinart, *The Icarus Syndrome: A History of American Hubris* (New York: Harper, 2010); and Steve Sestanovich, *Maximalist: America in the World from Truman to Obama* (New York: Knopf, 2014).

11. A typical example of Putin's views on Western decadence could be taken from a 2013 speech Putin gave. "We can see many EuroAtlantic countries rejecting their own roots," Putin argued, "including Christian values, which form the foundation of Western civilization. They reject their own moral foundations as well as all

traditional identities: national, cultural, religious, and even gender. They pursue policies that place large families on equal footing with same-sex partnerships, and faith in God with Satan warship." Vladimir Putin quoted in Masha Gessen, *The Future Is History: How Totalitarianism Came to Russia* (New York: Riverhead, 2017), 408.

12. In the words of Mark Galeotti, Putin "began to believe [in the early 2000s] that, especially when faced with a fait accompli and a tough rebuttal, for all the West's economic and, indeed, military might, it lacked one crucial strategic asset: will. That, he seemed to have concluded, was Russia's strategic advantage." Mark Galeotti, *Putin's Wars: From Chechnya to Ukraine* (New York: Osprey, 2022), 103.

13. For a history of American missionary arrogance toward Russia, see David S. Fogelsong, *The American "Mission" and the Evil Empire: The Crusade for a "Free Russia" since 1881* (New York: Cambridge University Press, 2007).

14. Dara Massicot analyzes the distance between the actual Russian military and the military Putin thought he had on February 24, 2022, in "What Russia Got Wrong: Can Moscow Learn from Its Failures in Ukraine?," *Foreign Affairs* (March/April 2023), https://www.foreignaffairs.com/ukraine/what-russia-got-wrong-moscow-failures-in-ukraine-dara-massicot.

15. A history of the Cold War that integrates de-colonization, non-aligned states, and Cold War competition and that sheds light on global reactions to the 2022 war in Ukraine is Odd Arne Westad's *The Global Cold War: Third World Interventions and the Making of Our Times* (New York: Cambridge University Press, 2011). See also Jeremi Suri, *Power and Protest: Global Revolution and the Rise of Détente* (Cambridge, MA: Harvard University Press, 2005); and Adom Getachew, *Worldmaking after Empire: The Rise and Fall of Self-Determination* (Princeton, NJ: Princeton University Press, 2020).

16. See Eugene Rumer and Andrew Weiss, "Vladimir Putin's Russia Goes Global," *Wall Street Journal* (August 4, 2017). Angela Stent covers Russian foreign policy's global dimension in chapters 8–10 of *Putin's World: Russia against the West and with the Rest* (New York: Twelve, 2019), 208–292. Christopher Walker underscores the authoritarian impulse behind Russia's global outreach circa 2018 in "What Is 'Sharp' Power?," *Journal of Democracy* 29, no. 3 (July 2018): 9–23.

17. For background on the China-Russia relationship, see Bobo Lo, *Axis of Convenience: Moscow, Beijing and the New Geopolitics* (Washington, DC: Brookings Institution Press, 2008); and chapter 5, "A Turn to the East," in Bobo Lo, *Russia and the New World Disorder* (Washington, DC: Brookings Institution Press, 2015), 132–164.

18. Owen Matthews describes an Oval Office meeting about Russia's invasion plans with the president, vice president, and "top military and intelligence officials," which took place in early October. Matthews, *Overreach*, 196.

19. Two articles from the fall of 2021 that laid out the reasoning for a possible Russia invasion were Andrew Weiss and Eugene Rumer, "Ukraine: Putin's Unfinished Business," Carnegie Endowment for International Peace Publication (November 12, 2021); and Michael Kimmage and Michael Kofman, "Russia Won't Let Ukraine Go without a Fight," *Foreign Affairs* (November 22, 2021).

20. A detailed account of White House deliberations and actions during the lead-up to the war is Shane Harris, Karen DeYoung, Isabelle Khurshudyan, Ashley Parker, and Liz Sly, "Road to War: U.S. Struggled to Convince Allies, and Zelensky, of Risk of Invasion," *Washington Post* (August 16, 2022), https://www.washingtonpost.com/national-security/interactive/2022/ukraine-road-to-war/.

21. Zelensky's response to the pull-out of the US and British embassies from Kyiv was that "right now, the people's biggest enemy is panic," either playing it cool or still not willing to believe that war was coming. Volodymyr Zelensky quoted in Matthews, *Overreach*, 16. According to Matthews, Zelensky went to bed on February 23, 2022, "in the hope that the 'common sense' of which he had spoken earlier that evening [in a speech] would prevail"—that is, that the Russian invasion would not occur. Matthews, *Overreach*, 19.

22. On lying as a political modus vivendi, see Christopher Bort, "Why the Kremlin Lies: Understanding Its Loose Relationship with the Truth," Carnegie Endowment for International Peace (January 6, 2022), https://carnegieendowment.org/2022/01/06/why-kremlin-lies-understanding-its-loose-relationship-with-truth-pub-86132.

Chapter 9

1. As Jake Sullivan put it a June 2017 interview with NPR's Jim Gilmore: "The biggest challenge that we had [in 2014] was, we didn't have a clear answer to the question of how do you deter behavior when the other side is basically denying that it's even taking place? And then how do you de-escalate or use diplomacy to try to resolve a situation when the other side is saying, 'I don't even know what you're talking about; we're not involved?'" https://www.pbs.org/wgbh/frontline/interview/jake-sullivan/.

2. For the text of Putin's February 21 speech, see http://www.en.kremlin.ru/events/president/transcripts/70565.

3. Serhii Plokhy notes that Hostomel airport was lightly armed despite "a warning from CIA director William Burns to President Zelensky that the Russians were going to land at Hostomel." *The Russo-Ukrainian War: The Return of History* (New York: Norton, 2023), 160.

4. On the complexities of collaboration and occupation, see Joshua Yaffa, "The Hunt for Russian Collaborators in Ukraine," *New Yorker* (January 30, 2023), https://www.newyorker.com/magazine/2023/02/06/the-hunt-for-russian-collaborators-in-ukraine.

5. Claims about Zelensky's unpopularity before the war are sometimes exaggerated. Serhii Plokhy points to data "released in Ukraine on the day before the invasion, February 23, [which] rated Zelensky as the country's most popular politician, with 42 percent support." Plokhy, *The Russo-Ukrainian War*, 164.

6. On the "I don't need a ride" comment of Zelensky's, see Stephen Collinson, "Zelensky Taps National Psyches of Other Countries as He Appeals to Save His Own," *CNN Politics* (March 16, 2022), https://www.cnn.com/2022/03/16/politics/zelensky-speech-national-psyches/index.html.

7. On the fading away of territory as a source of national and imperial power after 1945, see Charles S. Maier, *Once within Borders: Territories of Power, Wealth, and Belonging since 1500* (Cambridge, MA: Belknap Press, 2016).

8. On the events in Bucha, see Carlotta Gall, "Bucha: The Epicenter of Russian Atrocity," *New York Times* (June 18, 2022), https://www.nytimes.com/live/2022/06/18/world/ukraine-russia-news-deaths?smid=nytcore-ios-share&referringSource=articleShare#bucha-the-epicenter-of-russian-atrocity.

9. Three articles that elucidate the horror of the war itself and of the Russian occupation are Joshua Yaffa, "The Prisoners in a Cellar in the Ukrainian Village of Novyi Bykov," *New Yorker* (April 8, 2022), https://www.newyorker.com/news/dispatch/the-prisoners-in-a-cellar-in-the-ukrainian-village-of-novyi-bykiv; Joshua Yaffa, "A Ukrainian City under a Violent New Regime," *New Yorker* (May 16, 2022), https://www.newyorker.com/magazine/2022/05/23/a-ukrainian-city-under-a-violent-new-regime; and Joshua Yaffa, "The Psychologists Treating Rape Victims in Ukraine," *New Yorker* (July 14, 2022), https://www.newyorker.com/news/dispatch/the-psychologists-treating-rape-victims-in-ukraine.

10. On Russia's creation of filtration camps in Ukraine, see the OSCE report of July 14, 2022: https://www.osce.org/files/f/documents/3/e/522616.pdf.

11. On deportation of Ukrainian children to Russia, see Carly Olson, "Over 4,300 Ukrainian Children Have Been Deported to Russia or Russian-Occupied Areas, a Ukrainian Official Says," *New York Times* (March 28, 2023), https://www.nytimes.com/live/2023/03/28/world/russia-ukraine-news?smid=nytcore-ios-share&referringSource=articleShare#over-4300-ukrainian-children-have-been-deported-to-russia-or-russian-occupied-areas-a-ukrainian-official-says.

12. On sanctions and the war, see Edward Fishman and Chris Miller, "The New Russian Sanctions Playbook," *Foreign Affairs* (February 28, 2022), https://www.foreignaffairs.com/articles/russia-fsu/2022-02-28/new-russian-sanctions-playbook; Edward Fishman and Chris Miller, "Time for Even Tougher Sanctions on Russia," *Foreign Affairs* (April 5, 2022), https://www.foreignaffairs.com/articles/ukraine/2022-04-05/time-even-tougher-sanctions-russia; Edward Fishman and Chris Miller, "The Right Way to Sanction Russian Energy," *Foreign Affairs* (May 17, 2022), https://www.foreignaffairs.com/articles/russian-federation/2022-05-17/right-way-sanction-russian-energy; and Edward Fishman, "A Tool of Attrition," *Foreign Affairs* (February 23, 2023), https://www.foreignaffairs.com/ukraine/tool-attrition.

13. The US diplomat, Christopher M. Smith, stationed at the US Embassy in Kyiv in 2013, recalls seeing people streaming into Maidan Square (on December 1) "decked out in Ukrainian colors and EU ribbons." Christopher M. Smith, *Ukraine's Revolt, Russia's Revenge* (Washington, DC: Brookings Institution Press, 2022), 71.

14. One reason China would not go over more comprehensively to Russia's side in the war was economic. "In 2021 China's trade with the US was worth some $1.3 trillion, with the EU just over $1 trillion—and with Russia just under $70 billion," Owen Matthews writes. *Overreach: The Inside Story of Putin's War against Ukraine* (London: Harper Collins, 2022), 339.

15. On Patriarch Kirill, the leader of the Russian Orthodox Church, and his use of cultural traditionalism to justify the war, see Jason Horowitz, "The Russian Orthodox Leader at the Core of Putin's Ambitions," *New York Times* (May 22, 2022), https://

www.nytimes.com/2022/05/21/world/europe/kirill-putin-russian-orthodox-chu
rch.html?smid=nytcore-ios-share&referringSource=articleShare.

16. India's position on the 2022 Russian invasion is consistent with its position on Russia's conduct in Ukraine in 2014. This was to pursue its economic interests outside the scope of US and other sanctions on Russia. As Kathryn Stoner observes, after 2014, "India has not only continued its high volume of defense purchases from Russia, it has increased investment in Russia's Arctic oil interests . . . at a time when the West imposed sanctions on companies exploring there." *Russia Resurrected: Its Power and Purpose in a New Global Order* (New York: Oxford University Press, 2021), 113.

17. On Russia's military woes in the spring and summer of 2022, see Dara Massicot, "The Russian Military's People Problem," *Foreign Affairs* (May 18, 2022), https://www.for eignaffairs.com/articles/russian-federation/2022-05-18/russian-militarys-people-problem; and Dara Massicot, "Russia's Repeat Failures," *Foreign Affairs* (August 15, 2022), https://www.foreignaffairs.com/ukraine/russia-repeat-failures.

18. Given Russia's stated war aims, it is striking that mass civilian suffering was inflicted on Mariupol, a city that before the war had been 44 percent ethnic Russian and was predominantly Russian speaking. See Plokhy, *The Russo-Ukrainian War*, 188.

19. On the annexation of four Ukrainian *oblasts*, or provinces, see Anton Troianovsky and Valerie Hopkins, "With Bluster and Threats, Putin Casts the West as the Enemy," *New York Times* (September 30, 2022), https://www.nytimes.com/2022/09/30/world/europe/putin-speech-ukraine-russia.html.

20. On polling data (circa September 2022) on Russian attitudes toward the war, see "More Than Half of Russians Feel Anxious or Angry about Mobilization, Poll Indicates," *Reuters* (September 20, 2022), https://www.reuters.com/world/europe/more-than-half-russians-feel-anxious-or-angry-about-mobilisation-poll-indicates-2022-09-29/.

21. On Zelensky's speech to the US Congress, see Philip Bump, "How Zelensky Appealed to History, Explained," *Washington Post* (December 22, 2022), https://www.washing tonpost.com/politics/2022/12/22/zelensky-congress-speech-russia/.

Conclusion

1. In a series of books, Margaret MacMillan has explored the interconnected ends and beginnings of wars: *Paris 1919: Six Months That Changed the World* (New York: Random House, 2007); *Dangerous Games: The Uses and Abuses of History* (New York: Random House, 2009); *The War That Ended Peace: The Road to 1914* (New York: Random House, 2013); and *War: How Conflict Shaped Us* (New York: Random House, 2020).

2. On John Gaddis's role in the drafting of George W. Bush's Second Inaugural Address, see "The Historians Who Influenced the Writing of Bush's 2nd Inaugural," *History News Network*, http://hnn.us/articles/9805.html.

3. John Gaddis's paradigmatic triumphalist history of the Cold War is *We Now Know: Rethinking Cold War History* (New York: Oxford University Press, 1997). For a cultural history of Cold War triumphalism, see Penny M. von Eschen, *Paradoxes of Nostalgia: Cold War Triumphalism and Global Disorder since 1989* (Durham, NC: Duke University Press, 2022).

4. Hungary and Turkey, both NATO members, do not adhere to an interpretation of the war that blames Putin alone, which is one of the reasons both countries maintain a diplomatic relationship with Russia.

5. On the centrality of Ukraine to Hitler's planning and execution of World War II, see Timothy Snyder, *Bloodlands: Europe between Hitler and Stalin* (New York: Basic Books, 2022). In a microhistory of one town, Omer Bartov also demonstrates Ukraine's central position within the Second World War, among other wars and conflicts. See *Tales from the Borderlands: Making and Unmaking the Galician Past* (New Haven, CT: Yale University Press, 2022).

6. For Obama on Putin as a "bored kid," see Steve Holland and Margaret Chadbourn, "Obama Describes Putin as 'Like a Bored Kid,'" *Reuters* (August 9, 2013), https://www.reuters.com/article/us-usa-russia-obama/obama-describes-putin-as-like-a-bored-kid-idUSBRE9780XS20130809.

7. As Serhii Plokhy notes about Europe in general, it was war that "had been the main instrument used to create the European system of nation-states." *The Russo-Ukrainian War: The Return of History* (New York: Norton, 2023), 101.

8. Serhii Plokhy links the war in Ukraine to the Cold War through a Ukraine-Germany analogy. "Ukraine emerges on that map [of Sino-US competition] as a new Cold War Germany, its territories divided not just between two countries, but two global spheres and economic blocs." *The Russo-Ukrainian War*, 299.

9. William H. Hill emphasizes the distance between Russia and Europe after 1991 in his diplomatic history, *No Place for Russia: European Security Institutions since 1989* (New York: Columbia University Press, 2018).

10. Boris Yeltsin quoted in Philip Short, *Putin* (New York: Holt, 2022), 237.

11. On the motif of reactionary modernism, see Jeffrey Herf's *Reactionary Modernism: Technology, Culture, and Politics in Weimar and the Third Reich* (New York: Cambridge University Press, 1986).

12. Homer, *The Odyssey*, translated by Robert Fagles (New York: Penguin Books, 1996), 77.

13. Andrey Kurkov, *Diary of an Invasion*, 152.

Index